CEDAR RAPIDS.—St. Lawrence River.

A TRIP

THROUGH THE

LAKES OF NORTH AMERICA;

EMBRACING A FULL DESCRIPTION OF THE

ST. LAWRENCE RIVER,

TOGETHER WITH ALL THE

PRINCIPAL PLACES ON ITS BANKS,

FROM ITS SOURCE TO ITS MOUTH:

COMMERCE OF THE LAKES, ETC.

FORMING ALTOGETHER

A Complete Guide

FOR THE PLEASURE TRAVELER AND EMIGRANT.

With Maps and Embellishments.

NEW YORK:
PUBLISHED BY J. DISTURNELL,
No. 16 BEEKMAN STREET.
1857.

Stereotyped by V. DILL,
29 & 31 Beekman St., N. Y

PREFACE.

In presenting to the public the present volume, entitled "A Trip through the Lakes of North America," embracing a description of the St. Lawrence River, etc., the compiler wishes to return his sincere thanks for the liberal patronage and the many kind favors received from those who have doubly assisted him in his labors, by contributing reliable and useful information in regard to the many interesting localities in which the great Valley of the Lakes and the St. Lawrence abounds—affording altogether many new and interesting facts of great importance to the Tourist who may wish to visit the Inland Seas of America, or the noble St. Lawrence, at any point from its source to its mouth—the tour being one of the most healthy, picturesque, and wonderful on the face of the globe, when viewed, as a whole, from the Lake of the Woods to the Gulf of St. Lawrence.

In the arrangement and compilation of this work every attempt has been made to render the information it contains concise and truthful—taking up popular lines of travel as they now exist, and faithfully describing places and objects of interest as they occur on the route. We thus start from Niagara Falls, or Toronto, situated on Lake Ontario, and describe in succession Lake Simcoe, the Georgian Bay and North Channel, arriving at Saut Ste Marie, the gateway of the Lake Superior country. Here, among the Mineral Regions, may be found objects of interest sufficient to induce the intelligent traveler to spend some weeks or months; and if, added to this, should be included a Trip to the Upper Mississippi Valley, an entire season could be profitably employed.

Lake Superior, the *Ultima Thule* of many travelers, can now be easily reached by lines of steamers starting from Chicago, and running through Lake Michigan and the Straits of Mackinac; also, from Buffalo, Cleveland, and Detroit, passing through Lakes St. Clair and Huron to the St. Mary's River. All these routes are fully described, in connection with the Collingwood route, affording altogether ample and cheap opportunities to visit every portion of the Upper Lakes and their adjacent shores.

Lakes Erie, Ontario, and Champlain, and the St. Lawrence River, with its principal tributaries, are also faithfully described, together with the Rapids, Falls, Islands, and objects of interest along their shores—including the Steamboat Routes, with a description of the various Cities, Villages, and principal Landings from Lake Superior to the mouth of the St. Lawrence, or its entrance into the Gulf—thus forming a complete TRAVELER'S GUIDE for the seekers of health or pleasure, as well as for the emigrant or man of business.

The great changes and improvements constantly going on in the United States and Canada render this kind of compilation both laborious and expensive; therefore the productions of original authors ought to be protected by public opinion and favor, as well as by the laws of the land; but the latter, unfortunately, are often found insufficient.

In the compilation of a number of the Guide Books and geographical works now before the American public, many bearing the names of publishers, instead of the authors, great injustice has been done to the faithful compiler, or author, by trespassing upon their copyrights. A noted instance of this sort occurred a few years since, in the publication of an "AMERICAN GUIDE BOOK, or *Appleton's Hand-Book through the United States*." This work was an acknowledged infringement of the "PICTURESQUE TOURIST," edited by O. L. Holley, Esq., and issued, in 1844, by the present compiler. Since the above period two or three similar works have been issued, with the names of the publishers conspicuously attached to the title, although edited, or compiled, by persons of doubtful authority, and almost entirely unknown to the public. J. D

NEW YORK, *May*, 1857.

CONTENTS.

List of Embellishments.

RAILROAD AND STEAMBOAT ROUTES.

STEAMBOAT AND RAILROAD ROUTE FROM NEW YORK TO MONTREAL, *via* LAKE CHAMPLAIN.

Stations, etc.	Miles.		Usual Time. H. M.
NEW YORK..............	0	....	
ALBANY, (*Steamer*)........	145	....	10 00
TROY, (*Steamer*)..........	151	....	10 30
Saratoga Springs, (*Railroad*)	182	....	
Whitehall, (*Railroad*)......	223	....	14 00
Ticonderoga, (*Steamer*)..	247	....	
BURLINGTON, Vt. "	300	....	20 00
Plattsburgh, N. Y. "	325	....	
Rouse's Point, N. Y. "	350	....	24 00
St. John's, Can. (*Railroad*).	374	....	
MONTREAL, (*Railroad*)...	395	....	26 00

NOTE.—This line of travel affords one of the most delightful excursions during warm weather—passing through Lake Champlain, a most lovely and picturesque sheet of water, surrounded by romantic and mountainous scenery.

RAILROAD ROUTE FROM NEW YORK TO MONTREAL, *via* RUTLAND AND BURLINGTON, VT.

Stations, etc.	Miles.		Usual Time. H. M.
NEW YORK..............	0	....	
Poughkeepsie	75	....	2 40
ALBANY..................	144	....	5 00
TROY	150	....	5 15
North Bennington	182	....	6 30
RUTLAND	234	....	8 30
Middlebury...............	266	....	10 30
BURLINGTON,(*S.to Plattsb'h*)	301	....	11 00
Rouse's Point	356	....	14 00
St. John's, C. E.	379	....	15 00
MONTREAL	400	....	16 00

USUAL FARE from New York to Montreal, $9 to $10 50.

RAILROAD AND STEAMBOAT ROUTE FROM NEW YORK TO NIAGARA FALLS AND TORONTO, C. W., LEAVING NEW YORK AT 6 P.M. BY STEAMER.

Stations, etc.	Miles.		Usual Time. H. M.
NEW YORK.............	• 0	....	
ALBANY, (*Steamer*).......	145	....	12 00
Schenectady, (*Railroad*) ...	162	....	13 00
Utica, "	240	....	16 00
Rome, "	254	....	16 30
Syracuse, "	293	....	18 00
ROCHESTER, (*St. to Toronto*)	374	....	22 45
Lockport, (*Railroad*)...	430	....	25 00
Suspension Bridge, " ...	448	....	26 00
LEWISTON, " ...	452	....	
TORONTO, (*Steamer*).....	494	....	30 00

RAILROAD AND STEAMBOAT ROUTE FROM NEW YORK TO OSWEGO, TORONTO, ETC., LEAVING NEW YORK AT 6 A.M. BY HUDSON RIVER RAILROAD.

Stations, etc.	Miles.		Usual Time. H. M.
NEW YORK.............	0	....	
Poughkeepsie, (*Railroad*)...	75	....	2 40
Hudson, "	116	....	4 00
ALBANY, "	144	....	5 00
Schenectady, "	162	....	6 00
Utica, "	240	....	8 30
Rome, "	254	....	9 00
Syracuse, "	293	....	10 30
OSWEGO, "	328	....	13 00
Lewiston, (*Steamer* 140 *m.*).	468	....	
TORONTO, (*Steamer* 150 *m.*)	478	....	27 00

NOTE.—Passengers by continuing on by Railroad from Syracuse, *via* Rochester and Lockport, will arrive at Suspension Bridge, 448 miles, in sixteen hours after leaving New York, stop at Niagara Falls if desired, and reach Toronto by Railroad, *via* Hamilton, C. W., 81 miles farther; making the total distance from New York to Toronto by Railroad, *via* Suspension Bridge, 529 miles.

RAILROAD AND STEAMBOAT ROUTE FROM TORONTO TO COLLINGWOOD AND SAUT STE MARIE, MICH.

TORONTO TO COLLINGWOOD (*Railroad Route*), 94 miles.

STEAMBOAT ROUTE.

(Collingwood to Saut Ste Marie, Mich., passing through Georgian Bay and North Channel.)

Ports, etc.	Miles.	Ports, etc.	Miles.
COLLINGWOOD	0	SAUT STE MARIE	0
Cape Rich	30	Sugar Island	4
Cabot's Head	80	Garden River Set	10
Lonely Island	100	*Church's Landing*	14
Cape Smyth	125	Lake George	20
She-ba-wa-nah-ning	145	Nebish Rapids	24
Man-i-tou-wah-ning (25 m.)		St. Joseph Island	25
Little Current, Great Manitoulin Is.	170	The Narrows	35
		Campement D'Ours Is	38
Clapperton Island	190	*Bruce Mines*	50
Barrie Island	220	Drummond's Island, Mich.	70
Cockburn Island	255	Cockburn Island, C. W.	85
Drummond's Island, Mich.	270	Barrie Island	120
Bruce Mines, C. W.	290	Clapperton Island	150
St. Joseph Island	296	*Little Current,* Great Manitoulin Is.	170
Campement D'Ours Is	302		
The Narrows	305	Man-i-tou-wah-ning (25 m.)	
Sugar Island, Mich.	315	*She-ba-wa-nah-ning*	195
Nebish Rapids	316	Cape Smyth	215
Lake George	320	Lonely Island	240
Church's Landing	326	Cabot's Head	260
Garden River Set	330	Cape Rich	310
SAUT STE MARIE	340	COLLINGWOOD	340

STEAMBOAT FARE, $8 50. Including meals. USUAL TIME, 36 hours.

NOTE.—Landings in *Italic*.

STEAMBOAT ROUTE FROM SAUT STE MARIE TO SUPERIOR CITY, WIS., PASSING ALONG THE SOUTH SHORE OF LAKE SUPERIOR.

Ports, etc.	Miles.	Ports, etc.	Miles.
SAUT STE MARIE	0	SUPERIOR CITY	0
Point Iroquois	15	Point de Tour	70
White Fish Point	40	*Bayfield*	80
Point au Sable	90	*La Pointe*	83
Pictured Rocks	110	*Ontonagon*	158
Grand Island	125	*Eagle River*	218
Marquette, (Fare, $6.)	170	*Eagle Harbor*	228
Manitou Island	235	*Copper Harbor*	244
Copper Harbor	250	Manitou Island	259
Eagle Harbor	266	*Marquette*	324
Eagle River	276	Grand Island	369
Ontonagon, (Fare, $9.)	336	Pictured Rocks	384
La Pointe, (Fare, $11)	410	Point au Sable	404
Bayfield	414	White Fish Point	454
Point de Tour	424	Point Iroquois	479
SUPERIOR CITY (Fare $13)	494	SAUT STE MARIE	494

USUAL TIME from Saut Ste Marie to Superior City, 54 hours, including landings.

ROUTE FROM NEW YORK TO THE FALLS OF ST. ANTHONY, *via* LAKE SUPERIOR.

Stopping Places.	Total Miles.	Usual Time.
New York to Albany, by (*Steamboat*)	145	12 hours.
Albany to Niagara Falls, (*Railroad*)	303 448	1 day.
Niagara Falls to Toronto, (*R.R. and St.*)	46–494	1¼ "
Toronto to Collingwood, (*Railroad*)	94–588	1½ "
Collingwood to Saut Ste Marie, (*Steamboat*)	340–928	3 "
Saut Ste Marie to La Pointe, (*Steamboat*)	350–1,278	4½ "
La Pointe to Superior City, (*Steamboat*)	84–1,362	5 "
Superior City to Falls St. Croix, (*Portage*)	120–1,482	8 "
Falls St. Croix to Stillwater, (*Steamboat*)	30–1,512	
Stillwater to St. Paul, (*Stage*)	18–1,530	
St. Paul to Falls of St. Anthony, (*Stage*)	8–1,538	9 "

From the *Falls of St. Anthony* to *Dubuque* .... 326 miles.
" *Dubuque* to *St. Louis*, (*Steamboat*) .... 474 "

Total........ 800 miles.

A TRIP

THROUGH THE

LAKES OF NORTH AMERICA.

RAILROAD ROUTE FROM TORONTO TO COLLINGWOOD, AND TRIP AROUND LAKE SIMCOE.

AFTER passing over the delightful and usually smooth waters of Lake Ontario, the Tourist, on approaching Toronto, either from Cape Vincent, Oswego, Rochester, Buffalo, or the FALLS OF NIAGARA, usually experiences sensations which incite him to further travel and enjoyment. From this place the tourist can proceed direct to Montreal and Quebec, by railroad or steamer, or to Hamilton and Detroit on the west—while the Collingwood route extends north through a beautiful section of country.

2*

On landing at Toronto from American ports, it is usual for the custom-house officers to question passengers in regard to the contents of their baggage, which if it consists of nothing but common wearing apparel, is passed without further delay, and the porters take charge of the same, delivering the articles as directed. All persons, however, taking into Canada manufactured goods, whether subject to pay duty or otherwise, are expected to enter the same at the custom house.

The hotels are principally situated on Front Street, facing the bay, Church Street, or King Street, the latter being the principal promenade, or Broadway, of Toronto. Yonge Street is another principal thoroughfare, extending from the Esplanade, or water's edge, for many miles into the interior, affording a delightful drive in pleasant weather. The attractions of this thriving city, in connection with the beautiful bay and harbor, are well worthy the attention of the tourist. For a further description of Toronto, *see page* 240.

The railroads diverging from Toronto are the *Ontario, Simcoe and Huron Railroad*, extending north to Collingwood, 94 miles; the *Grand Trunk Railnay*, extending northeast to Montreal and Quebec, and west through Guelph to Port Sarnia, situated at the foot of Lake Huron, and the *Hamilton and Toronto Branch* of the Great Western Railway of Canada, running from Clifton at the Suspension Bridge, to Hamilton, and thence through to Windsor, on the Detroit River. These railroads, in connection with the steamers, render Toronto a great thoroughfare and mart of commerce. It now takes about thirty hours to reach Toronto from New York; five hours from Buffalo, and only twelve hours from Montreal, since the completion of the Grand Trunk Railway: the favorite steamboat route down the St. Lawrence River consumes about twice as much time. In four hours more the traveler can be landed at Collingwood, at the head of Georgian Bay, from whence steamers leave almost daily, during the season of navigation, for Mackinac, Green Bay, Chicago, Saut Ste Marie, and other ports on the Upper Lakes.

Passenger trains leave Toronto morning and afternoon for Collingwood, etc., starting from the depôt near the corner of Front and Bay Streets. The first objects of interest passed are the Parliament House, University Building, Lunatic Asylum, the Barracks, and Old Fort,* the latter being situated near the water's edge, for the protection of the bay and harbor.

The Grand Trunk Railway also runs for two or three miles parallel with the Ontario, Simcoe and Huron Railroad. The farming land through which the latter road runs is very productive, being in part heavily timbered with maple, birch, beech, oak, elm, pine, and hemlock. For many miles there seems to have been a studied effort to avoid the villages and thriving settlements lying west of Toronto on Yonge Street road.

THORNHILL STATION, 14 miles from Toronto, is located four miles west from the village, which is situated on Yonge Street. Here are extensive flouring-mills, propelled by water-power derived from the river Don, flowing into Toronto Bay.

The highest summit of the Ontario, Simcoe and Huron Railroad, being 700 feet above Lake Ontario, and 226 feet above the level of Lake Simcoe, is passed about 25 miles north of Toronto. The highest grade ascending is sixty feet to the mile.

AURORA, 29 miles from Toronto, is a small village situated on Yonge Street, where the morning trains usually meet on their way to and from Collingwood.

NEW MARKET, 34 miles from Toronto, is an old and thriving town, surrounded by a fine section of country. Here are several mills and other manufacturing establishments, situated on a stream which passes through the village, flowing into Lake Simcoe on the north. Fruit of different kinds, of fine quality, as well as grain, is raised in large quantities in this vicinity.

HOLLAND LANDING, 38 miles north of Toronto by railroad, is

* The *Old Garrison*, as it is now called, is situated on the lake shore, commanding the entrance to the harbor. On the capture of Toronto, formerly called *Little York*, by the American army in 1813, the magazine of the fort was fired by the British on their retreat, causing the death of General PIKE, the American commander, and many other valuable men. Long may it be before the scourge of war again desolates the frontier bordering the waters of the lakes or the St. Lawrence River.

advantageously situated on Holland River, which empties into Lake Simcoe. It contains an Episcopal, Presbyterian, and Methodist church; steam and water power, grist and saw mills, an extensive tannery, a foundry, and about 1,500 inhabitants. The railway here again intersects Yonge Street, studded with fine dwellings, orchards, and farms, all the way through from Toronto, 36 miles, bearing evidence of wealth, intelligence, and comfort, not surpassed by any other section of Canada.

Bradford, 42 miles from Toronto, is a small village situated near Lake Simcoe. The afternoon train of cars meets at this station on its way to and from Toronto. Large quantities of wheat and other farming products are annually sent from this place to Toronto, and other markets.

Bell Ewart, 53 miles from Toronto, is situated on Cook's Bay, lying at the south end of Lake Simcoe. Here are a convenient steamboat landing, several stores and lumber yards, and a population of some 300 or 400 inhabitants. The stumps and decayed trees by which it is surrounded indicate that it is of recent origin, yet still the town-lots are held at a high price, showing that speculation is not entirely confined to the *Yankees*, as the Americans are here usually called.

During the summer of 1856 the author accepted an invitation to visit *Lake Simcoe*, and take a trip over its lovely waters, now plowed by one of the most comfortable steamers, named the J. C. Morrison, in honor of the President of the Ontario, Simcoe and Huron Railroad. This pioneer work of Upper Canada was first advocated and commenced through the untiring zeal of an enterprising citizen of Toronto, now entirely disconnected with its present management.

The running of the trains on the above road, and the steamer on the lake, is so arranged that pleasure travelers can leave Toronto in the morning, enjoy a most delightful sail around Lake Simcoe, and return to Toronto in the evening, or proceed onward toward Collingwood, reaching the latter place in ample time for the steamer for the Saut Ste Marie, which usually leaves soon after the arrival of the evening train.

THE beautiful steamer J. C. MORRISON daily leaves Bell Ewart, on the arrival of the morning train from Toronto, making a trip around LAKE SIMCOE, a most lovely and pure sheet of water, elevated 474 feet above Lake Ontario and 134 feet above Lake Huron. It is about 40 miles long from north to south, and 25 miles wide, embosoming several picturesque islands, the beauties of which are very much heightened by the effects of light and shade during the summer and autumn months. This romantic lake is elevated above Lake Superior about 100 feet; its surplus waters running through the Severn River into Georgian Bay or Lake Huron.

On leaving the landing in Cook's Bay, the steamer usually runs between *Bird* and *Snake Islands*, both being owned and inhabited by Indians of the Mohawk tribe, who here lead an idle life, neglecting the noble pursuit of agriculture for the less certain employment of fishing and hunting.

JACKSON'S POINT, twelve miles from Bell Ewart, is the first landing usually made on the upward trip. This is a picturesque spot, as yet unimproved, although affording a convenient steamboat landing.

GEORGIANA ISLAND, eight miles farther, is next passed, lying on the east, near the main shore. This is a large and fertile island, at present unimproved.

BEAVERTON, 29 miles from Bell Ewart and 21 miles distant from Orillia, is a flourishing village, containing about 1,000 inhabitants. Here is a long pier and good steamboat landing. A railroad, to be built, extending from Port Hope, lying on the north shore of Lake Ontario, to Lake Simcoe, will terminate at

Beaverton, which is surrounded by a fine section of agricultural lands, producing wheat and other kinds of grain of good quality.

Thora Island is next passed on the west, and Point Mora on the right, running in a N.W. direction toward the foot of the lake, which here increases in beauty.

Grape Island, lying near the foot of the lake, is a beautiful small uninhabited island; and near by on the west lies *Chief Island*, occupied by Indians. Here the islands and headlands appear to great advantage, being clothed with rich foliage, varied in tint by every passing cloud.

Atherly, 18 miles from Beaverton, is a steamboat landing and small settlement at the foot of Lake Simcoe. Half a mile below Atherly the steamer passes through a narrow channel and draw-bridge into *Lake Couchiching*, or *Severn River*, here some three or four miles wide, containing several beautiful small islands, where may usually be seen the Indians in bark canoes gliding from island to island, seeming in the distance to resemble fairies of by-gone days. The islands may be thus described:

"All the fairy crowds
Of islands, which together lie,
As quietly as the spots of sky,
Among the evening clouds."

Orillia, Simcoe Co., C. W., is pleasantly situated three miles beyond Atherly by steamboat route. This is a summer resort for invalids and seekers of pleasure. The village contains two churches, three hotels, and several boarding-houses for the accommodation of visitors. Population about 800. This place is destined no doubt to become a favorite and fashionable resort, being easily reached from Toronto or Collingwood.

Rama is the name of an Indian village situated across the lake from Orillia, about four miles distant. The Indians may here be seen engaged in fishing, or paddling from place to place, many of them leading a roving and idle life, no doubt being destined soon to fade away as the falling leaf of autumn.

The Rapids or Falls commence in the Severn River some seven or eight miles below Orillia, which stream empties into the Georgian Bay near Penetanguishene, after a succession of rapids and falls of 134 feet descent. In the lake and river are to be found good fishing, and game of different kinds, affording ample amusement to the angler and sportsman.

On returning from Orillia, the steamer runs in a southerly direction along the west shore of the lake, presenting a succession of picturesque headlands, and most beautiful water scenery.

HAWKSTONE, 15 miles south of Orillia, is a new settlement, where buildings are being erected for the accommodation of summer visitors. On leaving Hawkstone the steamer runs direct for Bell Ewart, passing the mouth of Kempenfeldt Bay, at the head of which lies the town of Barrie. *Big Bay Point*, eight miles from Hawkstone, is next passed, and the steamer soon enters Cook's Bay, on which is situated Bell Ewart, 33 miles south of Orillia. The steamer usually arrives at 5½ P.M., in time to take the afternoon cars for Collingwood or Toronto, thus affording the pleasure traveler an opportunity to visit one of the most beautiful lakes of Canada.

At LEFROY, one mile from Bell Ewart by branch road, and 52 miles from Toronto, the journey by railroad is resumed.

BARRIE STATION, 63 miles from Toronto and 31 miles from Collingwood, is situated on Kempenfeldt Bay, directly opposite the town of Barrie, about one mile distant, which is reached by a road running round the head of the bay, affording a fine view of the town and surrounding country.

BARRIE, the capital of Simcoe Co., is delightfully situated on the northwest shore of Kempenfeldt Bay of Lake Simcoe. Besides the county buildings there is a handsome market-house, an Episcopal, Presbyterian, Methodist, and Roman Catholic church; also, two or three well-kept hotels. The village contains about 1,500 inhabitants, being surrounded by a fine agricultural country. A stage road runs from Barrie to Penetanguishene, 32 miles; also, to Orillia, at the foot of the lake.

After leaving Barrie Station, the Ontario, Simcoe and Huron Railroad runs in a northwest direction to Collingwood, passing through a level section of country, abounding in lumber of different kinds; there being several large lumber establishments on the line of the road.

COLLINGWOOD, 94 miles north from Toronto, is most advantageously situated near the head of Nottawassaga Bay, an indentation of Georgian Bay. The town, although commenced in 1854, at the time of the completion of the Ontario, Simcoe and Huron Railroad, now contains (1857) about 2,000 inhabitants, and is rapidly increasing. The surprising growth is mainly owing to its being the northern terminus of the railway which connects the Georgian Bay with Lake Ontario at Toronto. Great numbers of travelers and emigrants are at this point transferred to magnificent steamers, bound for Mackinac, Green Bay, Chicago, and the Great West, as well as to the Saut Ste Marie and Lake Superior. Here are a long pier, 800 feet in length; a breakwater, and light-house; several large stores and storehouses; four hotels, and two or three churches in the course of erection.

The steamers leaving Collingwood for Mackinac and Chicago, running along the west shore of Lake Michigan, are of a large class, affording good accommodations for pleasure travelers. A steamer leaves weekly for Green Bay, sometimes proceeding to the Saut Ste Marie and into Lake Superior. The steamer *Canadian* runs every day to Owen's Sound, 50 miles distant; and the steamer *Collingwood* runs weekly to Bruce Mines and the Saut Ste Marie, affording a delightful steamboat excursion.

Immense quantities of fish are taken in the waters of Nottawassaga Bay, being principally carried to the Toronto market. The whole north shore of the Georgian Bay abounds in white fish, salmon, trout, maskalonge, and other fish of fine quality, affording profitable employment to the Canadians and Indians.

"Some idea of the value and extent of the fishing operations promiscuously pursued in Nottawassaga Bay may be formed from the knowledge that the average daily take exceeds one thousand fish, weighing from forty pounds down to one pound. At this rate, that of the season would not fall short of £40,000. At the mouth of the Nottawassaga River the white fish are netted in perfect shoals throughout the spawning season. Most of the larger kinds of trout spawn about the islands, upon beds of calcareous rock, over which a shifting drift of sand or gravel passes by the action of the waves, where the water is shallow; and from being exposed to the sun, the temperature of the lake is warmer at these localities than elsewhere. Thither the fishermen resort, and net the fish, vapid and placid as they are, in fabulous amounts."

THE TORONTO AND GEORGIAN BAY CANAL.

This is a new and noble project, which is now interesting the citizens of Upper Canada, as well as of the United States: Toronto and Oswego being alike interested in connection with the far North and West. The proposed canal will be 80 miles ong, extending from Nottawassaga Bay through the valley of the Nottawassaga and Humber rivers to Toronto, advantageously situated on the north shore of Lake Ontario. The summit is 650 feet above the waters of Lake Ontario, requiring a succession of locks in the ascent and descent to Georgian Bay, the latter descent being only 310 feet—Lake Ontario lying 340 feet below Lake Huron, or Georgian Bay.

(*Extract from the* Toronto Globe, *of Septem' er*, 1856.)

"The geographical position of the projected canal, as it regards the Atlantic sea-board and those cities of the United States, each now striving to grasp the trade and traffic of the great West (and as it regards the great West itself, the northwest and the north), would give to the city of Toronto the power to make all those vast countries, in a measure, tributary to her. Their productions would seek the sea-board through your canal, and their importations would likewise pay their tribute in return."

The writer adds: "He wished only to indulge in a few remarks, and to call attention, not to the United States alone, but to the British Possessions in America, which ere long would also be pouring its flood of trade and traffic through the proposed canal. Westward, we possess vast and fertile countries, adapted to all the pursuits of agricultural life—countries susceptible of the highest cultivation and improvement. Between Lake Superior and the Lake of the Woods (above the 49th degree of N. lat.) we possess a country of this description, in soil and character inferior to no part of Minnesota, and bordering upon this territory lies the valley of the Assiniboine, or the Red River country, as it is sometimes called. As a wheat-growing country it will rival Canada. It does so now in soil and climate. In order to give you some idea of the extent of that country, or, perhaps I should say, portion of Western Canada, I will call your attention to a few facts. All Canada, as now usually designated, not in connection with what is termed Hudson Bay Territories, contains about 350,000 square miles. The valley of the Assiniboine contains about as many square miles, and is intersected in every direction by navigable rivers. Beyond this, again, lies the magnificent valley of the Saskatchawan.

It contains about 400,000 square miles, larger again than Canada.

"Over the richest prairie lands, loaded carts now pass in any direction for hundreds of miles, to the foot of the Rocky Mountains. In its present wild and uncultivated state it affords sustenance to immense herds of wild cattle. What would it do if cultivated by the hand of man? The future products of these immense countries must seek the sea-board, and all the canals and railroads which can be constructed will scarce suffice to afford facilities for the products of the West. He wished to call their attention also to another source, whence a trade would arise, and contribute to swell the traffic along the canal. Hudson Bay would give to Canada a sea-coast of 3,000 miles. No maritime power has ever possessed so great a nursery for a mercantile navy as this. It abounds with whales, and every kind of fish; and, strange as it may appear, that great sea lies, as it were, in the center of Canada. From the proposed terminus of the canal it is about 650 miles, 350 miles of which is a navigation capable of bearing ships of any burden; from Lake Superior to Hudson Bay is 300 miles. If the route between Lake Superior and Hudson Bay was open and improved, they would speedily establish fisheries along the coasts of that bay. The oil and fish now consumed in those states is immense, and they will be furnished them from Hudson Bay cheaper and more speedily than from the source they now receive them. A trade like this will sooner or later spring up, and create along Hudson Bay an immense demand for all those manufactures and productions which the United States can supply, and these must find their way through their canal. A large trade at this moment is had along that bay.* The Hudson Bay Company, who have seven forts there, and one above York Factory, receive annual supplies to the amount of from £70,000 to £90,000. Many of these goods, perhaps, are of that description which Toronto merchants could supply with advantage. To the traffic which must exist all along the shores of Lakes Huron and Superior I make no allusion. It is evident to all that it must be tributary to the canal. It may be said that all that I have alluded to as regards the traffic to arise from our country is far in prospective, but there is no reason why we should not progress and advance westward as do the United States."

* "The Hudson Bay Company have long endeavored by rewards and arguments to excite an exportation of tallow, hides, wool, etc., to England; but the bulky nature of the exports, the long and dangerous navigation to Hudson Bay, and the habits of the half-breed race, who form the mass of the people, and generally prefer chasing the buffalo to agriculture or regular industry, have rendered their efforts ineffectual."—R. MONTGOMERY MARTIN.

TRIP FROM ORILLIA TO GEORGIAN BAY.

Extract from the CANADIAN TOURIST.

FROM ORILLIA, situated near the foot of Lake Simcoe, the author with his companions, four in number, passed in two birch canoes down the Severn, a distance of about 60 miles, to GEORGIAN BAY, and thence to Collingwood by steamer. The river is navigable only for canoes, and, except by sportsmen, is as yet rarely visited.

"In our eyes, its solitary character and the romantic scenery on its banks were its principal attractions. Having reduced our luggage to the smallest possible dimensions, and put our fishing-tackle into good order, it only remained for us to make ourselves comfortable by spreading a quantity of plucked fern and juniper branches at the bottom of our canoes. We re-reclined sumptuously in one, with about as much accommodation as a ship's hammock would afford two moderately stout individuals. However, as we were less likely to be upset by being so closely jammed together that we could scarcely move, we became reconciled to our position between Bonaquum ('Thunderbolt'), who knelt at the bows and paddled, and his brother Kabeshquum ('Triumphant'), who steered. The other canoe contained Captain A——, whose experience in such expeditions, and knowledge of Indian character and language, were most valuable—and Babehwum ('Snow-Storm'), whose son, as an exemplification of the effect of civilization over the elements, called himself simply John Storm. As the wind was fair, we rigged our blankets upon sticks cut for the purpose; and, with all sail set, we glided rapidly on (through the lovely waters of Lake Couchiching), sometimes threading our way through narrow channels, past low-wooded islands, until in about two hours we found ourselves upon the green waters of the Severn.

"The scenery at the point of *debouchure* was very beautiful. Masses of rich variegated foliage clothed the banks, and bent over until the river rippled among the leaves. Often dark shadows reached across it, or were checkered by sunbeams glancing through the branches upon the clear and singularly light-colored water. As we proceeded, we exchanged for the calm surface of the lake, and the islands which seemed to rest on its bosom, rock and rapid, until at last the torrent became too tumultuous for our frail canoes. Meantime, we had not been engaged only in enjoying the beauties of nature, we had adopted the usual mode of trolling in this part of the world, with copper spoons, which, twisting rapidly through the water, formed a bright and attractive bait; so that, upon arriving at the first portage, we congratulated ourselves upon the prospect of lunching off half-a-dozen black bass weighing from two to five pounds each; while the Indians were engaged in culinary preparations.

"We were up before daylight on the following morning, and, after a good fish breakfast, were again on our way. I had scarcely thrown my trolling-line, when it was nearly jerked out of my hand by a most unexpected and violent tug. A bark canoe is not the most convenient place from which to play a large fish; and, in my inexperienced eagerness, I hauled away pretty steadily, bringing to the surface with some difficulty a fine maskalonge, weighing at least twenty-five pounds. He came splashing and plunging up to the side of the canoe, and I had lifted him out of water, when the hook gave way, and I lost as fine a fish as I ever had at the end of a line. However, I was consoled soon after by taking some fine pickerel, weighing from five to eight pounds each; and, before luncheon, hooked another maskalonge, when my companion, profiting by experience, was ready with his gaff-hook, and jerked him most scientifically into the canoe, much to the delight of the Indians. Though not so large as the first, he was a respectable fish, weighing about eighteen pounds. The scenery in the place was bold and rocky, the banks often lofty and precipitous, and the current always strong, with an occasional rapid. We lunched at a portage, which we were obliged to make in order to avoid the falls of the Severn, which are here about twenty-five feet in height, and surrounded by fine scenery. There are rapids above and below the falls, so that the difference of level between the upper and lower banks of the portage is not less than fifty feet."

We regret that we can not make room for more extracts from these interesting "Notes on Canada and the Northwest States," but we do the next best thing by recommending the articles themselves to the perusal of our readers.

The above trip affords a favorable opportunity to visit Penetanguishene and the "Million Islands" of Georgian Bay.

Penetanguishene, C. W., 50 miles north of Collingwood by steamboat route, situated on a lovely and secure bay, is an old and very important settlement, comprising an Episcopal and Roman Catholic church, two hotels, a custom-house, several stores and storehouses, and has about 500 inhabitants. In the immediate vicinity is a naval and military depot and barracks, established by the British government. The natural beauties of the bay and harbor, combined with the picturesque scenery of the shores, make up a picture of rare beauty. Here may be seen the native Indian, the half-breed, and the Canadian *voyageur*, with the full-blooded Englishman or Scotchman, forming one community. This place, being near the mouth of the river Severn, and contiguous to the numberless islands of Georgian Bay, is no doubt destined to become a favorite resort for the angler and sportsman, as well as the invalid and seeker of pleasure.

CHRISTIAN ISLAND, lying about 25 miles from Penetanguishene, and 25 miles N. E. of Cape Rich, is a large and fertile island, which was early settled by the Jesuits. There are several others passed north of Christian Island, of great beauty, while still farther northwest are encountered innumerable islands and islets, forming labyrinths, and secluded passages and coves as yet almost unknown to the white man, extending westward for upward of one hundred miles.

ISLANDS ON NORTH SHORE, GEORGIAN BAY.

Extract from Letters from the North and Lake Huron.

SHE-BA-WA-NAH-NING, GEORGIAN BAY, C. W.,
August 16, 1856.

"AMONG the regions of the continent interesting to the traveler, and which are not frequently visited, is the north shore of Georgian Bay. Leaving Penetanguishene we crossed to the mouth of the river Mushkoss, a distance of about eighteen miles. From this place we proceeded up the shore in a small boat, making daily such journeys as suited, and lingering whenever we found an interest to repay.

"The Mushkoss is one of the lumber points on the bay. It is approached through a strip of numerous islands seven miles in width, and it is the first inhabited place on the shore above the mouth of the Severn. Here, as at the Severn, the only thing to attract a habitation is the lumber, which only receives attention. But one almost wonders, when he sees the country, where the lumber comes from, for the rock here again appears, and holds a dominion forever beyond the hopes of man to see subdued. The rock is throughout the country. It stands boldly along the shore, and forms the islands, sustains the water, and its bare surface appears everywhere. Yet the country has a vegetation which covers it with verdure. Bushes, wild flowers, and pine spring up everywhere, where a little earth has drifted and found a lodgment. Pine is almost the only timber, and we daily saw it growing in places so barren, that it seemed as if no vegetation could be sustained either in nutrition or uprightness of position. Some dwarfed oaks may be seen, and, perhaps, occasionally some birch. The pine which is sawed into lumber is cut a distance back, along the banks of the river, and is then drifted down. It is inferior in size to that of more southern regions, and, we believe, by no means has so good an average soundness of quality.

"The Mushkoss is a stream of moderate size, but sends a large division to the bay, to the westward, which diverges many miles above. The river, in the interior country, expands into lakes or pools, some of which are large and filled with numerous islands. This, with a dark-colored water, is characteristic of many of the streams which come down from the north. Even small streams sometimes form a small chain of numerous lakes, extending a great distance back. It is up these streams and around these lakes that many of the Indians find their hunting-grounds for the winter; sometimes going almost to the divide, beyond which the waters flow into Hudson Bay. They go in the fall, and return in the spring with furs, which fall into the hands of the Hudson Bay Company, or those of the various traders along the coast, and are paid for in goods at a large profit.

"Proceeding westward the traveler encounters a maze of innumerable islands, which commences at the eastern extremity of the bay, and continues in an almost unbroken stretch for one hundred miles and upward. There are myriads of them, and we have counted over fifty from a single stand-point. They are mostly small, although some of them are of large size. One may wander industriously amid them for months, and find new scenes to gladden his eyes every day, for the chain has a breadth of many miles. Countless channels run between them, many of which are sufficiently deep and clear for the largest vessels of the lakes. There are numerous small bays, and the channels sometimes have a considerable width; and, now and then, one runs a distance of ten and twenty miles with scarcely an interruption. It is almost impossible to tell when you approach the mainland. One may think himself upon it when he is miles away, or may pursue some lagoon projecting deep into it, when he supposes himself treading on an island channel, and at last be obliged to return.

"One is earnestly told before he starts, by those who have been on this shore, that if he would take his course through the islands, he must have a guide; and certainly without, the stranger can not be sure of great expedition. We were fortunate enough to have Bayfield's chart along, which we found a great help, although no attempt is, or could successfully be, made to chart in detail the interminable labyrinth of islands.

"The better way for one coasting thus is to take a course through the outer edge of the islands, keeping the broad waters in view. A certain guide and a cool, bracing atmosphere are thus obtained, while the splendor of its scenery is almost unrivaled. Along the islands and next to the bay are numerous and wide shoals. The rock floor, sometimes level and again broken, can often be seen through the clear water for a long distance. To the west the islands grow less numerous and the water between them wider, until you approach She-ba-wa-nah-ning, when the chain draws to a close. Islands after this are numerous, but may mostly be traced upon the chart. The islands have the same vegetation and the same physical conformation as the mainland.

"The course of the shore seems much nearer north and west, until you arrive at the French River, when it runs nearly west. The rock is continuous the whole distance. It is chiefly granite, but sandstone appears in considerable quantity this side of the French River. The rock attains at times considerable height and boldness, and as you near She-ba-wa-nah-ning, it sometimes rises into grandeur. Here a mountain chain hangs along the coast, standing up against the sky like a large blue cloud. Between this and the water are a few acres of tillable land, yet none is under cultivation save a very little which is mowed. Indeed, farming is a business which is not thought of on the north side Georgian Bay, even by the few white inhabitants scattered there. There may be a patch of a few acres now and then along the shore which might be cultivated, but we saw scarcely any. But there are probably some sections where a little may be found, for the Indians find somewhere here the maple for the manufacture of sugar. They told us that it is near the mouth of French River, on the east side, and that they there raise some potatoes and corn. But we believe that the shore can never be even sparingly settled. At some points there may be tillable lands a considerable distance back. Yet there are no indications of it along the shore. A large grant of land, we are informed, has been obtained to construct a railroad from the Ottawa to some point near the mouth of the French River on the bay

"The timber observed as far as She-ba-wa-nah-ning is almost entirely pine. One is almost surprised at the constancy of it. Some spruce, tamarac, birch, and poplar are seen, however, and probably cedar may be found also. The juniper shrub is abundant, and often very productive. There are exhaustless quantities of whortleberries, and as fine as the world anywhere produces. We hardly landed at a place where they were not plenty. Wild, red cherries, currants, gooseberries, raspberries, blackberries, and cranberries are frequently met with in considerable quantities. Such is the general character of the north shore, and the islands of Georgian Bay and their productions, up to She-ba-wa-nah-ning, which is situated nearly mid-way on the northern shore of the waters of Lake Huron."

TRIP FROM COLLINGWOOD TO THE SAUT STE MARIE.

THROUGH GEORGIAN BAY AND NORTH CHANNEL.

THIS is a new and highly interesting steamboat excursion, brought into notice by the completion of the *Ontario, Simcoe and Huron Railroad*, extending from Toronto to Collingwood, at the southern extremity of Georgian Bay.

NOTTAWASSAGA BAY, the southern termination of Georgian Bay, is a large expanse of water bounded by Cape Rich on the west and Christian Island on the east, each being distant about 30 miles from Collingwood. At the south end of the bay lies a small group of islands called the *Hen and Chickens*.

On leaving Collingwood for Bruce Mines and the Saut Ste Marie, the steamer usually runs direct across Georgian Bay to Lonely Island, passing Cabot's Head to the right, and the passage leading into the broad waters of Lake Huron, which is the route pursued by the steamers in the voyage to Mackinac, Green Bay, and Chicago. During the summer months the trip from Collingwood to Mackinac and Chicago affords a delightful excursion.

OWEN'S SOUND, or SYDENHAM, 50 miles west of Collingwood, although off the direct route to the Saut Ste Marie, is well worthy of a passing notice. Here is a thriving settlement, surrounded by a fertile section of country, and containing about 2,500 inhabitants. A steamer runs daily from Collingwood to this place, which will, no doubt, soon be reached by railroad.

LONELY ISLAND, situated about 100 miles west of Collingwood and 20 miles east of the Great Manitoulin Islands, is a large body of land mostly covered with a dense forest, and uninhabited, except by a few fishermen, who resort here at certain seasons of the year for the purpose of taking fish of different kinds. The steamer usually passes this island on its north side, steering for *Cape Smyth*, a bold promontory jutting out from the Great Manitoulin, and distant from Lonely Island about 25 miles.

SQUAW ISLAND and PAPOOSE ISLAND are seen on the north-east, while farther inland are the *Fox Islands*, being the commencement on the west of the innumerable islands which abound along the north shore of Georgian Bay.

LA CLOCHE MOUNTAINS, rising about 2,000 feet above the sea, are next seen in the distance, toward the north; these, combined with the wild scenery of the islands and headlands, form a grand panoramic view, enjoyed from the deck of the passing steamer.

SMYTH'S BAY is passed on the west, some eight or ten miles distant. At the head of this bay, on the Great Manitoulin Island, is situated a village of Indians, and a Jesuit's mission, called We-qua-me-kong. These aborigines are noted for their industry, raising wheat, corn, oats, and potatoes in large quantities. This part of the island is very fertile, and the climate is healthy.

SHE-BA-WA-NAH-NING, signifying, in the Indian dialect, "*Here is a channel*," is a most charming spot, 40 miles distant from Lonely Island, hemmed in by mountains on the north, and a high rocky island on the south. It is situated on the north side of a narrow channel, about half a mile in length, which has a great depth of water. Here is a convenient steamboat landing, a church, a store, and some ten or twelve dwellings, inhabited by Canadians and half-breeds. Indians assemble here often in considerable numbers, to sell their fish and furs, presenting with their canoes and dogs a very grotesque appearance. One resident at this landing usually attracts much attention—a noble dog, of the color of cream. No sooner does the steamer's bell ring, than this animal rushes to the wharf, sometimes assisting to secure the rope that is thrown ashore; the next move he makes is to board the vessel, as though he was a custom-house officer; but on one occasion, in his eagerness to get into the kitchen, he fell overboard; nothing daunted, he swam to the shore, and then again boarding the vessel, succeeded in his desire to fill his stomach, showing the instinct which prompts many a biped office-seeker.

On leaving She-ba-wa-nah-ning and proceeding westward, a most beautiful bay is passed, studded with islands—and mountains upward of 1,000 feet in height, presenting a rocky and sterile appearance, forming an appropriate background to the view—thence is passed Badgley and Heywood islands, the latter lying off Heywood Sound, situated on the north side of the Great Manitoulin.

MAN-I-TOU-WAH-NING, 25 miles northwest of She-ba-wa-nah-ning, is handsomely situated at the head of Heywood Sound. It is an Indian settlement, and also a government agency, being the place annually selected to distribute the Indian annuities.

LITTLE CURRENT, 25 miles west of She-ba-wa-nah-ning, is another interesting landing on the north shore of the Great Manitoulin, opposite La Cloche Island. Here the main channel is narrow, with a current usually running at the rate of five or six knots an hour, being much affected by the winds. The steamer stops at this landing for an hour or upward, receiving a supply of wood, it being furnished by an intelligent Indian or half-breed, who resides at this place with his family. Indians are often seen here in considerable numbers. They are reported to be indolent and harmless, too often neglecting the cultivation of the soil for the more uncertain pursuits of fishing and hunting, although a considerable large clearing is to be seen indifferently cultivated.

CLAPPERTON ISLAND and other islands of less magnitude are passed in the *North Channel*, which is a large body of water about 120 miles long and 25 miles wide. On the north shore is situated a post of the Hudson Bay Company, which may be seen from the deck of the passing steamer.

COCKBURN ISLAND, 85 miles west of Little Current, lies directly west of the Great Manitoulin, from which it is separated by a narrow channel. It is a large island, somewhat elevated, but uninhabited, except by Indians.

DRUMMOND ISLAND, 15 miles farther westward, belongs to the United States, being attached to the State of Michigan. This is another large body of land, being low, and as yet mostly uninhabited.

The next island approached before landing at Bruce Mines is ST. JOSEPH ISLAND, being a large and fertile body of land, with some few settlers.

BRUCE MINES VILLAGE, C. W., is situated on the north shore of Lake Huron, or the "North Channel," as it is here called, distant 290 miles from Collingwood, and 50 from the Saut Ste Marie. Here are a Methodist chapel, a public-house, and a store and storehouse belonging to the Montreal Copper Mining Company, besides extensive buildings used for crushing ore and preparing it for the market; about 75 dwellings and 500 inhabitants. The copper ore, after being crushed by powerful machinery propelled by steam, is put into puddling troughs and washed by water, so as to obtain about 20 per cent. pure copper. In this state it is shipped to the United States and England, bringing about $80 per ton. It then has to go through an extensive smelting process, in order to obtain the pure metal. The mines are situated in the immediate vicinity of the village, there being ten openings or shafts from which the ore is obtained in its crude state. Horse-power is mostly used to elevate the ore; the whims are above ground, attached to which are ropes and buckets. This mine gives employment to about 300 workmen. The capital stock of the company amounts to $600,000.

The *Wellington Mine*, about one mile distant, is also owned by the Montreal Mining Company, but is leased and worked by an English company. This mine, at the present time, is more productive than the Bruce Mines.

The Lake Superior *Journal* gives the following description of the Bruce Mine, from which is produced a copper ore differing from that which is yielded by other mines of that peninsula.

"Ten years ago this mine was opened, and large sums expended for machinery, which proved useless, but it is now under new management, and promises to yield profitably. Twelve shafts have been opened, one of which has been carried down some 330 feet. Some 200 or 300 men are employed, all from the European mines. Some of the ores are very beautiful to the eye, resembling fine gold. After being taken out of the shaft, they are taken upon a rail-track to the crushing-house, where they are passed between large iron rollers, and sifted till only a fine powder remains; from thence to the 'jigger works,' where they are shaken in water till much of the earthy matter is washed away, after which it is piled in the yard ready for shipment, having more the appearance of mud than of copper. It is now mostly shipped to Swansea, in Wales, for smelting. Two years since 1,500 tons were shipped to Baltimore and Buffalo to be smelted."

On resuming the voyage after leaving Bruce Mines, the steamer runs along St. Joseph Island through a beautiful sheet of water, in which are embosomed some few islands near the main shore.

CAMPEMENT D'OURS is an island passed on the left, lying contiguous to St. Joseph Island. Here are encountered several small rocky islands, forming an intricate channel called the "*Narrows.*" On some of the islands in this group are found copper ore, and beautiful specimens of moss. The forest trees, however, are of a dwarfish growth, owing, no doubt, to the scantiness of soil on these rocky islands.

About 10 miles west of the "Narrows," the main channel of the St. Mary's River is reached, forming the boundary between the United States and Canada. A rocky island lies on the Canadian side, which is reserved for government purposes, as it commands the main or ship channel.

SUGAR ISLAND is now reached, which belongs to the United States, and the steamers run a further distance of 25 miles, when the landing at the Saut Ste Marie is reached, there being settlements on both sides of the river. The British boats usually land on the north side, while the American boats make a landing on the south side of the river, near the mouth of the ship canal.

TRIP THROUGH GEORGIAN BAY AND THE NORTH CHANNEL OF LAKE HURON TO MANITOULIN AND SAUT STE MARIE.

(*Copied from a Toronto paper.*)

Dated on board the Steamer COLLINGWOOD, LAKE HURON, *August* 17, 1856.

" A LONG, dark tongue of land stretches out into the lake on our larboard quarter, and the opposite view is backed by a rugged coast, with mountains tall and grim. We are just off Cabot's Head, near where the Georgian Bay attains its greatest width (58 miles). The east coast of the Georgian Bay, as described by Mr. Murray, consists almost exclusively of a sterile rocky border. There are numerous harbors, many of which are, however, so hemmed in by reefs and sunken islets as to render them almost inaccessible to boats of any considerable draught. As we advance toward the north mainland past Lonely Island, the eastern extremity of the Great Manitoulin comes clearly within view. An abrupt escarpment here forms Cape Smyth, and inside a deep sheltered bend, called Smyth's Bay, is located the Jesuit Missionary village of Wequamekong. This neat little settlement being situated on a slope surrounded by extensive clearances, and covered with regularly-built frame houses, shows out favorably to the passer-by. Due north lies our first stopping-place. The distance from Collingwood to the head of the Georgian Bay is about 140 miles, and the point of measurement is a small trading port named She-ba-wa-nah-ning, which was reached early on the forenoon of Thursday. The entrance to it is by a strait so narrow as to be quite imperceptible at any considerable distance from shore, bounded on the east side by the mainland, and on the west by a high island. It forms a secure harbor at all times, and owing to the great depth of water and the steepness of both sides, it is not so difficult to pass, even in stormy weather, as one would suppose. This village, now for some unaccountable reason styled 'Killarney,' with the exception of a store, post-office, and diminutive Roman Catholic church, is a mere collection of fishing huts and Indian camps. It derives its original name, as indeed do most of these Indian localities – from a natural characteristic. That name signifies '*Here's a channel*,' and it amounts to a piece of great impertinence on the part of any one to destroy its adaptability by substituting Killarney, or any other, for it. The population numbers somewhere about 40 whites and half-breeds, with an occasional accession to the Indian residents, bringing it to an average between 60 and 70. They employ themselves almost entirely in the pursuits of trading, hunting, and fishing, but make no attempt at cultivation, not even so much as a cabbage-garden, although there is some tolerably good land in the vicinity. Now and again they have an odd visit from the Jesuit priests at the Wequamekong, and the Church of England Missionary at Manitouwahning; on which occasions the parishioners are called together by a tin horn instead of a bell. Just inside She-ba-wa-nah-ning is one of those lovely bayous so common along the rocky and indented northern coast, with countless small islets, very much resembling the famous '*Thousand Islands*' in the river St. Lawrence; and closing it in on three sides are the La Cloche Mountains, which here rise abruptly to a considerable altitude. The steamer does not return by the same channel, but passes around the island, forming its boundary on the lake side. Looking back through the narrow strip of water by which we have entered from the main lake, it seems a fairy-like performance to have threaded so small a gorge with this huge steamboat, and the enchanting wildness of the scenery that bounds us on every side adds delight to such surprise. On rounding the west point of this island, the lake opens out again before us, and our steamer heads toward Manitouwahning, distant about 27 miles. At the head of Heywood Sound, on the north side of the Grand Manitoulin, is situated the village, where we expect to find a host of "aborigines" awaiting the receipt of a cargo of trumpery by means of which the commissariat manages to annually amuse their uncultivated fancies and illustrate the marvelous solicitude entertained for them by their "Great Father," who, in the present instance, is a Mother. There is no wharf, but the water is so deep close in shore, that the steamboat sidles up to a low, gravelly beach, and our gangway is laid from her side to land with perfect ease. As it seems not altogether improbable that the chain of islands constituting an Indian Reserve in this locality must ere long be brought into the market for sale, it may prove serviceable to publish a few descriptive particulars relating to their position and quality. For such purpose, then, I shall here briefly relate them while the 'small-boy' in treasury uniform is superintending the embarkation of government presents to be distributed among that heterogeneous and expectant multitude before us.

"The belt of islands known as the Manitoulins embraces Fitzwilliam, an unimportant island southeast of the principal of this group, the Grand Manitoulin, and others, of which Barrie and Cockburn islands are the only ones worthy of note. The La Cloche and St. Joseph Island are sometimes erroneously included in the general denomination; but they are distinguished by being crown properties, while the Manitoulins form a portion of the Indian Reserves. With the exception of Great Manitoulin, none of these islands are of much consequence in point of value. The timber thereupon would indicate soil of a workable description, but their rocky elevation seems to deny the existence of fertile tracts of any appreciable extent. The *Grand Manitoulin* is eighty-one miles in length, and averages about twenty miles in width, and has an area of at least sixteen hundred square miles. Its geological features present nothing remarkable. The soil, over a limestone structure, with a lower fossiliferous bed of extraordinary depth, is rich; and there is an abundance of soft and hard lumber covering it throughout. I am unaware whether or not any portions of it have been surveyed. Certainly the sooner something practical is done in the way of cultivating it the better. It may be rather an easy administration of that heirloom of titled boobies and aristocratic sprigs, the Indian Department, to keep these reserved lands locked up in the chimerical pretense of *benefiting* the Indians. The majority of Indians derive no real advantage from them—will certainly never cultivate them—and, therefore, their continuous reservation operates but as a bar to the settlement of adjacent territories. The villages of Wequamekong and Manitouwahning are the only extensive settlements of pretension upon the Manitoulin Islands. The latter being the place where we had just landed at the above digression, is the locale of the government agency, and the appointed residence of Captain Ironsides, the local superintendent. In other words, it is the head-quarters of the Indian Department. As a cultivated spot it has a very enticing appearance. The site is favorable, in some respects, for a village, but building frame houses for savages, and neither clearing off the stones at similar cost, nor teaching the natives themselves to do so, and afterward to plant gardens, potatoes, corn and maize fields, is not a model plan of carrying out the objects of such selections. The present condition of this place is the best proof. The white inhabitants residing here number about thirty; the Indian population fluctuates between six or seven hundred and two thousand. These, however, seem never to have appreciated the wooden domiciles erected for them, as upward of sixteen frame houses in the village are forsaken, and the remainder may be said to merely serve as a shelter for the families living in them, as they have no signs of improvement near or far. There is a neat little church in the village, and a resident minister of the Church of England. There also is a 'medicine man.' The residences of these gentlemen and that of Captain Ironsides are very comfortable dwellings. About £600 worth of goods were landed as presents. They consist principally of blankets, trinkets, calicoes, pork, flour, and a small quantity of ammunition. It was the custom formerly to give them articles adapted to their habitual pursuits, such as shot, guns, rifles, knives, ammunition, kettles, hatchets, etc.; but the most serviceable of these things have been discontinued, in accordance with the wisdom of authority. It occupies the officers in charge sometimes two or three weeks dispensing these articles. The scraps of tribes now present to receive these gifts belong mostly to the Ottawas, Chippewas, and Pottawatamies. Some few Munsees and Delawares used at one time to frequent the station, but now there is no great variety of tribes about any part of the lake. Indeed, at this annual distribution but a very few Indians attended, in comparison with the multitudinous attendance of former years. The 'forest children' are annually fading away, and before many more winters and summers have elapsed it will most probably be as rare a thing to find a handful of them about these lakes, as it was in earlier days to discover the footsteps of the pale-face away up in these northern wilds.

"The next day we accompanied Captain Ironsides, and a party of friends, to the Indian village of Wequamekong. (This is the Jesuit mission mentioned in the preceding part of my letter.) It was reached by a portage of about seven miles across the neck of the peninsular promontory which forms the east side of Heywood Sound. The land through which we passed is said to be much more fertile than that in any other section of the island. The village of Wequamekong is quite romantically situated, and is altogether a very pretty little place. The Indians here are remnants of the Chippewa and Ottawa tribes, and they appear cleaner, more industrious, and civilized than I had seen elsewhere. They have fine fields of Indian corn, patches of beans, potatoes, etc., and quite a respectable show of garden vegetables. We witnessed an interesting sight in the 'numbering of the tribes' by Captain Ironsides. It gave us an opportunity to see some fine-looking old chiefs, several of whom were astonished at the idea of having their likenesses taken. The villagers also turned out in holiday attire. We could have scarce believed it possible they were so well to do in worldly goods as their 'fashionable' habiliments denoted. Certainly the Jesuits have carried out their mission at this village in the most praiseworthy manner. What with good spirits, ravenous appetites, an agreeable host, and the weather that an Italian might almost envy, our time glid swiftly away until the return of the steamboat on Sunday morning. And contented as we had been, the sight of Captain Butterworth's jovial countenance, and a renewal of our acquaintance with the 'quite at home' comforts of the *Collingwood*, were abundantly relished.

"After leaving Manitouwahning (on Friday), we have the Great Manitoulin on our left; and up to Little Current, the next stopping-place, 30 miles farther on, the course lies through picturesque clusters of low islands, scantily wooded, and covered in the open parts with a rank growth of dry-looking wild grass, and diversified by clumps of dwarfish pines and firs. There is here a small settlement of Indians and half-breeds. They furnish wood for the steamer, and likewise supply meat, fish, vegetables, etc. At dark we cast off from Little Current. Thence our passage was among woody islands, and through narrow but deep channels, the main shore of Manitoulin always within sight, and now and then opening out into a wider sheet of water, so that the whole course seems to be alternate narrow straits and small lakes. From Little Current to the Bruce Mines the distance is nearly 120 miles, and between the west end of Manitoulin and the north shore, for some distance, the channel is very broad. We passed this during the night-time. It was a clear moonlight night; and we could see by the drifting clouds that hovered above the Great Manitoulin, how rude Boreas was indulging himself with a jolly blow outside, in the lake, while not a gust moved the surface of this inside lake, through which our steamboat smoothly plowed her way. After a short stay at the mines, we proceeded onward to Saut Ste Marie, landing once more, *en voyage*, at Sugar Island. The village of St. Mary, or Saut Ste Marie, is so well known to most people, I shall not bore the reader with any description of it. Suffice to say, the canal on the American side has helped to build up that part at the expense of its opposite settlement. The inhabitants, however, seem to have nothing else to do besides smoking, drinking gin-slings and mint-juleps, and catching fish.

"Dr. Jackson states that the healthiness of the climate in these parts during summer months is unsurpassable, and, above all other places, is calculated to restore the health of invalids suffering from the depressive miasms of the fever-breeding Southwestern States, or the pent-up enervating atmosphere of Eastern cities.

"This route along the North Channel, for the safe conveyance of merchandise and all perishable goods, is infinitely preferable to that usually traveled across the lakes, filling up as it does a distance of not less than 460 miles of rough lake navigation by a pleasant course sheltered from storms and affording a diversity of scenery calculated to relieve the tedium of so long a voyage."

ST. JOSEPH ISLAND C. W.

This important island, lying in St. Mary's River, near its outlet into Lake Huron, is thus described by T. N. Molesworth, provincial land surveyor, and may answer in part for a description of Drummond and Sugar islands, lying contiguous and belonging to the United States.

"The surface along the southern and southwestern shores of St. Joseph Island is generally flat, low, and swampy, being in many places wet, and very thickly timbered. The northern, northeastern, and eastern shores, in general, rise with a gentle inclination from the shore, being swampy only for a short distance inward; and along the northerly shore of Point-au-Gravier there is a precipitous rise of about 30 feet in height. The highest hill, near the center of the island, has an elevation of about 400 feet.

"The island is generally well watered, a considerable number of streams rising in the swamps in the interior, and entering the lake. The principal one is that having its source in Lake Hilton, which enters Milford Haven with a rapid current, and having a very good mill-site near its mouth, and a constant supply of water, and also entering a safe and capacious harbor, is the best adapted for the use of the island. The other streams are of small size, but appear to have a constant supply of water.

"The surface soil is almost generally a red sandy loam, or clay and sand mixed with mold; but in some places a white sand appears; in others a brown or red clay; under this there is a stiff clay, in some places of a reddish color, in others nearly white, which crumbles when exposed to the surface.

"Very little rock appears anywhere on St. Joseph Island, and only on the shore; small particles of quartz rock rising about ten feet above the surface, appear at Payme-day-giundeg. In the channel opposite Campement D'Ours Island a mass of syenitic granite puts out in irregular points, some parts rising about 20 feet above the water. In Lot 10, Concession V., white sandstone appears just at the edge of the water, and at the level of its surface; and in the Point-au-Gravier Concession, blue limestone appears rising abruptly from the water to the height of 30 feet—in the horizontal strata, of from six inches to a foot in thickness. It is used for making lime and building at the Bruce Mines, and by the inhabitants.

"The island is closely wooded; the timber on the hills and dry surface being maple, beech, birch—often mixed with hemlock--cedar, spruce, basswood, and elm. In some parts the timber is all maple, and a great deal of it is bird's-eye and curly maple—the latter mostly where the surface is stony. In the swamps the timber is cedar, spruce, balsam, hemlock, pine, and tamarack—generally growing very densely in most of the swamps—the cedar predominating—in some, the tamarack or spruce.

"With regard to the capabilities of the island for settlement, about two thirds of its surface will probably be available—the remaining third being swamps of little use except as meadows at a future period.

"Its soil is of good quality for agricultural purposes, raising wheat, oats, potatoes, turnips, carrots, peas, beans, Indian corn, and melons equally well with lands in other parts of the province. The mining regions will afford a favorable market for the surplus agricultural produce raised upon the island, which lies in the course of, and possesses stopping-places for, the American and Canadian steamers proceeding to the Saut Ste Marie and Lake Superior.

"The snow disappearing off the clearings about the middle of April, the farmers commence farming operations a few days later: there are very few frosts after that time to injure any crops. The harvest commences about the middle of August. There is an abundance of fine fish in the waters around the island, and small fisheries are carried on in the following places. Tenby Bay. (White fish are caught extensively after the middle of October.) Campement des Matelots, or St. Joseph. (Black bass, pike, and white-fish very abundant.) Opposite Sugar Island there is a herring fishery; and in Mud Lake, opposite the Campement des Matelots, on the American shore, there is a considerable pickerel fishery. Besides these there are abundance of pike, trout, and maskalonge in all the waters round the island, which are very serviceable to the inhabitants. There are a few moose and red deer, and a number of black bears on the island, besides foxes, hares, etc.

"The lake freezes over generally before the middle of December, the ice clearing off in the spring about the 1st May; and the snow lies permanently on the ground from the middle of December to the middle of April; its average depth is from two to three feet, its greatest about four feet. The lowest range of the thermometer is in February, when it reaches 23° below zero (Fahr.), for perhaps a fortnight, the average cold being from 10° above to 10° below zero. In June, July, and August the highest range is sometimes 100° above zero; average range 70° to 80°."

This island has been recently surveyed, and the lands sold under the direction of the Crown Land Department of Canada, thus offering inducements for settlement and cultivation.

Saut Ste Marie, capital of Chippewa Co., Mich., is advantageously situated on St. Mary's River, or Strait, 350 miles N.N.W. of Detroit, and 15 miles from the foot of Lake Superior, in N. lat. 46° 31′. The rapids at this place, giving the name to the settlements on both sides of the river, have a descent of 20 feet, within the distance of a mile, and form the natural limit of navigation. The Ship Canal, however, which has recently been constructed on the American side, obviates this difficulty. Steamers of a large class now pass through the locks into Lake Superior, greatly facilitating trade and commerce. The village on the American side is pleasantly situated near the foot of the rapids, and contains a court-house and jail; a Baptist, a Methodist, and a Roman Catholic church; 15 or 20 stores and storehouses, besides a few manufacturing establishments, and about 1,000 inhabitants. Many of the inhabitants and Indians in the vicinity are engaged in the fur trade and fisheries, the latter being an important and profitable occupation. Summer visitors flock to this place and the Lake Superior country for health and pleasure. There are two hotels on the American side, and one on the Canadian side of the river, affording good accommodations.

Fort Brady is an old and important United States military post contiguous to this frontier village, where is stationed a regular garrison of troops. It commands the St. Mary's River and the approach to the mouth of the canal.

Saut Ste Marie, C. W., is a scattered settlement, where is located a part of the Hudson Bay Company. Here is a steamboat landing, an hotel, and two or three stores, including the Hudson Bay Company's; and it has from 200 to 300 inhabitants. Indians of the Chippewa tribe reside in the vicinity in considerable numbers, they having the exclusive right to take fish in the waters contiguous to the rapids. They also employ themselves in running the rapids in their frail canoes, when desired by citizens or strangers—this being one of the most exhilarating enjoyments for those fond of aquatic sports. *(See Engraving.)*

SAULT ST. MARIE—FROM AMERICAN SIDE.

THE SAINT MARY'S FALLS SHIP CANAL.

THIS Canal, which connects the navigation of Lake Superior with the Lower Lakes, is a little more than one mile in length, and cost about one million dollars.

It was built in the years 1853, '54, '55 by the Saint Mary's Falls Ship Canal Company, under a contract with commissioners appointed by the authorities of the State of Michigan to secure the building of the canal.

A grant of 750,000 acres of the public land had previously been made by Congress to the State of Michigan to aid in the construction of this important work.

This grant of 750,000 acres was given to the parties contracting for the building of the canal, provided the work should be completed within two years from the date of the contract.

The work was commenced in the spring of 1853, and completed within the time specified in the contract (*two years !*).

This result was accomplished under many disadvantages, during a very sickly season, and when great difficulty was experienced in obtaining laborers; but the unremitting vigor of those who had the charge of the work secured its completion in the most substantial, permanent, and acceptable manner.

During a great portion of the time there were from 1,200 to 1,600 men employed upon the work, exclusive of the force at the different quarries where the stone was cut and prepared for the locks, besides a large force employed in necessary agencies, getting timber, etc.

The stones for the locks were cut at Anderden, Canada (near Malden), and at Marblehead, near Sandusky, in Ohio. These were sent in vessels to the work, some twenty-five different sailing vessels being employed in this business.

On the completion of the canal in June, 1855, the Governor of the State, the State officers, and the Canal Commissioners proceeded to Saut Ste Marie for the purpose of inspecting the work. It was accepted, and thereupon, in accordance with the terms of the contract, the State authorities released to the Canal

Company and issued patents for the 750,000 acres of land. This was all the remuneration the company received for the work.

The lands were selected during the building of the canal by agents appointed by the Governor of Michigan.

Of the 750,000 acres, 39,000 acres were selected in the iron region of Lake Superior, 147,000 acres in the copper region, and the balance, 564,000 acres, in the Lower Peninsula.

The following figures will give some idea of the magnitude of this work:

Length of canal 5,584 feet, = 1 mile 304 feet.

Width at top 115 feet—at water-line 100 feet—at bottom 64 feet.

The depth of the canal is 12 feet.

A slope wall on the sides of the canal is 4,000 feet in length.

There are two locks, each 350 feet in length.

Width of locks 70 feet at top—61½ feet at bottom.

The walls are 25 feet high—10 feet thick at bottom.

Lift of upper lock 8 feet—lower do., 10 feet; total lockage 18 feet.

Lower wharf 180 feet long, 20 feet wide.

Upper wharf 830 feet long, from 16 to 30 feet wide.

There are three pairs of folding gates, each 40 feet wide.

Upper gate 17 feet high—lower gate 24 feet 6 inches high.

There are also upper and lower caisson gates, used for shutting off the water from the canal.

The amount of lumber, timber, and iron used in the building of the piers and gates is enormous.

There were 103,437 lbs of wrought iron used in the gates, and 38,000 lbs cast iron.

About 8,000 feet of oak timber, etc.

The tolls on the canal are collected by the State—are merely nominal—and only intended to defray the necessary expenses of repairs.

THE UPPER LAKE COUNTRY.

We copy the following extract from an address published in the Lansing (Mich.) *Republican*, as containing interesting information regarding the Commerce of the Upper Lakes:

C. T. Harvey, Esq., of Lake Superior, agreeably to appointment, made an address in the Hall of the House of Representatives on the subject of the "present state and future prospects of the Commerce of Lake Superior."

"As to the past, he observed that in 1839 the first steamer visited the Saut Ste Marie, to the great astonishment of the Indians who lived on St. Mary's River. That in 1844 Capt. Ward first established a regular steamboat line from Detroit to the entrance of Lake Superior *via* Mackinac. That in 1849 Mr. S. McKnight (a member of the house) did all the transportation of merchandise around the Falls of St. Mary's with one or two horses, and it was not till 1851 that the first steamer floated on the waters of Lake Superior only six years ago.

"After some further reminiscences showing at how very recent a date business in that quarter had commenced, the speaker proceeded to the present.

"He referred to the report of the Superintendent of the Saut Canal, to show that in the season of 1856 just closed there was over 11,000 tons of iron ore shipped through it to Detroit and eastward. An increase of 800 per cent. over 1855, when only 1,400 tons were sent down. That 1,040 tons of bloom iron were sent, an increase of 25 per cent.; but the most remarkable fact was that ten millions four hundred and fifty-two thousand pounds of copper were sent through the canal in the raw state—over two and a quarter millions of dollars—an increase of some 67 per cent. Mr. H. remarked that this noticeable increase did not look like a failure of the mining interests, although public excitement respecting them had subsided.

"The business eastward through the canal of mineral and fish exported from the lake, amounted to, as estimated by the Superintendent, $2,875,000; while the imports of merchandise and supplies were, in round numbers, $2,500,000; making a total of $5,375,000, of which he calculated full $5,000,000 was commerce of the Upper Peninsula. Remarking that a trade of this magnitude, which had sprung up out of nothing within fifteen years, must in the next fifteen years increase in almost the same ratio, till the results would be almost incredible, he hazarded the conjecture, that within 25 years as many vessels of all kinds would pass and re-pass in the St. Mary's River, as now frequent the waters of the St. Clair."

TRIP FROM COLLINGWOOD TO MACKINAC, GREEN BAY, CHICAGO, ETC.

THIS excursion is an interesting one for the pleasure traveler, as well as the man of business. The steamer on leaving Collingwood runs direct for *Cabot's Head*, 80 miles, skirting the main shore of Canada to *Cape Hurd*, about 20 miles farther, passing the Bear's Rump, Flower Pot, Echo and Cove islands.

YEO ISLAND and FITZ WILLIAM ISLAND (a large island) are seen on the north; several smaller islands are also passed, when the broad waters of Lake Huron are entered, the steamers usually running direct for Mackinac.

The GREAT MANITOULIN may be seen in the distance, toward the north, in pleasant weather, and the OUTER DUCK and GREAT DUCK islands are passed about 80 miles westward of Cape Hurd.

The steamer then pursues a westerly course toward Mackinac, about 100 miles farther, sighting Presque Isle on the main Michigan shore, and passing Bois Blanc and Round islands. The Straits of Mackinac are now entered, being here about twenty miles across, but soon diminishes in width; opposite old Fort Mackinac it is four or five miles in width.

The STRAITS OF MACKINAC, with the approaches thereto from Lakes Huron and Michigan, will always command attention from the passing traveler. Through this channel will pass, for ages to come, a great current of commerce, and its shores will be enlivened with civilized life, where at present the Indian now lingers, but, alas! is fast fading away.

It is proposed to construct a railroad running from Detroit or Saginaw to Old Fort Mackinac, which, when completed, will tend to open the whole northern portion of this part of the State of Michigan, one of the most favorably situated States of the whole Union; having two peninsulas, rich in soil and mineral productions, and from which are now exported immense quantities of lumber, copper, and iron ore.

In this great commercial route Lake Huron is traversed for about 180 miles, often affording the traveler a taste of sea-sickness and its consequent evils. Yet there often are times when Lake Huron is hardly ruffled, and the timid passenger enjoys the voyage with as much zest as the more experienced mariner.

MACKINAC, the gem of the Upper Lake islands, may vie with any other locality for the salubrity of its climate, for its picturesque beauties, and for its vicinity to fine fishing-grounds. Here the invalid, the seeker of pleasure, as well as the sportsman and angler, can find enjoyment to their heart's content during warm weather. For further description see page 110.

On leaving Mackinac for Green Bay the steamer generally runs a west course for the mouth of the bay, passing several islands in Lake Michigan before entering the waters of Green Bay, about 150 miles distant.

SUMMER ISLAND lies on the north side and ROCK ISLAND lies on the south side of the entrance to Green Bay, forming a charming view from the deck of the steamer.

POTAWATOMEE ISLAND, CHAMBERS' ISLAND, and other small islands, are next passed on the upward trip toward the head of the bay.

GREEN BAY, about 100 miles long and from 20 to 30 miles wide, is a splendid sheet of water, destined no doubt to be enlivened with commerce and pleasure excursions. Here are to be seen a number of picturesque islands and headlands. Several important streams enter into Green Bay, the largest of which is Neenah or Fox River, at its head, and is the outlet of Winnebago Lake. Menomonee River forms the boundary between the States of Wisconsin and Michigan, and empties into the bay opposite Green Island.

The town of GREEN BAY, the capital of Brown Co., Wis., is finely situated near the mouth of Fox or Neenah River, at its entrance into Green Bay, where is a good and secure harbor.

It lies 25 miles due west of Kewaunee, on the west shore of Lake Michigan, and 115 miles north from Milwaukee. The town is handsomely situated, and contains many large warehouses and elegant residences, together with several churches, hotels, and stores of different kinds, and about 3,000 inhabitants. The improvement of Fox River by dams and locks, in connection with the improvements on the Wisconsin River, afford an uninterrupted steam navigation from Green Bay to Prairie du Chien, on the Mississippi River—thus making Green Bay a great point for the trans-shipment of goods and produce of every variety; the largest class steamers running to Chicago on the south, Saut Ste Marie on the north, as well as to Collingwood, to Detroit, and to Buffalo on the east. The lumber trade of Green Bay is immense, this whole section of country abounding in timber of different kinds the most useful for building purposes.

ASTOR is the name of a suburb of Green Bay, lying at the mouth of Fox River, while on the opposite side of the stream stands *Fort Howard*, surrounded by a village of the same name.

NENOMONEE CITY, Oconto Co., Wis., is a new settlement, situated on the west side of Green Bay, near the mouth of Nenomonee River. The country to the west and north of this place is as yet a wilderness, inhabited only by a few roving Indians.

In regard to the route from Green Bay to Lake Superior, the *Advocate* says:

"A road from Green Bay to the most southerly point of Keewenaw would be less than 200 miles in length, and while it would shorten the travel over the present route (by water) at least 100 miles, would open one of the most beautiful and fertile sections in the Union—a section which will remain unknown and unoccupied until such a road is opened by the government. The Lake Superior people need it most especially for procuring supplies, driving cattle, etc.

"The traveler finds the whole distance, to within a few miles of Lake Superior, abounding in every resource which will make a country wealthy and prosperous. Clear, beautiful lakes are

..erspersed, and these have plenty of large trout and other ish. Water and water-powers are everywhere to be found, and the timber is of the best kind—maple groves, beech, oak, pine, etc. Nothing is now wanted but a few roads to open this rich country to the settler, and it will soon teem with villages, schools, mills, farming operations, and every industrial pursuit which the more southern portion of our State now exhibits."

Fox or *Neenah River* rises in Marquette Co., Wis., and passing through Lake Winnebago, forms its outlet. This important stream is rendered navigable for steamers of a small class by means of dams and locks, forming in connection with a short canal to the Wisconsin River a direct water communication from Green Bay to the Mississippi River, a distance of about 200 miles. The rapids in the lower part of Fox River afford an immense water-power, while the upper section of country through which it flows, produces lumber and grain in great abundance.

Appleton, Outaganie Co., Wis., is situated on Fox or Neenah River, 30 miles from its entrance into Green Bay, and five miles from Lake Winnebago, where are rapids called the *Grand Chute*. Here the river descends about 30 feet in one mile and a half, affording an inexhaustible amount of water-power. Here are located two flouring mills, four saw mills, a paper mill, and sash factory. This is the capital of the county. and is no doubt destined to become a large manufacturing and commercial place, from the facilities which it possesses, by means of navigation and hydraulic power. Steamers run south into Lake Winnebago, and north into Green Bay.

Neenah, situated at the foot of Lake Winnebago, where commences the river improvement, is a growing place. Here is a fine water-power, which gives motion to several mills.

The City of Oshkosh, situated on the west side of Lake Winnebago, is a flourishing place, and the capital of Winnebago County, Wis. It contains the county buildings, 7 churches, a land-office, several public houses, 40 or 50 stores of different kinds, 2 steam grist-mills, 12 steam saw-mills, 2 iron foundries, and a number of other manufacturing establishments, and about 7,500 inhabitants.

The *Fox* and *Wolf* rivers uniting, form a large and important stream, flowing into the lake at Oshkosh, which, together with plank-roads and a railroad to extend south to Fond du Lac, and another road to Ripon, give great facilities for trade and commerce, in connection with lake and river navigation. The *Fox River Improvement* here leaves Lake Winnebago, and extends in a southwest direction toward the junction with the Wisconsin River at Portage City.

FOND DU LAC, capital of Fond du Lac County, is a flourishing city favorably situated at the head of Lake Winnebago, 87 miles N.N.W. from Milwaukee by railroad route, and 42 miles west of Sheboygan, lying on Lake Michigan. Here are located the county buildings, a city hall, several churches and public houses, 60 stores of different kinds, two banking houses, a car factory, an iron foundry, and several other manufacturing establishments, and 7,000 inhabitants. Steamers run daily to Oshkosh, Appleton, Green Bay, and other ports.

The *Chicago, St. Paul* and *Fond du Lac Railroad*, when finished, will form a direct and speedy communication with almost every part of Wisconsin, Illinois, and Minnesota.

LAKE WINNEBAGO, which is a most beautiful sheet of water, about 30 miles long and 10 broad, forms a link in the chain of navigable waters, connecting Green Bay and Lake Michigan with the Wisconsin and Mississippi River at Prairie du Chien. Railroads will soon reach the waters of this lake from several points.

THE TRIP FROM CHICAGO TO MACKINAC, etc., connecting at the latter place with the *Green Bay* route, is fully described in another part of this work

MINERAL WEALTH OF THE LAKE SUPERIOR REGION.

NATIVE COPPER.—"This useful metal is in every respect the most interesting substance found in connection with the trappean rocks of the Lake Superior region, is widely distributed, and possesses great mineralogical interest. In addition to the enormous masses which occur in the veins of this region, sometimes attaining at the Cliff Mine the weight of several hundred tons, a great variety of crystalline forms are occasionally found. The most interesting localities of the crystallized copper are at the Copper Falls, the Cliff, the Phœnix, and the Eagle Harbor mines. Many of these beautiful specimens are highly valued by those interested in the mines, and, of course, difficult to be obtained, except by those residing at the localities where they occur."

NATIVE SILVER.—"This valuable metal occurs, diffused through the trap, at various localities on Keweenaw Point and Isle Royal. In fact, its distribution is coextensive with that of native copper; but the principal portion of that which has been obtained thus far was from the old Lake Superior (now Phœnix), the Cliff, the Copper Falls, and the Minnesota mines. The silver occurs in connection with the metallic copper, both metals being united together at their edges, and yet each being almost entirely pure and free from alloy with the other. The silver is almost invariably accompanied by a greenish, hydrous silicate of alumina and iron. The largest mass of silver obtained, up to this time, weighed more than six pounds. This was found at the Phœnix Mine. Beautiful specimens of native silver, in Prehnite, have also been picked up on the beaches of Washington Harbor, Isle Royal."

A DIAMOND FOUND.—We had been well aware that this country was very rich in minerals and some kinds of precious stones, but we had not expected to see a Lake Superior diamond, yet such is the case. We were shown one yesterday that would measure three fourths of an inch in length, and at least one fourth of an inch in thickness. It is a regular formed octagon, and all who have seen it pronounce it a diamond, but of what exact value is yet uncertain, it being in the rough state. It cuts glass and shows all the brilliancy of a diamond of the first water, which, if it should prove to be, will make its value not less than two thousand dollars. The diamond was found by the wife of Mr. Alfred Hauffman, while walking on the shore of the Lake. The waves washed it up, and on receding left it exposed to the rays of the sun, when its brightness attracted her attention, and she picked it up. Mr. H. is a poor laboring man, and should it prove as valuable as is supposed, it will be quite a handsome windfall (we might say *water*-fall) for him. This is a great country.—*Lake Superior Journal*—1856.

For a description of Lake Superior Iron Region, see page 66.

LAKE COMMERCE—IMPORTANT IMPROVEMENTS.

Deepening of the St. Clair Flats.—We understand, says the Detroit *Daily Advertiser* (June, 1857), that the contract for deepening the channel of the St. Clair Flats has been let to Mr. Barton, of Buffalo. The contract is subject to the approval of the War Department, and should it be approved by the first of next month, it will be prosecuted with vigor. Mr. Barton is also connected with Mr. Osgood in the contract for deepening the channel of the St. Mary River, which has been approved by the War Department. The machinery to be used in the work will be taken up in a few days, and every preparation is being made to commence the work about the 1st of July, and to drive it successfully forward. We hear that both the above-named gentlemen have had much experience in this kind of business, and being men of energy and perseverance, will push the work forward with all possible dispatch. The deepening of both these channels is all-important to the commercial community, and it is earnestly hoped that nothing may occur to hinder or retard its progress and speedy completion.

THE CHAPEL.—Pictured Rocks.

TRIP FROM SAUT STE MARIE TO THE DIFFERENT PORTS ON LAKE SUPERIOR.

SINCE the completion of the St. Mary's Ship Canal in the spring of 1855, steamers and propellers of a large class traverse the waters of Lake Superior, affording safe and excellent accommodations for travelers and emigrants. During the year 1856 three large steamers formed the Lake Superior Line running from Cleveland and Detroit through the canal to Superior City, at the head of Fond du Lac, and two large steamers, besides several propellers, ran from Chicago for the same destination, stopping at Mackinac, forming an almost daily communication with the different Lake Superior ports.

The steamer COLLINGWOOD also runs direct from Collingwood, C. W., to the Saut Ste Marie, enabling passengers taking the Toronto and Collingwood route to proceed direct into Lake Superior.

On leaving the Upper Landing at the Saut Ste Marie, above the rapids, the steamer soon enters Tequamenon Bay, passing IROQUOIS POINT, 15 miles distant on the south shore, while *Gros Cap*, on the north or Canada side, lies opposite, being about four miles asunder. This headland consists of hills of porphyry estimated to rise 6 or 700 feet above the waters of the lake. "Gros Cap is a name given by the *voyageurs* to almost innumerable projecting headlands; but in this case appropriate—since it is the conspicuous feature at the entrance of the lake."

North of Gros Cap lies *Goulais Bay*, and *Goulais Point*, another bold headland, is seen in the distance. The whole north shore, as seen from the deck of the steamer, presents a bold and grand appearance.

TEQUAMENON BAY is about 25 miles long and as many broad, terminating at *White Fish Point*, 40 miles above Saut Ste Marie. *Parisien Island* is passed, lying near the middle of the above bay, being attached to Canada. Opposite this island, to the north, is seen *Coulée Point*, and besides this, several small islands stud the north shore. *Tequamenon River* enters the bay from the east, discharging a large quantity of water.

MAMAINSE POINT (Little Sturgeon), opposite WHITE FISH POINT, is another bold headland, near where is situated the Quebec Copper Mining Co.'s Works, at present abandoned, owing to their being found unproductive. Some 15 or 20 miles north are located the Montreal Company's Copper Mine, which is being successfully worked. While still farther north, skirting Lake Superior, is to be found a vast *mineral region*, as yet only partially explored.

The scenery of Lake Superior, and the productions of its shores, which are so little known to even our professional tourists, are thus vividly described by an intelligent writer:

"Situated between latitudes forty-six and forty-nine—with an altitude of over two hundred yards above the level of the ocean, and a depth reaching far below that level—a coast of surpassing beauty and grandeur, more than twelve hundred miles in extent, and abounding in geological phenomena, varied mineral wealth, agates, cornelian, jasper, opal, and other precious stones—with its rivers, bays, estuaries, islands, presque isles, peninsulas, capes, pictured rocks, transparent lakes, leaping cascades, and bold highlands, limned with pure veins of quartz, spar, and amethystine crystals, full to repletion with mineral riches; reflecting in gorgeous majesty the sun's bright rays and the moon's mellow blush; o'ertopped with ever-verdant groves of fir, cedar, and the mountain ash; while the background is filled up with mountain upon mountain, until rising in majesty to the clouds, distance loses their inequality resting against the clear vault of heaven."

On passing *White Fish Point*, where may be seen a number of "sand-dunes," or hills, and a light-house 75 feet in height, the broad waters of Lake Superior are reached. The steamers usually pursue a westerly course toward Grand Island or Marquette, passing *Point au Sable*, 50 miles farther. During clear weather, the steep sandy hills on the south shore, ranging from 400 to 1,000 feet in height, may be seen from the deck of the steamer.

The PICTURED ROCKS, of which almost fabulous accounts are given by travelers, are about 110 miles west of Saut Ste Marie. Here also are to be seen the *Cascade Falls* and the *Arched Rock*, both objects of great interest. The Amphitheatre, Miners' Castle, Chapel, Grand Portal, and Sail Rock, are also points of great picturesque beauty, which require to be seen to be justly appreciated.

Extract from FOSTER and WHITNEY'S Report of the Geology of the Lake Superior Land District:

PICTURED ROCKS.

"The range of cliffs to which the name of the Pictured Rocks has been given, may be regarded as among the most striking and beautiful features of the scenery of the Northwest, and are well worthy the attention of the artist, the lover of the grand and beautiful, and the observer of geological phenomena.

"Although occasionally visited by travelers, a full and accurate description of this extraordinary locality has not as yet been communicated to the public.*

"The PICTURED ROCKS may be described, in general terms, as a series of sandstone bluffs extending along the shore of Lake Superior for about five miles, and rising, in most places, vertically from the water, without any beach at the base, to a height varying from fifty to nearly two hundred feet. Were they simply a line of cliffs, they might not, so far as relates to height or extent, be worthy of a rank among great natural curiosities, although such an assemblage of rocky strata, washed by the waves of the great lake, would not, under any circumstances, be destitute of grandeur. To the voyager coasting along their base in his frail canoe they would, at all times, be an object of dread; the recoil of the surf, the rock-bound coast, affording for miles no place of refuge; the lowering sky, the rising wind; all these would excite his appre-

* Schoolcraft has undertaken to describe this range of cliffs, and illustrate the scenery. The sketches do not appear to have been made on the spot, or finished by one who was acquainted with the scenery, as they bear no resemblance, so far as we observed, to any of the prominent features of the Pictured Rocks.

"It is a matter of surprise that, so far as we know, none of our artists have visited this region and given to the world representations of scenery so striking, and so different from any which can be found elsewhere. We can hardly conceive of any thing more worthy of the artist's pencil; and if the tide of pleasure-travel should once be turned in this direction, it seems not unreasonable to suppose that a fashionable hotel may yet be built under the shade of the pine groves near the Chapel, and a trip thither become as common as one to Niagara now is."

hension, and induce him to ply a vigorous oar until the dreaded wall was passed. But in the Pictured Rocks there are two features which communicate to the scenery a wonderful and almost unique character. These are, first, the curious manner in which the cliffs have been excavated and worn away by the action of the lake, which for centuries has dashed an ocean-like surf against their base; and, second, the equally curious manner in which large portions of the surface have been colored by bands of brilliant hues.

"It is from the latter circumstance that the name by which these cliffs are known to the American traveler is derived; while that applied to them by the French *voyageurs* ('Les Portails'*) is derived from the former, and by far the most striking peculiarity.

"The term *Pictured Rocks* has been in use for a great length of time, but when it was first applied we have been unable to discover.

"The Indian name applied to these cliffs, according to our *voyageurs*, is *Schkuee-archibi-kung* or "The end of the rocks," which seems to refer to the fact that, in descending the lake, after having passed them, no more rocks are seen along the shore. Our *voyageurs* had many legends to relate of the pranks of the *Menni-boujou* in these caverns, and in answer to our inquiries seemed disposed to fabricate stories without end of the achievements of this Indian deity.

"We will describe the most interesting points in the series, proceeding from west to east. On leaving Grand Island harbor,†

---

* Le Portail is a French term, signifying the principal entrance of a church or a portal, and this name was given to the Pictured Rocks by the *voyageurs* evidently in allusion to the arched entrances which constitute the most characteristic feature. Le Grand Portail is the great archway, or grand portal.

† The traveler desirous of visiting this scene should take advantage of one of the steamers or propellers which navigate the lake and land at Grand Island, from which he can proceed to make the tour of the interesting points in a small boat. The large vessels on the lake do not approach sufficiently near the cliffs to allow the traveler to gather more than a general idea of their position and outlines. To be able to appreciate and understand their extraordinary character, it is indispensable to coast along in close proximity to the cliffs and pass beneath the Grand Portal, which is only accessible from the lake, and to land and enter within the precincts of the Chapel. At Grand Island, boats, men, and provisions may be procured. The traveler should lay in a good supply, if it is intended to be absent long enough to make a thorough examination of the whole series. In fact, an old voyager will not readily trust himself to the mercy of the winds and waves of the lake without them, as he may not unfrequently, however auspicious the weather when starting, find himself weather-bound for days together. It is possible, however, in one day, to start from Grand Island, see the most interesting points and return. The distance from William's to the Chapel—the farthest point of interest—is about fifteen miles.

high cliffs are seen to the east, which form the commencement of the series of rocky promontories, which rise vertically from the water to the height of from one hundred to one hundred and twenty-five feet, covered with a dense canopy of foliage. Occasionally a small cascade may be seen falling from the verge to the base in an unbroken curve, or gliding down the inclined face of the cliff in a sheet of white foam. The rocks at this point begin to assume fantastic shapes; but it is not until having reached Miners' River that their striking peculiarities are observed. Here the coast makes an abrupt turn to the eastward, and just at the point where the rocks break off and the friendly sand-beach begins, is seen one of the grandest works of nature in her rock-built architecture. We gave it the name of "Miners' Castle," from its singular resemblance to the turreted entrance and arched portal of some old castle—for instance, that of Dumbarton. The height of the advancing mass, in which the form of the Gothic gateway may be recognized, is about seventy feet, while that of the main wall forming the background is about one hundred and forty. The appearance of the openings at the base changes rapidly with each change in the position of the spectator. On taking a position a little farther to the right of that occupied by the sketcher, the central opening appears more distinctly flanked on either side by two lateral passages, making the resemblance to an artificial work still more striking.

"A little farther east, Miners' River enters the lake close under the brow of the cliff, which here sinks down and gives place to a sand-bank nearly a third of a mile in extent. The river is so narrow that it requires no little skill on the part of the voyager to enter its mouth when a heavy sea is rolling in from the north. On the right bank, a sandy drift plain, covered with Norway and Banksian pine, spreads out, affording good camping-ground—the only place of refuge to the voyager until he reaches Chapel River, five miles distant, if we except a small sand beach about midway between the two points, where, in case of necessity, a boat may be beached.

"Beyond the sand beach at Miners' River the cliffs attain an altitude of one hundred and seventy-three feet, and maintain a nearly uniform height for a considerable distance. Here one of those cascades of which we have before spoken is seen foaming down the rock.

"The cliffs do not form straight lines, but rather arcs of circles, the space between the projecting points having been worn out in symmetrical curves, some of which are of large dimensions. To one of the grandest and most regularly formed we gave the name of 'The Amphitheatre.' Looking to the west, another projecting point—its base worn into cave-like forms—and a portion of the concave surface of the intervening space are seen.

"It is in this portion of the series that the phenomena of colors are most beautifully and conspicuously displayed. These can not be illustrated by a mere crayon sketch, but would require, to reproduce the natural effect, an elaborate drawing on a large scale, in which the various combinations of color should be carefully represented. These colors do not by any means cover the whole surface of the cliff even where they are most conspicuously displayed, but are confined to certain portions of the cliffs in the vicinity of the Amphitheatre; the great mass of the surface presenting the natural, light-yellow, or raw-sienna color of the rock. The colors are also limited in their vertical range, rarely extending more than thirty or forty feet above the water, or a quarter or a third of the vertical height of the cliff. The prevailing tints consist of deep-brown, yellow, and gray—burnt-sienna and French-gray predominating.

"There are also bright blues and greens, though less frequent. All of the tints are fresh, brilliant, and distinct, and harmonize admirably with one another, which, taken in connection with the grandeur of the arched and caverned surfaces on which they are laid, and the deep and pure green of the water which heaves and swells at the base, and the rich foliage which waves above, produce an effect truly wonderful.

"They are not scattered indiscriminately over the surface of the rock, but are arranged in vertical and parallel bands, extending to the water's edge. The mode of their production is undoubtedly as follows: Between the bands or strata of thick-bedded sandstone there are thin seams of shaly materials, which are more or less charged with the metallic oxides, iron largely predominating, with here and there a trace of copper. As the surface-water permeates through the porous strata it comes in contact with these shaly bands, and, oozing out from the exposed edges, trickles down the face of the cliffs, and leaves behind a sediment, colored according to the oxide which is contained in the band in which it originated. It can not, however, be denied that there are some peculiarities which it is difficult to explain by any hypothesis.

"On first examining the Pictured Rocks, we were forcibly struck with the brilliancy and beauty of the colors, and wondered why some of our predecessors, in their descriptions, had hardly adverted to what we regarded as their most characteristic feature. At a subsequent visit we were surprised to find that the effect of the colors was much less striking than before: they seemed faded out, leaving only traces of their former brilliancy, so that the traveler might regard this as an unimportant feature in the scenery. It is difficult to account for this change, but it may be due to the drynesss or humidity of the season. If the colors are produced by the percolation of the water through the strata, taking up and depositing the colored sediments, as before suggested, it is evident that a long period of drouth would cut off the supply of moisture, and the colors, being no longer renewed, would fade, and finally disappear. This explanation seems reasonable, for at the time of our second visit the beds of the streams on the summit of the table-land were dry.

"It is a curious fact, that the colors are so firmly attached to the surface that they are very little affected by rains or the dashing of the surf, since they were, in numerous instances, observed extending in all their freshness to the very water's edge.

"Proceeding to the eastward of the Amphitheatre, we find the cliffs scooped out into caverns and grotesque openings, of the most striking and beautiful variety of forms. In some places huge blocks of sandstone have become dislodged and accumulated at the base of the cliff, where they are ground up and the fragments borne away by the ceaseless action of the surge.

"To a striking group of detached blocks the name of 'Sail Rock' has been given, from its striking resemblance to the jib and mainsail of a sloop when spread—so much so, that when viewed from a distance, with a full glare of light upon it, while the cliff in the rear is left in the shade, the illusion is perfect. The height of the block is about forty feet.

"Masses of rock are frequently disloged from the cliff, if we may judge from the freshness of the fracture and the appearance of the trees involved in the descent. The rapidity with which this undermining process is carried on, at many points, will be readily appreciated when we consider that the cliffs do not form a single unbroken line of wall; but, on the contrary, they present numerous salient angles to the full force of the waves. A projecting corner is undermined until the superincumbent weight becomes too great, the overhanging mass cracks, and aided perhaps by the power of frost, gradually becomes loosened, and finally topples with a crash into the lake.

"The same general arched and broken line of cliffs borders the coast for a mile to the eastward of Sail Rock, where the most imposing feature in the series is reached. This is the Grand Portal —*Le Grand Portail* of the *voyageurs*. The general disposition of the arched openings which traverse this great quadrilateral mass may, perhaps, be made intelligible without the aid of a ground-plan. The main body of the structure consists of a vast mass of a rectilinear shape, projecting out into the lake about six hundred feet, and presenting a front of three hundred or four hundred feet, and rising to a height of about two hundred feet. An entrance has been excavated from one side to the other, opening out into large vaulted passages which communicate with the great dome, some three hundred feet from the front of the cliff. The Grand Portal, which opens out on the lake, is of magnificent dimensions, being about one hundred feet in height, and one hundred and sixty-eight feet broad at the water-level. The distance from the verge of the cliff over the arch to the water is one hundred and thirty-three feet, leaving thirty-three feet for the thickness of the rock above the arch itself. The extreme height of the cliff is about fifty feet more, making in all one hundred and eighty-three feet.

"It is impossible, by any arrangement of words, or by any combination of colors, to convey an adequate idea of this wonderful scene. The vast dimensions of the cavern, the vaulted passages, the varied effects of the light as it streams through the great arch and falls on the different objects, the deep emerald green of the water, the unvarying swell of the lake keeping up a succession of musical echoes, the reverberations of one's own voice coming back with startling effect, all these must be seen, and heard, and felt, to be fully appreciated.

"Beyond the Grand Portal the cliffs gradually diminish in height, and the general trend of the coast is more to the south-east; hence the rock being less exposed to the force of the waves, bears fewer marks of their destructive action. The entrance to Chapel River is at the most easterly extremity of a sandy beach which extends for a quarter of a mile, and affords a convenient landing-place, while the drift-terrace, elevated about thirty feet above the lake-level, being an open pine plain, affords excellent camping-ground, and is the most central and convenient spot for the traveler to pitch his tent, while he examines the most interesting localities in the series which occur in this vicinity—to wit, the Grand Portal and the Chapel.—*(See Engraving.)*

The Chapel—*La Chapelle* of the *voyageurs*—if not the grandest, is among the most grotesque, of Nature's architecture here displayed. Unlike the excavations before described, which occur at the water's edge, this has been made in the rock at a height of thirty or forty feet above the lake. The interior consists of a vaulted apartment, which has not inaptly received the name it bears. An arched roof of sandstone, from ten to twenty feet in thickness, rests on four gigantic columns of rock, so as to leave a vaulted apartment of irregular shape, about forty feet in diameter, and about the same in height. The columns consist of finely stratified rock, and have been worn into curious shapes. At the base of one of them an arched cavity or niche has been cut, to which access is had by a flight of steps formed by the projecting strata. The disposition of the whole is such as to resemble very much the pulpit of a church; since there is overhead an arched canopy, and in front an opening out toward the vaulted interior of the chapel, with a flat tabular mass in front, rising to a convenient height for a desk, while on the right is an isolated block, which not inaptly represents an altar; so that if the whole had been adapted expressly for a place of worship, and fashioned by the hand of man, it could hardly have been arranged more appropriately. It is hardly possible to describe the singular and unique effect of this extraordinary structure; it is truly a temple of nature—"a house not made with hands."

"On the west side, and in close proximity, Chapel River enters the lake, precipitating itself over a rocky ledge ten or fifteen feet in height.*

"It is surprising to see how little the action of the stream has worn away the rocks which form its bed. There appears to have been hardly any recession of the cascade, and the rocky bed has been excavated only a foot or two since the stream assumed its present direction.

"It seems therefore impossible that the river could have had any influence in excavating the Chapel itself, but its excavation must be referred to a period when the waters of the lake stood at a higher level.

"Near the Grand Portal the cliffs are covered, in places, with an efflorescence of sulphate of lime, in delicate crystallizations; this substance not only incrusts the walls, but is found deposited on the moss which lines them, forming singular and interesting specimens, which however can not be transported without losing their beauty.

"At the same place we found numerous traces of organic life in the form of obscure fucoidal markings, which seem to be the impressions of plants, similar to those described by Prof. Hall as occurring in the Potsdam sandstone of New York. These were first noticed at this place by Dr. Locke, in 1847."

GRAND ISLAND, 125 miles distant from the Saut, is about ten miles long and five wide, lying close in to the south shore. This is a wild and romantic island; the cliffs of sandstone, irregular and broken into by the waves, form picturesque caverns, pillars, and arches of immense dimensions. The main shore, also in

* "At this fall, according to immemorial usage among the *voyageurs* in ascending the lake, the *mangeurs de lard*, who make their first trip, receive baptism; which consists in giving them a severe ducking—a ceremony somewhat similar to that practiced on green-horns, when crossing the line.

sight, presents a magnificent appearance. Here are several other small islands, and a good harbor. It is proposed to construct a railroad from this harbor to the head of Big Bay de Noc, the most northern arm of Green Bay, only 30 miles distant, thus forming an almost direct north and south route to Chicago, etc.

MARQUETTE, Mich., 170 miles from the Saut, is one of the most flourishing places on the borders of Lake Superior, being the shipping port of the rich iron mines, which are from four to twelve miles distant from the village. These mines yield from 60 to 80 per cent. pure iron, which is exported in large quantities to Detroit, to Cleveland, and to Pittsburgh. A railroad extends some twelve or fourteen miles to the mines, affording the mines facilities for transporting the ore to Marquette, where is a good harbor. The village contains two churches, a large hotel, besides several taverns and stores, and about 1,000 inhabitants. A railroad will soon be constructed from this point to Little Bay de Noc, about 30 miles southeast, which, when completed, will greatly facilitate the traffic in iron and copper ores, in which this whole section of country abounds, as well as with other valuable metals, precious stones, etc.

LAKE SUPERIOR IRON REGION.

"THE discovery of the iron mountains and mines of Lake Superior was made in 1846, but owing to the cost of trans-shipment and transportation across the Portage at the Falls of St Mary's River, but little was done to develop them until the completion of the Saut Ste Marie ship canal, two years ago, which gave a new and lively impetus to the business; and it now forms an important feature of the Lake Superior trade.

"The mines are situated from three to sixteen miles from Marquette, a pleasant and thriving village of 1,000 inhabitants, overlooking Lake Superior, located near the mouth of Carp River, 140 miles above Saut Ste Marie.

"The mine nearest to the lake is the Eureka, about two and a half miles from Marquette. The ore here is not so easily or cheaply obtained as at the Sharon or Cleveland mountains, but it is of surpassing richness, and yields an iron of the finest and best quality for cutlery, etc. It has not been worked so extensively as the others, but it is being prosecuted with vigor.

"The Jackson Iron Mountain, owned by the Sharon Company, is situated 14 miles from Marquette; and the Cleveland Mountain, owned by Wm. H. Gordon and others, of Cleveland, is two miles beyond. A plank road, laid with flat iron rails, is in operation from Marquette to both of these mines, and the ore is transported in cars drawn by horses and mules. One span of horses or mules will draw a car containing five tons of ore, and make one trip a day. The operative forces at each of them the present season are about equal, and they send to Marquette an aggregate of from 800 to 1,000 tons per week. These mountains rise gradually to a height of six or seven hundred feet, and are a solid mass of iron ore, yielding from 50 to 60 per cent. of the best iron in the world.

"Two and a half miles beyond the Cleveland is the New England Iron Mountain, which is said to abound with ore of equal richness and quality with the others, but as the railroad is not yet completed to it, nothing has been done to develop it. A mile or two farther on we reach the Burt Iron Mountain; but as they all bear so strong a resemblance to each other in quantity, quality, and richness of ores, a description of one answers for them all. That the iron of this region is inexhaustible admits of no doubt, and that it is the richest and best in the world has been clearly proved by analysis and practical demonstration.

"The associates of the late Heman B. Ely, Esq., are constructing a substantial railroad from Marquette to the Burt Mountain, and a company has been formed to continue it on to Wisconsin State-line. Six or eight miles of this road is completed, laid with heavy T rail, and a locomotive is running upon it. The grading is nearly completed to the Jackson Mountain, 14 miles, and the iron will be laid this fall, or early in the spring. The completion of this road will have a tendency to reduce materially the price of ore at Marquette. It is now held at $5 per ton, delivered on the wharf; it can then be sold at $3 50, and yield as fair a profit as it now does at $5.

"The Sharon Iron Company have expended some $300,000 in the construction of a substantial breakwater and wharf, twelve hundred feet long, at Marquette. The harbor is well protected, except against an east wind, which blows directly in; but an expenditure of fifty thousand dollars, in extending the breakwater already constructed, would make it safe at all times.

"In 1848, two years after the discovery of iron, the first bloom forge on Lake Superior was built by the Jackson Iron Company. It is situated about ten miles from Marquette, in the vicinity of the Jackson Móuntain. It is a small affair, having only two fires, and as the machinery proved imperfect, but little has been done with it.

"The second forge was built by the Marquette Iron Company in 1850, located at the village of Marquette. This had four fires, and was worked by steam. It was in successful operation about eighteen months, when it was destroyed by fire, in 1852

"The third bloomery was built, in 1853, by Mr. M'Connell. It is situated on the Dead River, six miles from Marquette, has two fires, and is worked by water-power.

"The fourth and most extensive and successful bloom forge, on Lake Superior is that of the Collins Iron Company, situated on Dead River, three miles from Marquette. This was completed in 1855. It is worked by water-power, has eight fires, and is capable of manufacturing 2,000 tons blooms per annum.

"*Burt Mountain* is situated seventeen miles west from the lake, and forms the present terminus of the I. M. R. R. The surface indications of the iron ore at this point are of the first class, of which we procured some fine specimens. It has not yet been opened, yet those who understand such matters think it will pay richly to work it. We did not find all the surface-indications, yet what we did find contained but little jasper, being mostly diamond, granulated, and slate ore. The weight of it quite surprised us—we took hold of a piece about eight inches square and three in thickness, thinking to lift it with one hand, but our fingers slipped off as though it had been oiled, and no attempt was made afterward to lift any but small pieces. The bed of ore which we found lay within a few feet of the railroad track, and could be loaded on to cars at a very small expense. It will probably be opened as soon as the cars are running to this point; from this point we strike off nearly south to Lake Angelina.

"*Cleveland Mountain* is sixteen miles from the lake, and one mile east of the Burt Mountain. This mine is now actively worked, and sends down daily to the lake from forty to fifty tons of good ore. Mr. D. P. Moore, the foreman of the mining work, informed us they had some two hundred tons of ore ready for transportation, and were constantly gaining upon the teams that take it away. There are now about thirty men employed at this mine constantly, and additions are expected soon. It would be utterly impossible to give an adequate idea of the immense amount of ore at this point—it lies piled up in huge masses above the surface, and the depth of it can not be determined, but probably extends farther down than ever will be dug to get it. Indeed, there is now enough upon the surface to last for ages, to say nothing of other localities, to which this is but a commencement. The miners have struck a bed of jasper, where they are now at work, on a level with the road, which will not be very profitable working; yet this is no drawback at all, for it is thought that below it is as good ore as any obtained, and even if there was none, there is enough above ground, which can be got out cheaper than that. This the company will probably do now, as when the work of mining shall become thoroughly systematized, the cheaper ore can be worked as profitably as the best can now. Yet this is not necessary, as there is an unlimited amount of ore that yields from eighty to ninety per cent. of pure iron. There seems to be no obstacle now in the way of the successful and profitable working of this mine.

"*Jackson Mountain*, from the lake, is fourteen miles distant, and east from the Cleveland Mountain to the place where the miners are working, two miles. It will be seen at once, that thousands of tons can be prepared with but little labor, when a good face is cleaned off and ready for blasting. From Mr. Zimmerman, the foreman of the mining operations, we learned that the company have eleven men now at work excavating the ore and preparing it for removal. It may not be amiss to remark here, that the ore is broken up into a convenient size for handling and shipping, at all the mines, before it is taken away. They have now at the mines about five hundred tons ready for transportation. The quantity carried to the lake as yet, this season, is small, comparatively; but we understand the company have just received a stock of mules, and will probably commence the transportation of it on a large scale very soon. Where the miners are now excavating, the surface exhibits a thin layer of slaty rock, which, being removed, shows ore of the best quality, except in a few small veins which contain some jasper. The surface-indications upon the top of the mountain exhibit a rather large proportion of jasper; yet where the side has been faced down it shows that it is only at the surface; what it may be on penetrating to the heart of the mountain it is impossible to conjecture.

"The *Eureka Mine* is distant from the lake but two and a half miles, and but a short distance from the railway, with which it connects by a side track. Some difficulty has been experienced here in getting out the ore, in consequence of the veins being imbedded in the rock, but the work of excavating has been persevered in, until it now promises well. The ore improves as it progresses downward, and the veins grow wider. The close proximity of this mine to the lake gives it an advantage over those more distant, as the cost of transportation will be materially lessened. There are many locations within the district which we passed over, that we did not visit. They are not yet opened, and we did not think it proper to describe them until they should be, and their value ascertained. This will probably be done at no distant day."—*Report of* 1856.

Carp and *Dead* rivers both flow into Lake Superior, near Marquette, on each side of which there are rapids and falls of great beauty, affording good water-power. *Chocolate River* also flows into the lake some two or three miles east of Marquette, but through a different geological formation.

On leaving Marquette, the steamer usually runs in a N.W. direction, passing *Presque Ile*, *Granite Point*, and GRANITE ISLAND, the latter having two vertical walls of trap 20 feet high and 12 feet apart, forming a good boat-harbor.

STANARD'S ROCK, discovered by Captain Stanard in 1835, while in the employ of the American Fur Company, sailing the schooner John Jacob Astor, is a solitary and dangerous bare rocky projection, rising out of the lake, off the mouth of Keweenaw Bay, in the route of the steamers on their way from Marquette to Copper Harbor, 65 miles.

L'ANCE is an excellent harbor, where is a small settlement, situated at the head of Keweenaw Bay. A short distance north are located a Roman Catholic and Methodist mission house and church. The Catholic being on the west shore of the bay, and the Methodist on the east, both are surrounded by Indian tribes and settlements. This locality, at no distant day, must become an important point, being favorably situated between the iron and copper regions of Lake Superior.

PORTAGE ENTRY, situated on the west shore of Keweenaw Bay, about fifteen miles north of L'Ance, at the outlet of Portage Lake, is a new and important place, from whence some of the rich copper ore of this region is exported.

PORTAGE LAKE is an extensive and beautiful sheet of water, extending to within half a mile of the entire breadth of the peninsula of Keweenaw Point, in the county of Houghton. It receives a number of small streams, draining the rich copper region of Lake Superior. No portion of the south shore of Lake Superior exceeds this lake and its vicinity as a resort for health and pleasure.

KEWEENAW POINT* is a large extent of land jutting out into Lake Superior, from ten to twenty-five miles wide, and about sixty miles in length. This section of country for upward of 100 miles, running from southwest to northeast, abounds in silver and copper ores, yielding immense quantities of the latter; much of it being pure native copper, but often in such large masses as to render it almost impossible to be separated for the purpose of transportation. Masses weighing from 1,000 to 5,000 pounds are often sent forward to the Eastern markets. The geological formation is very interesting, producing specimens of rare beauty and much value.

MANITOU ISLAND lies off Keweenaw Point, on which is a light-house to guide the mariner to and from Copper Harbor. The island is about seven miles in length and four wide.

COPPER HARBOR, Houghton Co., Mich., situated on the north shore of Keweenaw Point, 250 miles from the Saut, is one of the best harbors on Lake Superior. The village contains about 600 inhabitants, a church, and two hotels, besides several stores and storehouses. Fort Wilkins, formerly a U. S. military post, has been converted into a hotel and water-cure establishment for the accommodation of visitors and invalids.

The copper mines are from four to six miles back of the landing, are very productive, and well worthy a visit.

AGATE HARBOR, ten miles west of Copper Harbor, is the name of a small settlement. This port is not much frequented as yet by steamers.

EAGLE HARBOR, 16 miles west of Copper Harbor, is a good steamboat landing. Here is a good public-house, together with several stores and storehouses. The mines are situated three miles and upward from the landing.

---

* "On many maps spelled *Keweewaiwona*, and otherwise. Pronounced by our Indians, 'Ki-wi-wai-non-ing,' now written and pronounced as above; meaning a portage, or place where a portage is made—the whole distance of some eighty or ninety miles around the Point being saved by entering Portage Lake and following up a small stream, leaving a portage of only about a half mile to Lake Superior on the other side."—*Foster and Whitney's Report.*

Eagle River Harbor and village are favorably situated at the mouth of a stream of the same name. Here is a thriving settlement, it being the outlet of the celebrated Cliff and North American Copper mines, two of the most successful copper mining companies probably in this or any other country. Here the lamented Dr. Houghton was drowned, October, 1845, while engaged in exploring this section of country—Keweenaw Point and adjacent country being very appropriately named Houghton County in honor of his memory.

The following is an account of the melancholy death of Dr Houghton:

"By a friend direct from Lake Superior, we have the painful intelligence of the death of Dr. Douglas Houghton, State Geologist of Michigan, who, with two *voyageurs* or half-breeds, was drowned by the swamping of their boat on Lake Superior during a storm on the 13th of October, 1845, as they were coming down from a portage to Copper Harbor. They were swamped about a mile and a half from Eagle River. Dr. Houghton had been for some time engaged in a geological and linear survey of the Copper Region for the Federal Government, and was engaged in the discharge of this duty when he met with his lamented end. He was about 50 years old, universally beloved by those who knew him, and had by years of patient toil and study acquired a knowledge of the Mineral Region which no living man possesses or can for years acquire. His death is not only a sore blow to his family and numerous friends, but a public calamity. His body had not been recovered on the 22d, when our informant left, though search had been made for it. The body of one of his *voyageurs* (Pequette) had been found, with a few pieces of the boat. There were four with him at the time of the disaster, two of whom were hurled by the waves upon the rocks, ten feet above the usual level of the waters."

Ontonagon, Ontonagon Co., Mich., 336 miles from the Saut Ste Marie, is advantageously situated at the mouth of the river of the same name. The river is about 200 feet wide at its mouth, with a sufficient depth of water over the bar for large steamers. Here is being erected an extensive pier and breakwater. The village contains an Episcopal, a Presbyterian, and a Roman Catholic church; three good hotels, the Bigelow

House being the largest; 2 steam saw-mills, and 10 or 12 stores and storehouses, and about 1,500 inhabitants.

In this vicinity are located the Minnesota, the Norwich, the National, the Rockland, and several other very productive copper mines. The ore is found from 12 to 15 miles from the landing, being imbedded in a range of high hills traversing Keweenaw Point from N.E. to S.W. for about 100 miles. Silver is here found in small quantities, beautifully intermixed with the copper ore, which abounds in great masses.

"During the month of July, 1856, the Minnesota Mine raised 152 tons 1,272 pounds of copper. One mass from this mine weighed 7,122 pounds—the largest, we believe, yet sent from that district.

"The Rockland raised in the same month 30 tons 848 pounds. Some of the masses raised were the most beautiful and pure which have ever been seen upon the lake."

LAKE SUPERIOR INTELLIGENCE.

"We have received a late copy of the Lake Superior *Miner*, and condense from its columns some interesting intelligence concerning Lake Superior matters.

"Ontonagon is said to be improving very rapidly, and the *Miner* thinks it destined to become the most important point on the lake shore. During 1856, some forty new buildings were erected, various streets graded and planked, and a large amount of real estate sold to actual settlers.

"The Minnesota Mine, fifteen miles from Ontonagon, shipped during the year ending January 1, 1857, 3,718,403 pounds of copper. Of this amount only 255,854 pounds was stamp work. The copper will probably be found of a high purity. There are now employed on the location, above and below ground, some 537 persons.

"The Rockland, National, Nebraska, and other mines, are also reported as raising large quantities of copper.

"Great improvements have been made on the Ontonagon harbor, and several new docks and piers erected.

"All the mines are making preparations to ship copper largely during the coming season, when 'lively times' are expected.

"It would be well for our Eastern merchants to open a larger trade with Lake Superior, in which there is a good chance, if we mistake not, for investments of a most profitable nature."

COPPPER MINING MATTERS.

"THE *Minnesota* has raised during the year ending Jan. 1st, 1857, 3,718,403 pounds of copper. They have built during the year one very fine warehouse and office, 25 by 60, an excellent agent's house, a minister's house, and a new engine-house.

"The following is the product of the year 1856, by months In that time the Minnesota leads the Cliff, in mine production, by more than 200 tons, and we think the difference in ingot copper will be still greater in favor of the former mine.

January	318,177	July	305,272
February	306,532	August	309,731
March	330,438	September	300,201
April	318,311	October	307,135
May	305,117	November	313,372
June	303,123	December	300,994

Total pounds, nett 3,718,403
Or 1,859 tons 403 pounds.

"The *Cliff* raised, during the year preceding December 1, 1856, at which their fiscal year terminates, 3,291,229 pounds of copper, or 1,654 tons and 1,239 pounds. They raised during the preceding year a little less than 1,489 tons, which shows an increase of about 149 tons in favor of the year just past.

"The following additional shipments were made by the various mines on the Point during the last season. We can only regret that we are not able to make the list complete at present.

North America	645,498	Central	105,487
Rockland	898,188	Northwestern	80,683
Connecticut	44,080	Copper Falls, about	396,000

"This last-named mine shipped some pounds more than the amount in the table.

"The following is the amount in round tons shipped from the Portage Lake District.

Isle Royale	293	Quincy	20
Portage	101	Pewabic	103
Huron	22		

LA POINTE, La Pointe Co., Wis., situated on Madeline Island, one of the group of the *Twelve Apostles*, 410 miles from the Saut, and 83 miles from Superior City, is a highly important place. It was early settled by the Jesuits and American Fur Traders. The population consists of a mixture of Indians, French Canadians, and Americans. In addition to its fur trade, La Pointe has long been the favorite resort of the "red man" and the "pale face;" the former will no doubt soon disappear, as the spirit of speculation has entered this whole region of country. Here, among the islands, are to be found some of the best fishing-grounds for which Lake Superior is so justly famed.

The TWELVE APOSTLES' ISLES consist of the Madeline, Cap, Line, Sugar, Oak, Otter, Bear, Rock, Cat, Ironwood, Outer, and Presque Isle, besides a few smaller islands, being grouped together a short distance off the mainland, presenting during the summer months a most picturesque and lovely appearance. Here are to be seen clay and sandstone cliffs rising from 100 to 200 feet above the waters, while most of the islands are clothed with a rich foliage of forest trees.

BAYFIELD, La Pointe Co., Wis., three miles west of La Pointe, has a good harbor. The village is situated on the mainland, from whence it is proposed to build a railroad for a distance of 120 miles to the St. Croix River, terminating at a point where the above river becomes navigable.

ASHLAND, 12 miles south of La Pointe, at the head of Chagwamegon Bay, is another new settlement no doubt destined to rise to some importance, it having a very spacious and secure harbor.

MASKEG RIVER, a considerable stream, the outlet of several small lakes, enters Lake Superior about 15 miles east of Ashland, some ten miles farther eastward enters MONTREAL RIVER, forming the boundary, in part, between the States of Michigan and Wisconsin.

On proceeding from La Pointe westward, the steamer usually passes around Point de Tour, ten miles north, and enters Fond du Lac, a noble bay situated at the head of Lake Superior. It may be said to be 50 miles long and 20 miles wide, abounding in good fishing-grounds.

SUPERIOR, OR SUPERIOR CITY, Douglass Co, Wis., is most advantageously situated on a bay of Superior, at the west end of the lake, near the mouth of St. Louis River. Here is a church, two hotels, and ten or fifteen stores and storehouses, and about 1,500 inhabitants A small river called the Nemadji runs through Superior, and enters into the bay. Perhaps no place on Lake Superior has commercial advantages equal to this town; its future is magnified almost beyond conception The *St. Croix and Superior Railroad* is proposed to terminate at this place, extending southward to Hudson on the St. Croix River, about 140 miles. Another railroad is proposed to extend westward to the Sauk Rapids, on the Upper Mississippi, either from this place or Portland, Min.

NOTES OF TRAVEL.

From a Correspondent of the Buffalo Courier.

ONTONAGON—LA POINTE—SUPERIOR CITY.

Dated, ST. PAUL, MINN., *August*, 1856.

"ON Sunday we attended church in Ontonagon, situated on the south shore of Lake Superior. There are, I believe, four congregations, viz., Presbyterian, Episcopalian, Methodist, and Catholic. Their houses of worship bear the characteristics of the place; they are hasty but comfortable edifices, which, as the place advances, must give way to more substantial and tasteful structures.

On Monday the steamer "*Lady Elgin*" arrived, bound for Superior City. We got on board about half-past three o'clock, and left, without any poignant regret, the young, but ambitious Ontonagon.

"We arrived at La Pointe at ten o'clock in the evening, situated on the southern extremity of Madeline Island, the largest of the group denominated the *Apostles' Islands*. La Pointe has been a place of considerable importance as a fur-trading post, and is still a common resort of the Indians desiring to sell furs or obtain supplies. Speculators have seized upon it, and to believe their representations, it is about the only place of any consequence upon the lake. How much of a village it is, or how it is situated, the shades of night prevented me from observing. I watched, however, when a passenger came on board, and observed his feet clogged with clay; so I concluded that the island had a clay soil.

"In the morning of the following day we found ourselves maneuvering to get into the harbor of Superior. This place has one of most beautiful natural harbors that I ever witnessed The town is situated on the extreme end of Lake Superior, on a gentle declivity overlooking the water. Immediately in front a long, narrow strip of land shoots across, cutting off a commo ous and perfectly secure harbor. This natural breakwater seems almost to have been placed there artificially, so exactly is it adapted to its purpose. The harbor has but one fault, and that is a serious one, yet which may be remedied by sufficient outlay. Boats of a sufficient capacity to undergo the weather of these lakes can not find sufficient depth of water, except in narrow and confined channels of the bay. A dredging-machine kept at work here for a few months would, I believe, entirely relieve it from these difficulties."

WAHBAGON is the name of a new town that has been laid out on the Wisconsin side of the St. Louis River, opposite to the Indian village of Fond du Lac, and at the end of navigation on the northern lakes and rivers. It is the farthest inland point accessible by vessels from the ocean—being fourteen miles west of Superior. It is said to be the only point on the St. Louis River that can be reached by roads from the south or west without crossing the river.

GORDON, the name of a new town located on the line of the St. Croix and Lake Superior Railroad, and about midway between Superior and Hudson, is now attracting the attention of capitalists.

DISTANCES from FOND DU LAC to ST. PAUL, Min.

		Miles.
FOND-DU-LAC, (St. Louis River)		
Pokagema, (*Portage*)		75
FALLS ST. CROIX, (*Canoe*)	40	115
Marine Mills, (*Steamboat*)	19	134
Stillwater, "	11	145
ST. PAUL, (*Stage*)	18	163

Distance from SUPERIOR CITY to ST. CLOUD (Sauk Rapids), by proposed railroad route, 120 miles. St. Cloud to St. Paul, 76 miles. Total, 196 miles.

DISTANCES from SUPERIOR CITY to PEMBINA, Min.

		Miles.
SUPERIOR		
CROW WING		80
Otter Tail Lake	70	150
Rice River	74	224
Sand Hills River	70	294
Grand Fork, (Red River)	40	334
PEMBINA	80	414

From St. Paul to Pembina, *via* Crow Wing........464 miles.

SUPERIOR CITY

THE Superior *Chronicle* of the 20th of Jan., 1857, arrived by mail a day or two since, and is pretty much taken up with a 'semi-annual review of the town of SUPERIOR, Wisconsin.' The statement is highly flattering to the enterprise of the citizens, as well as to the natural advantages of the location—the extreme western and northern point of lake navigation. The number of inhabitants is about 1,500, being an increase in one year of 900. The number of houses in June, 1856, 196, and in January, 1857, 340.

There are in and round the town five saw-mills in operation. Eight hundred thousand feet of lumber were imported, and one million feet of lumber made by the mills. The *Chronicle* says:

"The lands granted to build a road from Hudson to Superior, and from Superior to Bayfield, have passed into the hands of the St. Croix and Lake Superior Railroad Company, and that company have contracted with Messrs. Dillon, Jackson, Jarrett & Co. for the construction and entire equipment of that portion of the road between Superior and Hudson within two years from the 4th of July next. These contractors are also obligated to build a good wagon road from this place to the St. Croix River this winter; and also to complete, early next spring, an extensive pier and warehouse on the grounds of the company at the mouth of the Nemadji River. About sixty men are employed in constructing the wagon road, and parties are preparing the piles and timbers for the docks and warehouses The contractors have about $10,000 worth of provisions and supplies for next summer's operations distributed along this end of the line. Next season the work on the road is to be commenced at three different points—Superior, Gordon, and Hudson; and on this division one thousand men will be employed.

"The St. Croix and Lake Superior Railroad Company intend erecting next spring a substantial dock and warehouse on their depôt grounds at the mouth of the Nemadji River. The dock will be three hundred feet long by fifty wide, and the warehouse one hundred and ten feet front by forty deep, the timbers for which are now being got out, and the first installment is to be delivered on the ground the present week.

"The proprietors of Superior are constructing a very extensive dock on the river bank opposite to the depôt grounds of the railroad company. It commences on the bay front, about seven hundred feet from the mouth of the river, and runs from thence a distance of two thousand feet It is to be fifty feet wide, and connected with the mainland by a causeway over the marsh at the foot of Robinson Avenue

"A company to erect a Masonic Hall was organized last summer, with a capital stock of $7,000. It was placed under contract, and the work begun, but owing to the difficulty in collecting assessments in consequence of the absence of many of the stockholders, it was suspended until next spring. It is proposed to erect a very large hotel in the vicinity of this Hall next summer, at a cost of $80,000, but as the organization is not perfected, we can make but a brief allusion to it.

"Several years ago Congress made an appropriation of $15,000 to build a light-house at this place; but, like all other matters intrusted to government officials, its commencement has been unnecessarily delayed. It is under contract, and as the limitation allowed for its completion will expire next fall, we feel pretty sure that its construction will be commenced on the opening of navigation.

"The arrivals at this port for the past three years bear the following comparison:

Years.	Steamboats.	Sailing Vessels.	Total.
1854	2	5	7
1855	23	10	33
1856	40	16	56

"This table shows an increase in 1855 over 1854 of 26 vessels, and an increase in 1856 over 1855 of 23 vessels."

PORTLAND, St. Louis Co., Min., advantageously situated at the extreme west end of Lake Superior, seven miles N.W. from Superior City, is a place of growing importance, where is a good steamboat landing, with bold shore. This is the capital of the county, and bids fair to be a successful competitor with Superior City for the carrying trade of the Great West and Pacific coast. Along the shore of the lake northward are to be seen bold sandy bluffs and highlands, supposed to be rich in mineral wealth.

FOND DU LAC, St. Louis Co., Min., is situated on St. Louis River, 20 miles above its entrance into Lake Superior. Vessels of a large class ascend to this place, being within four miles of the St. Louis Falls, having a descent of about 60 feet, affording an immense water-power. Here are sandstone and slate quarries, from which stone and slate are quarried, and extensively used for building purposes. Iron and copper ore abound in the vicinity. These advantages bid fair to make this point a mart of commerce and manufacture.

St. Louis River, flowing into the S.W. end of Lake Superior, is a large and important stream, and is navigable for steamers and lake craft for upward of 20 miles from its mouth. Above the falls (where the water has a descent of 60 feet, presenting a beautiful appearance), the river is navigable for canoes and small craft for about 80 miles farther. This river is the recipient of the waters of several small lakes lying almost due north of its outlet, its head waters flowing south from near Rainy Lake.

Clifton, St. Louis Co., Min., situated 11 miles N.E. of the head of Lake Superior, is a new settlement. In the vicinity are rich copper mines and good farming lands.

Burlington is another new settlement, situated northeast of Clifton, possessing similar advantages.

Encampment is the name of a river, island, and village, where is a good harbor, the mouth of the river being protected by the island. On the river, near its entrance into the lake, are falls affording fine water-power. Cliffs of greenstone are to be seen, rising from 200 to 300 feet above the water's edge, presenting a handsome appearance. To the north of Encampment, along the lake shore, abound porphyry and greenstone. This locality is noted for a great agitation of the magnetic needle; the depth of water in the vicinity is too great for vessels to anchor, the shores being remarkably bold, and in some places rise from 800 to 1,000 feet above the water.

Hiawatha is another new settlement, situated on the west shore of Lake Superior, where is found copper ore and other valuable minerals, precious stones, etc.

Grand Portage, Min., advantageously situated on a secure bay, near the mouth of Pigeon River, is an old station of the American Fur Company. Here is a Roman Catholic Mission, a block-house, and some 12 or 15 dwellings. Mountains from 800 to 1,000 feet are here seen rising abruptly from the water's edge, presenting a bold and sublime appearance.

Pigeon Bay and River forms the northwest boundary between the United States and Canada, or the Hudson Bay

Company's territory. Pigeon River is but a second-class stream, and by its junction with Arrow River continues the boundary through Rainy Lake and River to the Lake of the Woods, where the 49th degree of north latitude is reached. The mouth of Pigeon River is about 48 degrees north latitude, and 89 degrees 30 minutes west from Greenwich.

Along the whole west shore of Lake Superior, from St. Louis River to Pigeon River, are alternations of metamorphosed schists and sandstone, with volcanic grits and other imbedded traps and porphyry, with elevations rising from 800 to 1,200 feet above the lake, often presenting a grand appearance.

Pie Island, lying northeast of Grand Portage, is a large island belonging to the British. Hills some 700 feet in height are here to be seen, presenting a wild and romantic appearance, being formed in part of green rock.

Thunder Cape is a bold promontory on the north, rising 1,350 feet above the waters of the lake; inside of this point lies *Thunder Bay*, a large and picturesque sheet of water.

Isle Royale, Houghton Co., Mich., being about 45 miles in length from N.E. to S.W., and from 8 to 12 miles in width, is a rich and important island, abounding in copper ore and other minerals, and also precious stones. The principal harbor and only settlement is on *Siskowit Bay*, being on the east shore of the island, about 50 miles distant from Eagle Harbor, on the main shore of Michigan.

The other harbors are—Washington Harbor on the southwest, Todd's harbor on the west, and Rock Harbor and Chippewa Harbor on the northeast part of the island. In some places on the west are perpendicular cliffs of greenstone, very bold, rising from the water's edge, while on the eastern shore conglomerate rock or coarse sandstone abounds, with occasional stony beach. On this coast are many islets and rocks of sandstone, rendering navigation somewhat dangerous. Good fishing grounds abound all around this island, which will, no doubt, before many years, become a favorite summer resort for the invalid and sportsman, as well as the scientific tourist.

Siskowit Lake is a considerable body of water lying near the center of the island, which apparently has no outlet. Other small lakes and picturesque inlets and bays abound in all parts of the island. Hills, rising from 300 to 400 feet above the waters of the lake, exist in many localities throughout the island.

Fort William, an Hudson Bay Company's post, situated at the mouth of Kaministequoi River, is a very important locality. Besides the fort and Company's buildings, here is a Roman Catholic Mission and some 200 resident inhabitants of a mixed character, mostly in the employ of the gigantic Company, which here holds undisputed sway. Here commences the Portage road to Pembina and the Red River Settlement.

The Kaministequoi River is a large and rapid stream, with a fall of about 200 feet perpendicular descent some 30 miles above its mouth. Canoes descended from this point in about four hours; but the ascent is long and tedious. The river is represented as containing many beautiful rapids and islands, also as abounding in fish of various kinds. It empties its pure waters into *Thunder Bay*. The scenery around Thunder Bay is very grand, the mountains, rising 1,000 feet and upward above the surface of the water, have a very imposing effect.

Black Bay and River is another important locality, being in part surrounded by high elevations, presenting a romantic and picturesque appearance.

Neepigon Bay and River, situated at the north extremity of Lake Superior, is a wild and almost unknown region of country. The bay contains several islands, and the river is represented as being a large and rapid stream rising far toward the north, and from thence flowing through a wilderness of great picturesque beauty.

RED RIVER OF THE NORTH.

This interesting section of country being closely connected with the trade of the Upper Lakes, and attracting much attention at the present time, we subjoin the following extract from "Minnesota and Dacotah," by C. C. Andrews—1857:

"It is common to say that settlements have not been extended beyond Crow Wing, Min. This is only technically true. A few facts in regard to the people who live four or five hundred miles to the north will best illustrate the nature of the climate and its adaptedness to agriculture.

"There is a settlement at Pembina, where the dividing line between British America and the United States crosses the Red River of the North. It didn't *extend* there from our frontier, sure enough. If it extended from anywhere, it must have been from the north, or along the confines of that mystic region called Rainy Lake. Pembina is said to have about 600 inhabitants. It is situated on the Pembina River. It is an Indian-French word meaning '*Cranberry*.' Men live there who were born there, and it is in fact an old settlement. It was founded by British subjects, who thought they had located on British soil. The greater part of its inhabitants are half-breeds, who earn a comfortable livelihood in fur-hunting and farming. It is 460 miles northwest of St. Paul, and 330 miles distant from Crow Wing. Notwithstanding the distance, there is considerable communication between the places. West of Pembina, about thirty miles, is a settlement called St. Joseph, situated near a large mythological body of water called *Miniwakin*, or Devil's Lake.

"Now let me say something about this *Red River* of the North, for it is beginning to be a great feature in this upper country. It runs north and empties into Lake Winnipeg, which connects with Hudson Bay by Nelson River. It is a muddy and sluggish stream, navigable to the mouth of the Sioux Wood River for vessels of three feet draught for four months in the year, so that the extent of its navigation within Minnesota alone (between Pembina and the mouth of Sioux Wood River) is 400 miles. Buffaloes still feed on its western banks. Its tributaries are numerous and copious, abounding with the choicest kind of game, and skirted with a various and beautiful foliage. It can not be many years before this magnificent valley (together with the Saskatchawan) shall pour its products into our markets, and be the theater of a busy and genial life.

"Red River Settlement is seventy miles north of Pembina, and lies on both sides of the river. Its population is estimated at 10,000 souls. It owes its origin and growth to the enterprise and success of the Hudson Bay Company. Many of the settlers came from Scotland, but the most were from Canada. They speak English and Canadian French. The English style of society is well kept up, whether we regard the church with its bishop, the trader with his wine-cellar, the scholar with his library, the officer with his sinecure, or their paper currency. The great business of the settlement, of course, is the fur traffic.

"An immense amount of buffalo skins is taken in summer and autumn, while in the winter smaller but more valuable furs are procured. The Indians also enlist in the hunts; and it is estimated that upward of $200,000 worth of furs are annually taken from our territory and sold to the Hudson Bay Company. It is high time indeed that a military post should be established somewhere on Red River by our government.

"The Hudson Bay Company is now a powerful monopoly. Not so magnificent and potent as the East India Company, it is still a powerful combination, showering opulence on its members, and reflecting a peculiar feature in the strength and grandeur of the British empire—a power, which, to use the eloquent language of Daniel Webster, 'has dotted over the whole surface of the globe with her possessions and military posts, whose morning drum-beat following the sun, and keeping company with the hours, circles the earth daily with one continuous and unbroken strain of martial music.' The company is growing richer every year, and its jurisdiction and its lands will soon find an availability never dreamed of by its founders, unless, as may possibly happen, *popular sovereignty steps in to grasp the fruits* of its long apprenticeship."

The charter of the Hudson Bay Company expires, by its own limitation, in 1860, and the question of annexing this vast domain to Canada, or forming a separate province, is now deeply agitating the British public, both in Canada and in the mother country.

THE HUDSON BAY COMPANY'S CHARTER.

From a Correspondent of the Toronto Globe, dated, July, 1856.

SIR—In the year 1670 Charles the Second created nine individuals a corporate body, and granted them a charter under the style and title of the "*Hudson Bay Company.*"

"The preamble of the charter sets forth, 'that whereas certain parties had at their own cost and charges undertaken an expedition for Hudson Bay, for the discovery of a new passage into the South Sea, and for finding some trade for furs, minerals, and other considerable commodities, etc.; now know ye that we, being desirous to promote all endeavors tending to the public good and encourage the said design, have granted.'

"The words of the grant are these following:

"'We do give, grant, and confirm unto the said governor and company, and their successors, the sole trade and commerce of all those seas, straits, bays, rivers, lakes, creeks and sounds, in whatsoever latitude they shall be, that lie within the entrance of the strait commonly called *Hudson Strait*, together with all the lands and territories upon the countries, coasts and confines of the seas, bays, lakes, rivers, creeks and sounds aforesaid, that are not already actually possessed by the subjects of any other Christian prince or state; with the fishery of all sorts of fish, whales, sturgeon, and all royal fishes in the seas, bays, inlets and rivers within the premises, and the fish therein taken, together with the royalty of the sea upon the coasts within the limits aforesaid, and all mines royal as well discovered as not discovered, of gold, silver, gems and precious stones, to be found or discovered within the territories, limits and places aforesaid; and that the said land be from henceforth reckoned and reputed as one of our plantations or colonies in America called *Rupert's Land.* And furthermore we do grant unto the said governor and company, and their successors, that they and their successors, and their factors, servants, and agents for them, and on their behalf, and not otherwise, shall forever hereafter have, use and enjoy, not only the whole, entire and only trade and traffic, and the whole, entire and only liberty, use and privilege, of trading and trafficing to and from the territory, limits, and places aforesaid, but also the whole and entire trade and traffic to and from all havens, bays, creeks, rivers, lakes, and seas, into which they shall find entrance or passage by water or land, out of the territories, limits and places aforesaid, and to and with all nations and people inhabiting or which shall inhabit within the territories, limits and places aforesaid, and to and with all other nations inhabiting any of the coasts adjacent to the said territories, limits and places, which are not already possessed as aforesaid, or whereof the sole liberty or privilege of trade or traffic is not yet granted to any other of our subjects.'

'Who can say what constituted Rupert's Land; or where it was supposed to be situated? And who can undertake to explain or give a true construction of the meaning of the absurdly vague and indefinite language in which the grant in question is supposed to be made?

"If this grant of land is worth any thing at all, or if it conveys any estate whatever to the Hudson Bay Company, it must be confined to those islands lying *within the entrance* of the strait, and can not be made to convey any other portion.

"The entrance of the strait is from the Atlantic, and the southern boundary of the strait is Labrador; its coast can not be said to be within the entrance of the strait, nor can Hudson Bay, distant some 800 miles from that entrance, in the common acceptation of the term, be said to be within the entrance of the strait; much less can the lands and shores of Hudson Bay be said to lie *within the entrance of the strait.*

"If ever the claims of the Hudson Bay Company are brought before a judicial tribunal for investigation, the interpretation which shall be given this charter (if charter it is) will be in the strictest and most limited sense, and not in the enlarged and extended one which that Company have given to it.

"At all events, '*within the strait*' must mean such a proximity to the strait as would give the lands spoken of an affinity or relation to Hudson Strait, and not such lands as from their immense distance have no such geographical affinity or relation to that strait. In this case the nearest point to Hudson Bay is 700 miles, nevertheless the Hudson Bay Company set up a claim to 1,500 miles beyond this point—2,200 miles from *within the entrance* of Hudson Strait.

"The immense extent of country claimed is not warranted by any possible construction of the charter, and is wholly inconsistent with the objects of a trading company, who evidently are not calculated to found kingdoms or establish states and empires.

"Although Henry Hudson is supposed to be the discoverer of Hudson Bay, for he sailed into the strait that now bears his name in 1610, and perished there that year, nevertheless France laid claim to all that territory as early as 1598. In that year letters patent were granted by Henry the 4th of France to Sieur de la Roche, creating him Governor-General of Canada, Hochelaga, Terres Nueves, Labrador, and the river of the great Bay of Norrembegue.

"On the 29th April, 1627, Louis the 13th granted a charter to a company called 'Le Compagnie de la Nouvelle France,' to which company was also granted the exclusive trade and possession of the country called *La Nouvelle France*, for a period of fifteen years. Now the boundaries of 'La Nouvelle France,' as described at that time, include the whole of Hudson Strait and Hudson Bay, and in fact all that country extending to the Pacific Ocean which the Hudson Bay Company now claim.

"By the treaty of Saint Germain-en-Laye in March, 1632, Charles the 1st of England resigned to Louis the 13th of France the sovereignty of Acadia, *La Nouvelle France*, and Canada.

"Some time about 1663, according to Charlevoix, a party of English adventurers, guided by two French deserters, built a trading establishment on Hudson Bay, and subsequently erected two or three others. This act was regarded by France as one of usurpation, and accordingly in 1686 an expedition was sent from Canada under the command of Chevalier de Troyes, who destroyed the establishments and drove away the possessors, alleging that the country thus occupied by them was in the dominions of the king of France. During the war that subsequently ensued between France and England, these places were taken by the English, and retained until the treaty of Ryswick in 1696. By that treaty they were again restored to France, and they remained in her possession until 1714, when by the treaty of Utrecht the whole of the Hudson Bay countries were ceded to England; since which period the whole country has continued in her possession.

"Thus it is clear that at the time when Charles made the grant to the Hudson Bay Company, it was not his to grant, even if there had been no doubt as to his power. The treaty of Ryswick actually destroyed the charter, by surrendering the country to France; and when by the treaty of Utrecht it was ceded to England in 1714, that country came to the crown of England clearly freed from any stipulations as to the reservation of any vested or other right whatever.

THE HUDSON BAY COMPANY.

To the Editor of the Toronto Globe:

SIR—In a city paper, of the 29th ultimo, I have read with much pleasure some observations relative to the Hudson Bay Company, and the charter under which that Company assume an exclusive control over half a continent.

"The period has now arrived when Canada should assert her right in relation to a matter of so important a nature, and in which her vital interests are most deeply involved. And it is time that her mercantile community should inquire by what authority it is that a company, consisting of some two hundred shareholders, in the city of London, claim the exclusive right to trade over a country extending from the coast of Labrador on the east to the Pacific Ocean on the west, and bounded on the north only by the Arctic seas?

"When we know that this community of commercial adventurers draw their wealth and influence and power solely from the traffic carried on within this immense circuit of country, we are induced to ask, how does it happen that the mercantile community of Canada, living, as it were, within the very sphere of their action, are dead to all those commercial enterprises which, for nearly a century past, has annually poured into the coffers of this monopoly a copious shower of wealth?

"The reply probably will be, 'It is not that our merchants are unenterprising or unpatriotic—but as the Hudson Bay Company possess an exclusive right to trade throughout that country, all others are by law prohibited.'

"While I admit that this is the general impression, I contend that it is an impression designedly created and artfully maintained by the Hudson Bay Company, in order that they may more securely profit by the monstrous imposture.

"There was a time when a company of Canadian merchants successfully disputed the assumed claims of the Hudson Bay Company.

"That which then was accomplished may now be done again.

"The Northwest Company of Montreal pushed their enterprises to an extent which this chartered one of Charles the Second had never then attempted. And the Northwest Company carried these enterprises into effect at a time when the means of transport were in its very infancy. The bark canoe was the only conveyance by which merchandise was conveyed from Montreal, or by which the rich productions of even in those times the mighty West were brought in return to that city.

"If we draw a comparison between the manner in which that trade was carried on, and the mode in which it could now be conducted, while we can not but admire the energy and the enterprise of the merchants of that day, we must admit that those of the present time are enabled to enjoy advantages which the Northwest Company could not have dreamed of.

"Where the light canoe of former times could scarcely float, or where these were obliged to discharge their cargoes and embark them at the extremity of some portage, ships of one thousand tons burden now float, and a ship navigation is now opened from Montreal to half way across the continent; instead of the canoe timidly hugging the shores of the great lakes, the steamer and propeller are now seen mid-lake pursuing their courses, undeterred by wind or wave.

"The course of trade, as conducted in those days, required two years' time to complete an order for goods sent by the trader in the West. The usual time for dispatching such orders was in the autumn, when the canoes were about to return for Montreal. Sometimes these orders did not arrive in time to be forwarded by the fall ships to England, in which case they had to lay over for the spring ships, or rather summer. When the goods arrived in the spring at Montreal, they were then embarked in canoes, and reached Lake Nippising *via* the Ottawa

River; from Lake Nippising they reached Lake Huron by the French River, thence along Lake Huron to the Ste Marie River to Lake Superior; and coasting Lake Superior they reached the Kaministequoi, up the Kaministequoi to Lac la Pluie, down Lac la Pluie and the La Pluie River to the Lake of the Woods, along the Lake of the Woods to the Winnipeg, thence to Lake Winnipeg, around Lake Winnipeg to the Saskatchawan River, by it to Great Slave Lake, thence to the plains of Athabasca, and across the Rocky Mountains to the Pacific Ocean, making the distance thus traveled over 4,000 miles, and having to unload and reload their canoes at innumerable portages between Montreal and the place of their destination. In conducting this traffic 500 French *voyageurs* were employed, and in addition to these were the numerous hunters and traders engaged in the service of this Company, in all, perhaps, to the number of 2,000 or more. And these men were all inhabitants of Canada who were thus early engaged in developing the rich productions of their country, and Canada at large was benefited by the trade, for the wealth it brought was freely flung back to circulate through those various industrial pursuits of life which a trade like this had called into action.

"Had the Northwest Company continued in existence, there is no doubt but the country along the great Lakes Huron and Superior would not now be the '*terra incognita*' that it is; the portals leading to the West, such as the Kaministequoi and Pigeon rivers, would not have been closed, as it were, under lock and key, but the *voyageurs* making these the thoroughfare of their traffic would have speedily opened out the country to population and production, other traders or merchants would have followed in their wake, and settlements would have sprung up along the channel down which this vast and important trade was conducted, by Canadian enterprise alone. The waters and the woods that were then enlivened by the stir and bustle of these active and enterprising merchants, and cheered by the lively songs of the happy *voyageur*, are now silent and deserted; for the whole of the trade of that western country is now directed to the shores of Hudson Bay, there to be stowed in Hudson Bay Company's ships for the city of London.

"Some idea may be formed of the magnitude of the trade of the Northwest Company by these facts. In four years from the time of the formation of that Company, the net return of the profits of that year was £50,000, a sum of money which exceeded the original capital invested. In three years afterward, the annual net profits had amounted to £150,000; and each ensuing year these profits were annually increasing, until the contests of the two companies led to open warfare, and this resulted in a union of interests.

"The Hudson Bay Company, however, had in fact been driven from all commercial rivalry, and it was only when they found that neither fraud nor force in Canada, nor courtly favor, nor parliamentary influence in England, could succeed in driving the Northwest Company from their pretended teniture, they offered to compromise their disputes, and proposed to share with the Northwest Company of Montreal their imaginary privileges, in order that all other adventurers to that country should be excluded a participation in the spoils.

"It was thus that the Hudson Bay Company bribed the rivals whom they could not defeat, and the Northwest Company subscribed to the existence of claims or rights which they had heretofore defied and disputed, fortified by the opinions of such men as Lord Brougham, Sir Vickery Gibbs, Sir Arthur Pigot, Mr. Sponkie, Mr. Braidoft, and others.

"Had the Hudson Bay Company dared to test the validity of their charter in a court of law, it would have been proclaimed to the world that every British subject had a right to trade and traffic, unfettered and uncontrolled, throughout that country, for that the Royal Charter under which the Hudson Bay Company claimed exclusive privileges there was illegal, was null and void.

"By changing the route of transport to and from the West, the shorter and better one, *via* the Lakes, became unfrequented, and its very existence almost forgotten, and the now limited companies traded without the apprehension of exciting the rivalry of others.

"Their trade was kept a secret—no one witnessed the passage of imports upward, nor the productions downward from hunting-grounds, claimed by a company irresponsible to any law, or to any country. So secret even now are all the operations of that Company, that the furs taken within ninety miles of Penetanguishene are transported to Lake Superior, thence to Hudson Bay for shipment to London.

"The very productions of our own country are sold here in Toronto, after having been purchased at the Hudson Bay House in London by our merchants.

"The very employés of the Hudson Bay Company, who are engaged in the Orkney Islands at low wages, are taken to Lake Superior *via* Hudson Bay, lest these men should learn that they could engage elsewhere at higher wages, which they would do if taken to Lake Superior *via* the St. Lawrence route. Within these few years past, since the mining interests have awakened attention to Lake Superior, these men frequently leave the employment of the Hudson Bay Company, and such acts are denominated by the Company's agents 'desertion,' and they are often arbitrarily imprisoned

"With this introduction, which is very far from being such as the merits of the subject require, let me now ask your readers to take the map of North America, trace the lines of that section of British North America styled Canada, containing about 350,000 square miles, then compare it with that which is denominated the Territories of the Hudson Bay Company, this portion will be found to comprise about *four millions* of square miles, and to this must be added very large portions of Canada which for years past have been subjected to the despotic control and blighting influences of this monstrous monopoly.

"Two hundred stockholders in London, without a single bond or tie of any nature to the true interests of Canada, claim to hold four millions of square miles in British America as their hunting-grounds. Of these four millions of square miles, one million four hundred thousand abound in all those materials which can contribute to agricultural and to natural wealth. Before, however, entering upon the subject of the capabilities and advantages which those sections of our country for agricultural, mechanical, and mercantile pursuits possess, I propose to show what, in fact, is this supposed charter of the Hudson Bay Company HURON."

"HUDSON BAY, or SEA, was discovered by Henry Hudson in 1610. It is about 900 miles in length, by 600 at its greatest breadth, with a surrounding coast of 3,000 miles. It lies between the parallels of 51° and 65° north latitude, and in extent is about six times as large as Lake Superior. The coasts are generally high, rocky, rugged, and sometimes precipitous. The bay is navigable for a few months in summer, but for the greater part of the remainder of the year is filled up with fields of ice. The transitions of the thermometer in summer are from 100° to 40° in two days, and the torrents of rain are surprising; the range of the thermometer throughout the year is 140°. The sea is entered by Hudson Strait, on the northeast, which is about 500 miles long, with a varying breadth, and with an intricate navigation obstructed by several islands. The principal bays and inlets in this great inland sea are, James' Bay, on the southeast, which is 240 miles long by 140 wide; Button's Bay and Port Nelson on the western coast, and Chesterfield Inlet on the northwest, which, after stretching far into the interior, terminates in a fresh-water lake."—*Hudson Bay Territories*, by R. M. MARTIN, Esq.

STE IGNACE ISLAND is a large and bold extent of land lying on the north shore of Lake Superior, forming, with other islands, the outward barrier to Neepigon Bay. Here may be seen mountains rising from 1,000 to 1,300 feet above the lake. Copper and other minerals abound in this region.

The SLATE ISLANDS, lying east of Ste Ignace, are also large bodies of land, lying some 10 or 12 miles south of the main shore, which is bold and precipitous, and supposed to abound with copper ore and other minerals.

PIC ISLAND and RIVER lie still farther east. At the mouth of the river is situated a post of the Hudson Bay Company. This is a large stream, affording six feet of water over the bar at its mouth.

MICHIPICOTEN ISLAND is a large and bold body of land; in some places the surface rises 800 feet above the waters of the lake. The shores abound with greenstone and amygdaloid, while in the interior is found copper and silver ores. Here was located the Lake Superior Silver Mining Company of Canada.

MICHIPICOTEN HARBOR and RIVER is another favorable and important locality. The river is navigable to the falls, 15 miles. It rises near the source of Moose River, which empties into James' Bay.

In this vicinity are found iron and copper ore of good quality. At the mouth of the river is situated a post of the Hudson Bay Company, from whence the Portage road extends northward about 300 miles to James' Bay, on the south end of Hudson Bay.

This road has been traveled in six days from Lake Superior to Moose Fort, situated on James' Bay, although the usual time is from eight to ten days. A chain of forts or trading-houses is passed along this line, situated for the most part on Moose River, emptying into the head of James' Bay, near 52° N. lat. The time, no doubt, will soon arrive, when the Canadian public will claim this route for the purpose of trade and commerce, it forming a most direct communication between the Arctic Ocean, Hudson Bay, Lake Superior, and the lower lakes.

MONTREAL ISLAND and RIVER is another ocality south of Michipicoten, which abounds in minerals of different kinds.

CARIBOU is a small island lying about 30 miles south of Michipicoten, near the middle of the lake. It is usually passed in sight when the steamers return along the north shore on pleasure excursions

---

In order to give an idea of these magnificent excursions, we copy the following advertisement which appeared in a Cleveland paper in August, 1856 :

Two Grand Pleasure Excursions around Lake Superior.

The new, staunch, upper-cabin and low-pressure steamer PLANET, Capt. Joseph Nicholson, will make two pleasure excursions to Lake Superior, as follows:

First.—Leave Cleveland on Monday, August 18th, and Detroit on Tuesday, August 19th. Second.—Leave Cleveland on Thursday, August 28th, and Detroit on Friday, August 29th; touching at Mackinac, passing through the Saut Ste Marie Canal, and also pass in view the Pictured Rocks and Grand Island by daylight; visit Marquette (the iron region), Copper Harbor, Eagle Harbor, Eagle River, Ontonagon (the copper region), La Pointe (the fairy region)—thence passing over to Pigeon Bay, Prince's Bay, Pie Island, and Isle Royale, on the north shore, and returning by the south shore. A fine view of the Michipicoten and Caribou islands is also obtained.

The *Planet* is new, 1,200 tons burden, low-pressure engine of 1,000 horse-power; has an upper cabin 210 feet long, and splendid accommodations for 300 passengers, but on these trips, that they may be in fact, as well as in name, Pleasure Excursions, the number will be limited to 175.

A good band of music will be in attendance to enliven the scene, and no expense will be spared to make these excursions the most agreeable that have been made to Lake Superior.

The price of tickets for the excursion round will be Forty Dollars from Cleveland, and Thirty-six Dollars from Detroit. Those wishing to remain over one trip can do so, and return the second trip of the *Planet*, without extra charge.

E. B. WARD, Detroit.

NORTHERN SHORE OF LAKE SUPERIOR.

EXTRACT from Report on the Geology of the Lake Superior Country, by FOSTER and WHITNEY:

NORTHERN SHORE.—"Beginning at Pigeon Bay, the boundary between the United States and the British Possessions (north latitude 48°), we find the eastern portion of the peninsula abounds with bold, rocky cliffs, consisting of trap and red granite.

"The Falls of Pigeon River, eighty or ninety feet in height, are occasioned by a trap dyke which cuts through a series of slate rocks highly indurated, and very similar in mineralogical characters to the old graywacke group. Trap dykes and interlaminated masses of traps were observed in the slate near the falls.

"The base of nearly all the ridges and cliffs between Pigeon River and Fort William (situated at the mouth of Kaministequoi River, the western boundary of Upper Canada) is made up of these slates, and the overlaying trap. Some of the low islands exhibit only the gray grits and slates. Welcome Islands, in Thunder Bay, display no traps, although, in the distance, they resemble igneous products, the joints being more obvious than the planes of stratification, thus giving a rude semi-columnar aspect to the cliffs.

"At Prince's Bay, and also along the chain of islands which lines the coast, including Spar, Victoria, and Pie islands, the slates with the crowning traps are admirably displayed. At the British and North American Company's works the slates are traversed by a heavy vein of calc-spar and amethystine quartz, yielding gray sulphuret and pyritous copper and galena. From the vein where it cuts the overlaying trap on the main shore, considerable silver has been extracted.

"At Thunder Cape, the slates form one of the most picturesque headlands on the whole coast of Lake Superior. They are made up of variously colored beds, such as compose the upper group of Mr. Logan, and repose in a nearly horizontal position. These detrital rocks attain a thickness of nearly a thousand feet, and are crowned with a sheet of trappean rocks, three hundred feet in thickness.

"At L'Anse à la Bouteille (opposite the Slate Islands, on the north shore of Lake Superior) the slates re-appear, with the granite protruding through them, and occupy the coast for fifteen miles; numerous dykes of greenstone, bearing east and west, are seen cutting the rocks vertically. The Slate Islands form a part of this group, and derive their name from their geological structure

"They are next seen, according to Mr. Logan, for about seven miles on each side of the Old Pic River. Near Otterhead a gneissoidal rock forms the coast, which presents a remarkable regular set of strata, in which the constituents of syenite are arranged in thin sheets and in a highly crystalline condition. From this point to the Michipicoten River the slates and granite occupy alternate reaches, along the coast, for the distance of fifty miles. 'With the exception of a few square miles of the upper trap of gargantua, these two rocks appear to hold the coast all the way to the vicinity of Pointe aux Mine, at the extremity of which they separate from the shore, maintaining a nearly straight southeasterly line across the Batchewanung Bay, leaving the trap of Mamainse between them and the lake. Thence they reach the northern part of Goulais Bay, and finally attain the promontory of Gros Cap, where they constitute a moderately bold range of hills, running eastwardly toward Lake Huron.'"*

FISHERIES OF LAKE SUPERIOR.

Good fishing-grounds occur all along the north shore of Lake Superior, affording a bountiful supply of white fish, Mackinac trout, and many other species of the finny tribe. On the south shore there are fisheries at White Fish Point, Grand Island, near the Pictured Rocks, Keweenaw Point, La Pointe, and Apostles' Islands, and at different stations on Isle Royale, where large quantities are taken and exported; but there are no reliable statistics as to the number of men employed or the number of barrels exported. Between the head of Keweenaw Point and the mouth of the Ontonagon River, considerable quantities of fish are taken, for which there is a ready market at the mining stations. In addition to the white fish and Mackinac trout, the siskawit is occasionally taken. Its favorite resort, however, is the deep water in the vicinity of Isle Royale.

Lake Superior Trout-Fishing in Winter.—The Lake Superior *Journal* says:

"Angling through the ice to a depth of thirty fathoms of

---

* Canadian Report, 1846-7.

water is a novel mode of fishing somewhat peculiar to this peculiar region of the world. It is carrying the war into fishdom with a vengeance, and is denounced, no doubt, in the communities on the bottom of these northern lakes as a scaly piece of warfare. The large and splendid salmon-trout of these waters have no peace; in the summer they are enticed into the deceitful meshes of the gill-net, and in the winter, when they hide themselves in the deep caverns of the lakes, with fifty fathoms of water above their heads, and a defense of ice two or three feet in thickness on the top of that, they are tempted to destruction by the fatal hook.

"Large numbers of these trout are caught every winter in this way on Lake Superior; the Indian, always skilled in the fishing business, knows exactly where to find them and how to kill them. The whites make excursions out on the lake in pleasant weather to enjoy this sport. There is a favorite resort for both fish and fishermen near Gros Cap, at the entrance of Lake Superior, through the rocky gateway between Gros Cap and Point Iroquois, about 18 miles above the Saut, and many a large trout, at this point, is pulled up from its warm bed at the bottom of the lake, in winter, and made to bite the cold ice in this upper world. To see one of these fine fish, four or five feet in length, and weighing half as much as a man, floundering on the snow and ice, weltering and freezing to death in its own blood, oftentimes moves the heart of the fisherman to expressions of pity.

"The *modus operandi* in this kind of great trout-fishing is novel in the extreme, and could a stranger to the business overlook at a distance a party engaged in the sport, he would certainly think they were mad, or each one making foot-races against time. A hole is made through the ice, smooth and round, and the fisherman drops down his large hook, baited with a small herring, pork, or other meat, and when he ascertains the right depth, he waits—with fisherman's luck—some time for a bite, which in this case is a pull altogether, for the fisherman throws the line over his shoulder, and walks from the hole at the top of his speed till the fish bounds out on the ice. We have known of as many as fifty of these splendid trout caught in this way by a single fisherman in a single day; it is thus a great source of pleasure and a valuable resource of food, especially in Lent, and the most scrupulous anti-pork believers might here 'lown pork and up fish' without any offense to conscience."

CHICAGO.

The City of Chicago is advantageously situated on the west side of Lake Michigan, at the mouth of Chicago River, in N. lat. 41° 52′, and W. long. from Greenwich 87° 35′. It is elevated six to eight feet above the lake, which secures it from ordinary floods, and extends westward on both sides of the river, about two miles distant from its entrance into Lake Michigan, the front on the lake being three or four miles from north to south. The harbor has a depth of from twelve to fourteen feet of water, which makes it a commodious and safe haven; and it has been much improved artificially by the construction of piers which extend on each side of the entrance of the river for some distance into the lake, to prevent the accumulation of sand upon the bar. The light-house is on the south side of the harbor, and shows a fixed light on a tower forty feet above the surface of the lake; there is also a beacon-light on the end of the pier. In a naval and military point of view, this is one of the most important ports on the upper lakes, and should be strongly defended, it being the "*Odessa*" of these inland seas.

The city contains a court-house, the county buildings, Rush Medical College, a commercial college, a marine hospital, a United States land-office, market houses, sixty churches, eight banks, several fire and marine insurance companies, and a number of large hotels; gas-works, and water-works. The manufacturing establishments of Chicago are numerous and extensive, consisting of iron-foundries and machine shops, railroad car manufactory, steam saw, planing, and flouring mills, manufactories of agricultural implements, etc. Numerous steamers and propellers ply between this place and Saut Ste Marie, Lake Superior ports, Collingwood, Detroit, Buffalo, and the various intermediate ports. Estimated population in 1856, 100,000.

The *Illinois and Michigan Canal*, connecting Lake Michigan with Illinois River, which is 60 feet wide at the top, 6 feet deep. and 107 miles in length, including five miles of river navigation, terminates here, through which is brought a large amount of produce from the south and southwest; and the numerous railroads radiating from Chicago add to the vast accumulation which is here shipped for the Atlantic sea-board. Chicago being within a short distance of the most extensive coal-fields to be found in Illinois, and the pineries of Michigan and Wisconsin, as well as surrounded by the finest grain region on the face of the globe, makes it the natural outlet for the varied and rich produce of an immense section of fertile country.

RAILROADS DIVERGING FROM CHICAGO.

		Miles.
1.	Chicago and Milwaukee	85
2.	Chicago, St. Paul and Fond du Lac*	360
3.	Fox River Valley and Wisconsin Central*	75
4.	Galena and Chicago Union, (to Dunleith) Beloit Branch, and Beloit and Madison.	188
5.	Chicago, Fulton and Iowa Air Line	136
6.	Chicago, Burlington and Quincy	210
7.	Chicago and Rock Island	182
8.	Chicago, Alton and St. Louis	290
9.	ILLINOIS CENTRAL—Chicago Branch†	365
10.	Pittsburgh, Fort Wayne and Chicago*	470
11.	Cincinnati, Peru and Chicago*	87
12.	Michigan Southern and Northern Indiana	247
13.	Michigan Central (and New Albany and Salem)	282
	Total	2,997

* Unfinished railroads.

† At this time the Illinois Central Railroad is the means of connecting Chicago with Cairo and St. Louis on the south, and with Galena and Dunleith on the west, forming a total line of road of 722 miles, as follows:

ILLINOIS CENTRAL RAILROAD—AND ITS BRANCHES.

Cairo to Lasalle—Main Line	308 miles.
Lasalle to Dunleith—Galena Branch	147 "
Chicago to Centralia—Chicago Branch	267 "
Total	722 miles.

PROGRESS OF CHICAGO AND THE GREAT WEST.

"TWENTY years ago the city of Chicago, Illinois, was an insignificant town at the southern end of Lake Michigan; now, her granaries, her storehouses, her railroad depôts, and her private dwellings are scarcely surpassed by those of any city in the Union for their solidity, enormous dimensions, and their unexampled cost, giving evidence of rapid wealth, caused by her lake commerce and her railroad concentrations.

"The '*Democratic Press*' of that city has just made up its annual statistical statement of the progress of Chicago, and from it we copy the annexed statistics, which the editor says may be relied on. It is headed 'Fifth annual review of the prospects, condition, traffic, etc., of the railroads centering in Chicago, with a general summary of the business of the city for 1856.'

GENERAL SUMMARY.

Total number of miles of railway in the State of Illinois now in operation	2,761
Increase in 1856	351
Increase in the State in five years (over 500 miles per year)	2,666
Total earnings of all the railways centering in Chicago for the year 1856	$17,343,242
Increase of 1856 over 1855	$4,045,041
Population of Chicago in 1850	29,963
" " in 1852	38,783
" " in 1854	74,500
" " in 1855	82,750
" " January 1, 1857 (estimated)	110,000
Total receipts of grain in Chicago for the year 1855, bushels	20,487,953
Total receipts of grain, being the largest primary grain port in the world, for the year 1856 (increase in 1856 over 20 per cent.), bushels	24,674,824
Total shipments of grain from the port of Chicago for the year 1856, bushels	21,583,221
Total amount of corn received in 1856, bushels	11,888,398
Total amount of wheat received in 1856, bushels	9,392,365
Total number of hogs, alive and dressed, received in Chicago for 1855–56	308,539
Total number of shipments, alive and dressed	170,831
Averaging the weight at only 200 pounds, and the price at $5 per hundred, the value of the hogs received would be	$3,585,880
Number of barrels of beef packed in 1856	33,038

Receipts of lumber at the port of Chicago for the year 1856, being the largest lumber market in the world, feet	456,673,169
Receipts of lead for the year 1856, pounds	9,527,506
Now laid up in the port of Chicago, steamers and sail vessels	245
Total number of vessels arriving in Chicago for the year 1856	7,328
Total tonnage of vessels arriving in this port for the year 1856	1,545,379
Amount of imposts received at the Chicago custom-house on foreign goods for the past year	$102,994
Total amount of capital invested in manufactures during the year 1856, showing an increase of $1,464,400 over 1855	$7,759,400
Total number of hands employed, showing an increase over 1855 of 1,838	10,573
Total value of manufactured articles, showing an increase of $4,483,572	$15,515,063
Total amount invested during the year 1856 in improvements, stores, dwellings, hotels, etc., showing an increase over 1855 of $1,973,370	$5,708,624
Total number of passengers carried west by four principal railways leading out of Chicago	639,666
Total number remaining west above those who returned on these four lines	107,653
Total number of passengers moved on all the roads centering in Chicago	3,350,000

"The editor remarks, in conclusion: 'The total movement on the principal railway lines centering at Chicago would be about 3,350,000 passengers.

"The above facts and figures will be regarded with special satisfaction by all our citizens, and by the people of the Northwest generally. They show a healthy, but rapid and most astonishing progress. It may be doubted whether the whole history of the civilized world can furnish a parallel to the vigorous growth and rapid development of the country which has Chicago for its commercial metropolis. When it is remembered that twenty years ago she was not an incorporated city, and less than a quarter of a century since the Indians still had possession of the largest portion of this magnificent country, these facts, stubborn and incontestable though they be, seem more like the dreams of some vagrant imagination than sober matters of reality, which scores of men still among us have themselves seen and realized."

PORTS OF LAKE MICHIGAN LYING ON THE EAST AND SOUTH SHORES.

MICHIGAN CITY, Ind., situated at the extreme south end of Lake Michigan, is distant 45 miles from Chicago by water, and 228 miles from Detroit by railroad route. The *New Albany and Salem Railroad,* 228 miles in length, terminates at this place, connecting with the Michigan Central Railroad. Several plank roads also terminate here, affording facilities for crossing the extensive prairies lying in the rear. Here are several large storehouses situated at the mouth of Trail Creek, intended for the storage and shipment of wheat and other produce; 15 or 20 stores of different kinds, several hotels, and a branch of the State Bank of Indiana. It was first settled in 1831, with the expectation that it would become a great emporium of trade; but owing to the want of a good harbor, and the rapid increase of Chicago, the expectation of its founders have not been realized. It now contains about 3,000 inhabitants, and is steadily increasing in wealth and numbers.

NEW BUFFALO, Mich., lying 50 miles east Chicago by steamboat route, is situated on the line of the Michigan Central Railroad, 218 miles west of Detroit. Here has been erected a lighthouse and pier, the latter affording a good landing for steamers and lake craft. The settlement contains two or three hundred inhabitants, and several stores and storehouses. It is surrounded by a light, sandy soil, which abounds all along the east and south shores of Lake Michigan.

ST. JOSEPH, Berrien Co., Mich., is advantageously situated on the east shore of Lake Michigan, at the mouth of St. Joseph River, 194 miles west of Detroit. Here is a good harbor, affording about 10 feet of water. The village contains about 1,000 inhabitants, and a number of stores and storehouses. An active trade in lumber, grain, and fruit is carried on at this place, mostly with the Chicago market, it being distant about 70 miles by water. Steamers of a small class run from St.

Joseph to Niles and Constantine, a distance of 120 miles, to which place the St. Joseph River is navigable. Stages also run to Niles and Dowagiac, connecting with trains on the Michigan Central Railroad.

St. Joseph River rises in the southern portion of Michigan and Northern Indiana, and is about 250 miles long. Its general course is nearly westward; is very serpentine, with an equable current, and flowing through a fertile section of country. There are to be found several flourishing villages on its banks. The principal are Constantine, Elkhart, South Bend, Niles, and Berrien.

NILES, situated on St. Joseph River, is 26 miles above its mouth by land, and 191 miles from Detroit by railroad route. This is a flourishing village, containing about 3,000 inhabitants, five churches, three hotels, several large stores and flouring mills; the country around producing large quantities of wheat and other kinds of grain. A small class of steamers run to St. Joseph below and other places above, on the river, affording great facilities to trade in this section of country.

The Ports extending from Grand Haven to Saginaw Bay are fully described in another portion of this work, as well as the bays and rivers falling into Lakes Michigan and Huron.

TRIP FROM CHICAGO TO MACKINAC AND SAUT STE MARIE.

On starting from the steamboat wharf near the mouth of the Chicago River, the Marine Hospital and depôt of the Illinois Central Railroad are passed on the right, while the Lake House and lumber-yards are seen on the left or north side of the stream. The government piers, long wooden structures, afford a good entrance to the harbor; a light-house has been constructed on the outer end of the north pier, to guide vessels to the port.

The basin completed by the Illinois Central Railroad to facilitate commerce is a substantial work, extending southward for near half a mile. It affords ample accommodation for loading and unloading vessels, and transferring the freight to and from the railroad cars.

The number of steamers, propellers, and sailing vessels annually arriving and departing from the harbor of Chicago is very great; the carrying trade being destined to increase in proportionate ratio with the population and wealth pouring into this favored section of the Union.

On reaching the green waters of Lake Michigan, the city of Chicago is seen stretching along the shore for four or five miles, presenting a fine appearance from the deck of the steamer. The entrance to the harbor at the bar is about 200 feet wide. The bar has from ten to twelve feet water, the lake being subject to about two feet rise and fall. The steamers bound for Milwaukee and the northern ports usually run along the west shore of the lake within sight of land, the banks rising from thirty to fifty feet above the water.*

* The thermometer stood at 70° Fahrenheit, Sept. 26, 1854, the day being thick and foggy with little or no wind.

LAKE MICHIGAN is about seventy miles average width, and 340 miles in extent from Michigan City, Ind., on the south, to the Strait of Mackinac on the north; it presents a great expanse of water, now traversed by steamers and other vessels of a large class running to the Saut Ste Marie and Lake Superior; to Collingwood, Can.; to Detroit, Mich.; to Cleveland Ohio; and to Buffalo, N. Y. From Chicago to Buffalo the distance is about 1,000 miles by water; while from Chicago to Superior City, at the head of Lake Superior, or Fond du Lac, the distance is about the same, thus affording two excursions of 1,000 miles each over four of the great lakes or inland seas of America, in steamers of from 1,000 to 2,000 tons burden. During the summer and early autumn months the waters of this lake are comparatively calm, affording safe navigation. But late in the year, and during the winter and early spring months, the navigation of this and the other great lakes is very dangerous.

WAUKEGAN, Lake Co., Ill., 36 miles north of Chicago, is handsomely situated on elevated ground, gradually rising to 50 or 60 feet above the water. Here are two piers, a light-house, several large storehouses, and a neat and thriving town containing about 6,000 inhabitants, six churches, a bank, several well-kept hotels, thirty stores, and two steam-flouring mills.

KENOSHA, Wis., 52 miles from Chicago, is elevated 30 or 40 feet above the lake. Here is a small harbor, a light-house, storehouses, mills, etc. The town has a population of about 5,000 inhabitants, surrounded by a fine back country. Here is a good hotel, a bank, several churches, and a number of stores and manufacturing establishments doing a large amount of business. The *Kenosha and Beloit Railroad*, when finished, will connect at the latter place with a railroad running to Madison, and thence to the Mississippi River.

The City of RACINE, Wis., 62 miles from Chicago and 25 miles south of Milwaukee, is built on an elevation some forty or fifty feet above the surface of the lake. It is a handsome and flourishing place. Here is a light-house, piers, storehouses, etc., situated near the water, while the city contains some fine public buildings and private residences. The population is about 9,000, and is rapidly increasing. Racine is the second city in the State in commerce and population, and possesses a fine harbor. Here are located the county buildings, fourteen churches, several hotels, and numerous stores of different kinds.

The *Racine and Mississippi Railroad*, extending from this place to Beloit, 68 miles, will be continued to the Mississippi River at Savanna. The Chicago and Milwaukee Railroad also runs through the town.

The City of Milwaukee, Wis., 86 miles from Chicago, by railroad and steamboat route, is handsomely situated on rising ground on both sides of the Milwaukee River, at its entrance into Lake Michigan. In front of the city is a bay or indentation of the lake, affording a good harbor, except in strong easterly gales. The harbor is now being improved, and will doubtless be rendered secure at all times of the season. The river affords an extensive water-power, capable of giving motion to machinery of almost any required amount. The city is built upon beautiful slopes, descending toward the river and lake. It has a court-house, city hall, a United States land-office, the University Institute, a college for females, three academies, three orphan asylums, thirty churches, several well-kept hotels, extensive ranges of stores, and several large manufacturing establishments. The city is lighted with gas, and well supplied with good water. Its exports of lumber, agricultural produce, etc., are immense, giving profitable employment to a large number of steamers and other lake craft, running to different ports on the upper lakes, Detroit, Buffalo, etc. The growth of this city has been astonishing; twenty years since its site was a wilderness; now it contains over 30,000 inhabitants, and of a class inferior to no section of the Union for intelligence, sobriety, and industry.

The future of Milwaukee it is hard to predict; here are centering numerous railroads finished and in course of construction, extending south to Chicago, west to the Mississippi River, and north to Lake Superior, which in connection with the Detroit and Milwaukee Railroad, terminating at Grand Haven, 80 miles distant by water, and the lines of steamers running to this port, will altogether give an impetus to this favored city, blessed with a good climate and soil, which the future alone can reveal.

During the past year an unusual number of fine buildings have been erected, and the commerce of the port has amounted to $60,000,000. The bay of Milwaukee offers the best advantages for the construction of a harbor of refuge of any point on Lake Michigan. The city has expended over $100,000 in the construction of a harbor; this needs extension and completion, which will no doubt be effected.

PORT WASHINGTON, Ozaukee Co., Wis., 25 miles north of Milwaukee, is a flourishing place, and capital of the county. The village contains besides the public buildings, several churches and hotels, twelve stores, three mills, an iron foundry, two breweries and other manufactories. The population is about 2,500. Here is a good steamboat landing, from which large quantities of produce are annually shipped to Chicago and other lake ports.

The unfortunate steamer Niagara, while on her passage from Collingwood to Chicago, was destroyed by fire off Port Washington in September, 1856, whereby sixty lives were lost

SHEBOYGAN, Wis , 50 miles north of Milwaukee and 130 miles from Chicago, is a thriving place, containing about 5,000 inhabitants. Here are seven churches, several public houses and stores, together with a light-house and piers; the harbor being improved by government works. Large quantities of lumber and agricultural products are shipped from this port. The country in the interior is fast settling with agriculturists, the soil and climate being good.* A railroad is about being constructed from this place to FOND DU LAC, 42 miles west, lying

* September 27, 1854, the thermometer stood at 60° Fahr., with a light wind from the north.

at the head of Lake Winnebago; also, another railroad to extend to Milwaukee on the south and Green Bay on the north-west.

Manitouwoc, Wis., 70 miles north of Milwaukee and 33 miles east from Green Bay, is an important shipping port. It contains about 2,500 inhabitants; five churches, several public houses, twelve stores, besides several storehouses; three steam saw-mills, two ship-yards, light-house, and pier. Large quantities of lumber are annually shipped from this port. The harbor is being improved so as to afford a refuge for vessels during stormy weather.

The west bank of Lake Michigan is here elevated about 60 or 80 feet, presenting a rough appearance in many places, with sundry bluffs rising from the water's edge to the level of the country, above which it is clothed with heavy timber of different kinds.

"Manitouwoc is the most northern of the harbors of Lake Michigan improved by the United States government. It derives additional importance from the fact that, when completed, it will afford the first point of refuge from storms for shipping bound from any of the other great lakes to this or to the most southern ports of Lake Michigan."

Two Rivers, Wis., eight miles north from Manitouwoc, is a new and thriving place at the entrance of the conjoined streams (from which the place takes its name) into Lake Michigan. Two piers are here erected, one on each side of the river; also a ship-yard and three steam saw-mills. The village contains about 2,000 inhabitants. This section of country, extending back to Green Bay, abounds in good timber, which is prepared and shipped to Chicago and other ports. Fish are taken in large quantities, and sent to different markets.

Kewaunee, Wis., 25 miles north of Two Rivers and 102 miles from Milwaukee, is a small shipping town, where are situated several saw-mills and lumber establishments. Green Bay is situated about 25 miles due west from this place.

From Manitouwoc and Two Rivers, in a northerly direction, the country is still, for the most part, a wild wilderness, inhabited sparsely by Indians of different tribes. The following is an extract from the Manitouwoc *Tribune* of March, 1857 :

ROMANCE OF THE FOREST.

"Some months since we gave the particulars of a horrible occurrence which happened in our immediate neighborhood, rivaling in interest the thrilling story of the eagle's victim, on the mountain of Switzerland No traces of the child which the bear carried off in such a daring manner have as yet been found; but the excitement which such an incident awakens is gradually dying away, and is now replaced by that of one of more recent date, scarcely less thrilling in its detail.

"Last week a Mr Woodward, living near Sandy Bay, had some difficulty with an Indian. The next day his little girl, three years of age, was standing near the house, when an Indian sprang out of the thickets, and clasped her in his arms, and bounded away through the underbrush. Pursuit was commenced immediately, but up to Saturday without success, though information had been received which, it was hoped, would lead to the recovery of the child—an Indian and a squaw having been seen the day after the abduction carrying a child which was closely wrapped in a blanket, and was crying bitterly."

On leaving Two Rivers, the steamers usually run for the Manitou Islands, Mich., a distance of about 100 mi es. Soon after the last vestige of land sinks below the horizon on the west shore, the vision catches the dim outline of coast on the east or Michigan shore at Point aux Betsie, which is about 30 miles south of the Great Manitou Island. From this point, passing northward by *Sleeping Bear Point*, a singular shaped headland looms up to the view. It is said to resemble a sleeping bear. The east shore of Lake Michigan presents a succession of high sand-banks for many miles, while inland are numerous small bays and lakes.

LITTLE, or SOUTH MANITOU ISLAND, 250 miles from Chicago and 100 miles from Mackinac, lies on the Michigan side of the lake, and is the first island encountered on proceeding northward from Chicago. It rises abruptly on the west shore 2 or 300 feet from the water's edge, sloping toward the east shore, on which is a light-house and a fine harbor. Here steamers stop for wood. The GREAT or NORTH MANITOU is nearly twice as large as the former island, and contains about 14,000 acres of land. Both islands are settled by a few families, whose principal occupation is fishing and cutting wood for the use of steamers and sailing vessels.

FOX ISLANDS, 50 miles north from South Manitou, consist of three small islands lying near the middle of Lake Michigan, which is here about 60 miles wide. On the west is the entrance to Green Bay, and on the east is the entrance to Grand Traverse Bay, and immediately to the north is the entrance to Little Traverse Bay.

GREAT and LITTLE BEAVER islands, lying about midway between the Manitou Islands and Mackinac, are large and fertile bodies of land, and are at present occupied by Mormons, who have here their most eastern settlement.

GARDEN and HOG islands are next passed before reaching the Strait of Mackinac, which, opposite Old Fort Mackinac, is about six miles in width. The site of Old Fort Mackinac is on the south main or Michigan shore, directly opposite Point Ste Ignace, on the north main shore. St. Helena Island lies at the entrance of the strait from the south, distant about fifteen miles from Mackinac.

OLD FORT MACKINAC is an important and interesting location; it was formerly fortified and garrisoned for the protection of the strait and this section of country when inhabited almost exclusively by various tribes of Indians. This place can be easily reached by sail-boat from the island of Mackinac.

PTE LA GROS CAP, lying to the west of Old Fort Mackinac, is a picturesque headland well worthy of a visit.

The STRAIT OF MACKINAC is from five to twenty miles in width, and extends east and west about thirty miles, embosoming several important islands besides Mackinac Island, the largest being BOIS BLANC ISLAND, lying near the head of Lake Huron. Between this island and the main north shore the steamer GARDEN CITY was wrecked, May 16, 1854; her upper works were still visible from the deck of the passing steamer in the fall of the same year

GROSSE ILE ST. MARTIN and Ile St. Martin lie within the waters of the strait, eight or ten miles north of the island of Mackinac. In the neighborhood of these different islands are the favorite fishing-grounds both of the Indian and the "pale face."

The town and fortress of MACKINAC is most beautifully situated on the east shore of the island, and extends for a distance of about one mile along the water's edge, and has a fine harbor protected by a water battery. This important island and fortress is situated in N. lat. 45° 54′, W. lon. 84° 30′ from Greenwich, being seven degrees thirty minutes west from Washington. It is 350 miles north from Chicago, 100 miles south of Saut Ste Marie by the steamboat route, and about 300 miles northwest from Detroit. *Fort Mackinac* stands on elevated ground, about 200 feet above the water, overlooking the picturesque town and harbor below. In the rear, about half a mile distant, stands the ruins of old *Fort Holmes*, situated on the highest point of land, at an elevation of about 350 feet above the water, affording an extensive view.

The town contains two churches, two hotels, ten or twelve stores, 100 dwelling-houses, and about 600 inhabitants. The climate is remarkably healthy and delightful during the summer months, when this favored retreat is usually thronged with visitors from different parts of the Union, while the Indian warriors, their squaws and their children, are seen lingering around this their favorite island and fishing-ground.*

The island of MACKINAC, lying in the Strait of Mackinac, is about three miles long and two miles wide. It contains many deeply interesting points of attraction in addition to the village and fortress; the principal natural curiosities are known as the Arch Rock, Sugar Loaf, Lover's Leap, Devil's Kitchen, Robinson's Folly, and other objects of interest well worthy the attention of the tourist. The Mission House and Grove House are the principal hotels.

---

* Sept. 28, 1854, the thermometer stood at 50° Fahr. Very pleasant weather with light wind, not having seen a wave break for two days.

ISLAND OF MACKINAC.

THE view given represents the Island, approaching from the eastward. "A cliff of limestone, white and weather-beaten, with a narrow alluvial plain skirting its base, is the first thing which commands attention;" but, on nearing the harbor, the village (2), with its many picturesque dwellings, and the fortress (3), perched near the summit of the Island, are gazed at with wonder and delight. The promontory on the left is called the "Lover's Leap" (1), skirted by a pebbly beach, extending to the village. On the right is seen a bold rocky precipice, called "*Robinson's Folly*" (5), while in the same direction is a singular peak of nature called the "*Sugar Loaf.*" Still farther onward, the "*Arched Rock,*" and other interesting sights, meet the eye of the explorer, affording pleasure and delight, particularly to the scientific traveler and lover of nature. On the highest ground, elevated about 350 feet above the waters of the Strait, is the signal station (4), situated near the ruins of old *Fort Holmes.*

The settlement of this Island was commenced in 1764. In 1793 it was surrendered to the American government; taken by the British in 1812; but restored by the treaty of Ghent, signed in November, 1814.

ARCHED ROCK—Mackinac.

The whole island of Mackinac is deeply interesting to the scientific explorer, as well as to the seeker of health and pleasure. The following extract, illustrated by an engraving, is copied from "FOSTER *and* WHITNEY'S *Geological Report*" of that region:

"As particular examples of denuding action on the island, we would mention the 'Arched Rock' and the 'Sugar Loaf.' The former, situated on the eastern shore, is a feature of great interest. The cliffs here attain a height of nearly one hundred feet, while at the base are strewn numerous fragments which have fallen from above. The *Arched Rock* has been excavated in a projecting angle of the limestone cliff, and the top of the span is about ninety feet above the lake-level, surmounted by about ten feet of rock. At the base of a projecting angle, which rises up like a buttress, there is a small opening, through which an explorer may pass to the main arch, where, after clambering over the steep slope of debris and the projecting edges of the strata, he reaches the brow of the cliff.

"The beds forming the summit of the arch are cut off from direct connection with the main rock by a narrow gorge of no great depth. The portion supporting the arch on the north side, and the curve of the arch itself, are comparatively fragile, and can not, for a long period, resist the action of rains and frosts, which, in this latitude, and on a rock thus constituted, produce great ravages every season. The arch, which on one side now connects this abutment with the main cliff, will soon be destroyed, as well as the abutment itself, and the whole be precipitated into the lake.

"It is evident that the denuding action, producing such an opening, with other attendant phenomena, could only have operated while near the level of a large body of water, like the great lake itself; and we find a striking similarity between the denuding action of the water here in time past, and the same action as now manifested in the range of the *Pictured Rocks* on the shores of Lake Superior. As an interesting point in the scenery of this island, the Arched Rock attracts much attention, and in every respect is worthy of examination." *(See Engraving.)*

Other picturesque objects of great interest, besides those enumerated above, occur at every turn on roving about this enchanting island, where the pure, bracing air and clear waters afford a pleasurable sensation, difficult to be described, unless visited and enjoyed.

Round Island is a small body of land lying a short distance southeast of Mackinac, while Bois Blanc Island is a large body of land lying still farther in the distance, at the head of Lake Huron, here about 30 miles wide, which width it averages for about 50 miles, when it widens to 100 miles and upward.

Point de Tour, 40 miles east from Mackinac, is the site of a light-house and settlement, at the entrance of St. Mary's River, which is here about half a mile in width; this passage is also called the West Channel. At a distance of about two miles above the Point is a new settlement, where has been erected a steamboat pier, a hotel, and several dwellings.

Drummond Island, a large and important body of land belonging to the United States, is passed on the right, where is to be seen the ruins of an old fort erected by the British. On the left is the mainland of Northern Michigan. Ascending St. Mary's River next is passed Round or Pipe Island, and other smaller islands on the right, most of them belonging to the United States.

On Drummond Island is said to exist a fine and valuable quality of stone, as will be seen by the following extract:

"A correspondent of the New Haven *Journal* denies the accuracy of the assertion that the deposit of lithographic stone lately found in Kentucky is the first discovery of that species of stone in the United States. The writer says that he obtained a specimen of the same kind of stone in 1825 at Drummond Island, at the entrance of the strait between Lakes Huron and Superior, where the supply was apparently inexhaustible. The stone was carried to Boston and tested by a lithographer, who said it was equal, if not superior, to the German stone. At that time, however, Drummond Island was far less accessible than Germany, and the discovery was, therefore, of no practical value."

St. Joseph Island, 10 miles above Point de Tour, is a large and fertile island belonging to Canada, which is more fully described on page 43. It is about 20 miles long from east to west, and about 15 miles broad, covered in part with a heavy growth of forest trees. Here is seen the ruins of an old fort erected by the British on a point of land commanding the channel of the river.

Carltonville is a small settlement on the Michigan side of the river, 12 miles above the De Tour. Here is a steam sawmill and a few dwelling-houses.

Lime Island is a small body of land belonging to the United States, lying in the main channel of the river, about 12 miles from its mouth. The channel here forms the boundary between the United States and Canada.

Mud Lake, as it is called, owing to its waters being easily riled, is an expansion of the river about five miles wide and ten miles long, but not accurately delineated on any of the modern maps, which appear to be very deficient in regard to St. Mary's River and its many islands—presenting at several points most beautiful river scenery In the St. Mary's River there are about 50 islands belonging to the United States, besides several attached to Canada.

Nebish Island and *Sailor's Encampment,* situated about half way from the Point to the Saut, are passed on the left while sailing through the main channel.

Sugar Island, a large body of fertile lánd belonging to the United States, is reached about 30 miles above Point de Tour, situated near the head of St. Joseph Island. On the right is passed the *British* or *North Channel,* connecting on the east with Georgian Bay. Here are seen two small rocky islands belonging to the British Government, which command both channels of the river.

The *Nebish Rapids* are next passed by the ascending vessel, the stream here running about five knots per hour. The main land of Canada is reached immediately above the rapids, being clothed with a dense growth of forest trees of small size. To the north is a dreary wilderness, extending through to Hudson Bay, as yet almost wholly unexplored and unknown, except to the Indian or Canadian hunter.

Lake George, twenty miles below the Saut is another expansion of the river, being about five miles wide and eight miles long. Here the channel is only from eight to ten feet in depth for about one mile, forming a great impediment to navigation.

CHURCH'S LANDING, on Sugar Island, twelve miles below the Saut, is a steamboat landing; opposite it is SQUIRREL ISLAND, belonging to the Canadians. This is a convenient landing, where is situated a store and dwelling. The industrious occupants are noted for the making of *raspberry jam*, which is sold in large quantities, and shipped to Eastern and Southern markets.

Garden River Settlement is an Indian village ten miles below the Saut, on the Canadian shore. Here is a missionary church and several dwellings, surrounded by grounds poorly cultivated, fishing and hunting being the main employment of the Chippewa Indians who inhabit this section of country. Both sides of the river abound in wild berries of good flavor, which are gathered in large quantities by the Indians, during the summer months.*

Extract from a letter dated SAUT STE MARIE, Sept., 1854:

"The scenery of the St. Mary's River seems to grow more attractive every year. There is a delicious freshness in the countless evergreen islands that dot the river in every direction from the Falls to Lake Huron, and I can imagine of no more tempting retreats from the dusty streets of towns, in summer, than these islands; I believe the time will soon come when neat summer cottages will be scattered along the steamboat route on these charming islands. A summer could be delightfully spent in exploring for new scenery and in fishing and sailing in these waters.

"And Mackinac, what an attractive little piece of *terra firma* is that island—half ancient, half modern! The view from the fort is one of the finest in the world. Perched on the brink of a precipice some two hundred feet above the bay—one takes in at a glance from its walls the harbor, with its numerous boats and the pretty village; and the whole rests on one's vision more like a picture than a reality. Every thing on the island is a curiosity; the roads or streets that wind around the harbor or among the grove-like forests of the island are naturally pebbled and macadamized; the buildings are of every style, from an Indian lodge to a fine English house. The island is covered with charming natural scenery, from the pretty to the grand, and

* Sept. 30, 1854, the thermometer stood at 42° Fahr., at the Saut Ste Marie, in the morning, a fine day for the season, with little or no wind.

one may spend weeks constantly finding new objects of interest and new scenes of beauty. It is unnecessary to particularize—every visitor will find them, and enjoy the sight more than any description.

"The steamers all call there, on their way to and from Chicago, and hundreds of small sail vessels, in the fishing trade, have here their head-quarters. Drawn upon the pebbled beach or gliding about the little bay are bark canoes and the far-famed "Mackinac boats," without number. These last are the perfection of light sail-boats, and I have often been astonished at seeing them far out in the lake beating up against winds that were next to gales. Yesterday the harbor was thronged with sail-boats and vessels of every description, among the rest were the only two iron steamers that the United States have upon all the lakes, the "Michigan" and the "Surveyor," formerly called the "Abert," employed in the coast survey.

"For a wonder, Lake Huron was calm and at rest for its entire length, and the steamer Northerner made a beautiful and quick passage from Mackinac to this place. The weather continues warm and dry, and hundreds are regretting they have so early left the Saut and Mackinac, and we believe you will see crowds of visitors yet. JAY."

A SUNDAY ON LAKE HURON.

During the autumn of 1856 the steamer Illinois arrived at Saut Ste Marie on Saturday evening, on her return from a trip through Lake Superior, having proceeded to La Pointe, situated on one of the "Twelve Apostles," and thence crossed over to the extreme western shore of the lake, near the mouth of Pigeon River, returning along the north or Canada shore to the Saut, with a pleasure party on board.

While the steamer was detained at the wharf, below the mouth of the ship canal, most of the passengers, and many of the citizens of this ancient and romantic village, together with a few Canadians from the opposite shore, amused themselves by music and dancing; while not a few drank deep from the intoxicating bowl. This scene of pleasure was kept up until near midnight, when, one by one, the passengers retired to their rest, and the villagers bade adieu to their new-made and old acquaintances.

The next morning the steamer was coursing her way through the pure and lovely waters of the St. Mary's River, with every appearance of a fine day. After passing Sugar Island, Nebish Rapids, and the island of St. Joseph, and entering broad waters of Lake Huron, a most beautiful view was sented to our gaze. In the rear was seen the entrance to De Tour passage, just passed, and the British island of Joseph—on the north lay Drummond Island, attached to stars and stripes, although bearing a foreign name—while in the far distance southward were seen the romantic island of Mackinac and the main shore of Michigan.

At this time, the hour of breakfast having passed, the Rev. Mr. ——, an Episcopal minister from Ontonagon, Mich., was invited to read the church service and preach a sermon, for the benefit of the passengers on board, among whom were persons of different creeds and nations. Never was a discourse more appropriately selected, or received with more devout attention, considering the mixed, and mostly strange, persons assembled in the after-cabin.

The lake, when seen, presented a serene and quiet calmness, alone disturbed by the powerful machinery propelling us through the waters at a most rapid rate; while the sentiments and rich melody of the speaker's voice lent a charm to the scene never to be forgot by many then present. Thus should it always be on a Sabbath, while journeying over these magnificent waters, if the weather will permit—blending serious thoughts with the most grand and lovely objects of nature—that produced by the view of land and water, as seen at times on the great lakes of North America.

A bounteous dinner was next served up, affording delight to those blessed with good appetites; while every passenger, male and female, seemed to enjoy the scenery that during the entire day was visible from the deck of the steamer.

Thunder Bay, Saginaw Bay, and Point au Barque were passed in succession—the mainland on the Canada or Michigan shore being, for most of the time, seen in the far distance; while occasionally the smoke of a passing steamer or a sail vessel caught the eye, silently gliding over the broad waters of Lake [illegible]on.

[illegible]e it not for the almost criminal carelessness or reckless-[illegible] many of the owners and masters of steamers navigating [illegible]es, whereby hundreds of valuable lives have been lost [illegible]ions of property destroyed, no more safe, instructive, [illegible]d excursion could be found on the face of the globe.

STEAMBOAT ROUTE FROM CHICAGO TO MACKINAC AND SAUT STE MARIE.

PASSING THROUGH LAKES MICHIGAN AND HURON.

Ports, etc.	Miles.	Ports, etc.	Miles.
CHICAGO, Ill.	0	SAUT STE MARIE	0
Waukegan	36	Garden River Set.	10
Kenosha, Wis.	52	*Church's Landing,* Sugar Island,	14
Racine	62		
MILWAUKEE	86	Nebish Rapids	25
Port Washington	111	St. Joseph Is., C. W.	26
Sheboygan	136	*Point De Tour*	50
Manitouwoc	156	*Mackinac,* Is. and town	95
Two Rivers	173	Old Fort Mackinac	105
Kewaunee, (25 miles)...		Hog and Garden Islands	120
South Manitou Is. Mich.	250	Great Beaver Is.	130
North Manitou Is.	260	Fox Islands	145
Fox Islands	300	North Manitou Is.	185
Great Beaver Is	315	*South Manitou Is.*	195
Hog and Garden Islands	325	Kewaunee, Wis.	
Old Fort Mackinac	340	*Two Rivers*	272
*Mackinac,** Is. and town	350	*Manitouwoc*	289
Point De Tour	395	*Sheboygan*	309
St. Joseph Is., C. W.	400	*Port Washington*	334
Nebish Rapids, Sugar Island, Mich.	420	MILWAUKEE	359
		Racine	383
Church's Landing	431	*Kenosha*	393
Garden River Set., C. W.	435	*Waukegan,* Ill.	409
SAUT STE MARIE, Mich.	445	CHICAGO	445

USUAL FARE, $8, including meals. USUAL TIME, 48 hours.

* The steamers running from Detroit and Collingwood to Green Bay and Chicago all stop at this port.

STEAMBOAT ROUTE FROM SAUT STE MARIE TO DETROIT.

PASSING THROUGH LAKES HURON AND ST. CLA.R.

Ports, etc.	Miles.	Ports, etc.	Miles.
SAUT STE MARIE......	0	DETROIT	0
Garden River Set., C. W.	10	Lake St. Clair	7
Church's Landing.....	14	St. Clair Flats	30
Lake George	20	Algonac	40
Nebish Rapids.........	24	Newport	46
St. Joseph Is., C. W.....	25	St. Clair	56
Mud Lake	30	*Port Sarnia*, C. W. } *Port Huron*, Mich. } ...	73
Lime Island, Mich......	43		
Drummond Island......	48	Fort Gratiot, } Lake Huron, }	75
Point De Tour, } Lake Huron, }	50		
		Point au Barque.......	140
Mackinac, (40 miles)...		Saginaw Bay..........	150
Presque Isle...........	105	Thunder Bay Is.	215
Thunder Bay Is.	135	Presque Isle, ...	245
Saginaw Bay	190	Mackinac, (70 miles)	
Point au Barque.......	210	*Point De Tour*, } St. Mary's River, }	300
St. Clair River, } Fort Gratoit, }	275		
		Drummond Island	302
Port Huron, Mich. } *Port Sarnia*, C. W. } ..	277	St. Joseph Island, C. W.	310
		Lime Island...........	312
St. Clair, Mich.........	294	Mud Lake	320
Newport	304	Sugar Island	325
Algonac	310	Lake George	330
St. Clair Lake.........	313	*Church's Landing*.....	336
Detroit River..........	343	Garden River Set., C. W.	340
DETROIT	350	SAUT STE MARIE......	350

FARE, $7, including meals. USUAL TIME, 30 hours.

TRIP FROM DETROIT TO MACKINAC AND SAUT STE MARIE, PASSING THROUGH LAKE HURON.

DURING the season of navigation, steamers of a large class, with good accommodations for passengers, leave Detroit almost daily for Mackinac, for Green Bay, for Chicago, situated on Lake Michigan, or for the Saut Ste Marie; from thence passing through the ship canal into Lake Superior, forming delightful excursions during the summer and the early autumn months.

On leaving Detroit the steamers run in a northerly direction, passing *Belle*, or *Hog Island*, two miles distant, which is about three miles long and one mile broad, presenting a handsome appearance. The Canadian shore on the right is studded with dwellings and well-cultivated farms.

PECHE ISLAND is a small body of land attached to Canada, lying at the mouth of Detroit River, opposite which, on the Michigan shore, is *Wind Mill Point* and light-house.

LAKE ST. CLAIR commences seven miles above Detroit; it may be said to be 20 miles long and 25 miles wide, measuring its length from the outlet of St. Clair River to the head of Detroit River. Compared with the other lakes it is very shallow, having a depth of only from 8 to 24 feet, as indicated by Bayfield's chart. It receives the waters of the Upper Lakes from the St. Clair Strait by several channels forming islands, and discharges them into the Detroit River or Strait. In the upper portion of the lake are several extensive islands, the largest of which is *Walpole Island*; it belongs to Canada, and is inhabited mostly by Indians. All the islands to the west of Walpole Island belong to Michigan. The Walpole, or "Old Ship Channel," forms the boundary between the United States and Canada. The main channel, now used by the larger class of vessels, is called the "North Channel." Here are passed the "St. Clair Flats," a great impediment to navigation, for the removal of which Congress will no doubt make ample appropriation sooner or later. The northeastern channel, separating Walpole Island from the main Canada shore, is called "*Chenail Ecarte.*" Besides the waters passing through the Strait of St. Clair, Lake St. Clair receives the river Thames from the Canada side, which is navigable to Chatham, some 24 miles; also the waters of Clinton River from the west or American side, the latter being navigable to Mt. Clemens, Michigan. Several other streams flow into the lake from Canada, the principal of which is the River Sydenham. Much of the land bordering on the lake is low and marshy, as well as the islands; and in places there are large plains which are used for grazing cattle.

ASHLEY, or NEW BALTIMORE, situated on the N.W. side of Lake St. Clair, 30 miles from Detroit, is a new and flourishing place, and has a fine section of country in the rear. It contains three steam saw-mills, several other manufactories, and about 1,000 inhabitants. A steamboat runs from this place to Detroit.

MT. CLEMENS, Macomb Co., Mich., is situated on Clinton River, six miles above its entrance into Lake St. Clair, and about 30 miles from Detroit by lake and river. A steamer plies daily to and from Detroit during the season of navigation. Mt. Clemens contains the county buildings, several churches, three hotels, and a number of stores and manufacturing establishments, and about 2,500 inhabitants. Detroit is distant by plank-road only 20 miles.

CHATHAM, C. W., 46 miles from Detroit by railroad route, and about 24 miles above the mouth of the river Thames, which enters into Lake St. Clair, is a port of entry and thriving place of business, where have been built a large number of steamers and sail-vessels.

ALGONAC, Mich., situated near the foot of St. Clair River, 40 miles from Detroit, contains a church, two or three saw-mills, and about 600 inhabitants

NEWPORT, Mich., seven miles farther north, is noted for steamboat building, there being extensive ship-yards, where are annually employed a large number of workmen. Here are fou.

steam saw-mills, machine shops, etc. Population about 800. Belle River here enters the St. Clair from the west.

St. Clair Strait connects Lake Huron with Lake St. Clair, and discharges the surplus waters of Lakes Superior, Michigan, and Huron. It flows in a southerly direction, and enters Lake St. Clair by six channels, the north one of which, on the Michigan side, is the only one at present navigated by large vessels in ascending and descending the river. It receives several tributaries from the west, or Michigan; the principal of which are Black River, Pine River, and Belle River, and several rivers flow into it from the east, or Canadian side. It has several flourishing villages on its banks. It is 48 miles long, from a half to a mile wide, and has an average depth of from 40 to 50 feet, with a current of three miles an hour, and an entire descent of about 15 feet. Its waters are clear and transparent, the navigation easy, and the scenery varied and beautiful—forming, for its entire length, the boundary between the United States and Canada. The banks of the upper portion are high; those of the lower portion are low, and in parts inclined to be marshy. Both banks of the river are generally well settled, and many of the farms are beautifully situated. There are several wharves constructed on the Canada side, for the convenience of supplying the numerous steamboats passing and repassing with wood. There is also a settlement of the Chippewa Indians in the township of Sarnia, Canada; the Indians reside in small log or bark houses of their own erection.

St. Clair, Mich., is pleasantly situated on the west side of St. Clair Strait, 56 miles from Detroit and 14 miles from Lake Huron. This is a thriving place, with many fine buildings, and is a great lumber depôt. It contains the county buildings for St. Clair Co., several churches and hotels, one flouring-mill, and five steam saw-mills, besides other manufacturing establishments, and about 3,000 inhabitants. St. Clair has an active business in the construction of steamers and other lake craft. The site of old *Fort St. Clair*, now in ruins, is on the border of the village

Southerland, C. W., is a small village on the Canada shore, opposite St. Clair. It was laid out in 1833 by a Scotch gentleman of the same name, who here erected an Episcopal church, and made other valuable improvements.

Moore, C. W., is a small village ten miles below Port Sarnia

Fromefield, or Talfourd's, C. W., is another small village, handsomely situated four and a half miles below Port Sarnia. Here is an Episcopal church, a wind-mill, and a cluster of dwellings.

Port Sarnia, C. W., 68 miles from Detroit, is an important place and port of entry, handsomely situated on the east bank of the river St. Clair, opposite Port Huron on the American shore, and near the foot of Lake Huron. It now contains about 2,500 inhabitants, and is the proposed terminus of the *Grand Trunk Railway* of Canada, which will afford a speedy communication with Hamilton, Toronto, Kingston, Montreal, and Quebec. Steamers run from Port Sarnia to Goderich, and different places on the Upper Lakes, and to Detroit, etc.

Port Huron, St. Clair Co., Mich., is very advantageously situated on the west bank of the river St. Clair, at the mouth of Black River, two miles below Lake Huron and 68 miles from Detroit by water. It contains several churches, two or three public houses, fifteen stores, one steam flouring-mill, four steam saw-mills, and several other manufacturing establishments. Population about 3,000. It is an important depôt for lumber, fish, etc. A railroad is to be constructed from Port Huron to Corunna and Grand Rapids, connecting with the Detroit and Milwaukee Railroad; another railroad will extend to Detroit, thus forming a direct route from Lake Huron to Lake Michigan, and to Toledo, Cincinnati, etc. During the season of navigation there is daily intercourse by steamboat with Detroit.

Fort Gratoit, two miles above Port Huron, is situated at the foot of Lake Huron, at the commencement of the St. Clair Strait. It was built in 1814, at the close of the war with Great Britain, and consists of a stockade, including a magazine, barracks, and other accommodations for a garrison of one battalion. It fully commands the entrance to Lake Huron, from the American shore, and is an interesting landmark to the mariner.

POINT EDWARD, on the opposite Canadian shore, is a military reserve, where is usually stationed a small British force. It also commands the entrance to Lake Huron. In the vicinity is an excellent fishery, where upward of 1,000 barrels of fish are annually taken and exported.

During the season of navigation, steamers run daily from Detroit to Port Sarnia, Goderich, Saugeen, and other ports in Canada West.

BAYFIELD, 108 miles from Detroit, is a new and flourishing place, situated at the mouth of a river of the same name.

GODERICH, 120 miles north of Detroit, is situated on elevated ground at the mouth of Maitland River, where is a good harbor. This is a very important and growing place, where will terminate the *Buffalo and Huron Railroad*, 160 miles in length. (*See page* 153.)

KINCARDINE, thirty miles from Goderich, is another port on the Canadian side of Lake Huron, where the British steamers land and receive passengers on their trips to Saugeen.

SAUGEEN, C. W., is situated at the mouth of a river of the same name, where is a good harbor for steamers and lake craft. This is the most northern port to which steamers now run on the Canada side of Lake Huron, and will no doubt, ere long, be reached by railroad.

LAKE HURON, off the mouth of Saginaw Bay, presents a wide expanse of waters, attaining its greatest width after passing Point au Barque; the steamer usually takes a northerly direction for many miles, when running toward the Strait of Mackinac. On the east lies the Canada shore and Georgian Bay.

FORRESTVILLE, Mich., 120 miles north of Detroit, situated on the west side of Lake Huron, is a new settlement, where is erected an extensive steam saw-mill. It has some three or four hundred inhabitants, mostly engaged in the lumber trade. A steamer runs from Detroit to this landing, which is distant 47 miles from Port Huron.

SAGINAW BAY is a very large body of water, it being about 30 miles wide and 60 miles long, penetrating far into the lower peninsula of Michigan. There are several islands near the center of the bay and along its eastern shore; while different kinds of fish are taken from its waters in large quantities. *Saginaw River*, flowing into the head of the bay, is a large and navigable stream, draining a rich section of country.

LOWER SAGINAW, near the mouth of the river, is a flourishing settlement, from whence a large amount of lumber is annually exported.

SAGINAW CITY, Saginaw Co., Mich., is handsomely situated on the left bank of the river, 23 miles above its mouth. It contains a court-house and jail, several churches, two hotels, 15 stores, two warehouses, and six steam saw-mills. Population about 4,000. There is a fine section of country in the rear of Saginaw, much of which is heavily timbered; the soil produces grain in abundance, while the streams afford means of easy transportation to market. Steamers run daily from Saginaw City to Detroit, during the season of navigation.

EAST SAGINAW, situated on the right bank of the river, about one mile below Saginaw City, is a new and flourishing place, also largely engaged in the lumber trade, where are located several extensive steam saw-mills and other manufacturing establishments.

The other important points passed on a trip from Detroit to Mackinac or the Saut Ste Marie are Thunder Bay Island and light, and Presque Isle, on the Michigan shore; while the Great Manitoulin Island, Great Duck Island, and Cockburn Island are on the Canada side.

If the steamer is bound for Mackinac, a westerly course is pursued after passing Presque Isle light until Bois Blanc Island is reached and passed, the steamer then gliding through the Strait of Mackinac, where the water-surface narrows to the width of about 20 miles.

BAYS AND RIVERS—SOIL, CLIMATE, ETC., OF THE LOWER PENINSULA OF MICHIGAN.

THE *Lower Peninsula of Michigan* is nearly surrounded by the waters of the Great Lakes, and, in this respect, its situation is naturally more favorable for all the purposes of trade and commerce than any other of the Western States.

The numerous streams which penetrate every portion of the peninsula, some of which are navigable for steamboats a considerable distance from the lake, being natural outlets for the products of the interior, render this whole region desirable for purposes of settlement and cultivation. Even as far north as the Strait of Mackinac, the soil and climate, together with the valuable timber, offer great inducements to settlers; and if the proposed railroads, under the recent grant of large portions of these lands by Congress, are constructed from and to the different points indicated, this extensive and heavily timbered region will speedily be reclaimed, and become one of the most substantial and prosperous agricultural portions of the West.

It is well that in the system of compensation, which seems to be a great law of the universe, the vast prairies which comprise so large a portion of this great Western domain are provided so well with corresponding regions of timber, affording the necessary supply of lumber for the demand of the increasing population which is so rapidly pouring into these Western States.

The State of Michigan—all the waters of which flow into the basin of the St. Lawrence—Northern Wisconsin, and Minnesota are the sources from which the States of Ohio, Indiana, Illinois, and Iowa, and a large portion of the prairie country west of the Mississippi, must derive their supply of this important article (lumber).

The quantity of pine lumber manufactured in Michigan alone

is estimated for the past year to amount to nearly one thousand millions of feet. The amount sold in Chicago in 1856 was upward of 450 millions, at an average price of, say $14 per thousand.

This great commodity is to a considerable degree undervalued. The supply in the West is now equal to the demand, but the consumption is so great, and the demand so constantly increasing with the development and settlement of the country, that of necessity, within comparatively a very few years, these vast forests will be exhausted. It is estimated that in ten years a very large proportion of the pine timber, accessible to navigable streams, will be consumed. But as the timber is exhausted the soil is prepared for cultivation, and a large portion of the northern part of the southern peninsula of Michigan will be settled and cultivated, as it is the most reliable wheat-growing portion of the Union.

Natural points for harbors are found at the mouths of nearly all the large streams in the State. Besides the ports and towns already described, there are on *Lake Huron*, after leaving Saginaw Bay going north, several settlements and lumber establishments, fisheries, etc. These are at Sauble River, Black River, and Devil River. At *Thunder Bay* a very flourishing town is being built up, with a superior water-power on the river. This is the county seat of Alpena County. The next important point on the coast is *Cheboygan River*. The U. S. Land Office for this district is located here, at a small town on the bay called *Duncan*. This point is nearly opposite the island of Mackinac.

Passing around the western extremity of the peninsula, at the Waugoshance Light and Island, the next point is Little Traverse Bay. This is the terminus of the Amboy and Traverse Bay Railroad.

About fifteen miles southwesterly from Little Traverse we enter *Grand Traverse Bay*, a large and beautiful arm of the lake, extending about thirty miles inland. This bay is divided into two parts by a point of land from two to four miles wide extending from the head of the bay about eighteen miles toward the lake. The country around this bay is exceedingly picturesque, and embraces one of the finest agricultural portions of the State

The climate is mild, and fruit and grain of all kinds suitable to a northern latitude are produced, with less liability to injury from frost than in some of the southern portions of the State.

Large quantities of these lands have been located, and several settlements and towns are rapidly growing up. *Grand Traverse City* is located at the head of the west arm of the bay, and is the terminus of the proposed railroad from Grand Rapids, a distance of about 140 miles.

Passing out of the bay and around the point dividing the west arm from the lake, we first arrive at the river *Aux Becs Sceis.* There is here a natural harbor, capable of accommodating the larger class of vessels and steamboats. A small settlement has been commenced at this place, but with its natural advantages, and the capital and enterprise of parties who now contemplate making further improvements, it will soon become a very desirable and convenient point for the accommodation of navigators.

The islands comprising the Beavers, the Manitous, and Fox isles should here be noticed. The *Beavers* lie a little south of west from the entrance to the Strait of Mackinac, the Manitous a little south of these, and the Fox's still farther down the lake. These are all valuable for fishing purposes, and for wood and lumber. Lying in the route of all the steamboat lines from Chicago to Buffalo and the Upper Lakes, the harbors on these islands are stopping-points for the boats, and a profitable trade is conducted in furnishing the necessary supplies of wood, etc.

The settlement of Mormons on the Big Beaver Island has recently been abandoned, and the people have mostly dispersed.

We next arrive at *Manistee*, a small but important settlement at the mouth of the Manistee River. The harbor is a natural one, but requires some improvement. A large trade is carried on with Chicago in lumber. The river passes through a fine pine district, and is one of the largest in the State.

The next point of importance is the mouth of the *Père Marquette* River. Here is the terminus of the proposed railroad from Flint, in Genesee County, connecting with Detroit by the Detroit and Milwaukee Railway, a distance of about 180 miles.

The harbor is very superior, and the country in the vicinity is well adapted for settlement. About 16 miles in the interior is situated one of the most compact and extensive tracts of pine timber on the western coast.

About forty miles south of this, in the county of Oceana, a small village is located at the mouth of *White River*. The harbor here is also a natural one, and the region is settled to considerable extent by farmers. Lumber is, however, the principal commodity, and the trade is principally with the Chicago market.

The next point is *Muskegon*, at the mouth of the *Muskegon River*. It is supported principally by the large lumber region of the interior. Numerous steam saw-mills are now in active operation here, giving the place an air of life and activity.

The harbor is one of the best on the lake, and is at present accessible for all the vessels trading between Muskegon and Chicago. A small steamboat runs up the Muskegon River about forty miles to *Newaygo*, the capital of Newaygo County. This village is in a beautiful region of farming country, and also in close proximity to the extensive pineries stretching along the valley of the river. One of the largest lumber mills in the State, running 114 saws, is in operation at this place. About seventy millions of feet of lumber are manufactured annually on this river.

GRAND HAVEN, Ottawa Co., Mich., is situated on both sides of Grand River, at its entrance into Lake Michigan, here eighty miles wide; on the opposite side lies Milwaukee, Wis. The different settlements comprising Grand Haven contain about 5,000 inhabitants. Here is a court-house and jail, two churches, six hotels and taverns, a number of stores; eight large steam saw-mills, pail and tub factories, a foundry and machine shop, and other manufacturing establishments.

Steamers run from Grand Haven to Chicago, to Milwaukee, and also to other ports on Lake Michigan. Steamers also run from Grand Haven to Grand Rapids, about forty miles up the river, bringing down immense quantities of lumber and produce. Above Grand Rapids, where is a fall of twenty-two feet, steamers run to Lyons, about sixty miles distant, where steamboat navigation ceases.

The *Detroit and Milwaukee Railroad*, when finished, will extend from Detroit to Grand Haven, 185 miles, running for most of the distance through a rich section of country. It will form a through line of travel, by means of steamers across the lake to Milwaukee, and through Wisconsin to the Mississippi River and the Far West.

GRAND RAPIDS, situated forty miles above Grand Haven, although in her *teens*, can truly assume the title of a city. With a busy, enterprising population of more than 8,000, and rapidly increasing, possessing a water-power unequaled by any in the State, affording to manufacturers and others tempting inducements; surrounded by a new, fertile, and rapidly improving country, it can not fail shortly to become one of the most prominent cities in the Northwest.

"Extensive and inexhaustible beds of gypsum, a valuable and almost indispensable soil-fertilizer in any country, are found near this place. Building stone of good quality, easily attainable, as well as other desirable building materials, are abundant, and much in requisition, of which fact there is sufficient satisfactory evidence in the noble structures to be seen here, both of stores and dwellings, many of which evince good taste and correct architectural judgment. I was credibly informed that there were mercantile houses, in this *remote* city, doing business to the extent of one to two hundred thousand dollars each, yearly. It is confidently expected that the Detroit and Milwaukee Railroad will be completed and in operation from Detroit to this place during the summer of 1857. This road extends through an exceedingly rich agricultural section; that portion lying between the eastern bound of Shiawassa County and Grand

Rapids may safely be classed as the very best in the whole State, and I will venture the assertion that a very few years only will be required to demonstrate the truth of this, in the large amount of its surplus products seeking a market eastward, through the agency of this railroad."

THE GRAND RIVER PINERIES.—" Up in the northern part of the Grand River valley, and along and beyond the Muskegon River, an immense amount of pine timber is to be found. The mills upon the Muskegon River are, most of them, of later date than those of Grand River, and some of them are the finest in the world. One of the mills upon Grand River is so complete an automatic machine that it draws up and arranges its own logs, feeds them to any required thickness of boards, gigs back and sets itself, carries off and piles up the lumber, registers the number of boards cut—all by the aid of the most simple and beautiful machinery.

" At a low estimate," says the Grand Rapids *Enquirer*, from which we gather these facts, " the value of this trade foots up between five and seven millions of dollars. There is every prospect that these figures will be largely increased in ensuing years, there being thousands of acres of better pine lands than have yet been cut, yet lying untouched, north of these two rivers."

The following table shows, to some extent, the amount of lumber business now done on the Grand and Muskegon rivers and their tributaries:

Number of saw-mills on Grand and Muskegon rivers and their tributaries	115
(These mills run from 1 to 130 saws each.)	
Amount of lumber cut per year—feet	173,000,000
" lath " " "	48,000,000
" staves " " "	3,000,000
" shingles " " "	200,000,000
Number of hands constantly employed in mills	1,150
Number of hands employed in pineries in winter	3,460
Number of hands employed in rafting and loading vessels	660
Average load of vessels, feet	80,000
Annual number of arrivals of vessels carrying lumber from Grand and Muskegon rivers	1,920

DETROIT.

THE City of DETROIT, a port of entry, and the great commercial mart of the State, is favorably situated in N. lat. 42° 20′, W. long. 82° 58′, on a river or strait of the same name, elevated some 30 or 40 feet above its surface, being seven miles below the outlet of Lake St. Clair and twenty above the mouth of the river, where it enters into Lake Erie. It extends for the distance of upward of a mile upon the southwest bank of the river, where the stream is three fourths of a mile in width. The principal public and private offices and wholesale stores are located on Jefferson and Woodward avenues, which cross each other at right angles, the latter running to the water's edge. There may usually be seen a great number of steamboats, propellers, and sail vessels of a large class, loading or unloading their rich cargoes, destined for Eastern markets or for the *Great West*, giving an animated appearance to this place, which is aptly called the *City of the Straits*. It was incorporated in 1815, being now divided into nine wards, and governed by a mayor, recorder, and board of aldermen. Detroit contains the old State-house, from the dome of which a fine view is obtained of the city and vicinity; the City Hall, Masonic Hall, Firemen's Hall, Mechanics Hall, Odd Fellows Hall, the Young Men's Society Building, two Market Buildings, twenty churches, ten hotels, besides a number of taverns; a United States custom-house and post-office, a theater, a museum, two orphan asylums, four banks, and a savings' fund institute, besides a great number of manufacturing establishments. There are also several extensive ship-yards and machine shops, where are built and repaired vessels of almost every description. The population in 1850 was 21,891; in 1856, 48,000.

Detroit may be regarded as one of the most favored of all the Western cities of the Union. It was first settled by the French explorers as early as 1701, as a military and fur trading port. It changed its garrison and military government in 1760 for a British military commander and troops, enduring under the latter régime a series of Indian sieges, assaults, and petty but vigilant and harassing warfare, conducted against the English garrison by the celebrated Indian warrior Pontiac. Detroit subsequently passed into the possession of the American revolutionists; but on the 16th August, 1812, it was surrendered by Gen. Hull, of the United States army, to Gen. Brock, commander of the British forces. In 1813 it was again surrendered to the Americans.

The railroads finished and in progress of construction in Michigan afford facilities of an immense importance to Detroit, and the State at large. The following lines diverge from Detroit:

1. The *Detroit, Monroe and Toledo Railroad*, 62 miles in length, connecting with the Michigan Southern Railroad at Monroe, and with other roads at Toledo.

2. The *Michigan Central Railroad*, 282 miles in length, extends to Chicago, Ill. This important road, running across the State from east to west, connects at Michigan City, Ind., with the New Albany and Salem Railroad—thus forming a direct line of travel to Louisville, St. Louis, etc., as well as Chicago and the Far West.

3. The *Detroit and Milwaukee Railroad* runs through a rich section of country to Grand Haven, on Lake Michigan, opposite Milwaukee, Wis., and will soon be completed.

4. The *Detroit and Port Huron Railroad* is also under construction, which, when completed, will connect Lake Huron by rail with the valley of the Ohio River.

5. The *Great Western Railway* of Canada has its terminus at Windsor, opposite Detroit, the two places being connected by three steam ferries—thus affording a speedy line of travel through Canada, and thence to Eastern cities of the United States.

The DETROIT RIVER, or *Strait*, is a noble stream, through which flow the surplus waters of the Upper Lakes into Lake Erie. It is 27 miles in length, and from half a mile to two miles in width, forming the boundary between the United States and Canada. It has a perceptible current, and is navigable for vessels of the largest class. Large quantities of fish are annually taken in the river, and the sportsman usually finds an abundance of wild ducks, which breed in great numbers in the marshes bordering some of the islands and harbors of the coast.

There are altogether seventeen islands in the river. The names of these are, *Clay*, *Celeron*, *Hickory*, *Sugar*, *Bois Blanc*, *Ella*, *Fox*, *Rock*, *Grosse Isle*, *Stoney*, *Fighting*, *Turkey*, *Mammy Judy*, *Grassy*, *Mud*, *Belle* or *Hog*, and *Ile la Peche*. The two latter are situated a few miles above Detroit, near the entrance to Lake St. Clair, where large quantities of white-fish are annually taken.

ILE LA PECHE, attached to Canada, was the home of the celebrated Indian chief *Pontiac*. Parkman, in his "History of the Conspiracy of Pontiac," says: "Pontiac, the Satan of this forest-paradise, was accustomed to spend the early part of the summer upon a small island at the opening of Lake St. Clair." Another author says: "The king and lord of all this country lived in no royal state. His cabin was a small, oven-shaped structure of bark and rushes. Here he dwelt with his squaws and children; and here, doubtless, he might often have been seen carelessly reclining his naked form on a rush-mat or a bear-skin, like an ordinary Indian warrior."

The other fifteen islands, most of them small, are situated below Detroit, within the first twelve miles of the river after entering it from Lake Erie, the largest of which is GROSSE ISLE, attached to Michigan, on which are a number of extensive and well cultivated farms. This island has become a very popular retreat for citizens of Detroit during the heat of summer, there being here located good public houses for the accommodation of visitors.

Father Hennepin, who was passenger on the "Griffin," the first vessel that crossed Lake Erie, in 1679, in his description of the scenery along the route, says: "The islands are the finest in the world; the strait is finer than Niagara; the banks are vast meadows, and the prospect is terminated with some hills covered with vineyards, trees bearing good fruit, groves and forests so well disposed that one would think that Nature alone could not have made, without the help of art, so charming a prospect."

COMPARATIVE PURITY OF DETROIT RIVER WATER.

The following Table shows the solid matter in a gallon of water, taken from Lakes and Rivers in different cities:

	Grs. solid matter.		Grs. solid matter.
Albany, Hudson River	6.320	Rochester, N. Y. — Hemlock L.	1.330
Troy, Mohawk River	7.880	Rochester, N. Y. — Lake Ont.	4.160
Boston, Cochituate Lake	1.850	Rochester, N. Y. — Genesee R.	11.210
New York, Croton River	6.998	Detroit, Detroit River	5.722
Brooklyn, L. I. Ponds	2.367	Cleveland, Lake Erie	5.000
Philadelphia, Schuylkill R.	4.260	Montreal, St. Lawrence R.	5.000
Cincinnati, Ohio River	6.736		

Of the Detroit River water, Prof. Douglass, in his report of the analysis, says: "In estimating the value of your city water, as compared with other cities, due allowance must be made for the fact, that the total solid matter is materially increased by the presence of silica, alumina, and iron, elements that can produce little or no injury; while the chlorides, much the most injurious compounds, are entirely absent. The presence of such large quantities of silica and iron is accounted for by the fact, that Lakes Superior and Huron are formed, for the most part, in a basin of ferruginous sandstone and igneous rock."

LAKE AND RIVER FISHERIES.

"THE early French explorers of the Upper Lakes, in 1615, make mention of the white fish and trout as being luxurious, and much used for the sustenance of life by the sons of the forest. From the time civilization dawned upon the shores of the lakes, the French settlers supplied themselves with them; and during the war of 1812, they were found of substantial benefit to the soldiers in appeasing their hunger, for the want of other supplies.

"Previous to the completion of the Erie Canal, salt was mostly transported by the St. Lawrence, and thence up the lakes, and obtained only at enormous prices. After the canal was completed, in 1827, it became comparatively cheap, and the fisheries were made profitable. In 1830, emigration to Michigan rapidly commenced, and increased to such a degree in 1834, that the new-comers found it difficult to purchase produce, on account of the scarcity, as nearly every thing consumed was imported from sister States. This caused a great consumption of fish, and gave birth to the extension of river and lake fisheries.

"From this time the business increased, and several grounds were cleared on the St. Clair River, and as the market increased they were extended to the shores of Lake Huron. Several houses in Detroit became extensively engaged in the business, employing vessels exclusively in the trade. The American Fur Company also engaged in it; and, in 1841, two schooners were taken over the falls at the Saut Ste Marie into Lake Superior, for the purpose of fishing on that lake.

"There are a great variety of fish in the lakes besides white fish and trout. Lake Superior abounds with the siskowit, a delicious fish, weighing from three to ten pounds. They are exceedingly fat, and when tryed will yield 25 per cent. of oil Sturgeon weighing upward of 100 pounds have been taken; trout, 60 pounds; maskalonge, 40 pounds; pickerel, 15 pounds; mullet, 10 pounds; bill-fish, six pounds; also cat-fish, herrings, eels, etc. In the vicinity of the Saut Ste Marie, and al' the streams emptying into Lake Superior, large quantities of small speckled, or brook-trout, are taken.

"In 1840 there were 35,000 barrels of fish of various kinds packed, and it is estimated that the quantity now annually taken in American waters can not be less than 100,000 barrels, besides what find their way to the Canadian markets. Detroit is the most extensive mart, where large quantities are sold for home consumption; and market is found for them in New York, Pennsylvania, Ohio, Indiana, and other Western States."—See "*Sketches of the City of Detroit*," pub. in 1855.

The White Fish is regarded as the prince of fresh-water fish Henry R. Schoolcraft, in his poem, "The White Fish," says:

" All friends to good living by tureen and dish,
Concur in exalting this prince of a fish;
So fine in a platter, so tempting a fry,
So rich on a gridiron, so sweet in a pie;
That even before it the salmon must fail,
And that mighty *bonne-bouche*, of the land-beaver's tail.
* * * * *
'Tis a morsel alike for the gourmand or faster,
While, white as a tablet of pure alabaster!
Its beauty or flavor no person can doubt,
When seen in the water or tasted without;
And all the dispute that opinion ere makes
Of this king of lake fishes, this '*deer of the lakes*,'*
Regard not its choiceness to ponder or sup,
But the best mode of dressing and serving it up.
* * * * *
Here too, might a fancy to descant inclined,
Contemplate the love that pertains to the kind,
And bring up the red man, in fanciful strains,
To prove its creation from feminine brains."†

STEAMBOAT ROUTE FROM CLEVELAND TO DETROIT.

Ports, etc.	Miles.	Ports, etc.	Miles.
Cleveland, Ohio	0	Detroit, Mich.	0
Point Pelée Is., and Light	60	*Windsor*, C. W.	1
Bar Point, C. W.	97	Fighting Island	8
Bois Blanc Is. Light, Detroit River,	100	Fish Island	9
		Wyandotte, Mich.	11
Malden, C. W.	101	Mama Juba Is. and Light	12
Gibraltar, Mich.		Grosse Isle	13
Grosse Isle, "	102	Gibraltar, Mich.	
Mama Juba Is. and Light	108	*Malden*, C. W.	19
Wyandotte, Mich.	109	Bois Blanc Is. Light, Lake Erie,	20
Fish Island Light	111		
Fighting Island	112	Bar Point, C. W.	23
Windsor, C. W.	119	Point Pelée Island	60
Detroit	120	Cleveland	120

Fare, $3 00. Usual Time, 7 hours.

---

* A translation of *Ad-dik-keem-maig*, the Indian name for this fish.
† *Vide* "Indian Tales and Legends."

CLEVELAND AND DETROIT STEAMERS—DAILY.

May Queen, 688 tons............Capt. E. Vesie
Ocean, 900 " .... " C. C. Blodgett.

STEAMERS RUNNING FROM CLEVELAND AND DETROIT TO DIFFERENT PORTS ON THE UPPER LAKES.

LAKE SUPERIOR LINE, STOPPING AT MACKINAC AND SAUT STE MARIE.

Steamer Illinois, 926 tons...........Capt. Wilson.
" North Star, 1,106 tons..... " B. G. Sweet.
" Planet, 1,154 tons......... " Nicholson.
Propeller Manhattan, 320 tons...... " John Spalding.
" Mineral Rock, 560 " ..... " John Fraser.
" Gen. Taylor, 462 " ...... " R. Rider.

GREEN BAY LINE, STOPPING AT MACKINAC, RUNS BETWEEN BUFFALO, CLEVELAND, DETROIT, AND GREEN BAY.

Steamer Michigan, 642 tons...............Capt. A. Stewart.
" Sultana, 650 " .... " Mead

DETROIT TO SAGINAW CITY.

Steamer Sam Ward, 433 tons..............Capt. H. Fish

RUNNING FROM DETROIT.

Steamer Ploughboy, 300 tons, Capt. D. Rowan, runs to Port Sarnia and Goderich, C. W.

Steamer Mazeppa, 250 tons, runs to Goderich and Saugeen

DETROIT TO PORT HURON AND FORRESTVILLE.

Steamer Forrester................Capt. J. Robertson.
" Forest Queen............ " S. D. Woodworth.
Steamer Ariel, 165 tons, runs to New Baltimore, Mich.
" Albion, 132 tons, runs to Mt. Clemens.

STEAMBOAT ROUTES FROM DETROIT TO TOLEDO, SANDUSKY, ETC.

DETROIT AND TOLEDO STEAMBOAT LINE.

ARROW, 373 tons................Capt. J. W. Keith.
DART, 297 " .... " S. Dustin.

One of the above steamers runs daily to and from Toledo, stopping at Wyandotte, Trenton, Monroe, and other ports on the Michigan shore. Distance from Detroit to Toledo, by steamboat route, 70 miles.

DETROIT TO SANDUSKY.

The steamer BAY CITY, 479 tons, Capt. J. M. Lundy, runs from Detroit to Sandusky, Ohio, connecting with railroad lines running to Newark, Columbus, Cincinnati, etc.

WYANDOTTE, ten miles below Detroit, is a new and flourishing manufacturing village, where are located the most extensive iron works in Michigan.

TRENTON, six miles farther, is the next steamboat landing.

The City of MONROE, capital of Monroe Co., Mich., is situated on both sides of the river Raisin, three miles above its entrance into Lake Erie, and about 40 miles from Detroit. It is connected with the lake by a ship canal, and is the terminus of the *Michigan Southern Railroad*, which extends west, in connection with the Northern Indiana Railroad, to Chicago, Ill. The town contains about 5,000 inhabitants, a court-house and jail, a United States land-office, eight churches, several public-houses, and a number of large stores of different kinds. Here are two extensive piers, forming an outport at the mouth of the river, where the steamers land and receive passengers; the railroad track running to the landing. A plank-road also runs from the outport to the city, which is an old and interesting locality, being formerly called *Frenchtown*, where a sanguinary battle was fought during the war of 1812. The *Detroit, Monroe and Toledo Railroad*, just completed, passes through this city; it being about 40 miles to Detroit and 22 miles to Toledo by railroad route. This line of travel will be extended south to Cincinnati. Steamers run from Detroit to Toledo, stopping at Monroe daily during the season of navigation.

The City of SANDUSKY, capital of Erie Co., Ohio, is a port of entry and flourishing place of trade. It is advantageously situated on Sandusky Bay, three miles from Lake Erie, in N. lat. 41° 27′, W. long. 82° 45′. The bay is about 20 miles long, and five or six miles in width, forming a capacious and excellent harbor, into which steamers and vessels of all sizes can enter with safety. The average depth of water is from ten to twelve feet. The city is built on a bed of limestone, producing a good building material. It contains about 10,000 inhabitants, a court-house and jail, eight churches, two banks, several well-kept hotels, and a number of large stores and manufacturing establishments of different kinds. This is the terminus of the Mad River and Lake Erie Railroad, running to Dayton, 153 miles, and the Sandusky, Mansfield and Newark Railroad, 116 miles in length. The Cleveland and Toledo Railroad, northern division, also runs through Sandusky, affording altogether great facilities to travelers, in connection with a line of steamers running to Detroit, Cleveland, and Buffalo

The City of TOLEDO is situated on the Maumee River, four miles from its mouth, and ten miles from the Turtle Island Light, at the outlet of the Maumee Bay into Lake Erie. The harbor is good, and the navigable channel from Toledo to the lake is of sufficient depth for all steamers or sail vessels navigating the lakes, with the exception of a short distance through the bay, which requires deepening from one to two feet. Toledo is the eastern terminus of the *Wabash and Erie Canal*, running through the Maumee and Wabash valleys, and communicating with the Ohio River at Evansville, a distance of 474 miles; also of the *Miami and Erie Canal*, which branches from the above canal 68 miles west of Toledo, and runs southwardly through the Miami Valley in Western Ohio, and communicates with the Ohio River at Cincinnati.

"The railroads diverging from Toledo are the *Michigan Southern and Northern Indiana Railroad*, running through the southern counties of Michigan and the northern counties of Indiana, and making its western terminus at Chicago, Illinois, at a distance of 243 miles; also, the Air Line Railroad, running due west from Toledo, through Northwestern Ohio and the northern counties of Indiana to Goshen, a distance of 110 miles, where it connects with the Northern Indiana Railroad, running to Chicago; also the terminus of the Jackson Branch of the Michigan Southern Road, and the Detroit, Monroe and Toledo Railroad.

"It is also the eastern terminus of the *Toledo, Wabash and Western Railroad*, running in a southwesterly direction through the Maumee and Wabash valleys, crossing the eastern line of the State of Illinois, about 125 miles south of Chicago, and continuing in a southwesterly course through Danville, Springfield, Jacksonville, Naples, etc., in Central Illinois, to the Mississippi River, and connecting with the Hannibal and St. Joseph Road, which stretches nearly due west through the State of Missouri to St. Joseph, on the Missouri River. It also, in connection with other roads, affords a through line of travel to St. Louis. The *Dayton and Michigan Railroad* (to be completed the present year), which connects Toledo with Cincinnati, is much the shortest railroad line connecting Lake Erie with the Ohio River. Besides the above important roads, the *Cleveland and Toledo Railroad* terminates here.

"Toledo is the nearest point for the immense country traversed by these canals and railroads, where a transfer can be made of freight to the more cheap transportation by the lakes, and thence through the Erie Canal, Welland Canal, or Oswego Canal, to the sea-board. It is not merely the country traversed by these canals and railroads that send their products, and receive their merchandise, through Toledo, but many portions of the States of Kentucky, Tennessee, Missouri, and Iowa find Toledo the cheapest and most expeditious lake-port for the interchange and transfer of their products and merchandise."

This city is the capital of Lucas County, Ohio, where is situated a court-house and jail, several fine churches and school edifices, six hotels, and a great number of stores and storehouses, also several extensive manufacturing establishments.

The population of Toledo in 1850 was about 4,000, and now it is supposed to contain 12,000 inhabitants, and is rapidly increasing in wealth and numbers. The shipping interest is increasing, here being transhipped annually an enormous amount of grain, and other kinds of agricultural product of the great West; it being, no doubt, destined, like Chicago, to export direct to European ports, lying as it does on the direct railroad and steamboat route from St. Louis to Montreal.

At this time there are in process of erection in Toledo many handsome dwellings, numerous handsome blocks of stores, a post-office and custom-house by the general government, and a first-class hotel; these two latter buildings, from the plans we have seen, would do credit to any city, and when completed can be classed among the most elegant structures. No city in the State can boast of finer private residences than Toledo; and the general character of the buildings erected in the past three years is substantial and elegant.

PERRYSBURG, capital of Wood Co., Ohio, is situated on the right bank of the Maumee River, 18 miles above its entrance into Maumee Bay, the southern termination of Lake Erie. It contains a court-house and jail, four churches, 20 stores of different kinds, three steam saw-mills, a tannery, and several other manufacturing establishments. Population about 1,500. Here is the head of steamboat navigation on the Maumee River, affording thus far a sufficient depth of water for steamers of a large class.

MAUMEE CITY, capital of Lucas Co., Ohio, and a port of entry, is situated on the Maumee River, opposite Perrysburg, at the foot of the rapids and at the head of navigation, nine miles above Toledo. A side cut here connects the *Wabash and Erie Canal* with the river The Toledo and Illinois Railroad also passes through this place. It contains a court-house, five churches, 30 stores, four flouring-mills, three saw-mills, one oil-mill, and other manufacturing establishments propelled by water-power, the supply being here almost inexhaustible.

MAUMEE RIVER rises in the northeast part of Indiana, and flowing northeast enters Lake Erie, through *Maumee Bay*. It is about 100 miles long, navigable 18 miles, and furnishing an extensive water-power throughout its course.

TRIP FROM BUFFALO TO DETROIT—DIRECT.

Commodious steamers of about two thousand tons burden leave Buffalo direct for Detroit, daily, Sundays excepted, at ten o'clock P.M., or on the arrival of the Eastern express train of cars, leaving Albany the same morning; also, connects with cars from Niagara Falls, etc.

On leaving the wharf at Buffalo, the steamers usually run direct for Long Point on the Canada, or north shore of Lake Erie, proceeding for most of the distance in British waters, to the mouth of Detroit River.

Long Point, 65 miles from Buffalo, is a long strip of land, nearly 20 miles long and from one to three miles in width, covered for the most part with a stunted growth of forest trees. It was formerly a peninsula, running out from the land in an easterly direction, nearly half way across the lake; but the waters having made a wide breach across its western extremity, has converted it into an island. There is an important light-house on the east end to guide the mariner on his passage through Lake Erie, here about 40 miles wide, and where is found the greatest depth of water. To this Point both shores of the lake can be seen in a clear morning from the deck of the steamer, affording a most grand sight when the sun rises on a cloudless day. Then may usually been seen a fleet of vessels wending their way toward Buffalo or the mouth of the Welland Canal, through which channel annually passes a great number of steam propellers and sail vessels on their way to Lake Ontario and the St. Lawrence River.

Port Colborne, C. W., situated about 20 miles west of Buffalo, lies at the mouth of the Welland Canal, while Port Maitland, some 20 miles farther, is situated at the mouth of Grand River, where is a navigable feeder communicating with the canal, thus affording two entrances to the above canal.

Port Dover, about 70 miles west of Buffalo and 40 miles distant from Hamilton by proposed railroad route, is situated on the north shore of Lake Erie, at the mouth of the river Lynn. Here is a good harbor, and the village is a place of growing importance, containing about 1,000 inhabitants.

Port Ryerse and Port Rowan are small villages on the Canada shore, situated on the bay formed by Long Point. Inland there is to be found a rich and fine farming district, consisting of some of the best lands in Canada West.

The *Sand Hills*, immediately west of Long Point, are seen for some distance as the steamer pursues her onward course toward *Point aux Pins*, passing through the widest part of the lake, where both shores are lost sight of for a number of miles. The water usually presents a clear green color in the middle, but near the shore is more or less tinged with muddy water, proceeding from the streams emptying into the lake.

Port Burwell, C. W., about 35 miles west of Long Point, is handsomely situated at the mouth of Otter Creek. Here is a light-house and good harbor. A large amount of lumber and other products are annually exported from this place to Eastern markets.

Port Stanley, about 25 miles farther west, is handsomely situated at the mouth of Kettle Creek, being in part surrounded by high and picturesque hills in the immediate vicinity. The harbor is well protected, and much frequented by British and American vessels running on Lake Erie. It is nine miles south of St. Thomas and twenty-four from London, the chief town of the county of Middlesex, for which place it may be considered the out-port. A plank-road runs between the two places; also, the *London and Port Stanley Railroad*, connecting with the Great Western Railway of Canada. Steamers run from Port Stanley to Buffalo, Cleveland, and other ports on Lake Erie.

Point aux Pins, or Rond' Eau (usually called by the American navigators *Round O*), about 100 miles west of Long Point, is a cape which projects from the Canada shore, inclosing a natural basin of about 6,000 acres in extent, with a depth of from ten to twelve feet, thus forming an excellent and secure harbor, the entrance to which has been improved by the Canadian government by running out piers, etc. It is proposed to construct a ship canal from this port to the St. Clair River, a distance of about 35 miles, thus avoiding the *St. Clair Flats*. Another Canadian project is to construct a canal from Goderich to Hamilton, C. W., about 120 miles in length.

Point Pelée, lying about 40 miles east of the mouth of Detroit River, projects a number of miles into Lake Erie, and forms, in connection with the island of Point Pelée and other islands in the vicinity, the most picturesque portion of lake scenery to be met with on this inland sea.

Point Pelée Island, belonging to Canada, is about seven miles long and two or three miles in width. It is inhabited by a few settlers. The island is said to abound with red cedar, and possesses a fine limestone quarry. A light-house is situated on the east side.

The steamers bound for Detroit River usually pass to the north side of Point Pelée Island, and run across *Pigeon Bay* toward *Bar Point*, situated at the mouth of Detroit River. Several small islands are passed on the south, called *East Sister*, *Middle Sister*, and *West Sister;* also, in the distance, may be seen the Bass Islands, known as the "North Bass," "Middle Bass," and "South Bass." On the west side of the latter lies the secure harbor of Put-in-Bay, celebrated as the rendezvous of Com. Perry's fleet, before and after the glorious naval victory which he achieved over the British fleet, September 10th, 1813.

Detroit River, forming one of the links between the Upper and Lower Lakes, is next approached, near the mouth of which may be seen a light on the Michigan shore called *Gibraltar Light*, and another light on an island attached to Canada, the steamers usually entering the river through the east or *British Channel* of the river, although vessels often pass through the west or *American Channel*

AMHERSTBURG, C. W., 18 miles below Detroit, is an old and important town. The situation is good; the banks of the river, both above and below the village, but particularly the latter, where the river emerges into Lake Erie, are very beautiful; several handsome residences may here be seen, surrounded by highly cultivated grounds. About a mile below the town is a chalybeate spring, which is said to resemble the waters of Cheltenham, in England. British and American vessels frequently land at Amherstburg, on their trips to and from the Upper Lakes.

FORT MALDEN, capable of accommodating a regiment of troops, is situated about half a mile above Amherstburg, on the east bank of the river, the channel of which it here commands.

At BROWNSTOWN, situated on the opposite side of the river, in Michigan, is the *battle-ground* where the Americans, under disadvantageous circumstances, and with a slight loss, routed the British forces, which lay in ambush, as the former were on their way to relieve the fort at Frenchtown, which event occurred August 5, 1812.

SANDWICH, C. W., is beautifully situated on the river, two miles below Detroit, and nine miles below Lake St. Clair. It stands on a gently sloping bank a short distance from the river, which is here about a mile wide. This is one of the oldest settlements in Canada West.

WINDSOR, C. W., situated in the township of Sandwich, is a village directly opposite Detroit, with which it is connected by three steam ferries. It was laid out in 1834, and is now a place of considerable business, having a population of about 2,000 inhabitants. Here terminates the *Great Western Railway* of Canada, which extends from Niagara Falls or Suspension Bridge, *via* Hamilton and London, to opposite Detroit—thus forming an important link in the great line of railroads, now finished, running from the sea-board at different points to the Mississippi River

STEAMERS RUNNING FROM BUFFALO TO DIFFERENT PORTS ON LAKE ERIE, ETC.—1857.

MICHIGAN CENTRAL RAILROAD LINE

Steamer PLYMOUTH ROCK, 2,000 tons....Capt. P. J. Ralph.
" MISSISSIPPI, 1,830 " .... " S. G. Langley.
" WESTERN WORLD, 2,000 " .... " J. S. Richards.

One of the above splendid steamers leaves the foot of Erie Street, Buffalo, every evening (Sundays excepted) at 9 P.M., direct for Detroit, connecting with trains on the Michigan Central Railroad, running to Chicago, etc.

C. E. NOBLE, *Gen. Agent*, Buffalo

MICHIGAN SOUTHERN RAILROAD LINE

SOUTHERN MICHIGAN, 1,470 tons .... Capt. L. B. Goldsmith.
WESTERN METROPOLIS, 1,830 " .... " I. T. Pheatt.
CITY OF BUFFALO, 2,200 " .... " A. D. Perkins.

One of the above new and popular steamers usually leaves the foot of Main Street, Buffalo, daily (Sundays excepted), direct for Toledo, connecting with trains on the Michigan Southern and Northern Indiana railroads, running to Chicago, etc. This line also connects with trains of cars running from Toledo tc Lafayette, Ind., St. Louis, etc.

C. FORBES, *Gen. Agent*, Buffalo.

CLEVELAND, COLUMBUS AND CINCINNATI RAILROAD LINE.

Steamer CRESCENT CITY......1,740 tons, Capt. Wm. T. Pease.
" QUEEN OF THE WEST, 1,850 " " D. H. McBride.

One of the above steamers usually leaves Buffalo at 8 o'clock P.M., direct for Cleveland, O., connecting with trains on the Cleveland, Columbus and Cincinnati Railroad.

J. C. HARRISON, *Gen. Agent*, Buffalo.

Steamer CLIFTON, Capt. H. Van Allen, runs from Buffalo to Chippewa, C. W., daily, connecting with the Erie and Ontario Railroad, forming a through line of travel to Niagara Falls, Toronto, etc.

Steamer MOHAWK runs from Buffalo to Port Stanley, etc., connecting with the London ana Port Stanley Railroad.

RAILROAD ROUTE FROM NIAGARA FALLS TO HAMILTON AND DETROIT, *via* GREAT WESTERN RAILWAY OF CANADA.

THIS great International Line, extending from Niagara River to Detroit River, opposite the city of Detroit, a distance of 229 miles, passes through a fine and interesting section of country, equal in many respects to Western New York. It connects with the New York Central and Buffalo and Niagara Falls Railroad, forming a great through route of travel.

Starting from the *Suspension Bridge* at CLIFTON, two miles below the Falls of Niagara, the passenger train soon reaches the verge of the mountain ridge overlooking the plain below, while in the distance may be seen the broad waters of Lake Ontario, usually studded with sail vessels and propellers on their way to or from the mouth of the Welland Canal.

> "Traced like a map, the landscape lies
> In cultured beauty stretching wide."

THOROLD, nine miles, is situated on the line of the Welland Canal, where is abundant water-power propelling five or six flouring-mills. A railroad extends to Port Dalhousie, some five or six miles distant, connecting with a steamer running to Toronto. This road will be extended to Port Colbourne, on Lake Erie, about twenty miles distant.

ST. CATHERINES, 12 miles from the Suspension Bridge, is a flourishing town, also situated on the line of the Welland Canal, which connects Erie and Ontario. This has become of late a fashionable place of resort during the summer months, caused by the mineral waters of the "*Artesian Wells*" obtaining great celebrity, owing to their curative properties. Here are two or three well-kept hotels for the accommodation of visitors. For further description of this place, see page 238.

BEAMSVILLE, twenty-two miles from the Suspension Bridge, is a thriving village, about one mile from the station.

GRIMSBY, five miles farther, is situated on Forty-mile Creek, the scene of some hard fighting during the war of 1812. It is a small village of 350 inhabitants; there are two churches, a hotel, and several stores; also, a grist and saw-mills propelled by water-power.

HAMILTON, 43 miles from Suspension Bridge, is the principal station on the line of the Great Western Railway, where are located the principal offices and workshops connected with the company. Here is a commodious depôt and steamboat landing. Carriages and omnibuses are always in readiness to convey passengers to the hotels in the city, which is more fully described on page 238.

The *Toronto Branch* of the Great Western Railway commences at Hamilton, and extends a distance of thirty-eight miles to the city of Toronto, running near the shore of Lake Ontario.

On leaving Hamilton for Windsor or Detroit, the road passes near the mansion of Sir Allan M'Nab, and over the Des Jardines Canal, entering the head of Burlington Bay.* Here is also a Suspension Bridge in sight, thrown over the stream as it cuts its way through the high bank which encircles the bay or lake. This point presents a beautiful view, both on leaving or arriving at the head-waters of Lake Ontario.

DUNDAS, five miles from Hamilton, is situated on rising ground on the side of the mountain, and is a thriving manufacturing place, having the advantage of a stream which flows, or rather rushes, with great impetuosity through its center, working on its way numerous mills. The *Des Jardines Canal* runs from hence to Burlington Bay, enabling the manufacturers to ship their goods at their own doors. Among the manufactories are flouring-mills, a paper-mill, a foundry, which is an extensive establishment, where machinery of every kind and steam-engines are made to a large extent; an axe factory, a woolen factory; two newspapers, and several places of worship. Population 3,500.

* On Thursday, March 12th, 1857, the most fearful accident on record occurred at this bridge, killing about seventy passengers, men, women, and children, being on their way from Toronto to Hamilton.

HARRISBURG, nineteen miles from Hamilton, is the station of the *Galt Branch* of the Great Western Railway.

PARIS, with the Upper and Lower Town, contains about 3,500 inhabitants; so called from its contiguity to beds of gypsum or plaster of Paris. It possesses a considerable amount of water-power, which works numerous mills. There are two foundries. a tannery, machine-shop, distillery, saw-mill, etc. The *Buffalo and Lake Huron Railway* intersects the Great Western at this point, running to Goderich, on Lake Huron.

WOODSTOCK, 48 miles from Hamilton and 138 from Windsor, is a county town, well situated on rolling ground, and contains about 4,500 inhabitants. It may be called a town of magnificent distances; East and West Woodstock forming a street upward of a mile in length. The vacant spaces, however, are fast being filled up with stately edifices, and it will thus in a short time become one of the handsomest thoroughfares in Canada. In this locality, noted for its handsome country seats —and indeed all the way from Hamilton—the land as seen from the road (the railroad for the most part passes through a new country) is rolling and well cleared of trees and stumps, presenting more the appearance of "merrie England" than any other section of the Province.

INGERSOLL, nine miles farther, formerly an Indian village, now contains about 2,000 inhabitants. A small arm of the Thames runs through it, and furnishes some water-power, by which several mills are worked. Since the opening of the railway it has risen in a surprising manner; and the town, which before then had a very dingy appearance, the houses being of wood and wanting paint, is now gay with white brick, and the streets resound with the hum of an enterprising population.

LONDON, 119 miles from Suspension Bridge and 110 from Windsor, if not, like her English namesake,

> ———— The great resort
> Of all the earth—checkered with all
> Complexions of mankind—

is nevertheless a very stirring business place, and presents another instance of the energy and enterprise of the Canadian. Ten years ago, this then very small village of wooden houses was entirely burned down, and now on its ashes is raised a most flourishing city, containing four banks, several wholesale houses, fifteen churches, many of them handsome structures, and the English Church having a fine peal of bells; life and fire insurance offices, breweries and distilleries. It has three newspapers and several good hotels. Population nearly 18,000. It is well watered by the river Thames, which, however, is only navigable up to Chatham, sixty miles distant.

The *London and Port Stanley Railroad* here joins the Great Western Railway; length twenty-four miles, running south to Lake Erie.

Chatham, forty-six miles from Windsor, situated on the river Thames, possesses the great advantage of a navigation, and is therefore a place of considerable business. It contains eight churches; and being the county town of Kent, it has a court-house, a very handsome building, several grist and saw-mills, woolen factory, two foundries, machine shop, etc. Numerous steamers and sail vessels have been built at this place. Steamers ply between Chatham, Detroit, and Amherstburg. Population about 5,000.

Windsor, 229 miles from Suspension Bridge, opposite Detroit, prettily situated on the banks of the river, is a place of considerable business, and is rapidly increasing in wealth and population, owing to the advantage it has of being the western terminus of the Great Western Railway. Of course Windsor must have a " Castle," and the hotel of that name will be found excellent. Population, 2,000.

Three steam-ferries ply between Windsor and Detroit, making close connections for the benefit of railroad passengers.

For further information in regard to this route—*See Canada Railway and Steam Navigation Guide.*

BUFFALO TO GODERICH, C. W., *via* BUFFALO AND LAKE HURON RAILWAY.

Office, 37 *Exchange Street, Buffalo, N. Y.*

This important line of travel extends from Buffalo, N. Y., crossing Niagara River by means of a steam ferry at Black Rock to Fort Erie, on the Canada side. It is proposed to construct a permanent railroad bridge of about one mile in length, a short distance above the present ferry. From Fort Erie the line of the railway extends westward within a short distance of Lake Erie for forty miles, to Dunnville, situated at the mouth of Grand River, crossing the Welland Canal.

From Dunnville the road runs along the valley of the river on the north side to Brantford, thirty-eight miles farther, and from thence extends westward to Paris, where it connects with the Great Western Railway of Canada. The line thence runs to Stratford, C. W., where it connects with the Grand Trunk

Railway, a total distance from Buffalo of 116 miles. To this point the road is now completed and in running order, and will be finished through to Goderich, situated on Lake Huron, during the year 1857.

DUNVILLE is advantageously situated on the Grand River, at a point where it is intersected by the feeder of the Welland Canal. It is a place of considerable business, and contains several grist, saw, and plaster mills, and a tannery. Population, about 1,500.

The *Welland Canal* is one of the many works of the same kind of which Canadians may be proud. This Canal affords a passage for propellers, sloops and schooners of 125 tons burden, around the Falls of Niagara, and connects Lake Erie with Lake Ontario. It is 42 miles long, including feeder, 56 feet wide, and from 8½ to 16 feet deep. The whole descent from one lake to the other is 334 feet, which is accomplished by 37 locks.

BRANTFORD, 78 miles from Buffalo and 82 miles from Goderich, is beautifully situated on Grand River, and named after Brant, the renowned chief of the Six Nations Indians, who, with his tribe, steadily supported the British Crown during the American War. "In '*Gertrude of Wyoming*' he is alluded to in disparaging terms:

'The mammoth comes—the fiend, the monster Brant.'

But some years afterward Campbell was obliged to apologize to Brant's son, who happened to visit London; as it appeared, on satisfactory evidence, his father was not even present at the horrible desolation of Wyoming. This much is due to the memory of Brant, who was a brave warrior and a steadfast ally of the British, and always exerted himself to mitigate the horrors of war."

Brantford, until the opening of the Great Western Railway, was a great wheat market, the streets being crowded with hundreds of wagons daily; but that road created other markets, and to this extent the town has suffered. It has, however, other sources of prosperity. There is no place in the Province which commands such extensive water-power, and which is made available for the working of numerous mills. The iron foundries, machine shops, and potteries are on a large scale, and have caused the place to be regarded as the Birmingham of Canada. It has a goodly number of churches of various denominations, and one of the largest and handsomest hotels in the Province—" The Kirby House." Population about 6,000.

STRATFORD, is a new and thriving town, favorably situated on the line of the *Grand Trunk Railway* of Canada. This section of Canada enjoys a good climate and fertile soil, producing cereal grains in great abundance.

The distance from Stratford to Goderich, by railroad route, is 44 miles, which, when completed, will afford a direct and speedy route from Buffalo to Lake Huron, a total distance of 160 miles.

GODERICH, C. W., is advantageously situated at the mouth of Maitland River, here affording a safe and good harbor for vessels of a large size. The village is beautifully situated on elevated ground, rising about 150 feet above the waters of Lake Huron. The population now amounts to about 4,000, and is rapidly increasing in numbers and wealth. Steamers run from this port to Port Sarnia, Detroit, and Saginaw, and other harbors on the Upper Lakes.

The *Buffalo and Lake Huron Railway Company* is pushing with energy the completion of this road, and the improvement of its passenger and freight capacity. We learn that the board of directors, at a late meeting in London, England, appropriated $1,300,000 for the construction of a steam ferry to run between Fort Erie and Black Rock, which shall be able to transfer six cars at a time from one side of the river to the other; for the construction of slips and docks on both sides to accomodate the steamer; for the construction of a track from Black Rock into the city of Buffalo, and to improve the harbor at Goderich, the terminus of the road on Lake Huron.

TABLE OF DISTANCES

FROM BUFFALO TO TOLEDO.—LAKE ERIE ROUTE.

Ports, etc.	Miles.	Ports, etc.	Miles.
BUFFALO, N. Y.	0	TOLEDO, Ohio...........	0
Silver Creek, "	34	Maumee Bay	7
DUNKIRK, "	42	Turtle Island...........	10
Portland, "	52	West Sister Island	22
ERIE, Pa...............	90	South Bass Island.......	40
Conneaut, Ohio.........	117	Kelley's Island	45
Ashtabula, "	131	SANDUSKY, Ohio.......	50
Painesville, "	156	CLEVELAND, "	100
CLEVELAND, "	185	Painesville, "	129
Kelley's Island	240	Ashtabula, "	154
SANDUSKY "	245	Conneaut, "	168
South Bass Island.......	245	ERIE, Pa.	195
West Sister Island	263	Portland, N. Y.	233
Turtle Island...........	275	DUNKIRK, "	243
Maumee Bay	278	Silver Creek, "	251
TOLEDO, Ohio	285	BUFFALO, "	285

NOTE.—The direct through route as run by the steamers from Buffalo to Toledo is about 250 miles; the circuit of Lake Erie being about 560 miles.

COMPARATIVE INCREASE OF LAKE CITIES.

	1840.	1850.	1853.	1856.
BUFFALO, N. Y......	18,213	42,261	60,000*	85,000
CHICAGO, Ill.	4,470	28,269	60,000	100,000
CLEVELAND, O.	6,071	17,034	40,000†	50,000
DETROIT, Mich.	9,102	21,019	34,436	48,000
MILWAUKEE, Wis....	1,700	20,061	25,000	42,000
OSWEGO, N. Y.......	....	12,205	.....	16,000
SANDUSKY, O.	1,434	6,008	8,000	10,000
TOLEDO, O.	1,222	3,829	6,412	12,000

* *Black Rock* annexed. † *Ohio City* annexed.

TRIP FROM BUFFALO TO CLEVELAND, SANDUSKY, TOLEDO, ETC.

STEAMERS of a large class leave Buffalo, daily, Sundays excepted, for the different ports on the American or south shore of Lake Erie, connecting with railroad cars at Cleveland, Sandusky, and Toledo.

On leaving Buffalo harbor, which is formed by the mouth of Buffalo Creek, where is erected a breakwater by the United States government, a fine view is afforded of the city of Buffalo, the Canada shore, and Lake Erie stretching off in the distance, with here and there a steamer or sail vessel in sight. As the steamer proceeds westward through the middle of the lake, the landscape fades in the distance, until nothing is visible but a broad expanse of green waters.

STURGEON POINT, 20 miles from Buffalo, is passed on the south shore, when the lake immediately widens by the land receding on both shores. During the prevalence of storms, when the full blast of the wind sweeps through this lake, its force is now felt in its full power, driving the angry waves forward with the velocity of the race-horse, often causing the waters to rise at the lower end of the lake to a great height so as to overflow its banks, and forcing its surplus waters into the Niagara River, which causes the only perceptible rise and increase of the rush of waters at the Falls.

DUNKIRK, N. Y., 42 miles from Buffalo, is advantageously situated on the shore of Lake Erie where terminates the *New York and Erie Railroad*, 460 miles in length. Here is a good and secure harbor, affording about twelve feet of water over the bar. A light-house, a beacon light and breakwater, the latter in a dilapidated state, have here been erected by the United States government. As an anchorage and port of refuge this harbor is extremely valuable, and is much resorted to for that purpose by steamers and sail vessels during the prevalence of storms; there is twelve feet of water over the bar.

The village was incorporated in 1837, and now contains about 4,000 inhabitants, 500 dwelling-houses, five churches, a bank, three hotels, and 20 stores of different kinds, besides several extensive storehouses and manufacturing establishments.

The *Buffalo and State Line Railroad*, extending to Erie, Pa., runs through Dunkirk, forming in part the Lake Shore line of railroad, which in connection with the railroad leading direct to the city of New York, affords great advantages to this locality, which is no doubt destined to increase with the growing trade of the lake country.

FREDONIA, three miles from Dunkirk, with which it is connected by a plank-road, is handsomely situated, being elevated about 100 feet above Lake Erie. It contains about 2,300 inhabitants, 300 dwelling-houses, five churches, one bank, an incorporated academy, four taverns, twenty stores, besides some mills and manufacturing establishments situated on Canadoway Creek, which here affords good water-power. In the village, near the bed of the creek, is an inflammable spring, from which escapes a sufficient quantity of gas to light the village. A gasometer is constructed which forces the gas through tubes to different parts of the village, the consumer paying $4 per year for each burner used. It is also used for lighting the streets of the village. The flame is large, but not so strong or brilliant as that obtained from gas in our cities; t is, however, in high favor with the inhabitants.

BARCELONA, N. Y., 58 miles from Buffalo, is the westernmost village in the State. It is a port of entry, and is much resorted to by steamers and large vessels navigating the lake, affording a tolerable good harbor, where is situated a light-house which is lighted by inflammable gas; it escapes from the bed of a creek about half a mile distant, and is carried in pipes to the light-house.

The City of Erie, Pa., 90 miles from Buffalo and 95 miles from Cleveland, is beautifully situated on a bluff, affording a prospect of Presque Isle Bay and the lake beyond. It has one of the largest and best harbors on Lake Erie, from whence sailed Perry's fleet during the war of 1812. The most of the vessels were here built, being finished in seventy days from the time the trees were felled; and here the gallant victor returned with his prizes after the battle of Lake Erie, which took place September 10th, 1813. The remains of his flag-ship, the *Lawrence*, lie in the harbor, from which visitors are allowed to cut pieces as relics. On the high bank, a little distance from the town, are the ruins of the old French fort, Presque Isle. The city contains a court-house, nine churches, a bank, three hotels, a ship-yard, several extensive manufacturing establishments, and about 7,000 inhabitants. In addition to the *Lake Shore Railroad*, the *Sunbury and Erie Railroad* will terminate at this place, affording a direct communication with New York and Philadelphia.

Presque Isle Bay is a lovely sheet of water, protected by an island projecting into Lake Erie. There is a light-house on the west side of the entrance to the bay, in lat. 42° 8′ N.; it shows a fixed light, elevated 93 feet above the surface of the lake, and visible for a distance of 15 miles. The beacon shows a fixed light, elevated 28 feet, and is visible for nine miles.

Conneaut, Ohio, 117 miles from Buffalo and 68 from Cleveland, situated in the northeast corner of the State, stands on a creek of the same name near its entrance into Lake Erie. It exports large quantities of lumber, grain, pork, beef, butter, cheese, etc., being surrounded by a rich agricultural section of country. The village contains about 3,000 inhabitants. The harbor of Conneaut lies two miles from the village, where is a light-house, a pier, and several warehouses.

Ashtabula, Ohio, 14 miles farther west, stands on a stream of the same name, near its entrance into the lake. This is a thriving place, inhabited by an intelligent population estimated at 2,500. The harbor of Ashtabula is two and a half miles from the village, at the mouth of the river, where is a light-house.

FAIRPORT stands on the east side of Grand River, 155 miles from Buffalo. It has a good harbor for lake vessels, and is a port of considerable trade. This harbor is so well defended from winds and easy of access, that vessels run in when they can not easily make other ports. Here is a light-house and a beacon to guide the mariner.

PAINESVILLE, O., three miles from Fairport and 30 miles from Cleveland, is a beautiful and flourishing town, being surrounded by a fine section of country. It is the county seat for Lake County, and contains a court-house, five churches, a bank, 20 stores, a number of beautiful residences, and about 3,000 inhabitants.

The City of CLEVELAND is situated on an elevated plain at the entrance of Cuyahoga River into Lake Erie, in N. lat. 41° 30′, W. lon. 81° 47′. It is distant 185 miles from Buffalo, and 107 miles from Toledo by railroad route; 120 miles from Detroit by steamboat route. Its harbor is spacious and safe when once entered, being formed by the mouth of the river. The city is regularly and beautifully laid out, ornamented with numerous shade-trees, from which it takes the name of "*Forest City*;" near its center is a large public square. It is the mart of one of the greatest grain-growing States in the Union, and has a ready communication by railroad with Albany, New York, and Philadelphia. The bluff on which it is built is 80 feet above the level of the lake, where stands a light-house, from which an extensive and magnificent view is obtained, overlooking the meandering of the Cuyahoga, the line of railroads, the shipping in the harbor, and the vessels passing on Lake Erie.

The city contains a court-house, city hall, custom-house, college buildings, a lyceum, a public reading-room, a literary institution, which sustains a course of lectures during the winter season; 25 churches of different denominations, six banks, an insurance company, and several large and well-kept hotels, among which may be named the Weddell House, the

Angier House, the American Hotel, and the Johnson House. It now boasts of 50,000 inhabitants, and is rapidly increasing in numbers and wealth. The *Ohio Canal* terminates here, forming a water communication with the Ohio River at different points.

The railroads diverging from Cleveland are the *Cleveland and Erie*, 95 miles; *Cleveland and Pittsburgh*, 100 miles, with several branches; *Cleveland and Mahoning*, 67 miles finished; *Cleveland, Columbus and Cincinnati*, 135 miles; and *Cleveland and Toledo*, Northern Division, 107 miles. These roads all run into one general depôt, situated near the water's edge, affording great facilities to the trans-shipment of freight of different kinds. The trade with the Upper Lakes is one of great and growing importance; steamers leave daily for Detroit, Mackinac, Green Bay, Chicago, the Saut Ste Marie, and Lake Superior.

For list of steamers sailing from Cleveland and Detroit to the Upper Lakes, see page 140.

Black River, 28 miles from Cleveland, is a small village with a good harbor, where is a ship-yard and other manufacturing establishments.

Vermilion, 10 miles farther on the line of the Cleveland and Toledo Railroad, is a place of considerable trade, situated at the mouth of a river of the same name.

Huron, Ohio, 50 miles from Cleveland and 10 miles from Sandusky, is situated at the mouth of Huron River, which affords a good harbor. It contains several churches, 15 or 20 stores, several warehouses, and about 2,000 inhabitants

The islands lying near the head of Lake Erie, off Sandusky, are Kelley's Island, North Bass, Middle Bass, and South Bass islands, besides several smaller islands, forming altogether a handsome group. Kelley's Island is the largest and most important, but on the north side of South Bass Island lies the secure harbor of Put-in Bay, made celebrated by being the rendezvous of Com. Perry's flotilla before and after the decisive battle of Lake Erie, which resulted in the capture of the entire British fleet.

NAVAL BATTLE ON LAKE ERIE.

September 10th, 1813, the hostile fleets of England and the United States on Lake Erie met near the head of the lake, and a sanguinary battle ensued. The fleet bearing the "red cross" of England consisted of six vessels, carrying 64 guns, under command of the veteran Com. Barclay; and the fleet bearing the "broad stripes and bright stars" of the United States, consisted of nine vessels, carrying 54 guns, under command of the young and inexperienced, but brave, Com. Oliver H. Perry. The result of this important conflict was made known to the world in the following laconic dispatch, written at 4 P.M. of that day:

"*Dear General:* We have met the enemy, and they are ours. Two ships, two brigs, one schooner, and one sloop.

"With esteem, etc., O. H. Perry.

"Gen. William Jones."

Mr. Powell, the artist, who painted the De Soto picture for Congress, has been appointed by the Ohio Legislature to paint a representation of Perry's Victory on Lake Erie—the price not to exceed $5,000. It will be placed in one of the panels of the rotunda of the new State House in Columbus, the capital of the State.

RAILROAD ROUTE AROUND LAKE ERIE.

This important body of water being encompassed by a band of iron, we subjoin the following *Table of Distances:*

	Miles.
Buffalo to Paris, C. W., via *Buffalo and Lake Huron Railroad*	84
Paris to Windsor or Detroit, via *Great Western Railway.*	158
Detroit to Toledo, Ohio, via *Detroit and Toledo R.R.*	63
Toledo to Cleveland, via *Cleveland and Toledo R.R.*	107
Cleveland to Erie, Pa., via *Cleveland and Erie R.R.*	95
Erie to Buffalo, via *Lake Shore Road*	88
Total miles	595

The extreme length of Lake Erie is 250 miles, from the mouth of Niagara River to Maumee Bay; the circuit of the lake about 560 miles, being about 100 miles less distance than has been stated by some writers on the great lakes.

OHIO RIVER AND LAKE ERIE CANALS

The completion of the Miami Canal makes four distinct channels of communication from the Ohio River through the State of Ohio to Lake Erie, namely:

1. The *Erie Extension Canal,* from Beaver, twenty or thirty miles below Pittsburgh, to Erie, 136 miles. 2. The *Cross-Cut Beaver Canal,* which is an extension or branch from Newcastle, Pa., on the Beaver Canal, to Akron, Ohio, where it unites with the Portsmouth and Cleveland Canal—making a canal route from Beaver to Cleveland of 143 miles. 3. The *Ohio Canal,* from Cleveland to Portsmouth, through the center of the State, 309 miles. 4. The *Miami Extension,* which is a union of the Miami Canal with the Wabash and Erie Canal, through Dayton, terminating at Toledo, at the mouth of the Maumee River on Lake Erie, 247 miles. The vast and increasing business of the Ohio Valley may furnish business for all these canals. They embrace rich portions of Pennsylvania, Ohio, and Indiana; but are not so located as to be free from competition with one another. At no distant time, they would unquestionably command a sufficient independent business, were it not probable that they may be superseded by railways. The capacity of railways—both for rapid and cheap transportation—as it is developed by circumstances and the progress of science, is destined to affect very materially the value and importance of canals.

OPENING OF NAVIGATION IN LAKE ERIE.

The following table, prepared by the Detroit *Advertiser*, from back files, shows the time when navigation has opened at this port for the past seventeen years:

1840..March 8....	Steamer	Star arrived from Cleveland.
1841..April 18....	"	Gen. Wayne arrived from Buffalo.
1842..March 3....	"	Gen. Scott cl'd for Buffalo.
1843..April 18....	"	Fairport cl'd for Cleveland.
1844..March 11....	"	Red Jacket cl'd for Fort Gratiot.
1845..Jan'y 4....	"	United States arrived from Buffalo.
1846..March 14....	"	John Owen arrived from Cleveland.
1847.. " 30....	"	United States " "
1848.. " 22....	Prop.	Manhattan cl'd for Buffalo.
1849.. " 21....	Steamer	John Owen cl'd for Cleveland.
1850.. " 25....	"	Southerner arrived from Buffalo.
1851.. " 19....	"	Hollister " " Toledo.
1852.. " 22....	"	Arrow cl'd for Toledo.
1853.. " 14....	"	Bay City arrived from Sandusky.
1854.. " 24....	"	May Queen " " Cleveland.
1855..April 2....	"	Arrow cl'd for Toledo.
1856.. " 15....	"	May Queen cl'd for Cleveland.
1857..March 24....	"	Ocean cleared for Cleveland.

DISCOVERY OF A NEW HARBOR IN LAKE HURON.

We learn from a Michigan paper that Capt. W. Gilmore, of the brig Sultan, having come into collision with a vessel off the Middle Island, on the night of October 27th, 1856, was driven by stress of the accident into *Bail du Derd*, on the north side of Lake Huron, about eighty miles above Goderich. Captain Gilmore, in a letter to the editor of the Port Bruce *Pioneer*, states that there is plenty of water in the harbor for the largest vessel on the lakes, and a safe anchorage. A pier inside the harbor is alone wanted to render the accommodations perfect. The captain expresses the opinion, that a light-house and a pier would render this bay one of the finest harbors on the lakes. Since this letter was written, we are informed that a small town has been planted in that locality.

BUFFALO

Buffalo City, Erie Co., N. Y., possessing commanding advantages, is distant from Albany 298 miles by railroad, and about 350 miles by the line of the Erie Canal; in N. lat. 42° 53′, W. long. 78° 55′ from Greenwich. It is favorably situated for commerce at the head of Niagara River, the outlet of Lake Erie, and at the foot of the great chain of Western lakes, and is the point where the vast trade of these inland seas is concentrated. The harbor, formed of Buffalo Creek, lies nearly east and west across the southern part of tne city, and is separated from the waters of Lake Erie by a peninsula between the creek and lake. This harbor is a very secure one, and is of such capacity, that although steamboats, ships, and other lake craft, and canal boats, to the number, in all, of from three to four hundred, have sometimes been assembled there for the transaction of the business of the lakes, yet not one half part of the water accommodations has ever yet been occupied by the vast business of the great and growing West. The harbor of Buffalo is the most capacious, and really the easiest and safest of access on our inland waters. Improvements are annually made by dredging, by the construction of new piers, wharves, warehouses, and elevators, which extend its facilities, and render the discharge and trans-shipment of cargoes more rapid and convenient; and in this latter respect is without an equal.

Buffalo was first settled by the whites in 1801. In 1832 it was chartered as a city, being now governed by a mayor, recorder, and board of aldermen. Its population in 1830, according to the United States Census, was 8,668; in 1840, 18,213; and in 1850, 42,261. Since the latter period the limits of the city have been enlarged by taking in the town of Black Rock; it is now divided into thirteen wards, and, according to the State Census of 1855, contained 74,214 inhabitants, being now the third city in point of size in the State of New York The public buildings are numerous, and many of them fine specimens of architecture; while the private buildings, particularly those for business purposes, are of the most durable construction and modern style. The manufacturing establishments are also numerous, and conducted on a large scale, producing manufactured articles for the American and Canadian markets.

The lines of steamers and railroads diverging from Buffalo tend to make it one of the greatest thoroughfares in the Union. Steamers and propellers run to Cleveland, Toledo, Detroit, Mackinac, Saut Ste Marie, Green Bay, Milwaukee, Chicago, etc.

The railroads diverging from Buffalo are the New York Central, extending to Albany 298 miles by direct route; Buffalo Division of the New York and Erie Railroad; Lake Shore Railroad; Buffalo, Niagara Falls, and Lewiston Railroad; and the Buffalo and Huron Railroad, the latter running through Canada to Goderich on Lake Huron, and connecting with the Great Western Railway, terminating at Windsor, opposite Detroit.

The principal hotels are the American, Clarendon, Commercial, and Mansion House, on Main Street, and the Western Hotel, facing the Terrace.

"The climate of Buffalo is, without doubt, of a more even temperature than any other city in the same parallel of latitude from the Mississippi to the Atlantic coast. Observations have shown that the thermometer never ranges as low in winter, nor as high in summer, as at points in Massachusetts, the eastern and central portions of this State, the northern and southern shores of Lake Erie, in Michigan, Northern Illinois, and Wisconsin. The winters are not as keen, nor the summers, cooled by the breezes from the lake, as sultry; and in a sanitary point of view, it is probably the healthiest city in the world.

"London, usually considered the healthiest of cities, has a ratio of one death in forty inhabitants. The ratio of Buffalo is one in fifty-six. The favorable situation of the city for drainage, and for a supply of pure water; its broad, well-paved streets, lined with shrubbery and shade-trees; its comparatively mild winters; its cool summers; its pleasant drives and picturesque suburbs, and its proximity to the '*Falls*,' combine to render it one of the most desirable residences on the continent."

In regard to the commerce of the "Far West," much of which centers in Buffalo, a writer justly remarks:

"Few men have duly estimated the value of our 1,500 miles of uninterrupted lake navigation. A coast of upward of 3,000 miles, connecting with numerous canals and railroads, whose aggregate length, when they shall be completed, will greatly exceed the length of all our inland seas and coasts, must create an amount of commerce far greater than has ever yet been witnessed on the waters of the Mediterranean. The completion of the ship canal at the Saut Ste Marie alone opens an inland sea of vast and growing importance."

TRADE AND COMMERCE OF BUFFALO—1856.

IMPORTS BY LAKE.

THE annual tables of the Lake Trade during the year, with some additional comparative statements showing the course of trade, the increase and decrease in the general average value of most articles, and other matters of interest concerning this trade during the year 1856, are copied from the Buffalo *Courier*. The value of Imports by Lake for the past six years is as follows:

1851	$31,889,951	1854	$45,030,931
1852	34,943,855	1855	50,346,819
1853	36,881,230	1856	45,684,079

This table exhibits a steady increase in the yearly valuation of the Lake Imports until last year, when there is a decrease as compared with 1855 of $4,662,740. This large decrease has been occasioned, not by a falling off in the receipts of the more valuable articles of import, but by the decline in the average value of nearly every description of produce.

The following table will show the different States through whose ports have been shipped the following produce received at this port. Through Cleveland, Sandusky, Toledo, and a few smaller ports, we have received the products of Ohio, Indiana, Southern Illinois, and Kentucky, and through Chicago, the products of Illinois, Iowa, Indiana, and Missouri.

	Flour.	Wheat.	Corn.	Oats.
Ohio ports	641,155	826,016	1,717,130	1,094,015
Michigan	203,125	495,289	164,497	42,314
Illinois	122,472	5,127,947	7,922,461	548,326
Wisconsin	115,427	1,707,798	52,702	39,146
Canada	60,906	386,067	......	......
Total	1,143,085	8,543,117	9,846,790	1,723,801

The following Table will show the entrances and clearances of foreign and American vessels, together with their tonnage and crews during the year 1856, and the total for the past 7 years:

Arrived.	No.	Tons.	Crews.
American vessels from foreign ports	112	17,745	598
Foreign do., do.	718	71,039	5,314
Total	830	88,784	5,912
Cleared.			
Amer. vessels to foreign ports	181	30,607	1,193
Foreign do., do.	632	62,833	5,580
Total	813	93,440	6,773
Coasting trade.			
Inward	3,292	1,441,663	49,556
Outward	3,193	1,424,702	49,210
Total	6,485	2,866,365	98,766
Grand Total for 1856	8,128	3,048,589	111,451
" " " 1855	9,231	3,360,233	111,515
" " " 1854	8,972	3,995,284	120,838
" " " 1853	8,298	3,252,978	128,112
" " " 1852	9,441	3,092,247	127,491
" " " 1851	9,050	3,087,533	120,542
" " " 1850	8,444	2,743,700	125,562

The amount of new tonnage now on the stocks both at this and other Western ports, and destined for the trade of this city and the West, will, we believe, increase the tonnage entering and departing from this district very materially during the coming season (1857), and that it must exceed any former year.

LOSSES ON THE LAKES.—If the losses on the great Lakes during the past year are any indication of the amount of commerce on our inland seas, it must have grown enormously since 1848. In that year the losses amounted to but a little over $400,000; in 1853 they had increased to nearly a million; in 1854 they were a little over two millions; in 1855 over two and a half millions; but the present year, 1856, they have reached the fearful sum of over three millions. But, large as this amount is, it does not seem so great when it is viewed in connection with the statement that the commerce of the Lakes passing the St. Clair Flats amounted in 1856 to more than three hundred millions of dollars, while the coasting trade not included in that estimate amounts to at least a hundred millions more. This looks very much like the course of empire taking a westerly direction.

RECAPITULATION OF LOSSES ON THE LAKES—1856.

Losses in May, steam and sail		$142,600
" June, " "		118,550
" July, " "		266,130
" August, " "		67,750
" September, " "		342,860
" October, " "		882,039
" November, " "		1,059,395
" December, " "		159,550
Total loss, steam and sail, in 1856		$3,038,874
" " " in 1855		2,797,839
Increased loss		241,035
Total loss of life in 1856	407	
" " in 1855	118	
Increase	289	
Loss on steam hulls		$732,800
Loss on cargoes by steam		645,300
Total loss by steam in 1856		1,378,100
" " in 1855		1,692,700
Decrease in 1856		$314,600
Loss on sail hulls		863,675
Loss on cargoes by sail		797,099
Total loss by sail in 1856		1,660,714
" " in 1855		1,105,139
Increase in 1856		$555,635

Synopsis of the Marine Register of the Board of Lake Underwriters of vessels in commission on the lakes in the fall of 1856.

	Number.	Tonnage.	Cash Value.
Steamers	107	62,863	$3,320,400
Propellers	135	54,675	2,741,200
Barques	56	21,773	673,800
Brigs	108	27,045	701,850
Schooners	850	173,380	5,487,100
Total	1,256	339,736	$12,944,350

D. P. DOBBINS, *Sec'y*
Board of Lake Underwriters.

EXPORTS FROM UP-LAKE PORTS TO BUFFALO.

STATEMENT, showing the several amounts of Flour and Grain exported by Lake from various ports to Buffalo, during the season of 1856:

	Flour, bbls.	Wheat, bush.	Corn, bush.	Oats, bush.	Rye, bush.
Ashtabula	....	2,500	....	....	....
Allensburgh	1,200	....	....	....	....
Bayfield, C. W	....	59,115	....	....	....
Black River	....	....	1,600	....	....
Brantford, C. W.	16,231	32,008	....	....	....
Port Burwell, C. W	....	18,164	....	....	....
Caledonia, C. W	....	2 726	....	....	....
Cayuga	7,628	41,127	....	....	18
Cleveland	245,512	72,577	117,239	172,087	39,786
Chicago	119,772	5,100,293	7,834,615	587,936	....
Conneaut	....	1,200	....	....	263
Detroit	189,309	833,398	64,997	43,411	....
Port Dover, C. W	13,036	89,718	....	....	....
Dunnville, C. W	2,223	19,502	....	....	....
Erie	....	....	....	6,995	27,990
Fremont	....	9,675	84,292	85,000	11,808
Fort Erie, C. W	7,077	....	....	....	....
Grand Haven	8,955	37,391	....	....	....
Green Bay	1,364	150	....	....	....
Goderich, C. W	600	26,164	....	....	....
Huron	327	20,889	281,423	252,916	88,182
Indiana	1,671	....	....	....	....
Kenosha	605	106,843	....	....	....
Maitland, C. W	....	3,780	....	....	....
Milwaukee	106,366	1,440,337	34,000	43,241	....
Michigan City	....	26,829	31,269	....	....
Milan	....	40	6,700	38,792	....
Monroe	995	73,909	....	....	....
Morpeth, C. W	....	5,000	....	....	....
Port Washington	1,463	3,210	....	....	....
Perrysburg	2,875	....	....	....	....
Racine	1,622	53,768	....	....	....
Port Robinson, C. W	....	4,636	....	....	....
Port Rowan, C. W	367	465	....	....	....
Ryerse, C. W	2,977	5,400	....	....	....
Saginaw	766	....	....	....	....
Sandusky	178,664	69,218	210,587	421,147	53,756
Sheboygan	893	37,082	....	....	....
Port Stanley, C. W	2,295	99,716	....	....	....
Toledo	208,417	621,164	937,579	81,157	24,002
Venice	100	....	8,000	20,000	....
Vermilion	....	2,810	20,038	30,650	....
Waukegan	124	51,870	138	....	....
York	2,624	1,997	....	....	....
Totals	1,126,048	8,465,671	9,632,477	1,733,382	245,810

TRIP FROM BUFFALO TO MACKINAC, CHICAGO, ETC.

THIS is a deeply interesting excursion, calculated to give the traveler a just conception of the great *inland seas* of North America, inasmuch as the route traverses Lakes Erie, St. Clair, Huron, and Michigan, a total distance of more than a thousand miles.

If to this is added a trip to the Falls of St. Mary (Saut de Ste Marie), in the outlet of Lake Superior, and connecting it with Lake Huron—to the *Manitoulin Islands* in the northern quarter of Lake Huron, their very name implying scenery fitted to excite sublime emotions, and suggesting the strong sentiment of religious awe which characterized the primitive red man—if these be added to the tour, no excursion of equal extent can be found that presents a greater variety of picturesque and magnificent scenery. Besides the above grand excursion, Lake Superior alone affords ample inducements for the tourist to extend his visit to this greatest of all the inland seas of America.

As this excursion begins on Lake Erie, we begin our guidance with a brief description of that noble and most useful body of water.

LAKE ERIE, washing the shores of *four* of these United States—New York, Pennsylvania, Ohio, and Michigan—and spreading between them and a large segment of the British province of Canada West, with the line of division as settled by treaty, running through the middle of the lake, is 250 miles long by 40 to 60 miles wide. Its surface, as ascertained by the engineers of the Erie Canal, is 565 feet above the Hudson River at Albany, and 330 feet above Lake Ontario. The greatest depth of the lake yet observed is 204 feet. This is comparatively shallow; and the relative depths of the great series of lakes may be illustrated by saying, that the surplus waters poured from the vast *basins* of Superior, Huron, and Michigan flow across the *plate* of Erie into the deep *bowl* of Ontario.

Lake Erie is reputed to be the only one of the series in which any current is perceptible. The fact, if it is one, is usually ascribed to its shallowness; but the vast volume of its outlet—the Niagara River—with its strong current, is a much more favorable cause than the small depth of its water, which may be far more appropriately adduced as the reason why the navigation is obstructed by *ice* much more than either of the other great lakes. The New York shore of Lake Erie extends about 60 miles, in the course of which the lake receives a number of streams, the most considerable of which are the Buffalo and Cattaraugus creeks; and presents several harbors, the most important of which at present are Buffalo Creek and Dunkirk.

As connected with trade and navigation, this lake is far the most important of all the great chain, not only because it is bordered by older settlements than any of them, except Ontario, but still more because, from its position, it concentrates the trade of the vast West.

When we consider the extent, not only of this lake, but of Huron, 260 miles long; of Michigan, 330 miles long; of Superior, 420 miles long, the largest body of fresh water on the globe, we may quote with emphasis the words of an English writer: "How little are they aware, in Europe, of the extent of commerce upon these inland seas, whose coasts are now lined with flourishing towns and cities; whose waters are plowed with magnificent steamers, and hundreds of vessels crowded with merchandise! Even the Americans themselves are not fully aware of the rising importance of these lakes, as connected with the West."

THE FIRST VESSEL WHICH NAVIGATED THE UPPER LAKES.

THE following account is translated from an old French work, printed in 1688, entitled, "*An Account of the Discovery of a very great Country situated in America,*" by Father Hennepin. It will be read with interest.

"It now became necessary for La Salle, in furtherance of his object, to construct a vessel above the Falls of Niagara, sufficiently large to transport the men and goods necessary to carry on a profitable trade with the savages residing on the western lakes. On the 22d of January, 1679, they went six miles above the falls to the mouth of a small creek, and there built a dock convenient for the construction of their vessel.*

"On the 26th of January, the keel and other pieces being ready, La Salle requested Father Hennepin to drive the first bolt, but the modesty of the good father's profession prevented.

"During the rigorous winter, La Salle determined to return to Fort Frontenac;† and leaving the dock in charge of an Italian named Chevalier Tuti, he started, accompanied by Father Hennepin as far as Lake Ontario; from thence he traversed the dreary forests to Frontenac on foot, with only two companions and a dog, which drew his baggage on a sled, subsisting on nothing but parched corn, and even that failed him two days' journey from the fort. In the mean time the building of the vessel went on under the suspicious eyes of the neighboring savages, although the most part of them had gone to war beyond Lake Erie. One of them, feigning intoxication, attempted the life of the blacksmith, who defended himself successfully with a red-hot bar of iron. The timely warning of a friendly squaw averted the burning of their vessel on the stocks, which was designed by the savages. The workmen were almost disheartened by frequent alarms, and would have abandoned the work had they not been cheered by the good father, who

---

* There can be but little doubt that the place they selected for building their bark was the mouth of the Cayuga Creek, about six miles above the falls. Governor Cass says "the vessel was launched at Erie;" Schoolcraft, in his journal, says, "near Buffalo;" and the historian Bancroft locates the site at the mouth of Tonawanda Creek. Hennepin says the mouth of the creek was two leagues above the great falls; the mouth of the Tonawanda is more than twice that distance, and the Cayuga is the only stream that answers to the description.

† Now Kingston, Canada

represented the great advantage their perseverance would afford, and how much their success would redound to the glory of God. These and other inducements accelerated the work, and the vessel was soon ready to be launched, though not entirely finished. Chanting *Te Deum*, and firing three guns, they committed her to the river amid cries of joy, and swung their hammocks in security from the wild beasts, and still more dreaded Indians.

"When the Senecas returned from their expedition, they were greatly astonished at the floating fort. 'which struck terror among all the savages who lived on the great lakes and rivers within fifteen hundred miles.' Hennepin ascended the river in a bark canoe with one of his companions as far as Lake Erie. They twice pulled the canoe up the rapids, and sounded the lake for the purpose of ascertaining the depth. He reported that with a favorable north or northwest wind the vessel could ascend to the lake, and then sail without difficulty over its whole extent. Soon after the vessel was launched in the current of Niagara, about four and a half miles from the lake. Hennepin left it for Fort Frontenac, and returning with La Salle and two other fathers, Gabriel and Zenobe Mambre, anchored in the Niagara the 30th July, 1679. On the 4th of August they reached the dock where the ship was built, which he calls distant eighteen miles from Lake Ontario, and proceeded from thence in a bark canoe to their vessel, which they found at anchor three miles from the 'beautiful Lake Erie.'

"The vessel was of 60 tons burden, completely rigged, and found with all the necessaries, arms, provisions, and merchandise; it had seven small pieces of cannon on board, two of which were of brass. There was a griffin flying at the jib-boom, and an eagle above. There were also the ordinary ornaments and other fixtures which usually grace a ship of war.

"They endeavored many times to ascend the current of the Niagara into Lake Erie without success, the wind not being strong enough. While they were thus detained, La Salle employed a few of his men in clearing some land on the Canadian shore, opposite the vessel, and in sowing some vegetable seeds for the benefit of those who might inhabit the place.

"At length the wind being favorable, they lightened the vessel by sending most of the crew on shore, and with the aid of their sails and ten or a dozen men at the tow-lines, ascended the current into Lake Erie. Thus on the 7th of August, 1679, the first vessel set sail on the untried waters of Lake Erie. They steered southwest, after having chanted their never-failing *Te Deum*, and discharged their artillery in the presence of a vast number of Seneca warriors. It had been reported to our voyagers that Lake Erie was full of breakers and sand-banks, which rendered a safe navigation impossible; they therefore kept the lead going, sounding from time to time, to avoid danger.

"After sailing, without difficulty, through Lake Erie, they arrived on the 11th of August at the mouth of the Detroit River, sailing up which they arrived at St. Clair, to which they gave the name it bears. After being detained several days by contrary winds at the bottom of the St. Clair River, they at length succeeded in entering Lake Huron on the 23d of August, chanting *Te Deum* through gratitude for a safe navigation thus far. Passing along the eastern shore of the lake, they sailed with a fresh and favorable wind until evening, when the wind suddenly veered, driving them across Saginaw Bay (Sacinaw). The storm raged until the 24th, and was succeeded by a calm, which continued until next day noon (25th), when they pursued their course until midnight. As they doubled a point which advanced into the lake, they were suddenly struck by a furious wind, which forced them to run behind the cape for safety. On the 26th, the violence of the storm compelled them to send down their topmasts and yards, and to stand in, for they could find neither anchorage nor shelter.

"It was then the stout heart of La Salle failed him; the whole crew fell upon their knees to say their prayers and prepare for death, except the pilot, whom they could not compel to follow their example, and who, on the contrary, 'did nothing all that time but curse and swear against M. La Salle, who had brought him thither to make him perish in a nasty lake, and lose the glory he had acquired by his long and happy navigation on the ocean.' On the 27th, favored with less adverse winds, they arrived during the night at Michilimackinac, and anchored in the bay, where they report six fathoms of water and a clay bottom. This bay they state is protected on the southwest, west, and northwest, but open to the south. The savages were struck dumb with astonishment at the size of their vessel and the noise of their guns.

"Here they regaled themselves on the delicious trout, which they described as being from 50 to 50 pounds in weight, and as affording the savages their principal subsistence. On the 2d of September, 1679, they left Mackinac, entered Lake Michigan (Illinois), and sailed 40 leagues to an island at the mouth of the Bay of Puara (Green Bay). From this place La Salle determined to send back the ship laden with furs to Niagara. The pilot and five men embarked in her, and on the 10th she fired a gun and set sail on her return with a favorable wind. Nothing more was heard from her, and she undoubtedly foundered in Lake Huron, with all on board. Her cargo was rich and valued at 60,000 livres.

"Thus ended the first voyage of the first ship that sailed over the Western Lakes. What a contrast is presented between the silent waves and unbroken forests which witnessed the course of that adventurous bark, and the busy hum of commerce which now rises from the fertile bottoms, and the thousand ships and smoking palaces which now furrow the surface of those inland seas!

NAVIGATION OF THE LAKES.

From the Buffalo Commercial Advertiser—1846.

"I HAVE noticed several communications in your paper recently, in relation to the early Navigation of the Lakes by American vessels, and as you solicit further communications on the subject, I give you such facts as I am acquainted with, and will add, that in regard to many of them I have vouchers to establish their correctness.

"I first visited Lake Erie and the Niagara River in August, 1795; and from an early period, until within the last twenty years, have been more or less interested in the navigation of the lakes.

"It is well known that the military posts of Oswego, Niagara, Detroit, and Mackinac were not surrendered to the United States until the fore part of the year 1796, under Jay's treaty. Boats had not been permitted to pass Oswego into Lake Ontario, and as no settlements of importance had been made previous to that time on the American shores of the lakes (excepting the old French settlements in the neighborhood of these ports, and they were under the jurisdiction and influence of the British government), no vessels were required, and, of course, none had been built.

"In August, 1795, I left Canandaigua on a journey to Presque Isle—now Erie, Pennsylvania. The country west of Genesee River, excepting a tract twelve miles in width extending from opposite Avon along the river to its mouth, had not then been purchased of the Indians, and no roads opened. We, of course, followed the Indian trail to Buffalo.

"At that time the only residents at that place, as far as I recollect, were William Johnson, the British Indian interpreter, whose house stood on the site of the present Mansion House, an Indian trader named Winnee, a negro named Joe, also a trader, both of whom resided on the flats near the mouth of Little Buffalo, and a Dutchman by the name of Middough, with a family, who resided some forty or fifty rods east of Johnson's. A large portion of the ground now occupied by your beautiful city was then an unbroken wilderness.

"At that time I am not aware that a single vessel was owned on the United States side of the lakes, and remember that Capt. Lee, who would have known, informed me that there were none

"In 1796 I was employed by the Connecticut Land Company to survey the Western Reserve, and I prepared to go on early in the season, with several other surveyors, and a party of men to perform the work. At Schenectady we fitted out three batteaux, manned by four hands each, with the necessary articles for the expedition, such as tents, blankets, cooking utensils, groceries, etc., with a quantity of dry goods, designed as presents to the Indians.

"These boats were put under the care of Mr. Joshua Stow, uncle of Judge Stow, of Buffalo. Understanding that the military posts at Oswego and Niagara were to be given up to the United States early this spring, under a stipulation in Jay's treaty, Mr. Stow took the route by Oswego and Niagara to Queenston. On his arrival at Oswego, that port had not been surrendered, and the boats were not permitted to pass. Determined not to be delayed, Mr. Stow took the boats a mile or two up the river, and the night following ran them past the fort into the lake and pursued his voyage, and before arriving at Niagara that post had passed into the possession of our troops. He landed at Queenston, had his boats and loading taken to Chippewa, where he took in provisions to complete his cargoes, which had been purchased at Canandaigua, and forwarded by the way of Irondequoit and the lake in open boats, and arrived a day or two before.

"At Buffalo he was met by others of the party, who had come on by land, among these, Gen. Moses Cleveland, one of the directors of the Connecticut Land Company (from whom the city of Cleveland took its name), who, by way of securing the good-will of the Indians to the expedition, held a council and distributed presents among them. The expedition went on from here, a part by the boats, and a part by land with pack-horses, and arrived at the mouth of Conneaut Creek on the 4th of July, 1796, and celebrated the day. The party then consisted of fifty-two persons.

At this time, as we ascertained, there was not a white person residing on the Reserve, excepting a French family just within the mouth of Sandusky Bay.

"One of our boats was employed during the season in bringing up supplies of provisions from Chippewa, and in October, on her up trip, was wrecked in a gale off the mouth of Chatauque Creek, and Tinker, the master, drowned.

"No American vessels had yet been built, and some of the baggage and stores for the troops at Detroit had been transported from Western Pennsylvania by the contractor, Gen

O'Hara, up the valley of the Big Beaver, and through the wilderness to Detroit, on pack-horses.

"Between the years of 1796 and 1800 (I am unable to particularize the year), the schooner Gen. Tracy was built at Detroit, and in August, 1808, purchased by Porter, Barton & Co. and thoroughly repaired, and on her second or third trip was wrecked on the Fort Erie reef in 1809.

"The brig Adams, a government vessel, was built about the same time as the Gen. Tracy, and was sailed by Capt. Brevoort for a number of years. She was built at Detroit.

"A small vessel called the Good Intent was built at Presque Isle by Capt. Wm. Lee, and I believe was partly, and perhaps wholly, owned by Rufus S. Reed. She, I think, was built about 1800, and wrecked near Point Abino in 1805.

"In 1802 the schooner Gen. Wilkinson, of 70 tons, was built at Detroit, and in 1811 thoroughly repaired, and her name changed to Amelia. She was sold to the United States during the war.

"In the winter of 1802 and '3 the sloop Contractor, of 64 tons, was built at Black Rock by the company having the government contract for the supply of the military posts, under the superintendence of Captain William Lee, by whom she was sailed until 1809, and afterward by Capt. James Beard. In 1803 or '4 a small sloop called the Niagara, of 30 tons, was built at Cayuga Creek, on the Niagara River, by the U. S. government, but not put in commission. She was purchased by Porter, Barton & Co. in 1806, and her name changed to the Nancy, and sailed by Captain Richard O'Neil.

"In 1806 the schooner Mary, of 105 tons, was built at Erie by Thomas Wilson, and purchased the one half by James Rough and George Bueshler, and the other half by Porter, Barton & Co. in 1808, and sailed by Captain Rough until the war, and then sold to the United States.

"In 1808 Porter, Barton & Co. purchased the schooner Ranger of George Wilber, then several years old—she was repaired and sailed by Capt. Hathaway. In 1810 the sloop Erie was built at Black Rock by Porter, Barton & Co., and sold to the United States in time of the war. The schooner Salina, sailed by Capt. Dobbins, and the schooner Eleanor, and probably others that I do not recollect, were built and sailed before the war, but I am unable to say where and when they were built, or by whom owned.

"On Lake Ontario I find that previous to 1809, and during that year, the following vessels had been built, and were engaged in the commerce of the lake: Schooner Fair American, owned by Matthew M'Nair, of Oswego, Theophilus Pease, master; also, schooners Lark, Island Packet, Eagle, Mary, Farmer, Two Brothers, Experiment, and Democrat

"Some time previous to the war the United States brig Oneida was built, and commanded by Captain Woolsey.

"In 1809 the schooner Ontario, of 70 tons, was built by Porter, Barton & Co. at Lewiston, and sold to the United States during the war.

"In 1809 the schooner Cambria was built on an island at the lower end of Lake Ontario, and brought in an unfinished state to Lewiston, where she was purchased and fitted out by Porter, Barton & Co., and her name changed to Niagara.

"In addition to the foregoing vessels, the following were in commission in 1810: Schooner Diana, sloop Marion, schooners Charles and Ann, Gold Hunter, and Genesee Packet.

"A number of vessels on both lakes, owned and armed during the war by the United States, were afterward sold and employed in the commerce of the lakes.

"The foregoing is a very imperfect history of the American vessels owned and employed on the lakes previous to the war, and it is not probable that any individual can furnish a complete one. As far as it goes, I believe it to be tolerably correct.

"AUG'S PORTER."

NOTE.—In 1818 the first steamboat, "Walk-in-the-Water," was built at Black Rock; at which time there were, in all, about thirty sail of vessels on the Upper Lakes.

In 1822 the Superior (1st.) was built; in 1824 the Chippewa was built; and in 1825 three more were added; from this period to 1830 four more steamers were added to the list. Since 1830 about two hundred steamers have been built on Lake Erie and the Upper Lakes, a list of which is hereafter added.

MAGNITUDE OF THE LAKES.

Lake Superior, at a height of 600 feet above the sea, is 420 miles long, 160 miles broad, and 1,000 feet deep. It discharges its waters by the strait, or river St. Mary, 50 miles long, into Lake Huron, which lies 27 feet below.

Lake Michigan, 576 feet above the sea, is 320 miles long, 82 miles broad, and 900 feet deep. It discharges its surplus waters through the Strait of Mackinac, 50 miles in length, into Lake Huron, nearly on a level.

Green Bay, at about the same elevation as Lake Michigan, is 100 miles long, 20 miles broad, and 60 feet deep.

Lake Huron, at a height of 574 feet above the sea, is 260 miles long, 110 miles broad, and 900 feet deep.

Georgian Bay, lying northeast of Lake Huron and of the same altitude, is 130 miles long and 55 miles broad. All the above bodies of water, into which are discharged a great number of streams, find an outlet by the river and Lake St. Clair, and Detroit River or Strait, in all about 90 miles long, with a fall of 14 feet into

Lake Erie, the fourth great lake of this immense chain. This latter lake again, at an elevation above the sea of 564 feet, 250 miles long, 60 miles broad, and 204 feet at its greatest depth, but, on an average, considerably less than 100 feet deep, discharges its surplus waters by the Niagara River and Falls into Lake Ontario, 330 feet below; 51 feet of this descent being in the rapids immediately above the Falls, 160 feet at the Falls themselves, and the rest chiefly in the rapids between the Falls and the mouth of the river, 35 miles below Lake Erie.

Lake Ontario, the fifth and last of the Great Lakes of America, is elevated 234 feet above tide-water at Three Rivers on the St. Lawrence; it is 180 miles long, 60 miles broad, 600 feet deep. Thus *basin* succeeds *basin*, like the locks of a great cana · the whole length of waters from Lake Superior to the Gulf of St. Lawrence being rendered navigable for vessels of a large class by means of the Welland and other canals—thus enabling a loaded vessel to ascend or descend 600 feet above the level of the ocean, or tide-water. Of these lakes, Lake Superior has by far the largest area, being nearly equal in superficial extent to Lakes Huron and Michigan together, and Lake Ontario has the least, having a surface only about one fifth of that of Lake Superior, and being somewhat less in area than Lake Erie, although not much less, if any, in the circuit of its shores. Lake Ontario is the safest body of water for navigation, and Lake Erie the most dangerous. The ascertained temperature in the midde of Lake Erie, August, 1845, was temperature of air 76° Fahrenheit, at noon—water at surface 73°—at bottom 53°. The lakes of greatest interest to the tourist or scientific traveler are Ontario, Huron, together with Georgian Bay and North Channel, and Lake Superior. The many picturesque islands and headlands, together with the pure waters of the Upper Lakes, form a most lovely contrast during the summer and autumn months.

The altitude of the land which forms the water-shed of the *Upper Lakes* does not exceed from 600 to 2,500 feet above the level of the ocean, while the altitude of the land which forms the water-shed of Lake Champlain and the lower tributaries of the St. Lawrence River rises from 4,000 to 5,000 above the level of the sea or tide-water, in the States of Vermont and New York.

The divide which separates the waters of the Gulf of Mexico, from those flowing northeast into the St. Lawrence, do not in some places exceed ten or twenty feet above the level of Lakes Michigan and Superior; in fact, it is said that Lake Michigan, when under the influence of high water and a strong northerly wind, discharges some of its surplus waters into the Illinois River, and thence into the Mississippi and Gulf of Mexico—so low is the divide at its southern terminus.

COAST LINE OF THE GREAT LAKES AND SHORES OF THE ST. LAWRENCE RIVER, ETC.

AMERICAN SIDE.

States, etc.	Coast Line.	Boundaries.
Minnesota, *L. Superior*,	150 ms.	Pigeon River to mouth St. Louis River.
Wisconsin, " ...	120 "	St. Louis River to mouth Montreal River.
Michigan, " ...	430 "	Montreal River to mouth St Mary's River.
" St. Mary's River	50 "	Saut Ste Marie to Pt. de Tour.
" Huron and Strait	100 "	Pt. de Tour to Pt. Seuil Choix.
" *L. Michigan*,	50 "	Pt. Seuil Choix to Green Bay.
Wisconsin, " ...	200 "	Green Bay to Ill. State line.
Illinois, " ...	60 "	Illinois State line to Indiana State line.
Indiana, " ...	40 "	Indiana State line to Michigan State line.
Michigan, " ...	300 "	State line to Strait of Mackinac.
" Strait of Mackinac	50 "	Fox Point to Lake Huron.
" *L. Huron*,	260 "	Strait of Mackinac to mouth St. Clair River.
" St. Clair River...	38 "	Fort Gratiot to Lake St. Clair
" St. Clair Lake...	30 "	West shore.
" Detroit River ...	27 "	Lake St. Clair to Lake Erie.
Michigan, *Erie*,	30 "	Detroit River to Maumee Bay.
Ohio, " ...	180 "	Maumee Bay to Penn. State line.
Pennsylvania, " ...	40 "	State line to N. York State line.
New York, " ...	70 "	State line to mouth Niagara River.
" Niagara River...	35 "	Lake Erie to Lake Ontario.
New York, *L. Ontario*,	180 "	Mouth Niagara River to St. Lawrence River.
" St. Lawrence R.	100 "	Lake Ontario to 45th degree N. lat.
Lower Canada, " ...	666 "	St. Regis to Gulf of St. Lawrence.
Total miles ...	3,206	

COAST LINE—CANADIAN SIDE.

Lake Superior.......	450 ms.	Pigeon River to St. Mary's R.
St. Mary's River.....	50 "	Saut Ste Marie to foot St Joseph Island.

L. Huron, (*N. Chan.*)	145 ms.	St. Joseph Island to Georgian Bay.
" (*Georgian Bay*)	230 "	Shebawanahning to Collingwood and Cabot's Head.
Lake Huron, (*proper*)	200 "	Cabot's Head to mouth St. Clair River.
St. Clair River.......	38 "	Port Sarnia to Lake St. Clair.
St. Clair Lake.......	30 "	East shore
Detroit River........	27 "	Lake St. Clair to Lake Erie.
Lake Erie...........	250 "	Mouth of Detroit River to Niagara River.
Niagara River.......	35 "	Lake Erie to Lake Ontario.
Lake Ontario........	230 "	Mouth Niagara River to Hamilton and foot of Lake.
St. Lawrence River...	766 "	Lake Ontario to Gulf of St. Lawrence.
Total miles......	2,451	

Grand Total, Lake and River Coast, 5,657 miles.

TRIBUTARIES OF THE ST. LAWRENCE RIVER.

UNLIKE the tributaries of the Mississippi, the streams falling into the Great Lakes or the St. Lawrence River are mostly rapid, and navigable only for a short distance from their mouths.

The following are the principal rivers that are navigable for any considerable length:

AMERICAN SIDE.

		Miles.
St. Louis River, Min..........	Superior to Fond du Lac.	20
Fox, or Neenah, Wis..........	Green Bay to L. Winnebago	36
St. Joseph, Mich..............	St. Joseph to Niles	26
Grand River, "	Grand Haven to Gd. Rapids	40
Muskegon, "	Muskegon to Newaygo	40
Saginaw, "	Saginaw Bay to Upper Sag.	26
Maumee, Ohio...............	Maumee Bay to Perrysb'h.	18
Genesee, N. Y	Charlotte to Rochester	6

CANADIAN SIDE.

		Miles.
Thames.....................	Lake St. Clair to Chatham	24
Ottawa	La Chine to Carillon......	40
"	(*By means of locks to Ottawa City*)..........	70
Richelieu or Sorel	Sorel to Lake Champlain (*by means of locks*) ..	75
Saguenay....................	Tadusac to Chicoutimi .... (thence to Lake St. John, 50 m.)	70

ST. LAWRENCE RIVER AND LAKE NAVIGATION, FROM FOND DU LAC, LAKE SUPERIOR, TO ANTICOSTI.

Lakes, Rivers, etc.	Length in miles.	Greatest breadth.	Av. breadth.	Depth in feet.	El. above sea.
Superior	420	160	80	1,000	600
St. Mary's River	50	4	1		
Michigan	330	82	58	900	576
Green Bay	100	25	18	100	576
Strait of Mackinac	30	20	10	40 to 200	
Huron	260	110	70	900	574
North Channel	160	20	10	200	574
Georgian Bay	140	55	40	500	574
St. Clair River	38		1		
St. Clair Lake*	20	25	15	8 to 20	568
Detroit River	27	3	1		
Lake Erie	250	60	38	204	565
Niagara River	35	3	1		
Lake Ontario	180	58	40	600	235
St. Lawrence River	766	60	2		
Lake St. Francis			3		142
Lake St. Louis, Mouth Ottawa River,			5		58
Elevation at Montreal					13
Tide-water at Three Rivers.					0
Total miles	2,806				

* The *St. Clair Flats*, which have to be passed by all large steamers and sail vessels running from Lake Erie to the Upper Lakes, now affords only eight or ten feet of water, the channel being very narrow and intricate. An appropriation, however, has recently been made by the government of the United States for improving the channel through the St. Clair Flats, which, no doubt, will effectually remove the obstruction to navigation.

Note.—Lake Baikal, the most extensive body of fresh water on the Eastern Continent, situated in Southern Siberia, between lat. 51° and 55° north, is about 370 miles in length, 45 miles average width, and about 900 miles in circuit; being somewhat larger than Lake Erie in area. Its depth in some places is very great, being in part surrounded by high mountains. The *Yenisei*, its outlet, flows north into the Arctic Ocean

LIST OF STEAMERS BUILT ON LAKE ERIE, ETC., SINCE THEIR FIRST INTRODUCTION IN 1818.

Built.	Name.	Tons.	Where built.	Remarks.
1818	Walk-in-the-Water.	342	Black Rock, N. Y.	wrecked Nov., 1821.
1822	Superior (1st)	300	Buffalo, N. Y.	changed to a ship.
1824	Chippewa	100	Buffalo, N. Y.	broken up.
1825	Henry Clay	348	Lake Michigan	broken up.
"	Pioneer	230	Black Rock, N. Y.	broken up.
"	Niagara (1st)	180	Black Rock, N. Y.	burnt in 1842.
1826	William Penn	275	Erie, Penn.	broken up.
"	Enterprise	250	Cleveland, O.	broken up.
1829	Wm. Peacock	120	Barcelona, N. Y.	exploded boiler 1830.
"	Newburyport	75	Erie, Penn.	broken up.
1830	Sheldon Thompson.	242	Huron, Mich.	broken up.
"	Ohio (1st)	187	Sandusky, O.	sunk 1837.
"	Adelaide (British)	230	Chippewa, C. W.	wrecked 1840.
1831	Gratiot	63	Charleston	broken up.
1832	Pennsylvania	395	Erie, Penn.	broken up.
"	Gen. Brady	100	Detroit, Mich.	broken up.
"	Uncle Sam	280	Grosse Isle, Mich.	broken up.
"	Perseverance	50	Erie, Penn.	broken up.
1833	Washington (1st)	600	Huron, Mich.	wrecked 1838.
"	New York	325	Black Rock, N. Y.	broken up.
"	Michigan (1st)	472	Detroit, Mich.	broken up.
"	Daniel Webster	358	Black Rock, N. Y.	burnt 1835.
"	Detroit (1st)	240	Toledo, O.	wrecked 1836.
"	Lady of the Lake	60	Mt. Clemens, Mich.	broken up.
"	Gov. Marcy	161	Black Rock, N. Y.	broken up.
"	North America	362	Conneaut, O.	broken up.
"	Newberry	170	Palmer, Mich.	broken up.
"	Delaware	170	Huron, Mich.	wrecked 1834.
1834	Victory	77	Buffalo, N. Y.	broken up.
"	Gen. Porter	342	Black Rock, N. Y.	name ch. to Toronto.
"	Jefferson	428	Erie, Penn.	broken up.
"	Com. Perry	352	Perrysburg, O.	boiler exploded 1835.
"	Monroe	341	Monroe, Mich.	broken up.
"	Mazeppa	130	Buffalo, N. Y.	changed to schooner.
"	Sandusky	377	Sandusky, O.	burnt 1843.
"	Minnessotunk (Br.)	250	Goderich, C. W.	broken up.
"	Jackson	50	Mt. Clemens, Mich.	broken up.
"	Jack Downing	80	Sandusky, O.	changed to schooner.
"	Little Western (Br.)	60	Chatham, C. W.	burnt 1842.
1835	Robert Fulton	308	Cleveland, O.	wrecked in 1842.
"	Columbus	391	Huron, Mich.	broken up.
"	Charles Townsend.	312	Buffalo, N. Y.	broken up.
"	United States	366	Huron, Mich.	broken up.
"	Chicago	166	St. Joseph, Mich.	wrecked in 1842.
"	W. F. P. Taylor	95	Silver Creek, N. Y.	wrecked 1838.
"	Thames (British).	160	Chatham, C. W.	burnt 1838.
1836	De Witt Clinton	493	Huron, Mich.	broken up.
"	Julia Palmer*	300	Buffalo, N. Y.	broken up.
"	Don Quixote.	80	Toledo, O.	wrecked 1836.
"	Crockett	18	Brunersburg	wrecked 1844.

---

* Taken over the portage at the Saut Ste Marie in 1846.

Date. Name. Tons. Where built. Remarks.

1836..Little Erie........ 149..Detroit, Mich.—lost in 1842.
" ..Barcelona (British). 102..Dunnville, C. W.—changed to schooner.
" ..United (British)... 40..Detroit, Mich.—blown up.
" ..St. Clair........... 250..Sandusky, O.
" ..Cincinnati......... 116. Sandusky, O.—changed to schooner.
1837..Illinois (1st)....... 755..Detroit, Mich.—broken up.
" ..Rochester......... 472..Richmond—changed to sail vessel.
" ..Madison.......... 630..Erie, Penn.—broken up.
" ..Cleveland.... .... 580..Huron, Mich.—burnt in 1854.
" ..Wisconsin......... 700..Conneaut, O.—broken up.
" ..Erie......... ..... 497..Erie, Penn.—burnt Aug., 1841.
" ..Constellation...... 483..Charleston—broken up.
" ..Bunker Hill...... 457..Charleston—broken up.
" ..Constitution....... 443..Conneaut, O.—broken up.
" ..New England..... 416..Black Rock, N. Y.—broken up.
" ..Milwaukee........ 400..Grand Island—wrecked 1842.
" ..Anthony Wayne... 390..Perrysburg, O.—blown up 1850.
" ..Macomb........... 100..Mt. Clemens, Mich.—tow boat.
" ..Rhode Island...... 164..Sandusky, O.—wrecked.
" ..Star............... 128..Belvidere, Mich.—broken up.
" ..Goderich (British). 200..
" ..Commerce........ 80..Sandusky, O.
" ..Mason............ 33..Grand Rapids, Mich.
1838..Great Western..... 780..Huron, Mich.—broken up.
" ..Buffalo............ 613..Buffalo, N. Y.—changed to sail vessel.
" ..Chesapeake....... 412..Maumee, O.—sunk 1846.
..Vermilion......... 385..Vermilion, O.—burnt 1842.
" ..Lexington......... 363..Charleston, O.—broken up.
" ..Fairport..... ..... 259..Fairport, O.—name changed.
" ..Red Jacket........ 148..Grand Island, N. Y.
" ..Gen. Vance....... 75..Perrysburg, O.
" ..James Allen....... 258..Chicago, Ill.
" ..Washington (2d)... 380..Ashtabula, O.—burnt 1838.
" ..G. W. Dale........ 162. Chicago, Ill.
" ..C. C. Trowbridge.. 52..Kalamazoo, Mich.
" ..Marshall.......... 51..Perrysburg, O.
" ..Wabash........... 84..
" ..Owashenonk...... 45..Grand Haven, Mich
" ..Patronage......... 56..St. Joseph, Mich.
1839..Gen. Scott......... 240..Huron, Mich.—sunk 1847.
" ..Chautauque....... 200..Buffalo, N. Y.
" ..Brothers (British).. 150..Chatham, C. W.—broken up.
" ..Kent (British)..... 180..Chatham, C. W.
" ..Huron............ 140..Newport, Mich.—broken up.
" ..Harrison (1st)...... 63..Erie, Penn.—broken up.
1840..Detroit (2d)........ 350..Newport, Mich.—sunk in Lake Huron.
" ..Missouri........... 612..Vermilion—broken up.
" ..Waterloo.......... 100..Black Rock, N. Y.—broken up.
" ..Harrison (2d)...... 362..Maumee, O.—broken up.
1841..Indiana........... 434..Toledo, O.—burnt 1848.
1842..Benj. Franklin..... 231..Algonac, Mich.—wrecked.
" ..John Owen......... 230..Detroit, Mich.—tow boat.
1843..Nile............... 600..Detroit, Mich.—wrecked 1849.
" ..Union............. 64..Black Rock, N. Y.
" ..Champion......... 270..Newport, Mich.—broken up.
1844..Emerald (British).. 250..Chippewa, C. W.
" ..Empire............1,136..Cleveland, O.—running on Lake Erie.
" ..Tecumseh. ...... 259..(Old Fairport)—wrecked in 1850.
" ..J. Wolcott......... 80..Maumee, O.—burnt in 1851.

Built.	Name.	Tons.	Where built.	Remarks.
1844	Indian Queen	112	Buffalo, N. Y.	—wrecked in 1846.
"	New Orleans	610	Detroit, Mich.	—wrecked 1849.
"	St. Louis	618	Perrysburg, O.	—wrecked in 1852.
"	U. S. St. Michigan	583	Erie, Penn.	—in commission.
"	" Abert	133	Buffalo, N. Y.	—in commission.
1845	Niagara (2d)	1,084	Buffalo, N. Y.	—burnt Sept., 1856.
"	Boston	775	Detroit, Mich.	—wrecked 1846.
"	Oregon	781	Newport, Mich.	—burnt 1849.
"	Troy	547	Maumee, O.	—laid up.
"	Superior (2d)	567	Perrysburg, O.	—wrecked Oct., 1856.
"	Lexington	363	Black River, O.	
"	Astor	200	Green Bay, Wis.	—wrecked.
"	Enterprise	100	Green Bay, Wis.	
"	London (British)	456	Chippewa, C.W.	—changed to sail vessel.
"	Helen Strong	253	Monroe, Mich.	—wrecked in 1846.
"	Romeo	180	Detroit, Mich.	—tow boat.
1846	Albany	669	Detroit, Mich.	—wrecked in 1854.
"	Hendrick Hudson	750	Black River, O.	—runs on Lake Erie.
"	Louisiana	900	Buffalo, N. Y.	—runs on Upper Lakes.
"	Saratoga	800	Cleveland, O.	—wrecked in 1854.
"	Canada (British)	800	Chippewa, C. W.	—changed to barque.
1847	Baltic	825	Buffalo, N. Y.	—changed to propeller.
"	Sultana	800	Trenton, Mich.	—runs on Upper Lakes.
"	A. D. Patchin	870	Trenton, Mich.	—wrecked in 1850.
"	Baltimore	500	Monroe, Mich.	—wrecked in 1855.
"	Diamond	336	Buffalo, N. Y.	—tow boat.
"	Pacific	500	Newport, Mich.	—changed to sail vessel.
"	Ohio (2d)	600	Cleveland, O.	—tow boat.
"	Samuel Ward	450	Newport, Mich.	—runs on Lake Huron.
"	Southerner	500	Trenton, Mich.	—wrecked in 1853.
1848	Arrow	350	Cleveland, O.	—runs on Lake Erie.
"	Alabama	600	Detroit, Mich.	—sunk in 1854.
"	Franklin Moore	300	Newport, Mich.	—tow boat.
"	J. D. Morton	400	Toledo, O.	—tow boat.
"	Empire State	1,700	St. Clair, Mich.	—laid up.
"	Queen City	1,000	Buffalo, N. Y.	—runs on Upper Lakes.
"	Globe	1,200	Detroit, Mich.	—changed to propeller.
"	Columbia	167	Fairport, O.	
"	Charter	350	Detroit, Mich.	—changed to propeller.
"	John Hollister	300	Perrysburg, O.	—burnt on Lake Erie.
1849	Atlantic	1,100	Newport, Mich.	—sunk in Lake Erie 1853.
"	May Flower	1,300	Detroit, Mich.	—wrecked in 1854.
"	Keystone State	1,500	Buffalo, N. Y.	—runs on Upper Lakes.
"	Telegraph	181	Truargo, Mich.	—runs on Lake Erie.
1850	Dart	297	Trenton, Mich.	—runs on Lake Erie.
"	Dover (British)	81	Port Dover, C. W.	
"	Ocean	900	Newport, Mich.	—runs on Lake Erie.
"	May Queen	688		runs on Lake Erie.
1851	Arctic	867	Newport, Mich.	—runs on Lake Michigan
"	Bay City	479	Trenton, Mich.	—runs on Lake Erie.
"	Buckeye State	1,274	Cleveland, O.	—runs on Upper Lakes.
"	Northerner	514	Cleveland, O.	—sunk in 1856.
"	Pearl	251	Newport, Mich.	—runs on Lake St. Clair.
"	Ploughboy (British)	450	Chatham, C. W.	—runs on Lake Huron.
"	Mazeppa (British)	250		runs on Lake Huron.
"	Queen (British)	64	Dunnville, C.W.	—runs on Lake St. Clair
"	Minnesota	749	Maumee, O.	
"	Caspian	1,050	Newport, Mich.	—wrecked in 1852.
"	Lady Elgin	1,037	Buffalo, N. Y.	—runs on Upper Lakes.

Built.	Name.	Tons.	Where built.	Remarks.
1852	Cleveland	574	Newport, Mich.	runs on Upper Lakes.
"	Golden Gate	771	Buffalo, N. Y.	wrecked in 1856.
"	Huron	348	Newport, Mich.	
"	Traveller	603	Newport, Mich.	runs on Upper Lakes.
"	Michigan (2d)	—	Detroit, Mich.	runs on Upper Lakes.
1853	Crescent City	1,740	Buffalo, N. Y.	runs on Lake Erie.
"	Queen of the West	1,851	Buffalo, N. Y.	runs on Lake Erie.
"	Mississippi	1,829	Buffalo, N. Y.	runs on Lake Erie.
"	St. Lawrence	1,844	Buffalo, N. Y.	laid up.
"	E. K. Collins	950	Newport, Mich.	burnt Oct., 1854.
"	Ariel	165	Sandusky, O.	runs on Lake Erie.
"	Garden City	—	Buffalo, N. Y.	wrecked May, 1854.
"	Canadian (British)	389	Chatham, C. W.	runs on Georgian Bay.
"	Collingwood (Br.)	—		runs on Georgian Bay
"	T. Whitney	238	Saginaw, Mich.	
"	Northern Indiana	1,470	Buffalo, N. Y.	burnt Aug., 1856.
"	Southern Michigan	1,470	Buffalo, N. Y.	runs on Lake Erie.
"	Forrester	504	Newport, Mich.	runs on Lake Huron.
1854	Plymouth Rock	1,991	Buffalo, N. Y.	runs on Lake Erie.
"	Western World	2,000	Buffalo, N. Y.	runs on Lake Erie.
"	North Star	1,106	Cleveland, O.	runs on Upper Lakes.
"	Illinois	926	Detroit, Mich.	runs on Upper Lakes.
"	R. R. Elliott	321	Newport, Mich.	tow boat.
"	Clifton (British)	247	Chippewa, C. W.	lake and river St. Clair.
1855	Forest Queen	462	Newport, Mich.	runs on Lake Huron.
"	Planet	1,154	Newport, Mich.	runs on Upper Lakes.
"	Island Queen	173	Kelley's Island	runs on Lake Erie.
1856	Amity (British)	217	Chatham, C. W.	
"	Magnet	256	Saginaw, Mich.	runs on Lake Huron
"	Western Metropolis	1,860	Buffalo, N. Y.	runs on Lake Erie.
"	Uncle Ben	155	Buffalo N. Y.	tow boat.
1857	City of Buffalo	2,200	Buffalo, N. Y.	runs on Lake Erie.

NOTE.—Besides the above list, there are a few small steamers of which nothing is known other than their names, among these are the Penetanguishene, Cynthia, Pontiac, Phenomenon, etc.

The Steamer CAROLINE, whose destruction filled so large a portion of public notice, was originally known as the *Carolina*, and is believed to have been built in New York, at an early date, then sent to Charleston, S. C., where she ran for several years. Before passing into Lake Erie she ran a couple of seasons on the Hudson River, between Albany and Troy, when her guards were shipped so as to admit her through the Erie and Oswego Canals. She was re-built at Ogdensburgh, N. Y., in 1834, and passed through the Welland Canal into Lake Erie. The date of her destruction by the British at Schlosser, near Niagara Falls, was Dec. 29, 1837, when five lives were supposed to be lost.

LAKE ERIE AND MICHIGAN SHIP CANAL.

From the Buffalo (N. Y.) Commercial, March, 1857.

"THIS project is attracting the attention of Western and Eastern papers. No doubt is expressed as to the practicability of the construction of the Canal. In fact, it is conceded that one can be built across the base of the peninsula without deep cutting, and the probability is that it would not exceed fifty feet at any particular point. But while they grant the feasibility of the plan, they occasionally express the opinion that it will be a long time before it will be built, if ever. Now, why not, pray? Because, we suppose, it would cost a pretty round figure to build it. Is this an insurmountable objection, if the construction of the work be entirely feasible? if all the shipping to and from Lake Michigan, present and to come, will pass through it? if the margin in the original cost and the time of a trip, *via* the straits and Lake Huron, and *via* the canal, be, as it would be, largely in favor of the latter, thus making it capable of producing a good per centage of tolls?—the accomplishment of which would yield a remunerative revenue."

The Toledo (Ohio) *Commercial* has the following:

"The harbor of Toledo affords the only suitable terminus for the proposed *Ship Canal* on Lake Erie, and there can scarcely be a doubt that it will be adopted by any company which may be organized for constructing the work. But in view of the immense importance of the canal to the interests of Toledo, would it not be well for our board of trade to look into the matter, and keep an eye open for any possible speculative movement which may be set on foot to select some other starting point? There should, indeed, be enterprise enough among our own citizens to take the initiative in this most important project. Under our general law, a company might be organized here for the portion of the line lying within the State of Ohio; and a similar organization could very readily be effected in Indiana, for the extension through that State. A large local interest in the stock would effectually secure to Toledo the advantages to which she is entitled by natural position; supposing, always, that the canal is to be opened—of which there really ought to be no doubt.

"A route for the canal, eminently practicable, and without deep cutting or heavy lockage, can be found, we are confident, through Ohio and Indiana."

The following is from the Monroe (Mich.) *Commercial:*

"For many years past the public attention has, at times, been directed to the importance of a *ship canal* from Monroe, on Lake Erie, to the waters of Lake Michigan. The project is perfectly feasible, but railroad enterprises have of late been so numerous, as to divert public attention from the benefits and objects of such a canal. The absolute necessities of commerce, however, are such as to bring the subject forcibly and favorably before the community, and the great commercial interests of certain locations are intimately connected with the completion of such a work. For instance, the project now on foot in Canada West, and portions of New York, of which Oswego is the commercial center, for constructing a ship canal, to connect Lakes Ontario and Huron, if carried forward to completion, would be a more fatal blow to the prosperity of Buffalo than any great work of improvement that could be made on the American continent. The immense trade between the great agricultural States in the West, and the Atlantic States in the East, now tributary to Buffalo, would seek the new route, and make Oswego, at the expense, and to the destruction of Buffalo, the great commercial metropolis of the lakes. The citizens of Western New York see this, and the necessity of availing themselves of a rival, and more ready and feasible route for a ship canal, to retain the ascendency they already possess, and secure forever, and beyond doubt, the trade, business, and profits of the business of the great West.

"A ship canal from Monroe to the navigable waters of Lake Michigan will accomplish this. The canal would be easily made, and would always be abundantly supplied with water from the lake, in the county of Hillsdale, which is now the source of four of the principal rivers of this State. The canal would make a direct line, and of course the shortest one that could be made, between Chicago and Buffalo and the Atlantic cities, and be certain of securing the transportation of the grain and provision trade of the West, and all the heavy freight business that now moves tediously by the protracted route of the lakes. The distance would be shortened more than half, or some five to six hundred miles, and that the expenses now incurred for insurance on produce, vessels, and goods, by the lakes, and the loss of property on Lakes Huron and Michigan, would pay the construction of the canal in a very few years.

"Why, then, should this great and important work be longer delayed? A discerning public can see its absolute necessity, and security and permanency of great commercial interests urge its construction, by every consideration of self-preservation and future greatness.

"We do say that Monroe and Michigan are also deeply interested in this great ship canal, and that they can do much to encourage its construction at an early day. Buffalo is moving, and let Monroe and Southern Michigan second the move. The object can not fail to enlist the hearty co-operation of Southern Michigan, and we call upon our citizens to wake up to the great work. It is not only a feasible improvement, but will prove an eminently successful one, and will work a revolution in the commerce of the Northwest that will make Monroe one of the greatest cities of the lakes."

DIRECT TRANSPORTATION FROM LAKE SUPERIOR TO LIVERPOOL.

From the St. Paul (Minnesota) Advertiser.

"AN article from the *European Times* recites the arrival at Liverpool, direct from Chicago, of the schr. 'DEAN RICHMOND,' whose departure we announced some three months ago. In this simple announcement is contained the initial fact of a new era in commercial history, and issues of startling and overwhelming significance crowd upon the calmest view of its relations with the future West. It seems to us—we know not if we apprehend its bearings correctly—that the results of this experiment must be an eventual revolution of the internal traffic of the Western States. It virtually makes our inland lakes the Mediterranean Sea of North America, and Chicago becomes the Alexandria of modern times. It peels off the littoral rind of the New World at a stroke—and splits the ripe apple of the continent to its core. Ocean commerce will follow that entering wedge. Direct transportation will inevitably supersede the expensive and complicated machinery employed in conveying Western grain through its present channels—which, besides involving several expensive trans-shipments, is attended with an important diminution of bulk. The Atlantic, the far Bosphorus, the Baltic, and the seas of the old hemisphere, will flow in through the rent torn by the keel of the 'Dean Richmond,' and the majestic commerce of the ocean overleaping the huge complications of human ingenuity—passing in triumph past the monuments of Clinton's genius, past canals and railroads, railroads and canals—through rivers and lakes, 2,000 miles into the interior—will plant its sea-worn flags upon the shores of Lake Michigan, and sit in royal state like another queen of Sheba, on the throne that Western industry shall build for her in the chief city of the interior plain of North America. Nobody can doubt that the demonstrated practicability of direct shipment from Chicago to Europe will eventually transfer the business of transportation to this channel. An inevitable consequence of this will be the enlargement of the Welland Ship Canal,* the ring-bolt in the chain of communication from the ocean to the lakes, to a capacity sufficient for a ship of any required size. The application of steam will overcome the delays of navigation, and the path opened by the 'Dean Richmond' will be thronged with the flags of every nation. But this is not all. What is true of Lake Michigan is true of Lake Superior. What is possible by the Welland Canal is equally possible with the Saut Ste Marie. The splendid chain of inland navigation does not end with Chicago. It is complete to the extreme western end of Lake Superior. Here, at the uttermost limit of ship-navigation, the town of Superior, some two years old, and containing not more than 1,000 inhabitants, is slowly rising on the shores of the queen lake, from the somber woods that surround it, to meet the majestic destiny that is creeping with slow pace up the St. Lawrence and through the lakes toward her, to cast the commerce of the ocean at her feet, and crown her with a diadem of ocean pearls. Nor is this all. The ocean highway, extending from the mouth of the St. Lawrence to the extremity of Lake Superior, will be the basis of the whole system of Western railroads. *A Northern Pacific Railroad, with a terminus at Superior*, is the necessary supplement of the navigable highway we have described. The arguments in its favor are irresistible, unanswerable. It is a logical deduction from the whole law of railroads. The paramount purpose of the Pacific Railroad, we take to be, to facilitate the commercial intercourse between the Atlantic and Pacific coasts, in other words, to facilitate transportation. Now transportation is impelled by an irresistible impulse in the cheapest route. Hence gravitation itself is scarcely more a law than the tendency of railroads to the nearest water-course in the direction of their destination. They break off at once by a sort of physical necessity, as transporting agencies, at the nearest navigable water communication. One always ends where the other begins. The commercial apparatus of the country is full of instances pertinent to this. By this long chain of inland lakes, covering nearly half of the distance between the Atlantic and Pacific coasts, nature seems to point with the force of a divine decree to a supplementary railroad route to the Pacific, to connect at its nearest span the ocean navigation of the opposite sides of the continent, and there can be no doubt that, other things being equal in feasibility of a route west of the Mississippi, the first road to the Pacific will abut on the shore of Lake Superior."

---

* Also the construction of a ship canal around the Falls of Niagara, on the American or New York side of the river.

THE COMMERCE OF THE LAKES.

EXTRACT from the Report of the Congressional Committee on the subject of the Commerce of the Lakes.

The following (from the Cleveland *Herald*) is the total Tonnage of the Lakes for 1854 and 1855, including the steam tonnage for the same years:

Districts.	Tonnage. 1854.	1855.	Steam Tonnage. 1855.
Sackett's Harbor	7,570	6,227	1,944
Oswego	24,365	42,460	5,199
Genesee	——	233	128
Niagara	868	468	128
Oswegatchie	3,744	4,485	3,042
Buffalo Creek	82,678	76,952	38,262
Cape Vincent	4,866	6,609	1,143
Presque Isle	8,210	9,269	4,720
Cuyahoga	45,483	51,078	15,012
Sandusky	6,084	8,051	306
Miami	5,479	3,763	115
DETROIT	52,363	65,058	32,180
Mackinac	4,393	4,431	2,397
Milwaukee	14,117	15,678	288
Chicago	31,041	50,972	3,207
Total tonnage	291,231	345,729	108,243

"Increase of lake tonnage (steam and sail) from June 30th, 1854, to June 30th, 1855, a fraction over 18 8-.0 per cent.

"Ratio of steam to sail tonnage for 1855, a small fraction less than 1-3.

TOTAL TONNAGE OF THE UNITED STATES FOR 1854 AND 1855.

	Registered.	Enrolled.	Total Tonnage.
1854	2,333,819	2,469,083	4,802,902
1855	2,535,136	2,676,864	5,212,000

"Ratio of increase of lake tonnage *over* the aggregate total tonnage of the United States, a fraction over 2 3-10 per cent. per annum more than double; or as 18 8-10 to 8-12 in favor of lake tonnage, *which thus constitutes* 1 1-15 *of the entire tonnage of the U. States.*

"The clearances of vessels from ports in the U. S. to Canada, and the entries of vessels from Canada to ports in the U. S., during the year 1855, show a greater amount of tonnage entered and cleared than between the U. States *a ıd any other foreign country.*

"From the U. S. to Canada there were 2,369 clearances of American vessels, and 6,638 of Canadian, making a total of 9,007. The total tonnage was 1,793,519. The clearances from Canada to the U. S. for the same time were 2,454 American vessels and 4,194 Canadian, making a total of 6,648, with a total tonnage of 1,767,730, and a total tonnage back and forth of 3,561,249.

"The value of lake tonnage for 1854, $10,185,000; at an average of $43 per ton, this would make the value of the increased tonnage for 1855 (viz., 345,000 tons) reach $14,835,000.

"The following table shows the value of the lake commerce for 1855, excluding the districts of Presque Isle and Mackinac, *and not including the freight and passenger trade:*

Districts.	Tonnage Ent'd & Cleared.	Val. of Imp'ts. & Exp'ts.
Cuyahoga	1,782,493	$162,185,640
Buffalo Creek	3,330,232	333,023,000
Sandusky	—	59,966,000
Maumee	1,034,644	94,107,000
Chicago	2,632,000	233,878,000
Detroit	1,538,000	140,000.000
Milwaukee	—	35,000,000
Oswego	1,607,000	145,235,000
Sackett's Harbor, Cape Vincent, Oswegatchie, Genesee, Niagara,	—	42,226,000
Exports and Imports		$1,216,620,640
Total value of lake commerce, excluding Presque Isle and Mackinac		$608,310,390

"This sum may seem incredible to those unacquainted with the immense carrying-trade of these lakes. But the figures will show that the trade between the U. S. and Canada, carried on over the lakes, is in value next to that between France and the U. S. The amount of American goods sent to Canada is $9,950,764, and the amount of foreign goods, but passing through American hands, is $8.769,280; while the amount of goods sent from Canada to the States is $12,182,314, making a total trade between the two countries of $30,902,658.*

* These figures are very convincing of the fact that the interests of the Canadas with the United States are o e and identical and the commercial and social good understanding happily existing between the two

"The actual value of property exposed to the perils of lake navigation is considerably greater than the *total value* of the merchandise of every description exported from the U. S. *to all* foreign countries, added to the total value of merchandise imported *from all* foreign countries into the United States.

"The dangers to which our lake commerce is exposed are three, viz., shipwreck, collision, and stranding. These are shown to be in a great measure attributable to the narrow area over which this commerce is carried on, the stormy character of the lakes, the exposed condition of the lake coasts, and the want of natural or artificial harbors of commerce or of refuge for the lake shipping.

"The following are the dimensions of the lakes and their connecting rivers:

Lakes.	Length.	Greatest breadth.	Av. breadth.	Areas.
Ontario....	180	52	40	5,400
Erie.......	240	57	38	7,800
Huron.....	270	105	70	20,400
Michigan ..	340	83	58	20,000
St. Clair...	20	25	25	300
	1,050		46¾	53,900
Str. Detroit.	27	—	—	—
St. Clair....	38	—	—	—
	1,115 total length.			

"Thus a vessel sailing from Cape Vincent, Lake Ontario, to Chicago, Lake Michigan, by *keeping the center lines* of the lakes, will sail 1,115 miles; and yet will average not more than 23 miles from shore throughout the whole distance.

"But the coast line of the lakes on the American side is much longer, and excluding Green Bay and the northwest coast of Lake Michigan, is for Lake Ontario 200 miles; Erie, 350; Huron, 440; Michigan, 850; or a total of 1,940 miles.

"A very large proportion of the extensive commerce above set forth is conducted by sail and steam vessels, at but a few miles' distance from the American coasts of these lakes, and over a surface not exceeding an area of 7,000 square miles; more than 1,400 miles of this coast constitutes to the numerous vessels by which this commerce is carried on, *a lee shore*, to the fear of which vessels navigating those lakes are constantly exposed.

"No reference has been made to the commerce and navigation

countries leaves no room for hope on the part of the *Oligarchal Mother of Colonies*, that Canada will remain long in servile subordination to a distant monarchy.—Ed.

of Lake Superior from the want of satisfactory data. In 1855, however, the exports of iron and copper alone from Lake Superior ports amounted to $2,700,000.

"The national importance of the lake commerce and navigation is clearly set forth—first with reference to the population of the seven States bordering on these lakes, and consequently interested in their navigation and commerce. Secondly, the position of those States relatively to the great valley of the Mississippi River; and the extent and cost of their railroads and lands, designed to open and facilitate commercial intercourse between the Atlantic Ocean, the lakes, and navigable waters and tributaries of the Mississippi River. Thirdly, the position of these seven lake States relatively to the British possessions and the valley of the St. Lawrence River. Fourthly, the importance of the commerce and navigation of the lakes as a nursery of seamen from which the navy of the United States may be supplied with the first class of seamen in the time of war, in which the tonnage of the lakes is compared with the tonnage engaged in the whale, cod, and mackerel fisheries.

"The white population of the United States, according to the census of 1850, was 19,553,038. There are seven States bounded in part with great lakes, with a population as follows:

New York	3,048,325
Pennsylvania	2,258,160
Ohio	1,955,050
Michigan	395,071
Indiana	977,154
Illinois	846,034
Wisconsin	304,756
White population of the 7 lake States..	9,784,550
" " " 24 other States.	9,768,488
Balance in favor of the lake States...	16,062

"Showing that the white population of the seven lake States is greater by 16,062* than the total white population of the remaining twenty-four States; and the difference has probably been still more increased since 1850.

"The total value of foreign imports for 1855 in this region is $274,403,935. If the seamen engaged in the lake navigation or in the fisheries are proportionate in number to the tonnage engaged in each, then those engaged in the navigation of the lakes must very considerably exceed those engaged in the whale, cod, and mackerel fisheries.

* The population of Minnesota (say 100,000) should be added to the above excess of white population.

"The amount of losses sustained by vessels and cargoes for want of suitable river and harbor improvements—number and kind of vessels sustaining losses on the lakes by "shipwreck, stranding, and collision," from 1848 to 1855 inclusive, with the amount of damage sustained:

STEAMBOATS.

	Shipwreck.		Stranding.		Collision.	
	No.	Loss.	No.	Loss.	No.	Loss.
1848.........	3	$25,000	9	$47,000	0	$——
1849.........	1	25,000	5	21,000	3	1,400
1850.........	5	98,000	8	13,400	8	28,800
1851.........	2	27,000	5	36,700	9	6,000
1852.........	3	125,000	5	14,700	16	158,350
1853.........	3	126,000	7	51,000	11	31,650
1854.........	4	110,000	2	110,000	8	31,200
1855.........	4	378,000	11	11,350	12	36,600
	25	914,000	52	305,150	67	286,000

PROPELLERS.

	Shipwreck. No.	Loss.	Stranding. No.	Loss.	Collision. No.	Loss.
1848.........	0	$——	1	$12,000	1	$400
1849.........	0	——	1	5,000	0	——
1850.........	0	——	4	2,500	3	2,400
1851.........	2	55,000	6	32,800	10	40,400
1852.........	4	85,000	5	6,900	9	73,000
1853.........	1	42,000	7	28,000	4	39,000
1854.........	5	370,000	0	——	8	69,500
1855.........	7	351,000	11	9,950	19	557,750
	19	903,000	35	99,050	54	667,800

SAIL VESSELS.

	Shipwreck. No.	Loss.	Stranding. No.	Loss.	Collision. No.	Loss.
1848........	23	$128,500	65	$73,020	3	$36,000
1849........	10	56,900	30	42,900	10	17,000
1850........	20	89,600	64	82,150	11	44,600
1851........	34	132,700	86	83,950	22	50,700
1852........	30	183,100	62	96,000	35	28,500
1853........	27	175,400	62	84,000	15	23,700
1854........	52	407,626	0	——	16	90,650
1855........	40	418,300	109	184,650	52	121,800
Sail.........	236	1,591,626	479	646,770	164	414,250
Propellers ...	19	903,000	35	99,050	54	667,800
Steamboats ..	25	914,500	52	305,150	67	286,000
Total ...	380	3,409,126	566	1,051,170	285	1,368,050

TOTAL LOSS IN EIGHT YEARS.

	Number	Damages.
By Shipwreck	380	$3,409,126
By Stranding	566	1,051,170
By Collision	285	1,368,050
Total	1,231	5,828,346

"Whole number of disasters to vessels and cargoes, or either of them, during these eight years, 2,117, of which 1,231 consist of shipwreck, stranding, and collision, a little over 4-6 of the whole, while the damage from these causes during the same period was nearly 5-7 of the whole, and amounted to $5,828,346; the total damage from disasters of all kinds being $8,852,649.

"The amount of damages to the commerce of the lakes during 1854, from the difficulty of crossing the St. Clair Flats with loaded vessels, was as follows:

VESSELS ENGAGED IN 1854 IN TRADE TO THE UPPER LAKES.

Steamboats	8	Tonnage,	6,880
Propellers	44	"	21,796
Sail Vessels (Barques)	32	"	12,234
Brigs	84	"	24,757
Schooners	198	"	48,323
Total Tons			110,990

SAIL VESSELS.

Paid towing and lighterage on Flats	$163,686 56
Time detained—days, 5,566	220,640 00
Damages by collision, paid for repairs	62,800 00
	$452,146 56
Steam vessels paid for like damages	208,000 00
Total damage on St. Clair Flats (for the season)	$660,146 56

"We call especial attention to the last item.

"The amount of duties collected in the fifteen collection districts of the Great Lakes from 1837 to 1855 was $5,511,129 90, and the whole amount of appropriations that have been made to these lakes from the beginning of the government till now is $2,884,125, showing that the United States have received from the lake revenue $2,267,004 98 more than it has given back to it in any shape. This balance will cover the amount expended on the light-houses on the lakes, with repairs, attendance of keepers, and the cost of the ship canal around the St. Mary's Falls, and still leave $1,000,000 for the U. States Treasury."

WESTWARD MOVEMENT OF THE CENTER OF POPULATION, COMMERCE, AND OF INDUSTRIAL POWER IN NORTH AMERICA.

Extract from Hunt's Merchant's Magazine.

"In the rapidly developing greatness of North America, it is interesting to look to the future, and speculate on the most probable points of centralization of its commercial and social power.

"Including with our nation, as forming an important part of its commercial community, the Canadas, and contiguous Provinces, the center of population, white and black, is a little west of Pittsburgh, situated at the head of navigation on the Ohio River. The movement of this center is north of west, about in the direction of Chicago. The center of productive power can not be ascertained with any degree of precision. We know it must be a considerable distance east, and north of the center of population. That center, too, is on its grand march westward. Both, in their regular progress, will reach Lake Michigan. The center of industrial power will touch Lake Erie, and possibly, but not probably, the center of population now move so far northward as to reach Lake Erie also. Their tendency will be to come together; but a considerable time will be required to bring them into near proximity. Will the movement of these centers be arrested before they reach Lake Michigan? I think no one expects it to stop eastward of that lake; few will claim that it will go far beyond it. Is it not, then, as certain as any thing in the future can be, that the central power of the continent will move to, and become permanent on, the border of the Great Lakes? Around these pure waters will gather the densest population, and on their borders will grow up the best towns and cities. As the centers of population and wealth approach, and pass Cleveland, that city should swell to large size. Toledo will be still nearer the lines of their movement, and should be more favorably affected by them, as the aggregate power of the continent will, by that time, be greatly increased. As these lines move westward toward Chicago, the influence of their position will be divided between that city and Toledo, distributing benefits according to the degree of proximity.

"If we had no foreign commerce, and all other circumstances were equal, the greatest cities would grow up along the line of the central industrial power, in its western progress, each new city becoming greater than its predecessor, by the amount of power accumulated on the continent for concentration from point to point of its progress. But as there are points from one resting-place to another possessing greatly superior advantages for commerce over all others, and near enough the center line of industrial power to appropriate the commerce which it offers, to these points we must look for our future great cities. To become chief of these, there must be united in them the best facilities for transport, by water and by land. It is too plain to need proof, that these positions are occupied by Cleveland, Toledo, and Chicago.

"But we have a foreign commerce beyond the continent of North America, by means of the Atlantic Ocean, bearing the proportion, we will allow, of one to twenty of the domestic commerce within the continent. This proportion will seem small to persons who have not directed particular attention to the subject. It is, nevertheless, within the truth. The proof of this is difficult, only because we can not get the figures that represent the numberless exchanges of equivalents among each other, in such a community as ours

* * * * * * * * * * *

"It can scarcely admit of a doubt, that the domestic commerce of North America bears a proportion as large as twenty to one of its foreign commerce. Has internal commerce a tendency to concentrate in few points, like foreign commerce Is its tendency to concentration ess than that of foreign commerce? No difference in this respect can be perceived. All commerce develops that law of its nature to the extent of its means. Foreign commerce concentrates chiefly at those ports where it meets the greatest internal commerce. The domestic commerce being the great body, draws to it the smaller body of foreign commerce. New York, by her canals, her railroads, and her superior position for coastwise navigation, has drawn to herself most of our foreign commerce, because she has become the most convenient point for the concentration of our domestic trade. It is absurd to suppose she can always, or even for half a century, remain the *best* point for the concentration of domestic trade; and as the foreign commerce will every year bear a less and less proportion to the domestic commerce, it can hardly be doubted that before the end of one century from this time the great center of commerce of all kinds for North America will be on a *lake harbor*. Supposing the center of population (now west of Pittsburgh) shall average a yearly movement westward, for the next fifty years, of twenty miles, this would carry it one thousand miles northwestward from Pittsburgh, and some five hundred or more miles beyond the central point of the natural resources of the country. It would pass Cleveland in five years, and Toledo in eleven years, reaching Chicago, or some point south of it, in less than twenty-five years. The geographical center of industrial power is probably now in northeastern Pennsylvania, having but recently left the city of New York, where it partially now for a time remains. This center will move at a somewhat slower rate than the center of population. Supposing its movement to be fifteen miles a year, it will reach Cleveland in twenty years, Toledo in twenty-seven years, and Chicago in forty-five years.

* * * * * * * * * *

"At the present rate of increase, the United States and the Canadas, fifty years from this time, will contain over one hundred and twenty millions of people. If we suppose it to be one hundred and five millions, and that these shall be distributed so that the Pacific States shall have ten millions, and the Atlantic border twenty-five millions, there will be left for the great interior plain seventy millions. These seventy millions will have twenty times as much commercial intercourse with each other as with all the world besides. It is obvious, then, that there must be built up in their midst the great city of the continent; and not only so, but that they will sustain several cities greater than those which can be sustained on the ocean border."

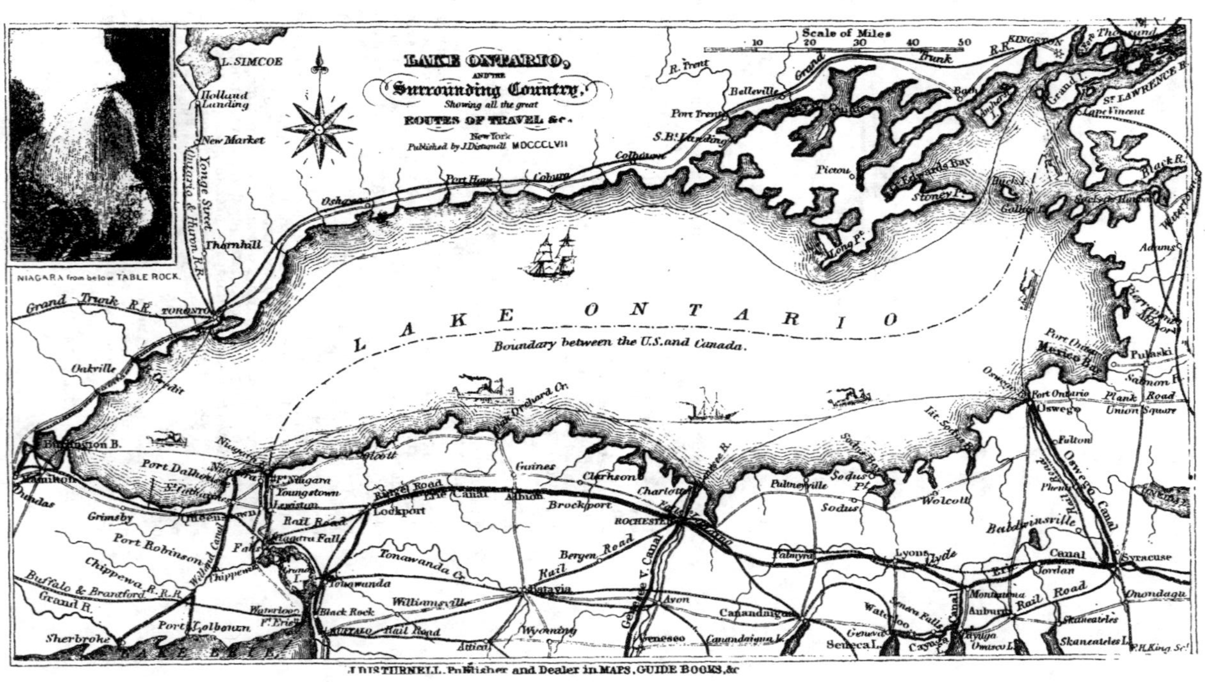

J. DISTURNELL, Publisher and Dealer in MAPS, GUIDE BOOKS, &c

RAILROAD AND STEAMBOAT ROUTES FROM BUFFALO TO NIAGARA FALLS, TORONTO, ETC.

THE most usual mode of conveyance from Buffalo to the Falls of Niagara, and thence to Lake Ontario, or into Canada, is by the *Buffalo, Niagara Falls and Lewiston Railroad*, 28 miles in length. It runs through Tonawanda, 11 miles; Niagara Falls, 22 miles; Suspension Bridge, 24 miles, connecting with the Great Western Railway of Canada, and terminates at Lewiston, the head of navigation on Niagara River, 28 miles.

American and Canadian steamers of a large class leave Lewiston several times daily, for different ports on Lake Ontario and the St. Lawrence River.

There is also another very desirable mode of conveyance, by Steamboat, descending the Niagara River, from Buffalo to Chippewa, C. W., thence by the *Erie and Ontario Railroad*, 17 miles in length; passing in full view of the Falls, to the Clifton House, three miles below Chippewa; Suspension Bridge, five miles; Queenston, eleven miles, terminating at Niagara, C. W., thirty-five miles from Buffalo.

As the Steamboat leaves Buffalo on the latter route, a fine view may be obtained of Lake Erie and both shores of Niagara River. On the Canada side, the first object of interest are the ruins of old FORT ERIE, captured by the Americans July 3d, 1814. It is situated at the foot of the lake, opposite the site of a strong fortress which the United States government have recently erected for the protection of the river and the city of Buffalo.

WATERLOO, C. W., three miles below Buffalo and opposite Black Rock (now a part of Buffalo), with which it is connected by a steam-ferry, is handsomely situated on the west side of Niagara River, which is here about half a mile wide. The *Buffalo and Lake Huron Railroad* runs from Fort Erie, near Waterloo, to Paris, C. W., where it connects with the Great Western Railway of Canada. It is now completed to Stratford, 116 miles, will soon be finished to Goderich, lying on L. Huron.

GRAND ISLAND, belonging to the United States, is passed on the right in descending the river. It is a large and valuable tract of good land, abounding with white oak of a superior quality.

NAVY ISLAND, belonging to the British, is next passed, lying within gunshot of the mainland. This island obtained great notoriety in the fall and winter of 1837–8, when it was occupied by the "Patriots," as they were styled, during the troubles in Canada. The steamer Caroline was destroyed on the night of December 29th, 1837, while lying at Schlosser's Landing, on the American shore, having been engaged in transporting persons to and from the island, which was soon after evacuated.

Opposite Navy Island, on the Canada side, near Chippewa battle-ground, is the house in which Capt. Usher resided when murdered in 1838. It is supposed he fell by the hands of some of the deluded patriots, having been shot by a secret foe, while in his own house.

CHIPPEWA, 20 miles below Buffalo and two miles above the Falls, is on the west side of Niagara River, at the mouth of a creek of the same name, which is navigable to PORT ROBINSON, some eight or ten miles west; the latter place being on the line of the Welland Canal. The village of Chippewa contains a population of about 1,000 souls. Steamboats and lake craft of a large size are built at this place for the trade of Lake Erie and the Upper Lakes. It has obtained a place in history on account of the bloody battle which was fought near it in the war of 1812, between the United States and Great Britain. The battle was fought on the 5th of July, 1814, on the plains a short distance south of the steamboat landing. The American forces were commanded by Major Gen. Jacob Brown, and the British, by Major General Riall, who, after an obstinate and sanguinary fight, was defeated with considerable loss.

At Chippewa commences the railroad extending to Niagara, at the mouth of the river, a distance of 17 miles. Steamboats continue the line of travel from both ends of this road, thus furnishing an interesting and speedy conveyance between Lakes Erie and Ontario.

On arriving in the vicinity of the FALLS OF NIAGARA, the cars stop near the *Clifton House*, situated near the ferry leading to the American side. The site of this house was chosen as giving the best view of both the American and Canadian or Horse-Shoe Falls, which are seen from the piazzas and front windows. This is the most interesting approach to the Falls.

In addition to the Falls, there are other points of attraction on the Canada side of the river. The collection of curiosities at the Museum, and the Camera Obscura, which gives an exact and beautiful, though miniature image of the Falls, are well worthy of a visit. The *Burning Spring*, two miles above the Falls, is also much frequented; and the rides to the battle-grounds in this vicinity make an exhilarating and very pleasant excursion. For further description of Falls, see page 211.

DRUMMONDSVILLE, one mile west of the Falls, and situated on *Lundy's Lane*, is celebrated as the scene of another sanguinary engagement between the American and British forces, July 25, 1814.

The following is a brief, though correct account of the engagement. "On the afternoon of the above day, while the American army was on their march from *Fort George* toward *Fort Erie*, ascending the west bank of the river, their rear guard, under the immediate command of Gen. Scott, was attacked by the advanced guard of the British army under Gen. Riall, the British having been reinforced after their defeat at Chippewa, on the 5th of the same month. This brought on a general conflict of the most obstinate and deadly character. As soon as attacked, Gen. Scott advanced with his division, amounting to about 3,000 men, to the open ground facing the heights occupied by the main British army, where were planted several heavy pieces of cannon. Between eight and nine o'clock in the evening, on the arrival of reinforcements to both armies, the battle became general and raged for several hours, with alternate success on both sides; each army evincing the most determined bravery and resistance. The command of the respective forces was now assumed by Maj. Gen. Brown and Lieut. Gen. Drummond, each having under his command a well-disciplined army. The brave (American) Col. Miller was ordered to advance and seize the artillery of the British, which he effected at the point of the bayonet in the most gallant manner. Gen. Riall, of the English army, was captured, and the possession of the battle-ground contested until near midnight, when 1,700 men being either killed or wounded, the conflicting armies, amounting altogether to about 6,000 strong, ceased the deadly conflict, and for a time the bloody field was left unoccupied, except by the dead and wounded. When the British discovered that the Americans had encamped one or two miles distant, they returned and occupied their former position. Thus ended one of the most bloody conflicts that occurred during the last war; and while each party boasted a victory, altogether too dearly bought, neither was disposed to renew the conflict."

CLIFTON is a new and flourishing village, situated at the western termination of the Great Western Railway, where it connects with the *Suspension Bridge.* For description of route to Detroit, etc., see page 150.

QUEENSTON, situated seven miles below the Falls, and about the same distance above the entrance of Niagara River into Lake Ontario, lies directly opposite the village of Lewiston, with which it is connected by a suspension bridge 850 feet in length. It contains about 500 inhabitants, 60 dwelling-houses, one Episcopal, one Scotch Presbyterian, and one Baptist church, four taverns, four stores, and three warehouses. This place is also celebrated as being the scene of a deadly strife between the American and British forces, Oct. 13, 1812. The American troops actually engaged in the fight were commanded by Gen. Solomon Van Rensselaer, and both the troops and their commander greatly distinguished themselves for their bravery, although ultimately overpowered by superior numbers. In attempting to regain their own side of the river many of the Americans perished, the whole loss in killed, wounded, and prisoners amounting to at least 1,000 men.

Major Gen. Brock, the British commander, was killed in the middle of the fight, while leading on his men. A new monument stands on the heights, near where he fell, erected to his memory. The first monument was nearly destroyed by gunpowder, April 17, 1840; an infamous act, said to have been perpetrated by a person concerned in the insurrection of 1837–38.

BROCK'S NEW-MONUMENT was commenced in 1853, and finished in 1856; being 185 feet high, ascended on the inside by a spiral staircase of 235 stone steps. The base is 40 feet square and 35 feet in height, surmounted by a tablet 35 feet high, with historical devices on the four sides. The main shaft, about 100 feet, is fluted and surmounted by a Corinthian capital, on which is placed a colossal figure of Major General Brock, 18 feet in height. This beautiful structure cost £10,000 sterling, being entirely constructed of a cream-colored stone quarried in the

Brock's Monument.—Queenston Heights.

vicinity. A massive stone wall, 80 feet square, adorned with military figures and trophies at the corners, 27 feet in height, surrounds the monument, leaving space for a grass-plot and walk on the inside of the inclosure.

The following is the inscription:

Upper Canada has dedicated this Monument
to the memory of the late
Major-General Sir ISAAC BROCK, K.B.,
Provisional Lieut.-Governor and Commander of the Forces in this Province,
whose remains are deposited in the vault beneath.
Opposing the invading enemy he fell in action, near the Heights,
on the 13th October, 1812, in the 43d year of his age,
Revered and lamented by the people whom he governed, and deplored by
the sovereign to whose service his life had been devoted.

The last words of Major General Brock, when he fell mortally wounded by a musket-shot through the left breast, were, "Never mind, my boys, the death of one man—I have not long to live" Thus departed one of the many noble spirits that were sacrificed on this frontier during the war of 1812.

The village of NIAGARA is advantageously situated on the Canada side, at the entrance of the river into Lake Ontario, directly opposite *Fort Niagara*, on the American side. It contains about 3,000 inhabitants; a court-house and jail; one Episcopal, one Presbyterian, one Methodist, and one Roman Catholic church; ten hotels and taverns, and twenty stores of different kinds; also, an extensive locomotive and car factory. This is the most noted place in Canada West for building steamboats and other craft navigating Lake Ontario. Here is a dockyard with a marine railway and foundry attached, capable of making machinery of the largest description, and giving employment to a great number of men. It is owned by the "Niagara Dock Company." Steamers leave daily for Toronto, etc.

FORT GEORGE, situated a short distance south or up-stream from the mouth of the river, is now in ruins. This was the scene of a severe contest in 1813, in which the Americans were victorious. A new fort has been erected on the point of land at the mouth of the river, directly opposite old *Fort Niagara* on the American side. The new fortification is called *Fort Massasauga.*

The whole frontier on the Canada side, from Fort George to Fort Erie, opposite Buffalo, was occupied by the American army in 1814, when occurred a succession of battles of the most determined and brilliant character.

NIAGARA RIVER,

ITS RAPIDS, FALLS, ISLANDS, AND ROMANTIC SCENERY.

"Majestic stream! what river rivals thee,
Thou child of many lakes, and sire of one—
Lakes that claim kindred with the all-circling sea—
Large at thy birth as when thy race is run!
Against what great obstructions hast thou won
Thine august way—the rock-formed mountain-plain
Has opened at thy bidding, and the steep
Bars not thy passage, for the ledge in vain
Stretches across the channel—thou dost leap
Sublimely down the height, and urge again
Thy rock-embattled course on to the distant main."

This most remarkable and romantic stream, the outlet of Lake Erie, through which flows all the accumulated waters of the Upper Lakes of North America, very appropriately forms the boundary between two great countries, the British province of Upper Canada on the one side, and the State of New York, the "Empire State" of the Union, on the opposite side. In its whole course, its peculiar character is quite in keeping with the stupendous Cataract from which its principal interest is derived.

The amount of water passing through this channel is immense; from a computation which has been made at the outlet of Lake Erie, the quantity thus discharged is about twenty millions of cubic feet, or upward of 600,000 tons per minute, all of which great volume of water, 20 miles below, plunges over the Falls of Niagara.

The Niagara River commences at Bird Island, nearly opposite the mouth of Buffalo harbor, and passes by the site of old Fort Erie and Waterloo on the Canada side. At the latter place a steam ferry-boat plies across the river to Black Rock, now forming a part of the city of Buffalo. It is here proposed to con struct a railroad bridge across the stream, about 1,800 feet in width.

SQUAW ISLAND and STRAWBERRY ISLAND are both small islands lying on the American side of the stream, near the head of Grand Island. The river is here used in part for the Erie Canal, a pier extending from Squaw Island to Bird Island, forming a large basin called Black Rock Harbor.

GRAND ISLAND, attached to Erie Co., N. Y., is a large and important body of land, about ten miles long from north to south, and seven miles wide. This island is partly cleared and cultivated, while the larger portion is covered with a large growth of oaks and other forest trees.

The ship or steamboat channel runs along the bank of Grand Island to nearly opposite Chippewa, where the whole stream unites before plunging over the Falls of Niagara, being again separated at the head of Goat Island. From this point the awe-struck traveler can scan the quiet waters above, and the raging rapids below, preparing to plunge over the cataract.

CAYUGA ISLAND and BUCKHORN ISLAND are small bodies of land belonging to the United States, situated immediately below Grand Island.

NAVY ISLAND, lying opposite the village of Chippewa, 18 miles below the head of the river, is a celebrated island belonging to the Canadians, having been taken possession of by the sympathizing patriots in 1837, when a partial rebellion occurred in Upper and Lower Canada.

TONAWANDA, 11 miles below Buffalo, is situated at the mouth of Tonawanda Creek, opposite Grand Island. The *Erie Canal* here enters the creek, which it follows for several miles on its course toward Lockport. A railroad also runs to Lockport, connecting with the *New York Central Railroad*, extending to Albany. A *ship canal* is proposed to be constructed from Tonawanda to some eligible point on Lake Ontario, thus forming a rival to the Welland Canal of Canada.

SCHLOSSER'S LANDING, two miles above Niagara Falls village, is a noted steamboat landing, opposite Chippewa, from whence the steamer *Caroline* was cut adrift by the British and destroyed, by being precipitated over the Falls during the Canadian rebellion, December 29th, 1837.

The Rapids.—Below Navy Island, between Chippewa and Schlosser, the river is nearly three miles in width, but soon narrows to one mile, when the Rapids commence, and continue for about one mile before reaching the edge of the precipice at the Horse-Shoe Fall.

At the commencement of the Rapids "the bed of the river declines, the channel contracts, numerous large rocks heave up the rolling surges, and dispute the passage of the now raging and foaming floods. The mighty torrent leaping down successive ledges, dashing over opposing elevations, hurled back by ridges, and repelled from shores and islands—plunging, boiling, roaring—seems a mad wilderness of waters striving against its better fate, and hurried on to destruction by its own blind and reckless impetuosity. Were there no cataract, these Rapids would yet make Niagara the wonder of the world."

Iris, or Goat Island, commences near the head of the Rapids, and extends to the precipice, of which it forms a part, separating the American Fall from the Canadian or Horse-Shoe Fall. It is about half a mile in length, eighty rods wide, and contains over sixty acres of arable land, being for the most part covered with a heavy growth of forest trees of a variety of species, and native plants and flowers. A portion of the island, however, has been cleared off, and a garden inclosed, in which are some excellent fruit trees, and a variety of native and foreign plants and flowers, and a fish-pond. The island is remarkably cool, shady, and pleasant, and is an object of unceasing admiration from year to year. Comfortable seats and arbors are placed at the most interesting points, where the visitor can sit at ease and enjoy the beautiful and sublime views presented to his sight—often entranced by a deafening roar of mighty waters in their descent, often accompanied by changing rainbows of the most gorgeous description.

NIAGARA.

WRITTEN BY LYDIA H. SIGOURNEY.

Flow on forever, in thy glorious robe
Of terror and of beauty; God hath set
His rainbow on thy forehead, and the cloud
Mantles around thy feet, and He doth give
Thy voice of thunder power to speak of Him
Eternally; bidding the lip of man
Keep silence, and upon thy rocky altar
Pour incense of awe-struck praise.

GOAT ISLAND BRIDGE.—The Niagara Falls *Gazette* gives the following description of this new structure:

"This bridge across the east branch of the Niagara River is situated in the Rapids, about sixty rods above the Cataract, on the site of the old wooden bridge. It is 360 feet long, and consists of four arches of ninety feet span each, supported between the abutments of three piers. The piers above water are built of heavy cut stone, and are twenty-two feet long and six feet wide, tapering one foot in the height. The foundations are formed of foot-square oak timber, strongly framed and bolted together in cribs, filled with stone, and covered with timber at the surface of the water. These timber-foundations are protected against wear and injury from ice by heavy plates of iron, and being always covered with water, will be as durable as the stone.

"The superstructure is of iron, on the plan of Whipple's iron-arched bridge. The whole width is twenty-seven feet, affording a double carriage-way of sixteen and a half feet, and two foot-ways of five and a fourth feet each, with iron railings. The arches are of cast iron, and the chords, suspenders, and braces of wrought iron. All the materials used in the construction are of the best quality, and the size and strength of all the parts far beyond what are deemed necessary in bridges exposed to the severest tests.

"This substantial and beautiful structure, spanning a branch of this majestic river in the midst of the rapids, and overlooking the cataract, is worthy of the site it occupies, and affords another instance of the triumph of human ingenuity over the obstacles of nature.

"The islands connected by this bridge with the American shore are the property of Messrs. Porter, and constitute the most interesting features in the scenery surrounding the cataract. This bridge has been erected by them to facilitate communication with these interesting localities not otherwise accessible."

This is a toll-bridge, every foot passenger being charged 25 cents for the season, or single crossing.

There are upward of thirty islands and islets in the Niagara River or Strait, above the cataract. Most of those not described are small, and scarcely worthy of enumeration, although those immediately contiguous to Goat Island form beautiful objects in connection with the rushing and mighty waters by which they are surrounded. *Bath Island*, *Brig Island*, *Chapin's Island*, and *Bird Island*, all situated immediately above the American Fall, are reached by bridges.

When on Goat Island, turning to the right toward the Falls, the first object of interest is *Hogg's Back*, a point of land facing the American Fall,—Bridge to Adington Island immediately above the Cave of the Winds, 160 feet below. Sam. Patch's Point is next passed on the right, from which he took a fearful leap some years since. Biddle's Stairs descend to the water's edge below and the Cave of the Winds, which are annually visited by thousands of visitors. Terrapin Bridge and Terrapin Tower afford a grand view of the Canadian or Horse-Shoe Fall and Rapids above the Falls. Three Sister Islands are contiguous to Goat Island, on the American side. Passing around Goat Island toward the south, a grand view is afforded of the river and rapids above the Canadian and American Falls.

CATARACT OF NIAGARA.

"Shrine of Omnipotence! how vast, how grand,
How awful, yet how beautiful thou art!
Pillar'd around thy everlasting hills,
Robed in the drapery of descending floods,
Crowned by the rainbow, canopied by clouds
That roll in incense up from thy dread base,
Hid by their mantling o'er the vast abyss
Upon whose verge thou standest, whence ascends
The mighty anthem of thy Maker's praise,
Hymn'd in eternal *thunders!*"

THE AMERICAN RAPIDS, FROM THE BRIDGE.

THE AMERICAN FALLS BY MOONLIGHT.

NIAGARA is a word of Indian origin—the orthography, accentuation and meaning of which are variously given by different authors. It is highly probable that this diversity might be accounted for and explained by tracing the appellation through the dialects of the several tribes of aborigines who formerly inhabited the neighboring country. There is reason to believe, however, that the etymon belongs to the language of the Iroquois, and signifies the "*Thunder of Waters.*"

"When the traveler first arrives at the cataract, he stands and gazes, and is lost in admiration. The mighty volume of water which forms the outlet of the great Lakes Superior, Michigan, Huron, and Erie, is here precipitated over a precipice 160 feet high, with a roar like that of thunder, which may be heard, in favorable circumstances, to the distance of fifteen miles, though, at times, the Falls may be nearly approached without perceiving much to indicate a tremendous cataract in the vicinity. In consequence of a bend in the river, the principal weight of water is thrown on the Canadian side, down what is called the *Horse-Shoe Fall,* which name has become inappropriate, as the edges of the precipice have ceased to be a curve, and forms a moderately acute angle. Near the middle of the fall, *Goat Island*, containing 75 acres, extends to the brow of the precipice, dividing the river into two parts; and a small projecting mass of rock at a little distance from it, toward the American shore, again divides the cataract on that side. Goat Island, at the lower end, presents a perpendicular mass of rocks, extending from the bottom to the top of the precipice. A bridge has been constructed from the American shore to Bath Island, and another connects the latter with Goat Island, and a tower is erected on the brow of the Horse-Shoe Fall, approached from Goat Island by a short bridge, on which the spectator seems to stand over the edge of the mighty cataract, and which affords a fine view of this part of it. The distance at the fall from the American shore to Goat Island is 65 rods; across the front of Goat Island is 78 rods; around the Horse-Shoe Fall, on the Canadian side, 144 rods; directly across the Horse-Shoe, 74 rods. The height of the fall near the American shore is 163 feet; near Goat Island, on the same side, 158 feet; near Goat Island, on the Canada side, 154 feet. Table Rock, a shelving projection on the Canadian side, at the edge of the precipice, is 150 feet high. This place is generally thought to present the finest view of the Falls; though if the spectator will visit the tower on the opposite side on Goat Island, at sunrise, when the whole cavity is enlightened by the sun, and the gorgeous bow trembles in the rising spray, he can not elsewhere, the world over, enjoy such an incomparable scene. A covered stairway on the American side descends from the top to the bottom of the precipice.

"It has been computed that 100 million tons of water are discharged over the precipice every hour. The Rapids commence about a mile above the Falls, and the water descends 57 feet before it arrives at the cataract. The view from the bridge to Goat Island, of the troubled water dashing tumultuously over the rocks of the American fall, is terrific. While curiosity constitutes an attribute of the human character, these falls will be frequented by admiring and delighted visitors as one of the grandest exhibitions in nature.

"This stupendous cataract, situated in N. lat. 43° 6,′ and W. long. 2° 6′ from Washington, is twenty-two miles north from the efflux of the river at Lake Erie, and fourteen miles south of its outlet into Lake Ontario. The whole length of the river is therefore thirty-six miles, its general course is a few points to the west of north. Though commonly called a river, this portion of the St. Lawrence is, more properly speaking, a *strait*, connecting, as above mentioned, the Lakes Erie and Ontario, and conducting the superfluous waters of the great seas and streams above though a broad and divided, and afterward compressed, devious, and irregular channel to the latter lake, into which it empties—the point of union being about forty miles from the western extremity of Lake Ontario.

"The climate of the Niagara is in the highest degree healthful and invigorating. The atmosphere, constantly acted upon by the rushing water, the noise and the spray, is kept pure, refreshing, and salutary. There are no stagnant pools or marshes near to send abroad their fœtid exhalations and noxious miasmas, poisoning the air and producing disease.

"Sweet-breathing herbs and beautiful wild flowers spring up spontaneously even on the sides, and in the crevices of the giant rocks; and luxuriant clusters of firs and other stately forest trees cover the islands, crown the cliffs, and overhang the banks of Niagara. Here are no mosquitoes to annoy, no reptiles to alarm, and no wild animals to intimidate, yet there is life and vivacity. The many-hued butterfly sips ambrosia from the fresh opened honey-cup—birds carol their lays of love among the spray-starred branches; and the lively squirrel skips chattering from tree to tree. Varieties of water-fowl, at certain seasons of the year, sport among the rapids, the sea-gull plays around the precipice, and the eagle—the banner bird of freedom—hovers above the cataract, plumes his gray pinions in its curling mists, and makes his home among the giant firs of its inaccessible islands.

"No place on the civilized earth offers such attractions and inducements to visitors as Niagara, and they can never be fully known except to those who see and study them, from the utter impossibility of describing such a scene as this wonderful cataract presents. When motion can be expressed by color, there will be some hope of imparting a faint idea of it; but until that can be done, Niagara must remain undescribed."

Below the Falls, the first objects of interest are the Ferry Stairs and Point View on the American side; while on the opposite side is a ferry and steamboat landing, where carriages are usually to be found to convey passengers to the Clifton House, Table Rock, and other places.

About 30 rods below the ferry stairs is the spot where the hermit Abbot was drowned. Half a mile below the latter point is Catlin's Cave, formerly much frequented.

The steamboat landing for the *Maid of the Mist* is situated on the American shore two miles below the Falls and about half a mile above the Suspension Bridge. This steamer, the second boat of the same name, first commenced running as an experiment boat in 1848; since then she has run annually without an accident of any kind. The first trip was made on September 18th, 1846, by Capt. H. Filkins, who with his small crew were the only persons on board, except an intrepid Canadian who was desirous of crossing the river with a horse, they both being safely landed on the Canadian shore.

The SUSPENSION BRIDGE, the greatest artificial curiosity in America, is situated two miles and a half below the Falls, where has recently sprung into existence *Niagara City*, or better known as the *Suspension Bridge*, on the American side, and *Clifton* on the Canadian side of the river, here being about 800 feet in width, with perpendicular banks of 325 feet.

The *Whirlpool* and *Rapids*, one mile below the Bridge, are terrific sights of great interest, and well worthy a visit.

The *Devil's Hole*, one mile farther down, is also a point of great attraction, together with the *Bloody Run*, a small stream where a detachment of English soldiers were precipitated in their flight from an attack by Indians during the old French war in 1759. An amphitheater of high ground spreads around and perfectly incloses the valley of the Devil's Hole, with the exception of a narrow ravine formed by Bloody Run—from which, against a large force, there is no escape, except over the precipice. The *Ice Cave* is another object of interest connected with the Devil's Hole.

The *Rapids* below the Whirlpool are the next object of attraction; then Queenston Heights and Brock's Monument on the Canadian side, and the *Suspension Bridge* at Lewiston; altogether forming objects of interest sufficient to fill a well-sized volume.

The Niagara River is navigable from Lewiston to its mouth at Fort Niagara, a farther distance of seven miles, or fourteen below the Falls of Niagara.

NEW STEAMER MAID OF THE MIST.

THIS steamboat will in future stop at both the Ferry landings, on the American and Canadian shores. She is of 170 tons burden, propelled by a powerful engine of over 100 horse-power, built expressly for this route, furnished with Francis' Life-boats, and all the modern improvements. The Cabins, Saloons, and Promenade Deck extend over the whole boat, so that passengers will be completely protected from the spray; now making her regular trips under the pilotage of J. R. Robinson, the celebrated navigator of the Rapids of Niagara.

The pleasure trip up to the Falls would seem to require little to recommend it, as the thousands who have repeated it in the old boat can bear witness to its great attractions. The novelty, beauty, and grandeur of the scene can not be over-estimated, passing as the boat does, for two miles through the gorge of the Niagara, directly in front of the New Railroad Suspension Bridge, the American Fall, Lunar Island, Cave of the Winds, to the Great Horse-Shoe Falls and Table Rock, all of which are presented at one view to the beholder in their most sublime and imposing aspect.

The boat will run daily (*Sundays excepted*), leaving Suspension Bridge Wharf morning and evening. The charge for the Pleasure Trip will be 50 cents.

☞ Omnibuses and Carriages run from all the depôts and hotels in connection with the boat.

The village of NIAGARA FALLS, Niagara Co., N. Y., is situated on the east side of Niagara River, in the immediate vicinity of the grand Cataract, 22 miles from Buffalo and 303 miles from Albany by railroad route. No place in the Union exceeds this favored spot as a fashionable place of resort during the summer and fall months, when hundreds of visitors may be seen every day flocking to Goat Island, or points contiguous to the Rapids and Falls. The village contains several large hotels for the accommodation of visitors, the most noted of which are the Cataract House and the International Hotel; the Monteagle Hotel, situated two miles below the Falls, near the Suspension Bridge, and the Clifton House, on the Canada side, are all alike popular and well-kept hotels; there are five churches of different denominations; 15 stores, in many of which are kept for sale Indian curiosities and fancy work of different kinds. The water-power here afforded by the descending stream, east of Goat Island, is illimitable. A paper-mill, a flouring-mill, two saw-mills, a woolen factory, a furnace and machine shop, together with other manufacturing establishments, here use the water-power so bountifully supplied. The population is about 3,000.

The railroads centering at the Falls are the *Buffalo, Niagara Falls and Lewiston Railroad*, the *New York Central Railroad*, and the *Canandaigua and Niagara Falls Railroad;* the latter road connecting with the *New York and Erie Railroad*, and forming with other roads a direct route to Philadelphia, Baltimore, and Washington

An *omnibus line* runs hourly from the village of Niagara Falls to Niagara City, or Suspension Bridge, during the summer months, and thence to the Clifton House and Table Rock on the Canada side, affording a cheap mode of visiting both sides of Niagara River.

NIAGARA CITY, situated two miles below the Falls, at the *Suspension Bridge*, is a new and flourishing place. Here is located the Monteagle Hotel, and other public houses, together with several stores and manufacturing establishments.

DIMENSIONS OF SUSPENSION BRIDGE.

LENGTH of span from center to center of towers.	822 feet.
Height of railroad track above water..........	250 "
Height of towers above rock on American side..	88 "
Height of towers above rock on Canada side....	78 "
Height of towers above floor of railway........	60 "
Number of wire cables......................	4
Diameter of each cable.....................	10 inches
Number of wires in each cable...............	3,659
Weight of superstructure.....................	750 tons.
Base of towers...............................	16 feet sq
Top of towers................................	8 "
Depth of anchor pits below surface of rocks.....	30 feet.

WEIGHT OF THE MATERIALS IN THE BRIDGE.

Timber of different kinds..................	919,130 lbs.
Wrought iron and suspenders..............	113,120 "
Castings.......	44,322 "
Iron rails.	66,740 "
Cable between towers................. ..	535,400 "
Total.....................	1,678,722 "

The *Great Western Railway of Canada*, which unites with the New York Central Railroad, terminating on the American side of the river, here commences and extends westward through Hamilton, London, and Chatham to Windsor, opposite Detroit, Mich., forming one of the great through lines of travel from Boston and New York to Chicago and the Far West.

This road also furnishes a speedy route of travel to Toronto, Collingwood, etc.

RATE OF CHARGES AT NIAGARA FALLS.

The following are the rate of charges usually exacted from persons visiting Niagara Falls—but, unfortunately, impositions are often practiced by unprincipled individuals, at this, as well as other fashionable resorts:

AMERICAN SIDE.

Board, from one to two and a half dollars per day.

For services of guide, from one to three dollars.

For guide behind the Central Fall, and visiting the Cave of the Winds, one dollar.

For crossing bridge to Goat Island, 25 cents.

Fare to and from Suspension Bridge, 12½ cents.

Fare for crossing Suspension Bridge, 25 cents.

Fare to the Whirlpool, 50 cents.

For use of steps or cars on Inclined Plane, 6¼ cents.

Ferriage to Canada side, 18¾ cents.

Omnibus fare and steam ferriage to Canada side, 25 cents.

CANADA SIDE.

Board, from one to two and a half dollars per day.

Visiting Barnett's Museum, Camera Obscura, and Pleasure Grounds, 25 cents.

For guide and use of dress to pass behind the Fall at Table Rock, one dollar.

Carriage fare from ferry to Clifton House, 6¼ cents.

Carriage fare to Whirlpool, Lundy's Lane Battle Ground, Burning Spring, and back to Ferry, 50 to 75 cents.

Guide to Battle Ground and visiting Monument, 25 cents.

Carriage fare to Brock's Monument on Queenston Heights, one dollar.

Carriage fare per day, four dollars.

The drives in the vicinity of the Falls, on both sides of the river, are unrivaled, and no visitor should lose the opportunity to visit all the objects of attraction above and below the mighty Cataract

Lewiston, Niagara Co., N. Y., is delightfully situated on the east bank of the Niagara River, seven miles below the Falls, and seven miles above the mouth of the river where it falls into Lake Ontario. It is an incorporated village and contains about 1,000 inhabitants, four churches, an incorporated academy; a custom-house, it being the port of entry for the district of Niagara; three hotels, nine stores, and three storehouses. Here is a very convenient steamboat landing, from which steamers depart daily for Oswego, Ogdensburgh, etc., on the American side, and for Toronto, Kingston, etc., on the Canadian side. The Buffalo, Niagara Falls and Lewiston Railroad terminates at this place, where is a magnificent Suspension Bridge thrown across the Niagara connecting Lewiston with Queenston, Canada. The mountain ridge here rises about 300 feet above the river, forming many picturesque and romantic points of great interest. On the American side of the river stands the site of old Fort Gray, erected during the war of 1812, while on the Canadian side are situated Queenston Heights, surmounted by a beautiful monument erected to the memory of Gen. Brock, of the British army, who was here killed in a sanguinary conflict, October 13th, 1812. From this height a most extensive and grand view is obtained of Lake Ontario and the surrounding country.

Youngstown, six miles below Lewiston, and one mile above old Fort Niagara at the mouth of the river, is a regular steamboat landing. The village contains about 800 inhabitants; three churches, two public houses, five stores, and two flouring-mills, besides other manufacturing establishments. A railroad is nearly completed, extending from this place to Niagara Falls, being a continuation of the Canandaigua and Niagara Falls Railroad, now completed to the Suspension Bridge A ferry plies from Youngstown to the village of Niagara on the Canada side of the river, here about half a mile in width. This is the first landing, on the American side of the river, after leaving the broad waters of Lake Ontario.

LAKE ONTARIO.

This Lake, the most eastern of the great chain of Lakes of North America, receives the surplus waters of Niagara River; it is 190 miles in length, and 60 miles in extreme breadth; being about 480 miles in circumference. The boundary line between the British Possessions and the United States runs through the middle of the lake, and so continues down the St. Lawrence to the 45th degree of north latitude, where the river enters Canada.

The lake is navigable throughout its whole extent for vessels of the largest size; and it is said to be in some places upward of 600 feet in depth. Its surface is elevated 234 feet above the Atlantic, and lies 330 feet lower than Lake Erie, with which it is connected by the Niagara River and by the Welland Canal in Canada. It has also been proposed to construct a ship canal on the American side. The trade of Lake Ontario, from the great extent of inhabited country surrounding it, is very considerable, and is rapidly increasing. Many sail vessels and splendid steamers are employed in navigating its waters, which, owing to its great depth, never freezes, except at the sides, where the water is shallow; so that its navigation is not so effectually interrupted by ice as some of the other large lakes. The most important places on the Canadian or British side of Lake Ontario are Kingston, Coburg, Port Hope, Toronto, Hamilton, and Niagara; on the American shore, Cape Vincent, Sacket's Harbor, Oswego, Charlotte or Port Genesee, and Lewiston on Niagara River. This lake is connected with the navigable waters of the Hudson River by means of the Oswego and Erie canals. It receives numerous streams, both from the Canadian and the American sides, and abounds with a great variety of fish of an excellent flavor. The bass and salmon, in particular, have a high reputation, and are taken in large quantities. The principal Bays are Burlington, Irondequoit, Great and Little Sodus, Mexico, Black River, Chaumont, and the picturesque waters of the Bay of Quinte.

The passage across Lake Ontario in calm weather is most agreeable. At times both shores are hidden from view, when nothing can be seen from the deck of the vessel but an abyss of waters. The refractions which sometimes take place in summer, are exceedingly beautiful. Islands and trees appear turned upside down; and the white surf of the beach, translated aloft, seems like the smoke of artillery blazing away from a fort.*

* **Beautiful Mirage.**—That grand phenomenon occasionally witnessed on the Lakes—mirage—was seen from the steamer Bay State, on a recent trip from Niagara to Genesee River (August, 1856), with more than ordinary splendor. The Lockport *Journal* says it occurred just as the sun was setting, at which time some twelve vessels were seen reflected on the horizon, in an inverted position, with a distinctness and vividness truly surprising. The atmosphere was overcast with a thick haze such as precedes a storm, and of a color favorable to represent upon the darkened background, vividly, the full outlines of the rigging, sails, etc., as perfect as if the ships themselves were actually transformed to the aerial canvas. The unusual phenomenon lasted until darkness put an end to the scene.

ROUTE AROUND LAKE ONTARIO.

	Miles.
Kingston, C. W., to Toronto, *via Grand Trunk Railway.*	160
Toronto to Hamilton, C. W., *Toronto and Hamilton R.R.*	38
Hamilton to Suspension Bridge, *via Great Western R.R.*.	43
Suspension Bridge to Rochester, N. Y, *via N. Y. Central Railway*	76
Rochester to Oswego, N. Y., by *stage*........	70
Oswego to Richland, N. Y., . "	35
Richland to Cape Vincent, *via Watertown and Rome R.R.*	55
Cape Vincent to Kingston, C. W., *via Wolfe Island*......	12
Total Miles	489

Note.—The extreme length of L. Ontario is 190 miles, from Cape Vincent to Hamilton, C. W.; being about four times as long as its greatest width. The circuit of the water is estimated at 480 miles. See *Lake Erie*, page 163.

AMERICAN STEAMBOAT ROUTE FROM LEWISTON TO OSWEGO, KINGSTON, AND OGDENSBURGH.

Ports, etc.	Miles.	Ports, etc.	Miles.
LEWISTON	0	OGDENSBURGH	0
Youngstown	6	*Morristown*	11
Niagara, Can.......	1–7	*Brockville*, Can......	1–12
Charlotte, or *Port Genesee*	80–87	Thousand Islands...	
Pultneyville.........	20-107	*Alexandria Bay*.....	22–34
Sodus Point..........	10–117	*Clayton*, or *French Creek*...........	12–46
OSWEGO	30–147	Grand, or Wolfe Island	
Stoney Point and Island	33–180	KINGSTON, Can......	24–70
Sacket's Harbor......	12–192	*Sacket's Harbor*.....	38–108
Grand, or Wolfe Island	28–220	Stoney Point and Island	12–120
KINGSTON, Can.	10–230	OSWEGO.............	33–153
Thousand Islands...		Sodus Point	30–183
Clayton, or *French Creek*...........	24–254	*Pultneyville*.	10–193
Alexandria Bay... .	12–266	*Charlotte*, or *Port Genesee*	20–213
Brockville, Can.	22–288	*Niagara*, Can.......	80–293
Morristown	1–289	*Youngstown*	1–294
OGDENSBURGH.......	11–300	LEWISTON...........	6–300

USUAL TIME from Lewiston to Ogdensburgh, *via* Oswego and Kingston, 28 hours.

USUAL TIME, *via* Toronto and Cape Vincent, 22 hours.

Cabin Fare, $5 50 (including meals). Deck Fare, $2 50.

STEAMBOAT ROUTE FROM LEWISTON TO TORONTO AND OGDENSBURGH, *via* EXPRESS LINE.

Ports, etc.	Miles.	Ports, etc.	Miles.
LEWISTON..........	0	OGDENSBURGH	0
NIAGARA	7	*Brockville*, Can,.....	11
TORONTO, Can......	42–49	*Clayton*, or *French Creek*..........	34–45
Point Peter and Light	128–177		
Duck Island........	30–207	CAPE VINCENT.....	13–58
Tibbet's Point and L.	19–226	Tibbet's Point	3–61

Ports, etc.	Miles.	Ports, etc.	Miles.
CAPE VINCENT.....	3–229	Duck Island........	19–80
Clayton, or *French Creek*.........	13–242	Point Peter and Light	30–110
Brockville, Can.....	34–276	TORONTO...........	128–238
OGDENSBURGH.....	11–297	NIAGARA..........	42–280
		LEWISTON..........	7–287

USUAL FARE, from Ogdensburgh to Montreal, $3 50
Through Fare, from Lewiston to Montreal, 9 00
" " from Buffalo to Montreal, 10 00

AMERICAN STEAMERS.

ONTARIO AND ST. LAWRENCE STEAMBOAT COMPANY'S OFFICE, OSWEGO, N. Y.

E. B. Allen, *Pres.*, Ogdensburgh.
Jas. Van Cleve, Sec. and Treas., Lewiston.

Steamer BAY STATE,	1,098 tons	....	Capt. John Ledyard.
" NEW YORK,	1,200 "	....	" R. B. Chapman.
" NORTHERNER,	905 "	....	" R. F. Child.
" CATARACT,	577 "	....	" Jas. R. Ester.
" NIAGARA,	473 "	....	" John Morley.
" ONTARIO,	832 "	....	" H. N. Throop.

One of the above steamers leaves Lewiston daily for Charlotte, Oswego, Sacket's Harbor, Kingston, and Ogdensburgh, returning by the way of Cape Vincent, Toronto, etc., to Lewiston.

A steamer of the same line also leaves Lewiston daily for Toronto, Cape Vincent, and Ogdensburgh, returning by the way of Sacket's Harbor, Oswego, Charlotte, etc., to Lewiston, connecting with cars running to Niagara Falls, Buffalo, etc.

ST. LAWRENCE RIVER STEAMERS,

RUNNING IN CONNECTION WITH THE ABOVE BOATS, FORMING A THROUGH LINE TO MONTREAL.

Steamer BRITISH QUEEN,	300 tons.	.....	Capt. A. Cameron.
" JENNY LIND,	300 "	......	" L. Moody.
" MONTREAL,	300 "	......	" John Laflame.

One of the above steamers leaves Ogdensburgh, daily, during the season of navigation, for Montreal, passing by daylight through the Rapids of the St. Lawrence, returning through the Canals.

Fort Niagara.—Mouth Niagara River.

TRIP FROM LEWISTON TO OSWEGO, KINGSTON, AND OGDENSBURGH.

DURING the season of navigation, steamers of a large class, belonging to the *Ontario and St. Lawrence Steamboat Company*, leave Lewiston daily, following the south or American shore to the foot of Lake Ontario, and thence to Ogdensburgh, on the St. Lawrence River.

On leaving the wharf at Lewiston, a most beautiful and extensive view is afforded of Niagara River, the lower Suspension Bridge, Brock's Monument on Queenston Heights, and the villages of Lewiston and Queenston, with the Mountain Ridge in the background. When are associated the stirring historical events connected with this vicinity, no spot exceeds it in interest. The banks of the river are here elevated from 40 to 50 feet, with bold shores, while the water rushes onward into Lake Ontario, the receptacle of all the waters of the Upper Lakes.

FORT NIAGARA, seven miles below Lewiston, lying on the American shore at the mouth of the Niagara River, is well worthy of a visit in connection with the ruins of *Fort George*, on the Canadian shore, near the village of Niagara. In 1679, M. De Salle, the explorer of the Mississippi, in the service of France, inclosed the spot on which the fort was here built in 1725, by palisades. In 1759 it was taken by the British, under Sir William Johnson, in whose hands it remained until 1796, when it was evacuated and given up to the United States. On the 19th of December, 1813, it was again taken by the British by surprise; and in March, 1815, again surrendered to the Americans. This old fort is as much noted for being the theater of tyranny and crime as for the scenes of military exploits. While in the hands of the French, there is no doubt of its having been at times used as a prison. In its close and impregnable dungeons, where light was not admitted, for many years there remained clear traces of the ready instruments for execution or for murder. During the war of the Revolution it was the head-quarters of all that was barbarous and unrelenting and cruel; this being the chief rendezvous of a savage horde that carried death and destruction into the remote American settlements. Of late years, the abduction of William Morgan, who was taken from the jail in Canandaigua, and conveyed more than 100 miles through a populous country, and lodged in the magazine at Fort Niagara, where he was kept three or four days, and then inhumanly drowned—has justly tended to continue its reputation for being the scene of tyranny and murder.

On passing out of the mouth of the Niagara River, and reaching the broad waters of Lake Ontario, a deeply interesting view is afforded of the town of Niagara and Fort Niagara, situated on opposite sides of the river, while in the distance may be seen Brock's Monument, rising nearly 500 feet above the waters of the lake, being eight or ten miles distant.

The steamer now pursues an easterly course in running for Charlotte, or Port Genesee, 80 miles from the mouth of Niagara River. The shores of the lake of a clear day are generally in sight, presenting an elevated and bold appearance for many miles. Eighteen Mile Creek, Thirty Mile Creek, and Oak Orchard River are passed in succession; at the mouth of each there are harbors and small settlements. *Braddock's Point* is a bold headland ten miles west of the mouth of the Genesee River.

Charlotte, or Port Genesee, 80 miles from the mouth of Niagara River, and 60 miles west from Oswego, is situated at the mouth of Genesee River, seven miles by railroad below the city of Rochester, it being the outport for that place. It is a port of entry, possessing a safe harbor, being protected by two long government piers, on one of which is located a light; there is also a light-house on the mainland. The village contains about 400 inhabitants, two churches, three hotels, four stores, four warehouses, one steam elevator, one steam saw-mill, and an extensive brick-yard. American and British steamers run direct from Charlotte to Cobourg, Port Hope, Toronto, etc., on the Canada side of the lake; also to Oswego, Sacket's Harbor, etc., on the American side, all connecting at Charlotte with railroad cars for Rochester.

The FALLS of the Genesee, near Rochester, are well worthy attention. The banks of the river immediately above Charlotte rise from 50 to 150 feet in height, presenting a fine appearance. The river is navigable for five or six miles to the first fall at Carthage, within the city bounds of Rochester; then other falls occur, the principal and most interesting being near the center of the city, it extending on both sides of the stream. The water-power here afforded is very great, being used to a great extent in propelling flour-mills, saw-mills, etc

GENESEE RIVER, a deeply interesting and romantic stream, rises in Potter Co., Pa., on the great table-land of Western Pennsylvania, interlocking with some of the head sources of the Alleghany and west branch of the Susquehanna River; it then pursues a north course to the New York State line, thence through the county of Allegany; then by many short turnings through the rich and fertile valley of the Genesee, which extends through Monroe County, where it falls into Lake Ontario, six miles below the city of Rochester. Its whole course is about 145 miles. Near its mouth, within the present city limits of Rochester, are two or three important falls, known as the *Genesee Falls;* within the distance of three miles there being an estimated descent of 226 feet; the great falls at Rochester are 96 feet, at Carthage 75, an intermediate one of 20, and the rest, rapids or small falls; altogether affording an immense amount of hydraulic power, which is used to a great extent, particularly at the Upper Falls, in propelling flouring-mills, and different kinds of manufacturing establishments. From the landing at Carthage, which constitutes a part of the city of Rochester, there is a steamboat navigation to Charlotte, or Port Genesee, a distance of four miles, where is a good harbor communicating with Lake Ontario. From the head of the rapids above Rochester it is navigable during high water for a considerable distance, passing through a rich and interesting region of country, celebrated for its fertility. This stream now constitutes the main feeder of the *Genesee Valley Canal*, which runs parallel to it for the greater part of its length through the State. There are also important falls on this river, both in Allegany and Livingston counties, where are to be found some of its most interesting features. In the town of Portage, Allegany Co., "there are three distinct falls on the river, respectively 60, 90, and 110 feet, within the space of two miles, each differing in character, and each having peculiar beauties. Although the cascades are highly admirable, they are almost disregarded in the wonder and fear caused by the stupendous, perpendicular walls of the river, rising to 400 feet in height, and extending along the stream for three miles, with almost as much regularity as if constructed by art. To this great depth the river has worn its bed in the solid rock, in turns as short and graceful as if winding through the softest meadow."

After leaving Charlotte for Oswego the steamer passes *Pultneyville* (occasionally stopping), Great Sodus Bay and Little Sodus Bay, running within sight of the south shore; the lake here presenting an irregular coast-line.

GREAT SODUS BAY is a fine sheet of water, affording a secure harbor for lake craft, being from one to three miles wide and five miles long. The fishing is here good, as well as in all the bays along the south shore of the lake.

SODUS POINT, Wayne Co., N. Y., situated at the entrance of Great Sodus Bay, is a port of entry, with a good harbor, and contains a church, a public house, two stores, a steam saw-mill, and about 300 inhabitants.

LITTLE SODUS BAY, 14 miles east of Great Sodus, is another important body of water. "At Little Sodus, in high winds, vessels can often come within the protection of Long Point on one side, and the protecting shores west, between it and Big Sodus, and ride out the storm in the indented shore of the lake, and can. when the improvements to Little Sodus harbor are completed, enter the bay with ease, and take refuge there. This fact gives great advantages to Little Sodus Bay, as it makes it accessible at all times."

The City of OSWEGO, 36 miles north of Syracuse by railroad, is advantageously situated on both sides of Oswego River, at its entrance into Lake Ontario. It is a port of entry, was chartered in 1848, being divided into four wards. In 1855 it contained 16,000 inhabitants, 1,500 dwelling-houses, two Presbyterian, two Episcopal, two Baptist, two Methodist, two Roman Catholic, one Universalist, and one African church, besides a Bethel congregation; a court-house and jail, a custom-house, four banking houses, two savings' banks; a gas company, a female seminary, and orphan asylum. There are several well-kept hotels; the Munger House and the Hamilton House on the east side of the river, and the Welland House on the west side, are the most frequented by pleasure travelers. The Pardee House is a new and commodious hotel which is nearly completed, situated on the west side of the river, near the steamboat landing.

The *Oswego and Syracuse Railroad*, 36 miles in length, connects this place with the Central Railroad of New York, while another railroad is being constructed on the east side of the Oswego River, to run to Syracuse and connect with the Syracuse and Binghamton Railroad, thus forming another direct route to the cities of New York and Philadelphia, and the coal region of Pennsylvania. The *Oswego Canal* also connects with the Erie Canal at Syracuse, altogether affording great facilities for trade and commerce, in connection with the lake navigation and water privilege. Here are now in operation 15 flouring-mills, with 84 run of stones, making 8,400 barrels of flour per day when in full operation; ten elevators capable of elevating 38,000 bushels of grain per hour, with storage room for 2,000,000 bushels. These huge edifices are so arranged as to unload and load vessels with great dispatch.

The *Oswego Starch Factory*, owned by an incorporated body, was erected in 1848, since which large additions have been made. The entire front of the building is now 510 feet, five stories high, extending back over the river 250 feet; it is capable of manufacturing twelve millions pounds of corn starch per year, consuming some 600,000 bushels of corn for the purpose, and giving employment to 300 persons. In addition to the above are two steam-engine and machine works, two iron and brass foundries, one cotton-mill, besides several other mills and factories.

The quantity of water flowing in the Oswego River at ordinary high water is 700,000 cubic feet per minute, at low water 200,000. Fall at the two lower dams in the city, 36 feet, affording altogether an immense and reliable water-power.

The number of vessels which arrive and depart annually from this port is very large; there being here owned eight steamers and propellers and about 100 schooners, averaging over 100 tons burden, besides a large number of canal boats. The harbor is capacious and safe, being well protected by two large stone piers, constructed by the United States government. On the end of the west pier is situated a light-house; about half a mile above are two bridges extending across the river, 600 feet in length. An extensive forwarding business is done at this place by means of lake, river, and canal navigation; goods passing through from New York to Oswego, and thence over the Collingwood route, or through the Welland Canal to the Upper Lakes.

Oswego now ranks as one of the greatest grain markets in the world, and will no doubt continue to increase with the growth and production of the Western States and Canada. The lumber trade is also very great, immense quantities being shipped from Canada to this port, and re-shipped to Eastern markets.

The impulse imparted to the commerce of Oswego by the late Reciprocity Treaty, which went into force October, 1854, is very great, as will be seen by the following returns made from official figures:

	1854.	1855.
Value of Foreign Imports........	$2,860,918	$6.139,743
" " Exports........	3,734,168	5,870,920
Total..........	$6,595,086	$12,010,663

Here it will be seen that the trade with Canada nearly doubled in the first year under the operation of the above treaty. The domestic or coastwise trade is also constantly and rapidly increasing.

One of the Steamers of the Ontario and St. Lawrence Steamboat Company leaves Oswego daily for Sacket's Harbor, Kingston, C. W., and Ogdensburgh, connecting with steamers running to Montreal and Rouse's Point, *via* the Northern Railroad of New York.

A steamer also leaves Oswego daily, for Rochester, Niagara, C. W., and Lewiston, connecting with steamers for Toronto, etc.

The *Toronto and Collingwood* line of steamers runs daily, Sundays excepted, from Oswego to Toronto, 150 miles, forming the most direct route through Lake Ontario to the Upper Lakes.

RAILROAD AND STEAMBOAT ROUTE FROM SYRACUSE TO NIAGARA FALLS, *via* OSWEGO AND LEWISTON.

This route, during the season of navigation on Lake Ontario, is a most interesting line of travel, affording the tourist a fine opportunity of viewing the scenery peculiar to Lake Ontario and Niagara River.

The *Oswego and Syracuse Railroad*, 35 miles in length, runs along the west side of Onondaga Lake to the Seneca River, which is passed near Baldwinsville, the first stopping-place after leaving Syracuse. From thence the road runs north on the west side of Oswego River, passing opposite to the village of Fulton, 11 miles from the city of Oswego. Passenger cars usually leave Syracuse and Oswego three times daily.

American steamers leave Oswego daily for Sacket's Harbor, Kingston, Canada, Ogdensburgh, etc., in the morning, on the arrival of the cars from Syracuse; while in the afternoon a steamer leaves for Rochester, Lewiston, etc., running up the lake. Passengers passing through Oswego are afforded a hasty glance of the city, the harbor, and Fort Ontario, the latter being located on the east shore of the river at its entrance into Lake Ontario.

DISTANCES AND FARE BETWEEN SYRACUSE AND NIAGARA FALLS, *via* OSWEGO AND LEWISTON.

Stopping Places.	Miles.	Fare.	Stopping Places.	Miles.	Fare.
SYRACUSE	0		NIAGARA FALLS	0	
OSWEGO	35	$1 00	LEWISTON	6	$0 50
Pultneyville	75	—	NIAGARA, C.W.	14	—
CHARLOTTE, or Port Genesee	100	—	CHARLOTTE, or Port Genesee	88	—
NIAGARA, C. W.	174	—	Pultneyville	113	—
LEWISTON	182	—	OSWEGO	153	—
NIAGARA FALLS	188	4 00	SYRACUSE	188	4 00

On resuming the trip from Oswego to Sacket's Harbor, the steamer runs in a northerly direction off *Mexico Bay*, being a large expanse of water at the east end of Lake Ontario, where lies PORT ONTARIO, at the mouth of Salmon River. On this stream is situated one of the most romantic falls in the country.

SALMON RIVER rises in Lewis Co., and flows west through Oswego Co. into Lake Ontario; discharging its waters into Mexico Bay, at the village of Port Ontario. This is a fine and durable stream, having a tolerably good harbor at its mouth, and is boatable during high water to the Falls in Orwell, a distance of 14 miles. "The *Falls of Salmon River* may be classed among the principal natural curiosities of the country. The current is gentle above for six or more miles, then two miles of rapids, and at the falls drops almost perpendicular 107 feet. At high water the sheet is 250 feet in width, but at low water it is narrowed down to about half that extent. The rocky strata seem to be composed of slate stone and granite, or gneiss, and the height of the banks immediately above the fall is variously estimated at from 70 to 90 feet; below it is said that the walls, perpendicular rock, are about 200 feet. At the foot of the cataract there is very deep water, abounding in fine fish, such as salmon, trout, etc."

Great Stoney Island and other islands are passed as the steamer approaches Black River Bay, which affords the most capacious and safe harbor on Lake Ontario. Here enters Black River, an important stream, which rises many miles to the eastward, interlocking with the waters of the Mohawk and other tributaries of the Hudson River.

Sacket's Harbor, 45 miles north of Oswego, and distant 38 miles from Kingston, Canada, possesses one of the best and most secure harbors on Lake Ontario, being situated on *Black River Bay*, ten miles below Watertown, with which place it is soon to be connected by a railroad. It was an important naval and military station during the war of 1812, with Great Britain; it being the rendezvous of the American fleet on Lake Ontario. Here now lies a large war vessel under cover, which was commenced at the above period. *Madison Barracks*, garrisoned by United States troops, is handsomely situated near the steamboat landing, being in full view from the water.

This place is an important port of entry, and no doubt destined to increase in wealth and numbers on the opening of railroad facilities. The village now contains four churches, two hotels, twenty stores, four storehouses, a ship-yard and rope-walk, three saw-mills, two furnaces, an iron foundry and machine-shop.

The *Sacket's Harbor and Ellisburgh Railroad*, 18 miles in length, connects with the Watertown and Rome Railroad.

Black River, so called from the color of its water, is the third in magnitude that has its whole course in the State of New York. Its whole course is about 120 miles, and is navigable from the High Falls in Leyden, where it has a fall of 63 feet, to the Long Falls at Carthage, a distance of 40 miles; thence, by a succession of rapids and falls, it continues a circuitous route, until it empties into *Black River Bay*, near the foot of Lake Ontario. It is a deep, sluggish stream, but the navigation is much obstructed by falls; affording, however, fine water-power. The land on the borders of the lower part of the river is very fertile and thickly settled; Jefferson County—and the vicinity of Watertown in particular, where is a good water power—is justly celebrated for its agricultural products.

CHAUMONT BAY, situated north of Sacket's Harbor at Black River Bay, is a large body of water abounding in fish of several kinds and fine flavor; here being extensive fisheries, where are annually taken large quantities of fish.

The trip across the foot of Lake Ontario from Sacket's Harbor to Kingston, Can., 38 miles, is a very interesting excursion during pleasant weather. Here may be seen beautiful headlands and several picturesque islands; the Fox and Grenadier islands are passed before reaching *Grand* or *Wolfe Island*, attached to Canada. This latter island, situated in the St. Lawrence River, at the foot of Lake Ontario, is a large and fertile body of land, being settled by Canadians.

CAPE VINCENT, Jefferson Co., N. Y., is situated at the head of the St. Lawrence River, where terminates the *Watertown and Rome Railroad*, and is a port of entry. It contains about 1,100 inhabitants, four churches, five hotels and taverns, ten stores, and an extensive storehouse connected with the railroad; one steam grist-mill, one foundry and machine-shop, one steam planing-mill, and a ship-yard. Steamers arrive and depart daily for different ports on Lake Ontario and the St. Lawrence River. A steamer also leaves Cape Vincent twice daily for Kingston, Canada, during navigation; while in winter, stages run across the ice to Grand or Wolfe Island, and thence to Kingston, distant 12 miles by direct route. Cape Vincent is a healthy and pleasant location, being much resorted to in warm weather by fishing and pleasure parties, being contiguous to the "Thousand Islands."

CLAYTON, or FRENCH CREEK, 18 miles below Cape Vincent, lies opposite Grindstone Island, attached to the State of New York. The village contains three churches, two public houses, ten stores, and a foundry and machine-shop. Here is an extensive ship-yard for the construction of steamers and other lake craft.

The *Black River and Utica Railroad*, when completed, will extend to Clayton, a distance of 109 miles from Utica.

ALEXANDRIA BAY, 12 miles below Clayton, is favorably situated on the southeast shore of the St. Lawrence, in the immediate vicinity of the greatest cluster of the Thousand Islands. The village contains one Presbyterian church, two good hotels for the accommodation of summer visitors, three stores, a steam saw-mill, a ship-yard, and about 350 inhabitants. No place on the St. Lawrence River exceeds this vicinity for its salubrity of climate and picturesque water scenery. The islands here, almost innumerable, are annually resorted to by visitors from almost every section of the country for health, and to enjoy the pleasure of fishing and hunting.

WELL'S ISLAND is settled by some 20 or 30 families, and is, no doubt, destined to become a favorite resort, as a hotel is projected, to be located near the foot of this lovely island.

MORRISTOWN, N. Y., 11 miles above Ogdensburgh, lies nearly opposite Brockville, C. W., with which it is connected by a ferry. This is a regular landing-place for the American steamers. The village contains two churches, two taverns, three stores, and about 350 inhabitants.

OGDENSBURGH, St. Lawrence Co., N. Y., is advantageously situated at the mouth of the Oswegatchie River where it empties into the St. Lawrence. It was first incorporated as a village in 1817, and now contains about 8,000 inhabitants, 1,000 dwelling-houses; one each Episcopal, Presbyterian, Baptist, Methodist, and Roman Catholic church—and a Universalist congregation; an incorporated academy, three banks, two insurance offices, a custom-house, six public houses, 100 stores of different kinds. The Oswegatchie River here furnishes an abundance of water-power, where are situated one woolen factory, two flouring-mills, three grist-mills, three saw-mills, one paper-mill, two planing-mills and two furnaces, a ship-yard and marine railway. This place is situated near the foot of sloop navigation on the St. Lawrence, although steamers of a large class run the Rapids to Montreal, 120 miles, ascending through the St. Lawrence canals.

Two daily lines of steamers leave Ogdensburgh for Cape Vincent, Kingston, Oswego Toronto, Lewiston, etc., while two daily lines leave Ogdensburgh or Prescott for Montreal, etc. Two steam ferry-boats run across the St. Lawrence, here one mile and a half wide, to Prescott, forming a close connection between the two shores. The *Northern Railroad* extends from Ogdensburgh easterly to Rouse's Point, N. Y., 118 miles, connecting with steamers and railroads extending to Boston and New York. A railroad is also projected to extend from Ogdensburgh and form a junction with the *Potsdam and Watertown Railroad.* Propellers and lake craft annually deposit an immense amount of Western produce, to be carried forward by railroads to Eastern markets. As a stopping-place for pleasure travelers, Ogdensburgh stands unrivaled, having the Thousand Islands above and the magnificent Rapids of the St. Lawrence below. Passengers are here usually transferred from the floating palaces of Lake Ontario to the equally safe but smaller steamers which run the Rapids to Montreal.

The *Northern Transportation Com.* has here its principal office for the trans-shipment of produce and merchandise going East and West. This company owns 15 propellers, of about 350 tons burden, running from Ogdensburgh and Oswego to Cleveland, Toledo, Detroit, Milwaukee, Chicago, etc. This line affords a cheap and speedy route of travel for travelers and emigrants.

The *Oswegatchie River*, which empties into the St. Lawrence at Ogdensburgh, is the outlet of *Black Lake*, lying in the county of St. Lawrence. The lake and river are navigable for about 25 miles, to within four miles of Ogdensburgh. At the mouth of this river, now a part of the village of Ogdensburgh, an early settlement was made by the French, and fortifications erected, all of which have gone to decay.

The Trip from Kingston to Ogdensburgh and Montreal is described in another part of this work, following the Canadian route from Hamilton and Toronto to Kingston, Prescott, and Montreal. For further information, see advertisements of Lake Ontario and River St. Lawrence Steamers.

TRIP FROM NIAGARA AND HAMILTON TO TORONTO AND KINGSTON, CANADA.

AMERICAN and CANADIAN steamers leave Lewiston, or Niagara, C. W., daily for Toronto, 40 miles from the mouth of Niagara River, connecting with railroad cars from Buffalo and Niagara Falls, running on both sides of the river.

A Canadian steamer also leaves Port Dalhousie daily for Toronto, connecting at St. Catherine's with cars on the Great Western Railway, altogether affording great facilities both in summer and winter to resort to the capital of Canada.

On leaving the mouth of Niagara River, the steamer pursues a N.W. course direct for Toronto, having, on a clear day, land constantly in sight from the deck of the steamer. Nothing can exceed the pleasure of this trip during pleasant weather. Usually may be seen propellers and sailing vessels on their way to or from Port Dalhousie, the mouth of the Welland Canal, a magnificent work, of which the Canadians are justly proud.

PORT DALHOUSIE, 12 miles west of the mouth of Niagara River, and distant 38 miles from Toronto, is a small village situated at the terminus of the Welland Canal, four miles below St. Catherine's, with which place it is connected by the *Port Dalhousie and Thorold Railroad,* five miles in length, connecting with the Great Western Railway.

The WELLAND CANAL, 28 miles in length, connecting Lake Erie with Lake Ontario, and overcoming the Falls of Niagara, is a work alike beneficial to the commercial interests of the United States and Canada, the former paying by far the greatest amount of tolls. The number of locks are 27, being 150 feet in length and 26½ feet wide. The total rise is 330 feet. The depth of water is 8½ feet, the canal being 45 feet wide at bottom and 81 feet at the surface. The feeder branch, from Junction to Dunnville, is 21 miles long. The Broad Creek branch from feeder to Port Maitland, the terminus on Lake Erie, is 1½ miles in length, with one lock each. The entire cost of the enlarged canal was about £1,000,000 Canadian currency, or $4,000,000.

St. Catherine's, 38 miles south of Toronto by water, 11 miles from Suspension Bridge, and 32 miles from Hamilton by railroad route, is advantageously situated on the line of the Welland Canal, here affording a large amount of water-power. This town is a place of great attraction and growing importance, being surrounded by a healthy and rich section of country. Here is a mineral fountain called the "*Artesian Well*," also several large and well-kept hotels, for the accommodation of invalids and seekers of pleasure. The Stevenson House, near the Spring, and the Welland Hotel, are the most frequented by pleasure travelers.

The village contains about 5,000 inhabitants, several fine churches and private edifices, here being exhibited a degree of taste and activity equal to any other town of its size in Canada or the United States. If the mineral waters prove as beneficial to invalids as is represented by many who have experienced their beneficial effects, it is no doubt destined to become a popular watering-place during the summer months. The "Well" is situated near the bank of the canal, and is 550 feet in depth; the water being raised by a steam pump to the bath-house, situated on the bank above.

The City of Hamilton, from its geographical position, and its peculiar natural and artificial advantages, lying on Burlington Bay, at the extreme west end of Lake Ontario, has within the last five or six years rapidly increased in wealth and numbers. But a few short years have passed away since the site on which now stands the crowded city, with its stately edifices and its elegant residences, its thronged streets, and its marts and factories teeming with life and business activity, was a dense forest, the residence and hunting-ground of the Indian. It was not many years ago that the waters of its beautiful bay, which now bear upon their bosom magnificent steamers and vessels of every grade, bringing to our port the treasures of other lands, and conveying to Eastern markets the products of the West, were calm and unruffled, save when the red man launched his barque upon the blue expanse, or when lashed into fury by the angry tempest.

Hamilton was first laid out in the year 1813, during the war with the United States, but for many years it progressed but slowly in population and importance. By the census of 1841 it numbered 3,446 inhabitants. During the succeeding four years the population nearly doubled, and by the census of 1851 the numbers had increased to 10,248. From that period to the present the city has progressed with almost unexampled rapidity for Canada. The commencement and completion of the Great Western Railway gave an impetus to all kinds of business. New streets were opened, and handsome edifices sprung up as if by magic in all parts of the city, as well as the more humble edifices. The population is now (1856) estimated at 25,000, the wealth having increased in greater proportion

By the following amounts of assessment of real and personal property during the past six years, it will be seen the value has more than trebled, and since 1852—three years—nearly doubled:

Valuation in	1850....	£61,574	Valuation in	1853...	£134,353
"	1851....	94,259	"	1854...	156,926
"	1852....	105,349	"	1855...	190,479

The city is governed by a mayor and board of aldermen and councilors, together with a police department. The public buildings are a city hall, city hospital, post-office building, twenty churches of different denominations, five banks, and a mechanics' institute. A new custom-house and market building are about being erected, both on a large scale and in a durable style of architecture.

The principal hotels are the Anglo-American, King Street, and City Hotel, James Street.

Steamers of a large class run from Hamilton to Toronto, Kingston, and other ports on both sides of Lake Ontario, affording a speedy and delightful mode of conveyance, not only through the lakes, but down the St. Lawrence River to Prescott, Ogdensburgh, and Montreal. For description of railroad route to Detroit, see page 150.

WELLINGTON SQUARE, seven miles below Hamilton, is a place of some importance, it being the outport for Hamilton during the winter months, when the lake is obstructed by ice.

BRONTE, 13 miles below Hamilton, is a small village containing about 400 inhabitants. Here are two public houses, two churches, a grist-mill, a cloth factory, and several lumber yards.

OAKVILLE, 19 miles from Hamilton, and about the same distance from Toronto, is a place of considerable business, having a good harbor. It contains about 1,000 inhabitants; four churches, several public houses and stores; a foundry, and other manufacturing establishments. The country in the rear is healthy and productive, being drained by several fine streams.

PORT CREDIT, 12 miles from Toronto, is a large shipping port for produce of different kinds. It is situated at the mouth of River Credit, here flowing into Lake Ontario. It was once a favorite resort of the Indians, receiving its name, in early times, from the circumstance of the fur traders here meeting the Indians, and delivering to them on *credit* their goods, for which the following year they received their value in furs.

TORONTO.

THE City of TORONTO, and capital of Canada, is favorably situated on Toronto Bay, in 43° 32′ N. lat., and 79° 20′ W long. from Greenwich. It is 40 miles N.E. Hamilton, 160 W. from Kingston, 333 from Montreal, and 413 from Quebec by railroad route. The bay is a beautiful sheet of water, about 4 miles long and 2 miles wide, separated from the main body of Lake Ontario, except at its entrance, by a long, narrow strip of sandy beach, the southwest termination of which is known as Gibraltar Point, on which is located a light-house.

"*Toronto* signifies, in the Indian language, *a place of meeting*. In 1793, when surveyed by the elder Bouchette, under the orders of Gov. Simcoe, two Massasauga families were the only inhabitants it contained, and the harbor was a resort for numerous wild fowl, while its waters produced an abundance of fish." It was incorporated as a city in 1834, when it contained 9,254 inhabitants. In 1842 it had increased to 15,436; in 1852, to 30,763; and in 1856, to over 50,000. It is laid out with wide streets, crossing each other at right angles. The esplanade fronting the bay extends for a distance of two miles. The city is lighted with gas, and is well supplied with pure water by companies incorporated for those purposes.

The principal public buildings are the Parliament House, the University of Toronto, Trinity College, Upper Canada College, the Lunatic Asylum, the Custom House, the Post Office, St. James' Church (the English cathedral), and the Roman Catholic Cathedral; besides which there are a great number of churches of different denominations. The Bank of Upper Canada has its head office here, and there are other banks and agencies; also several Fire and Marine Insurance Companies. This is the principal office of the Canada Land Company, which has nearly two millions of acres of land for sale, situated in various parts of the Province. The hotels and public houses are numerous and well kept, making this city a desirable sojourn. Russell's Hotel, the Clarendon, the American, Sword's Hotel, and a new hotel on King Street, are the principal public houses.

Toronto has become a great thoroughfare by means of steamers and railroads. A constant intercourse is thus kept up with the different ports on Lake Ontario, the Upper Lakes, and the St. Lawrence River. Steamers run from Toronto to Hamilton, St. Catherine's, Niagara, and Lewiston on the west and south; to Rochester and Oswego on the east; and to Cape Vincent, Kingston, Prescott, Montreal, etc., on the northeast.

The *Ontario, Simcoe and Huron Railroad*, 94 miles in length, terminates at Collingwood, on Georgian Bay, connecting with the waters of Lake Huron. The *Grand Trunk Railway* extends northeast to Montreal and Quebec, while its western termination will be at Port Sarnia, lying at the foot of Lake Huron. The *Toronto and Hamilton Railroad*, a branch of the *Great Western Railway* of Canada, also terminates here, affording altogether facilities of great benefit to Toronto and the whole of Canada.

The markets of Toronto are abundantly supplied with every description of provisions of the best quality, and at moderate prices. The climate is healthy and delightful during the summer and fall months, being modified by lake breezes.

"TRADE OF TORONTO.—The value of imports into Toronto last year (1856) amounted to £1,738,657, showing an increase on those of 1855 of £338,247. £822,335 were from Great Britain, £14,797 from B. A. Colonies, £365,404 from the United States, and from other foreign countries £36,119. The duties collected on these imports were £195,159, showing an increase of £42,584. The exports during 1856 were £551,333 (of which £176,703 was of flour, and £202,792 of wheat), showing an increase of £147,258.

"There were shipped during the year 1855 to American ports 601.524 bushels of wheat, and 118,807 barrels of flour; during 1856, 1,132,781 bushels wheat, and 97,935 barrels flour. To Canada ports 27,230 bushels wheat, and 32,370 barrels flour, in 1855; and 92,561 bushels wheat, and 73,824 barrels flour, in 1856.

"The increase in the shipments of wheat, it will be seen, are equal to 100 per cent. over those of last year, while the increase in flour, although not large, is respectable. Reducing the flour into wheat, at the rate of five bushels per barrel, we have the following for the two seasons:

	Bushels.		Value.
1856.............	2,084,007	at 7s.	£729,402
1855.............	1,384,639	at 10s.	692,319
Increase.....	699,368		£37,083

"The increase in value is not so great as the increase in quantity, owing to the fact that grain has sold at 25 per cent. lower in 1856 than it did in 1855.

"The returns of the Custom House set down the value of agricultural produce sent to the United States at £524,241. which is very correct; add, however, that sent to Canada ports—say £230,000—making the total exports upward of £750,000."

PORT WHITBY, 29 miles below Toronto, lies on the line of the Grand Trunk Railway, where is a steamboat landing, at which steamers land on their route from Toronto to Rochester, etc.

OSHAWA, 33 miles below Toronto by railroad route, is handsomely situated a short distance from the lake shore and has a good harbor. It contains five churches, two hotels, 15 stores, two woolen factories, two tanneries and a brewery, besides other manufacturing establishments. Population, 2,500.

BOWMANVILLE, 43 miles from Toronto, lying a short distance from the lake, is connected with *Darlington Harbor*, where is a steamboat landing.

PORT HOPE is a port of entry situated on the north shore of Lake Ontario, 62 miles from Toronto and 98 miles from Kingston by railroad route. This is a safe harbor, where steamers land daily from different ports on the lake, which together with sail vessels export large quantities of produce. The village contains a court-house, six churches, four hotels, 40 stores; two flouring-mills, a woolen factory, two iron foundries, a machine-shop, two tanneries, two breweries, and six distilleries. The lumber trade carried on at this port is very extensive and profitable. Population, 3,500. In addition to the *Grand Trunk Railway*, which runs through the town, a railroad runs from Port Hope to Beaverton, situated on Lake Simcoe, a distance of 41 miles, thus opening a fine section of Canada to emigration and trade.

From Port Hope, or Cobourg, going toward Kingston by railroad route, there is to be seen a fine section of Canada, passing through several flourishing towns, and near the Bay of Quinte.

COBOURG, handsomely situated on the north shore of Lake Ontario, nearly opposite the mouth of Genesee River, where the lake attains its greatest width, is 70 miles from Toronto, 90 miles from Kingston, and 263 miles from Montreal by railroad route. It possesses a good harbor and is much frequented by steamers and sailing vessels, it being one of the regular landings for the Royal Mail Steamers, which pass and repass, daily, on their way up and down the lake.

The principal public buildings in Cobourg are the court-house and jail, and the Victoria College, which was established in 1842, by Act of the Provincial Legislature, with power to grant degrees in the arts and sciences; there are also a number of fine church edifices. Here are the most extensive cloth manufactories in the Province; there are also iron, marble, and leather manufactories, with breweries and distilleries, six hotels and taverns, 40 or 50 stores of different kinds, and a number of mechanic shops. Population, 6,000. Few places in Canada present a more beautiful appearance from the water than Cobourg—the landscape being extensive and varied by a most delightful background.

The *Cobourg and Peterboro' Railroad*, 28 miles in length, commences at this place, which, together with the Grand Trunk Railway, tends greatly to benefit Cobourg and the towns lying on the rear, in the vicinity of *Rice Lake.*

Colborne, 14 miles below Cobourg, is situated on the line of the Grand Trunk Railway. Here is a good landing for vessels and a flourishing settlement.

On leaving Cobourg for Kingston on the downward trip, the steamer usually runs out into the broad waters of Lake Ontario, soon attaining their greatest width. Often during the prevalence of storms or high winds, the unacclimated voyager experiences sensations any thing but agreeable; sea-sickness often prostrating alike the athletic male and the delicate female. This however, on board the larger class steamers is no serious objection to journeying across Lake Ontario, it being considered the most safe navigation of any of the great lakes.

Nicholas Point and *Island* are passed about 40 miles from Cobourg. Next comes *Wicked Point*, and soon heaves in sight *Point Peter* and *Light.* This light is a conspicuous object for the mariner, who often, when off Prince Edward, the mainland, experiences the full force of easterly and westerly winds.

Duck Island, attached to Canada is another noted object for the mariner, either descending or ascending Lake Ontario, as this is the first important island to be met on descending from the head of the lake on the Canada side.

Outer Drake and *Inner Drake* are two small islands situated inland toward Prince Edward's Bay.

AMHERST ISLAND, a large and fertile body of land, is next passed on the left, while *Gage Island* and *Grand* or *Wolfe Island* may be seen on the right; these latter islands being situated at the foot of Lake Ontario, or mouth of the St. Lawrence River, where commences the celebrated "*Thousand Islands.*"

The City of KINGSTON, capital of Frontenac Co., Canada, 160 miles from Toronto, and 173 miles from Montreal by railroad route, is very advantageously situated on a beautiful harbor at the northeast extremity of Lake Ontario, and immediately above its outlet, "Cataraqui," or St. Lawrence River, in N. lat. 44° 8′, W. long. 76° 40′ from Greenwich. "The view of the city and surrounding scenery is not surpassed by the approaches to any other city in America. A few miles above Kingston the waters of Lake Ontario are divided by the first of the long series of islands so well known to Tourists as the "*Thousand Islands*," of which Simcoe and Grand or Wolfe Islands, opposite the city, may be looked upon as strongholds, designed by nature to withstand the encroaches of the waves of Ontario. On approaching from the west, by water, the first object that attracts the traveler's attention is *Fort Henry*, with the naval station of Fort Frederick at its base, and its attendant battlements, fortifications, towers, and redoubts. Fort Henry is a favorite resort for visitors, and its elevated position affords the best view that can be had of the city, lake, and surrounding country."

The principal public buildings are the City Hall, one of the finest and most substantial edifices in Canada, and built of cut limestone at a cost of $92,000. It contains all the public offices of the city, including a spacious hall, capable of seating over 1,000 persons; the court-house is a large stone building, which is about being removed, and another, more in accordance with the wants of the citizens, is to be erected on a ground more central, and its present site occupied by a custom-house and post-office. Here is a Roman Catholic cathedral and several fine church edifices, in all numbering sixteen. Queen's College, under the direction of the Presbyterians, has a president and four professors; the College of Regiopolis (Roman Catholic) has also a president and four professors; the General Hospital, Hotel Dieu, and a nunnery are also in the city, while two miles west is situated the Provincial Penitentiary. It has four banking-houses and several insurance offices; three well-kept hotels, and about 100 stores of different kinds; besides several breweries, distilleries, tanneries, foundries, machine-shops, and a marine railway and ship-yard for the building of lake craft; on *Navy Bay*, which lies between Point Frederick and Point Henry, is the naval dock-yard used for government purposes. Near the Penitentiary is a mineral spring of some celebrity, resembling in its component parts the Cheltenham spring of England; another spring exists which is unusually strong, resembling in some respects the "Artesian Well" of St. Catherine's. It has been analyzed by Prof. Williamson, and found to contain valuable medical properties.

Kingston occupies the site of *Fort Frontenac*, an old French post, this being one of a chain of posts extending from Quebec to Mackinac. Here are owned 20 steamers and about 40 schooners, sailing to and from the port, besides numerous other Canadian and American steamers and sailing vessels. It being the outlet for the productions of the fertile Bay of Quinte, and the *Rideau Canal*, terminating at Kingston, makes it an important and active mart of commerce.

STEAMBOAT ROUTE

F OM KINGSTON TO BELLEVILLE AND PORT TRENTON, PASSING THROUGH THE BAY OF QUINTE.

Landings.	Miles.	Landings.	Miles.
KINGSTON	0	PORT TRENTON	0
Amherst Island	13	BELLEVILLE	12
Bath	5–18	North Port	12–24
Fredericksburg	10–28	Indian Woods	8–32
Adolphustown	4–32	PICTON	15–47
Stone Mills	3–35	Stone Mills	5–52
PICTON	5–40	Adolphustown	3–55
Indian Woods	15–55	Fredericksburg	4–59
North Port	8–63	Bath	10–69
BELLEVILLE	12–75	Amherst Island	5–74
PORT TRENTON	12–87	KINGSTON	13–87

FARE from Kingston to Picton.............. $1 00
" " Belleville........... 1 50

Several steamers leave Kingston daily for Picton, Belleville, Port Trenton, and intermediate ports, during the season of navigation, connecting at Belleville and Port Trenton with the Grand Trunk Railway, and line of stages running to Rice Lake, Peterboro', etc.

On leaving the wnarf at Kingston the steamers run in a westerly direction, passing the *Brothers*, to AMHERST ISLAND, 13 miles. This is a large and fertile island, inhabited by an intelligent and prosperous class of citizens. Here commences the BAY OF QUINTE, a long, crooked, and picturesque body of water, into which empties the Napanee, Moira, and Trent rivers.

BATH, 18 miles from Kingston, is situated on the main shore, opposite Amherst Island. It contains about 600 inhabitants, with a fine back country.

FREDERICKSBURG, 28 miles from Kingston, is a settlement on the mainland.

ADOLPHUSTOWN, 32 miles from Kingston, is situated on the mainland, opposite MARYSBURG, located on Prince Edward's Island.

STONE MILLS, 35 miles from Kingston, is situated on Prince Edward's Island, near a most remarkable lake, elevated some 300 feet above the Bay of Quinte. It is called the *Lake of the Mountain*, being half a mile in length, and nearly as wide. It has no perceptible inlet, but discharges a large volume of water, which is used in propelling several mills of different kinds.

PICTON, 40 miles from Kingston, and 35 miles from Belleville by water, is the capital of Prince Edward Co., C. W., being handsomely situated. The Bay of Quinte, which here expands to a considerable width, is called Hallowell Bay. The village contains about 2,000 inhabitants; a court-house and jail, one Episcopal, one Presbyterian, one Methodist, and one Roman Catholic church, two hotels, and several taverns, twelve stores, one steam flouring-mill, one large tannery, and an extensive carriage manufactory.

On leaving Picton, the steamer runs north to the landing called *Indian Woods*, when a westerly course is again pursued to the head of the bay, passing *Morris*, or *Hall's Island*, and several beautiful headlands. Here is another expansion of water called *Hall's Bay*, on Capt. Owen's (R. N.) Chart of Lake Ontario.

BELLEVILLE, Hastings Co., C. W., is advantageously situated at the mouth of the river Moira, 75 miles by steamboat route, and only 47 miles by railroad from Kingston. This is a very thriving town, now containing about 8,000 inhabitants; the county buildings, a town hall and market building; a Methodist seminary, erected in 1855; one Episcopal, two Presbyterian, two Methodist, and one Roman Catholic church; four hotels, and a number of taverns; 50 stores of different kinds, and most kinds of mechanic workshops. The Moira River affords a good water-power, here being situated one woolen factory three flouring-mills, four saw-mills, one paper-mill, one axe factory, one extensive distillery, three foundries and machine-shops, and a ship-yard. This is a great market for lumber, grain, and other kinds of produce. It is proposed to extend a railroad from Belleville to Lake Simcoe, and thence to the Georgian Bay of Lake Huron.

Port Trenton, 87 miles from Kingston by steamboat route, and 59 miles by railroad, is another growing place and port of entry, situated near the head of the Bay of Quinte, at the mouth of Trent River. It contains about 1,200 inhabitants; one Episcopal and one Methodist church; three hotels, ten stores, one grist-mill, one extensive steam saw-mill, one large tannery, two distilleries, a foundry, machine-shop, and ship-yards. Steamers run from Port Trenton to Kingston, Prescott, Montreal, etc., trans-shipping a large amount of lumber and country produce.

The River Trent, which is the outlet of Pemedashcoutayong, or *Rice Lake*, is a fine stream of water, and is in part navigable for steamers running into the lake. Immense quantities of wild rice are found in the low waters of this lake and its vicinity, which abound in game of different kinds, affording ample sport and profit to the huntsman.

The principal inlet of Rice Lake is called *Otonibee River*, being the outlet of a succession of lakes, the most celebrated of which lies 823 feet above the ocean, and is called *Balsam Lake;* the other bodies of water are called Sturgeon Lake, West Lake, and East Lake. From Balsam Lake to the Bay of Quinte there is a succession of falls of 588 feet descent.

LIST OF STEAMERS.

AMERICAN STEAMERS BUILT ON LAKE ONTARIO AND RIVER ST. LAWRENCE SINCE THEIR INTRODUCTION IN 1816.

Built.	Name.	Tons.	Where built.	Remarks.
1816	Ontario	232	Sacket's Harbor	broken up.
1818	Sophia	75	Sacket's Harbor	broken up.
1823	Martha Ogden	150	Sacket's Harbor	lost in 1832.
1830	Brownville	150	Brownville	broken up.
1831	Charles Carroll	100	Sacket's Harbor	broken up.
"	Paul Pry	50	Ogdensburgh	broken up.
1832	United States	450	Ogdensburgh	broken up.
1833	Black Hawk	200	French Creek	broken up.
1834	Oswego	400	Oswego, N. Y.	broken up.
1836	Oneida	300	Oswego, N. Y.	broken up.
1837	Telegraph	200	Dexter, N. Y.	laid up.
1838	John Marshall	60	Lake Erie	lost in 1844.
1839	St. Lawrence	450	Oswego, N. Y.	broken up.
"	Express	150	Pultneyville	tow boat.
1841	George Clinton	100	Oswego, N. Y.	destroyed.
"	President	60	Oswego, N. Y.	lost in 1844.
1842	Lady of the Lake	425	Oswego, N. Y.	burnt in 1854.
1843	Rochester	350	Oswego, N. Y.	name changed.
1845	Niagara	473	Clayton, N. Y.	Lewiston to Ogdensburgh.
1847	Cataract	577	Clayton, N. Y.	Lewiston to Ogdensburgh.
1848	Bay State	1,098	Clayton, N. Y.	Lewiston to Ogdensburgh.
"	Ontario	832	Clayton, N. Y.	Lewiston to Ogdensburgh.
1849	Northerner	905	Oswego, N. Y.	Lewiston to Ogdensburgh.
1853	New York	1,200	Clayton, N. Y.	Lewiston to Ogdensburgh.

RUNNING ON THE ST. LAWRENCE RIVER.

Name.	Tons.	Where built.	Remarks.
Jenny Lind	300	Montreal, C. E.	Ogdensburgh to Montreal.
Montreal	300	Kingston, C.W.	Ogdensburgh to Montreal.
British Queen	300	Grand Island	Ogdensburgh to Montreal.

BRITISH STEAMERS BUILT ON LAKE ONTARIO AND THE RIVER ST. LAWRENCE SINCE 1816.

Built.	Name.	Tons.	Where built.	Remarks.
1816	Frontenac (1st)	500	Kingston, C. W.	broken up.
1817	Charlotte	150	Kingston.	
1819	Dalhousie	350	Prescott.	
1824	Toronto	200	Toronto.	
"	Queenston	350	Queenston.	
1825	Canada (1st)	250	Toronto.	
"	Niagara	400	Brockville.	
1828	Alciope	450	Niagara.	
1829	Sir James Kempt	200	Kingston.	
1830	Great Britain	700	Prescott.	
1831	Iroquois	100	Prescott.	
1832	John By	100	Kingston.	
"	William the Fourth	450	Gananoque	tow boat.
"	Transit	350	Oakville	wrecked.
1833	Britannia	200	Kingston	broken up.
"	Cobourg	500	Cobourg.	
"	Kingston (1st)	200	Kingston.	

Built.	Name.	Tons.	Where built. Remarks.
1833	Brockville	350	Brockville.
1834	Com. Barrie	275	Kingston—lost in 1842.
“	Enterprise	200	Kingston—broken up.
“	Union	300	Oakville—changed to barque.
1835	Traveller	350	Niagara—tow boat.
“	St. George	400	Kingston—laid up.
1837	Sir Robert Peel	350	Brockville—burnt in 1838.
“	Gore	200	Niagara—runs on Lake Huron.
“	Queen Victoria	200	Niagara—wrecked.
1838	Experiment	150	Niagara—broken up.
1839	Henry Gildersleeve	250	Kingston—tow boat.
“	Ontario*	300	Prescott—name changed.
1840	Highlander (1st)	300	Coteau du Lac—broken up.
“	Albion	200	Brockville.
“	America (1st)	300	Niagara—tow boat.
“	Sovereign	475	Niagara—broken up.
“	City of Toronto	500	Niagara—tow boat.
“	Prince Edward	200	Kingston—lost in 1848.
1841	Frontenac (2d)	200	Kingston—broken up.
“	Princess Royal	500	Niagara—tow boat.
“	Canada (2d)	450	Prescott—tow boat.
“	Despatch	200	laid up.
1842	Prince of Wales	200	Kingston—name changed.
“	Admiral	400	Niagara—runs on St. Lawrence.
“	Chief Justice Robinson	400	Niagara—Cobourg to Oswego.
“	Welland (1st)	300	burnt in 1856.
“	Mohawk (iron)	150	Kingston—runs on Lake Erie.
“	Cherokee (gov. steamer)	700	Kingston—sent to Halifax.
1843	Eclipse	400	Niagara—changed to schooner.

BRITISH STEAMERS RUNNING ON LAKE ONTARIO AND THE ST. LAWRENCE RIVER, 1856.

Name.	Commanders.	Tons.	From	To
Peerless	James Dick	400	Toronto	Niagara.
Zimmerman	D. Millory	500	“	“
Champion	W. Wilson	350	“	Oswego, N. Y.
Europa	J. Murdock	600	“	“
May Flower	D. Sinclair	300	....	....
Highlander (2d)	D. M‘Bride	250	Toronto	Rochester, N. Y.
Maple Leaf	R. Kerr	398	“	“
Welland (2d)	W. Donaldson	—	“	Port Dalhousie.
Ch. Just. Robinson	Jacob Young	315	Cobourg	Oswego, N. Y.
Arabian	Sclater	350	Hamilton	Prescott.
Kingston (2d)	C. Hamilton	400	“	“
Magnet	H. Twohy	500	“	“
Passport	Harbottle	400	“	“
Bowmanville	C. Perry	400	“	Montreal.
Monarch	A. Sinclair	400	“	“
Provincial	T. Kidd	300	“	Prescott.
Cora Linn	Sutherland	150	Kingston	Port Trenton.
Lady Elgin	Nosworthy	200	“	Belleville.
Bay of Quinte	F. Carrell	250	“	“
City of the Bay	W. R. Monroe	200	“	“
Sir Charles Napier	G. F. Creighton	200	“	Cape Vincent.
Trenton	H. De Witt	260	Port Trenton	Montreal.
St. Helen	C. Chrysler	100	“	“

* *Lord Sydenham*—running on the lower St. Lawrence—was the first steamer that run down the Rapids in 1840.

RUNNING ON THE ST. LAWRENCE RIVER.

Name.	Commanders.	Tons.	From	To
Banshee	T. Howard	300	Kingston	Montreal.
New Era	P. G. Chrysler	200	"	"
Ottawa	J. R. Kelley	270	"	"
St. Lawrence	T. Maxwell	200	"	"

NOTE.—The Tonnage of British Steamers is rated about one third less than by the American measurement, owing to deducting the space for engine and machinery.

The Steamers AMERICA and CANADA, two large vessels of about 800 tons each, were recently built, and run from Hamilton to Brockville, in connection with the Great Western Railway of Canada; but after the completion of the Grand Trunk Railway to Toronto they were found unprofitable, have since been condemned, and their engines taken out and sold.

CANADIAN VESSELS.

FROM a list of Canadian steamers, propellers, and schooners trading on the Lakes and the St. Lawrence River, recently compiled, we gather the following facts: In commission, 47 steamers, 17 propellers, and 171 schooners; the tonnage of which (British measurement) amounts to about 42,000 tons; the estimated value being about $3,500,000.

LIST OF BRITISH STEAMERS BUILT AND RUNNING ON THE ST. LAWRENCE RIVER, BELOW MONTREAL SINCE 1810.

Built.	Name.	Tons.	Where built.	Remarks.
1810	Accommodation	—	Montreal	broken up.
1812	Swiftsure	—	Montreal	broken up.
1814	Malsham	—	Montreal	broken up.
1816	Car of Commerce	—	Montreal	broken up.
1817	Lady Sherbrooke	—	Montreal	broken up.
"	Caledonia	—	Montreal	broken up.
"	Telegraph	—	Montreal	broken up.
1818	New Swiftsure	—	Montreal	broken up.
"	Quebec (1st)	—	Quebec	broken up.
1820	Montreal (1st)	—	Montreal	broken up.
"	Chambly	—	Montreal	broken up.
"	St. Lawrence (1st)	—	Montreal	broken up.
1822	La Prairie	—	Montreal	broken up.
1825	Hercules	300	Montreal	broken up.
"	Edmund Henry	—	Montreal	broken up.
1826	Waterloo	200	La Prairie, C. E.	lost in the ice.
1829	British America	391	Montreal	broken up.
"	John Molson	300	Montreal	broken up.
1832	Voyageur	300	Montreal	broken up.
"	Canada	350	Montreal	broken up.
"	Canadian Eagle	250	Montreal	broken up.
"	Patriot	100	Montreal	broken up.
1833	Britannia	135	Montreal	broken up.
1834	John Bull	500	Montreal	burnt in 1839.
1836	Princess Victoria	171	Montreal	tow boat.
1837	Charlevoix	200	Montreal	broken up.
1839	Lady Colborne	250	Montreal	broken up.
"	Lord Sydenham	—	Lake Ontario	broken up.
1840	Queen	372	Sorel, C. E.	laid up.
1841	Montreal (2d)	378	Montreal	wrecked 1853.
1842	North America	181	Montreal	broken up.
1843	Alliance	192	Montreal	laid up.
"	St. Louis	190	Sorel, C. E.	laid up.
"	Prince Albert (iron)	183	Montreal	Champlain & St. Lawr'nce Ferry.
1845	Lord Elgin	158	Lake Ontario	Montreal to Kingston.
"	Quebec (2d)	400	Quebec	Montreal to Quebec.
"	Rowland Hill	250	Quebec	tow boat.
1846	John Munn	400	Quebec	Montreal to Quebec.
"	Richelieu	70	Sorel, C. E.	Montreal to Chambly.
1847	Iron Duke (iron)	169	Montreal	Champlain & St. Lawr'nce Ferry.
"	Ottawa	270	Montreal.	
1848	Jaques Cartier	78	Sorel, C. E.	Montreal to Three Rivers.
1849	Crescent	72	Montreal	laid up.
1852	Castor	75	Montreal	Montreal to Three Rivers.
"	St. Lawrence (2d)	300		
1854	Montreal (3d)	300	Quebec	Burnt, June 27, 1857.
"	J. M'Kenzie	250	Quebec	Montreal to Quebec.
"	Saguenay	300	Sorel, C. E.	Quebec to Saguenay.
"	Princess Royal	--	Lake Ontario	Quebec to Saguenay.
"	Huron	350	Sorel, C. E.	
"	Musk Rat	150	Montreal	Montreal to Longueil.
1855	Cultivateur	60	Montreal	Montreal to Berthier.
"	Advance	—	Quebec	Quebec to River du Loup.
1856	Napoleon	114	Montreal	Montreal to Quebec.
"	Victoria	114	Montreal	Montreal to Quebec.

CANALS OF CANADA, SHOWING THEIR LENGTH, LOCKS, ETC.

NAMES, ETC.	Length in miles.	Locks.	Lockage in feet.	Cost.
WELLAND CANAL.				
Main Trunk, Port Colborne to Pt. Dalhousie	28	27	330	£1,061,497
Dunnville Feeder, junction to Dunnville	21	1	8	
Broad Creek Branch	1½	1	8	
ST. LAWRENCE.				
The Gallops	2	2	8	£1,052,601
Point Iroquois..............	3	1	6	
Rapid Plat	4	2	11½	
Farren's Point	¾	1	4	
CORNWALL................ (Long Saut Rapids)	11½	7	48	
BEAUHARNOIS............. (Cascade, Cedars, etc.)	11¼	9	82½	£365,331
LA CHINE.................	8½	5	45	£481,736
Total, from L. Erie to Montreal	69	54	535 feet.	
Add fall not requiring locks .			17	
Fall from Montreal to tide-water at Three Riv., C. E.			13	
Grand total			565 feet.	

NOTE.—Lake Huron is elevated nine feet above Lake Erie, and Lake Superior is elevated 26 feet above Lake Huron—making a total elevation above tide-water, or the ocean, of 600 feet, according to recent surveys.

	Length in miles.	Locks.	Lockage in feet.	Cost.
CHAMBLY CANAL.......... (River Richelieu)	11½	9	74	
St. Ours Lock, do.		1	5	
ST. ANNE'S LOCK. (Ottawa River)		1	8½	
RIDEAU CANAL. Kingston to Ottawa City ..	126	37	457	£965,000
OTTAWA CANAL and LOCKS .				£117,647

TRIP FROM KINGSTON TO MONTREAL.

THE American steamers on leaving Kingston on their trip to Ogdensburgh run between Grand Island and Howe Island, two large islands belonging to the British, when they enter the American Channel of the St. Lawrence and land at Clayton, situated at the mouth of French Creek, while the Canadian steamers usually run the North or British Channel, passing *Gananoqui,* 20 miles below Kingston. This is usually the first landing made by the British steamers in descending the river, unless they stop to take in wood at some of the numerous islands.

THE THOUSAND ISLANDS.—The remarkable group of islands in the River St. Lawrence called "*The Thousand Islands,*" commences opposite the city of Kingston, and stretches down the river for between 40 and 50 miles, for which distance the St. Lawrence is between six and twelve miles wide. They lie partly in Canada and partly within the bounds of the State of New York, the boundary line between the United States and Canada dividing them into about equal parts.

From an examination of Bayfield's chart of the St. Lawrence River, it appears that WOLFE or GRAND ISLAND, belonging to the British, is 18 miles long and from one to six miles wide. This is the largest island of the group, and contains much good land, being inhabited by a number of families. A canal is commenced, extending across this island, to facilitate trade with Cape Vincent.

GAGE ISLAND, lying west of Grand Island, is three miles long. On its southwest end may be seen a light-house as you approach Kingston from Toronto or Oswego. The American boats usually run between this island and Wolfe Island, through the *Packet* or *Bateau Channel.*

On GARDEN ISLAND, opposite Kingston, is situated a large lumber establishment, where may usually be seen vessels taking in lumber, destined for different ports.

Howe Island, also belonging to the British, is eight miles long, and from one to two miles wide, lying near the Canada shore. The usual steamboat route, on ascending and descending the river, is between this island and Wolfe Island, running through the *Kingston* or *British Channel*, a wide expanse of water, extending from near Kingston to French Creek, on the American side.

The *American Channel* runs east of Wolfe or Grand Island, between that and Cape Vincent, where extends the boundary line between the two countries, this being considered the main channel.

Carleton Island, belonging to the United States, is situated nearly opposite Cape Vincent. It contains about 1,200 acres of excellent land, and is an important island, as it commands the American Channel of the St. Lawrence, and has two fine coves or harbors at the upper end, where are extensive lumber stations. Here was erected a fort by the British in 1777, and it became their principal military and naval depôt for Lake Ontario during the Revolutionary War. Some years afterward, the shipping and public stores were removed to Kingston, but the island was retained and occupied by British troops until 1812, when the guard was surprised and taken by a party of New York militia.

The waters of the St. Lawrence among the islands here vary at different seasons from three to four feet in height, exposing some hundreds of islets at its lowest stage.

The fish most abundant are the maskalonge, pickerel, black bass, pike, perch, rock bass, cat-fish, and eels. The maskalonge, pickerel, and black bass are taken by trolling; the pike are taken in nets, and the perch, rock bass, etc., are taken by hook and line.

On the islands are found deer, foxes, raccoons, rabbits, squirrels, muskrats, and minks; also partridges, quail, and wild ducks in abundance.

Grindstone Island, five and a half miles long, belongs to the United States. This is a large island, lying in the middle of the river, a short distance below the mouth of French Creek. Here, it is said, the noted Bill Johnson has his favorite abode, either on the main island, or the small island in its immediate vicinity, called *Johnson's Island.*

WELL'S ISLAND, another large and important island, eight or nine miles in length, is attached to the State of New York; it lies mostly above the village of Alexandria, the boundary line running on its west side, where lies a beautiful body of water, called the "*Lake of the Thousand Islands,*" which is a favorite resort for the angler and sportsman.

THE ADMIRALTY ISLANDS are a group lying below Howe Island, and belong to the British. Here the Canadian Channel becomes a perfect labyrinth for a number of miles, and the navigation would be very dangerous were it not for the great depth of water and bold shores of the islets.

The FLEET GROUP, or NAVY ISLANDS, commence opposite Grindstone Island, on the Canadian side of the river, and extends for some distance below to opposite Well's Island. Here the boundary line runs close to the latter island, giving most of the small islands to the British.

The OLD FRIENDS are a small group immediately below Well's Island, belonging to the United States.

The INDIAN GROUP also lie on the American side of the channel, a few miles below the latter islands.

The AMATEUR ISLANDS lie in the middle of the river, opposite Chippewa Creek, and are, in part, attached to the State of New York, and a part belong to Canada, the boundary line running between them.

Immediately below the latter islands the river contracts to one or two miles in width, and the Thousand Islands, of which there are at least fourteen hundred, may be said to terminate, although a large collection of islands called *Brock's Group*, lying mostly on the Canada side, are passed a short distance below the village of Brockville, where the St. Lawrence River is about one mile wide, which width it averages for 30 or 40 miles, until you approach the rapids below Ogdensburgh, when it narrows to about half a mile in width, with banks elevated but a few feet above the water.

"The main stream of the St. Lawrence," says Buckingham, speaking of the Thousand Islands, "is so thickly studded with islands that it is like passing through a vast archipelago, rather than navigating a mighty river. They are for the most part rocky islets, sometimes rising in abrupt cliffs from the water, and so bold and steep that you may run the boat near enough to touch the cliffs from the vessel. A few only are low and flat, but being nearly all wooded, they form a perpetual succession of the most romantically beautiful and picturesque groups that can be conceived."

Among the Thousand Islands are usually found immense quantities of water-fowl and other kinds of wild game, which, during the spring and summer months, afford great pleasure to the sportsman. The fishing is also excellent for the most part of the year. During the months of July and August, pleasure parties from the surrounding country, and strangers from a distance, resort here for their amusement, enjoying themselves to their heart's content by hunting, fishing, and bathing, being surrounded by wild and interesting scenery and invigorating air, not exceeded by any section of the United States or Canada.

The St. Lawrence River, in fact for its entire length of several hundred miles, presents a magnificent appearance, well worthy the attention of the tourist. The *Rapids*, now successfully navigated on their downward trip by steamboats of a large class, returning through the canals, afford a deeply interesting excursion. The cultivated fields and settlements interchanging with bolder features, impart a grandeur as well as variety and beauty to the river and its shores which no other stream on the continent possesses in an equal degree.

BROCKVILLE, 50 miles below Kingston and 125 miles above Montreal by railroad route, is a beautiful and flourishing town of about 8,000 inhabitants; it contains a court-house and jail, a custom-house, several churches, two good hotels, and many fine buildings, besides several extensive manufacturing establishments. Here is a convenient steamboat landing, where the American and British passage-boats usually land on their trips up and down the river, the stream here being about two miles in width.

The *Grand Trunk Railway*, which runs through the town, has added much to the growth and trade of this place. The *Brockville and Ottawa Railroad*, which is in the course of construction, when finished, will further add to its prosperity, the country in the rear being very fertile and heavily timbered, producing large quantities of grain and lumber.

MAITLAND is a small village, five miles below Brockville, on the same side. It contains a church, a public house, and some 300 inhabitants.

The town of PRESCOTT, C. W., is situated on the north bank of the St. Lawrence, directly opposite Ogdensburgh, being 60 miles below Kingston and 113 miles above Montreal by railroad route. This point may be considered as the foot of lake and river navigation for sail vessels, as the Gallop Rapids occur about six miles below, where commences the first of the series of the St. Lawrence canals, terminating with the La Chine Canal, which enters Montreal. Prescott is a port of entry and contains a custom-house, a town-hall, four churches, six public houses, 20 or 30 stores, a foundry and machine-shop, together with several breweries and distilleries, and three extensive laundries. This is also a great depôt for lumber and country produce.

British and American steamers usually land at Prescott several times daily on their route up and down the St. Lawrence. Two steam ferry-boats are also constantly running between this place and Ogdensburgh. The *Grand Trunk Railway* passes through the town, and the *Ottawa and Prescott Railroad*, 53 miles in length, terminates here, affording a speedy and direct route to Ottawa City and the lumber region above.

No section of Canada has fairer prospects of advancement than Brockville and Prescott, if the advantages are embraced of forming lines of railroads to the upper Ottawa country, lying as they do nearer to that heavily timbered region than Montreal

Fort Wellington, adjoining the lower part of the town, is a strong fortification usually garrisoned by more or less British troops. WINDMILL POINT, one mile and a half below the fort, was the scene of an unfortunate attack by the patriots of 1838, who, after effecting a landing and maintaining their position with great determination for several days, were taken prisoners, many of whom were afterward executed at Kingston, and others transported to Van Dieman's Land.

RAPIDS OF THE ST. LAWRENCE

On resuming the downward trip, after leaving Prescott or Ogdensburgh, the most interesting objects are presented to view from the deck of the steamer. The depôt buildings of the Northern Railroad of New York, on the one side, and Windmill Point on the Canada side, are quickly passed and the Rapids soon reached.

Chimney Island, four miles below Prescott, is an interesting spot, where may be seen the remains of a fortification, erected by the French during the early settlement of Canada.

The Gallop Rapids, six miles below Prescott or Ogdensburgh, are easily passed by steamboats, although they prevent the navigation of the St. Lawrence by sail vessels. They extend for about two miles, around which is a ship canal on the Canada side of the river, overcoming a descent of seven feet.

Matilda, eight miles farther, is a convenient steamboat landing on the Canada side of the river, where is a canal one mile and three-quarters in length.

Waddington, on the American shore, 18 miles below Ogdensburgh, lies opposite Ogden's Island, which is passed to the right, descending through the main channel, forming the boundary line. Here commences Rapid Plat, and extends about two and a half miles. Another canal of the same length is built on the Canada shore, to overcome the descent in the river of eleven and a half feet.

Williamsburg, seven miles below Matilda, is a regular steamboat landing, where passage-boats usually touch ascending and descending the river. Here is another short canal.

Chrysler's Farm, a few miles below Williamsburg, is the place where was fought a battle in the war of 1812, between the English and Americans, in which the latter were defeated, with considerable loss in killed and wounded.

Louisville Landing, 28 miles below Ogdensburgh, is where passengers leave for *Massena Springs*, six miles distant by stage. This is a great resort for invalids during warm weather.

The LONG SAUT RAPIDS, extending from Dickinson's Landing, 40 miles below Prescott, to Cornwall on the Canada side, is one of the longest and most important rapids of the St. Lawrence. They are divided by islands into two channels, the *American Channel* and the *Lost Channel.** Formerly, the American, or East Channel, was mostly run by steamers in the downward trip, but of late the Lost Channel, on the Canadian side, is mostly used. This channel presents a grand and terrific appearance, the water being lashed into a white foam for several miles, yet still the steamer glides rapidly through them into the quiet and beautiful expanse of water below Cornwall.

The CORNWALL CANAL commences 72 miles above Montreal, on about the 45th degree of north latitude, the dividing line between the United States and Canada. It extends to Dickinson's Landing, 11½ miles, overcoming 48 feet descent in the St. Lawrence. Barnhart Island and Long Saut Island, two large and cultivated bodies of land, belong to the State of New York, while Cornwall Island and Sheek's Island belong to Canada, dividing the waters of the St. Lawrence into two channels, for most of the distance through the rapids.

CORNWALL, 112 miles from Kingston and 70 miles above Montreal, is situated on the northwest side of the river, at the

---

* PASSAGE OF THE LONG SAUT RAPID.—Those who have traveled on the St. Lawrence are aware that between Dickinson's Landing and Cornwall, a distance of from twelve to fourteen miles, there is a long rapid called the *Long Saut.* This rapid is divided into two channels by an island in the center, the channel on the south side being the one which has heretofore been descended by steamers and other large craft passing down the river. Capt. Maxwell, the enterprising commander of the mail steamer "Gildersleeve," having some time ago become impressed with an idea that the channel on the north side of the island was not only practicable for vessels of a large class, but that it was much safer and easier of descent than the channel on the south side, made, with much trouble, soundings and observations, for the purpose of ascertaining whether such was really the case.

Having well satisfied himself in the matter, he (with Mr. Hamilton's permission) made a descent down the North Channel, sometimes called *Lost Channel*, in the mail steamer "Gildersleeve." The passage was magnificent, the grandeur and beauty of the Rapid far surpassing even those of the Rapids at the Cedars, the Cascades, or La Chine. Owing to the great rapidity of the current, the water is much rougher than on the south side of the island, but the channel is straighter, and in every respect better than the one heretofore adopted, and there is little doubt that ere long the North Channel will be the one which the main traffic of the river will pass through.—*Montreal Herald.*

lower end of the *Cornwall*, or *St. Lawrence Canal*. The town contains about 2,500 inhabitants, 400 dwelling-houses, a court-house and jail, five churches, twenty stores, and several hotels. This is a regular steamboat landing for American and British steamers. The *Grand Trunk Railway* also passes through the rear part of the town.

St. Regis, four miles below, on the American side of the river, is situated on the line of the 45th degree of north latitude, the St. Lawrence below this point being entirely in Canada. St. Regis is an Indian village, part of its inhabitants living in the United States and part in Canada. It contains four or five hundred inhabitants, 80 dwelling-houses, one Roman Catholic church, one Protestant church, one tavern, and two stores. Here is a convenient steamboat landing, where during warm weather may sometimes be seen Indian boys, prepared to plunge into the water on having a piece of money thrown overboard: often it is caught by these expert swimmers before reaching the bottom.

Lake St. Francis, a most beautiful expanse of water, is an expansion of the St. Lawrence above Coteau du Lac, extending for a number of miles. It is studded with lovely and picturesque islands, giving a variety to the scenery of this river which is almost indescribable. The Indian village of St. Regis, and an island owned by the natives, lie near its upper termination.

Lancaster, 15 miles below Cornwall, lies on the west side of the lake, or river, here presenting a wide surface, the waters calmly pursuing their course downward before rushing impetuously down the several rapids below *Coteau du Lac*, or the foot of the lake.

At Coteau du Lac, 40 miles above Montreal, commences a rapid of the same name, extending about two miles. Seven miles below this commences the *Cedar Rapid*, which extends about three miles. *(See Frontispiece.)* Then comes the *Cascade Rapid*, which terminates at the head of Lake St. Louis, where the dark waters of the Ottawa, by one of its mouths, joins the

St. Lawrence. These three rapids, in eleven miles, have a descent of 82½ feet, being overcome by the Beauharnois Canal.

The grandeur of the scenery in the vicinity of these Rapids can not be conceived without being witnessed. The mighty St. Lawrence is here seen in all its magnificence and power, being lashed into a foam for miles by the impetuosity of its current. The *Cedar Rapids** have hitherto been considered the most formidable obstruction to downward-bound craft, but the new South Channel, or McPherson's Channel, as it is now called, affords an additional depth of water. The steamer *Bytown*, Capt. Wm. Sughrue, in 1843, was the first steamboat that descended this channel, which was brought into notice by D. S. McPherson, Esq., one of the late firm of the forwarding-house of McPherson, Crane & Co.

Beauharnois, 24 miles above Montreal, lies at the foot of the Cascade Rapids, where commences the *Beauharnois Canal*, 12 miles in length, overcoming altogether a descent of 82½ feet. Between Fond du Lac and Beauharnois, or the foot of the Cascade Rapids, is the most wild and romantic scenery that the St. Lawrence presents.

Caughnawaga, ten miles above Montreal, is an Indian village, numbering several hundred inhabitants. Here commences the *Montreal and Plattsburgh Railroad*, 52 miles in length. It is proposed to construct a ship canal from this place to the Richelieu River, the outlet of Lake Champlain, thus uniting the waters of the St. Lawrence and Hudson River, *via* Champlain Canal.

La Chine, eight miles above Montreal, is situated at the foot of an expansion of the St. Lawrence, called *Lake St. Louis*, where enter the black waters of the Ottawa River, the St. Lawrence presenting a greenish hue, the difference in the color of the waters being plainly visible for many miles below.

The La Chine Rapids, a few miles above Montreal, are the last rapids of importance that occur on the St. Lawrence. They

---

* It was here that Gen. Amherst's brigade of 300 men, on their way to attack Canada, then in possession of the French, were lost! At Montreal they received the first intelligence of the invasion, by the dead bodies floating down the river past the town.

are now considered the most dangerous and difficult of navigation. These rapids are obviated by the *La Chine Canal*, 8½ miles in length, overcoming a descent of 44½ feet. Canals of a large capacity now run round all the rapids, enabling steamers of a large size to ascend the river, although at a much less speed than the downward trip.

"The St Lawrence is perhaps the only river in the world possessing so great a variety of scenery and character, in the short distance of one hundred and eighty miles—from Kingston to Montreal. The voyage down this portion of the St. Lawrence in a steamer is one of the most exciting and interesting that our country affords to the pleasure-seeking traveler. Starting at daylight from the good old city of Kingston, we are at first enraptured by the lovely and fairy-like scenery of the 'Lake of the Thousand Isles,' and oft we wonder how it is that our helmsman can guide us through the intricate path that lies before him. Surely he will make some mistake, and we shall lose our way, and our steamer wander for ages ere the trackless path be once more discovered. However, we are wrong, and long before the sun has set we have shot the 'Long Saut,' and are passing through the calm and peaceful Lake St. Francis. Gently we glide along, and are lost in pleasing reveries, which grace the scenes of our forenoon's travel. Suddenly we are awakened from our dreams by a pitch, and then a quick jerk of our vessel, and rising to see the cause, we find ourselves receiving warning in the Coteau Rapids, of what we may expect when we reach the Cedars, a few miles farther on. Now the bell is rung for the engine *to slow* its speed, and glancing toward the beam, we find it merely moving sufficient to keep headway on the vessel; now looking toward the wheelman's house, we see four men standing by the wheel; backward we turn our gaze, and four more stand by the *tiller*, to assist those at the wheel in guiding our craft down the fearful leaps she is about to take. These preparations striking us with dread, we, who are now making our first trip, involuntarily clutch the nearest object for support, and checking our breath, await the first plunge. 'Tis over. We are reeling to and fro, and dancing hither and thither among billows of enormous size, caused solely by the swiftness of the current. With difficulty we keep our feet while rushing down the tortuous channel, through which only we can be preserved from total wreck or certain death. Now turning to the right, to avoid a half-sunken rock, about whose summit the waves are ever dashing, we are apparently running on an island situated immediately before us. On! on we rush! We must ground! but no; her head is casing off, and as we fly past the island, a daring leap might land us on its shores; and now again we are tossed and whirled about in a sea of foam; we look back to scan the dangers passed, and see a raft far behind, struggling in the waves. While contemplating its dangers, we forget our own, and the lines of Horace appear peculiarly applicable to the Indian who first intrusted his frail canoe to these terrific rapids:

Illi robur et æs triplex
 Circa pectus erat, qui fragilem truci
Commisit pelago ratem
 Primus ——.' "

RAPIDS OF THE ST. LAWRENCE—EXCITEMENT OF THE TRIP.

Extract from a Correspondent of the Detroit Advertiser—1856.

"LEAVING Hamilton in the evening, on board one of the splendid steamers navigating Lake Ontario, running direct for the St. Lawrence River, a distance of about 180 miles, we had a very pleasant night on the lake, and arrived at Cape Vincent, N. Y., at 7 next morning; discharged some freight, and proceeded to Brockville, Canada, and thence to Ogdensburgh, N. Y., where we arrived about noon; passing from Cape Vincent to Ogdensburgh (*via* the Express Line of steamers), we thread our winding way through among the *Thousand Islands;* here is no monotony, for the scenery is continually changing and ever beautiful.

"I have spoken of the route by which I came to Ogdensburgh; another very pleasant route is by way of the steamer from Detroit to Buffalo, thence to the Niagara Falls, taking the boat at Lewiston. By this route, passengers may see many points of interest, which they do not see in traveling by the direct route.

"On Wednesday, July 17th, we left Ogdensburgh on the steamer MONTREAL, Capt. J. Laflamme, ran across the St. Lawrence to Prescott—then headed down the river to Montreal. At six miles from Ogdensburgh we passed the first rapid (Gallop). This being the first of a series of rapids that we had to pass on our way to Montreal, we had the curiosity to notice the effect the scene had on the passengers. The first with whom we came in contact was a nervous old gentleman, and he was rushing from one side of the boat to the other, with fear and admiration depicted on his countenance, while excitement had taken possession of his whole frame.

"Here is a group of sentimental young ladies; so deeply are they absorbed in drinking in the sickly sentiments of the cheap, yellow-covered literature which they hold in their hands, that they know nothing of the wild and beautiful scene through which we are passing. This is not the case with all, for many are standing or seated near the railing of the deck, looking calmly at the turbulent waters, and discoursing upon the cause of all this commotion; others stand in the background, wishing, but fearing to look at the trembling of the waves. We are now past the first rapid, or the "Gallops," and the water is now in a state of perfect calmness, and so are the passengers.

"The boat stops a few moments at Louisville, 35 miles from Ogdensburgh. At this point the river is divided by an island, and here begins the *Long Saut,* a rapid of nine miles in length; formerly the boats passed down the south side, where the water runs with greater rapidity. The north side is called the 'Lost Channel,' a name given to it by the French boatmen, as they supposed that if a boat drifted into it, it would certainly be lost. A channel has been found on the north side, and now the steamers pass by it in preference to the south channel.

"As we approach the rapid, the grand and lofty tumbling of the waters, as they break upon the projecting rocks, have an angry appearance, and look as if they were preparing to engulph us. We are standing upon the bow of the boat, and are fascinated by the view of the scene, yet we involuntarily turn our eyes to the pilot-house, in front of which, on an elevation, stands the captain, and at the wheel are four strong men. Neither fear nor anxiety is to be perceived in either countenance; but with their eyes fixed upon the landmarks, and their strong hands upon the wheel, they guide the ship through the narrow and crooked channel with unerring precision. The grand and picturesque scene has now brought all to their feet; the novel-readers have dropped their books, and the excitement of reality now surpasses the excitement of their fiction. The nervous man is standing bareheaded against the pilot-house, with both hands elevated, mouth open, and an exclamation upon the end of his tongue, as his tongue refuses to act; but as the boat glides out of the last billow into smooth water, the exclamation drops from his lips, his mouth shuts with a sudden jerk; and as he subsides into a calm he wipes the sweat from his brow, and is glad that he has seen and passed over that rapid. Only a small portion of the Long Saut is very rough, the rest of it has much the appearance of Hell Gate, N. Y.

"After passing the Long Saut, the boat stops a few moments at Cornwall on the Canada side. In a short time after leaving Cornwall, the river widens into a lake, which is called *Lake St. Francis.* This lake is about forty miles in length. Having passed it, the boat stops a few moments at the village of Coteau du Lac.

"Soon after leaving the Coteau, we pass the *Coteau, Cedar,*

Split-Rock, and *Cascade Rapids*. The passage of these rapids is very exciting, particularly the Split-Rock; here, as the boat is by the action of the water lifted above the rocks, and then dropped down among them, the waters covering and then receding and leaving the rocks nearly bare, upon either side, looks fearfully dangerous; the channel is narrow, the current rapid, and the boat is carried along at a 2.40 pace; but the boat is strong, and a skillful pilot is at the helm, and the passage is very quickly and safely made.

"The river again widens, and is called *Lake St. Louis*. At the foot of this lake, on the south side, is the Indian village of Caughnawaga. Here a boat comes off from the village, and brings an Indian named Baptiste. He is a fine-looking man, apparently about sixty years of age; he comes on board to pilot the boat over the *La Chine*, which is the last but most dangerous of the rapids. No man but Baptiste has ever yet piloted a steamer over these rapids. As the boat moves onward to the rapids, all the passengers, even to the novel-readers, are anxious to get a good position in order to have a good view of the heaving, breaking, and laughing waters. As we enter the rapids, we appear to be running upon a small grass-covered rocky island. Indeed, as the bow of the boat is so near that it appears to be impossible to clear it, we look to see if the pilot is at the helm. Yes, there stands the captain at his post in front of the wheel-house, and the Indian pilot, with three other strong men are at the wheel; and as we look at the calm countenance of the Indian, and see that his bright eye does not so much as wink, but is fixed steadily upon his beacon, whatever it may be, and that the wheelsmen are fully under his control, we feel that, with his skill, care, and knowledge of the way, we may banish fear from our thoughts.

"Baptiste is a noble Indian; he guides the boats among the islands and the rocks, over the rapids and through the intricate channels, as easily as a skillful horseman reins a high-spirited charger. As quick as thought the boat glides away from those rocks which it appeared impossible to avoid, but the pilot apparently is insensible to fear, though not to the responsibility that rests upon him. He is aware, and all are aware, that one false move and all is lost; for the current is so swift, the seas run so high, and the boat is driven so rapidly, that one touch upon a rock would shiver her to atoms. Although the passage of the rapids appears to be dangerous, a sense of pleasure and excitement takes the place of fear. Just as we left the La Chine Rapids, looking for the nervous man—there he stood, shaking, laughing, and exclaiming, '*that caps the* CLIMAX.' In about half an hour after leaving this last rapid, we enter the harbor of Montreal."

RAILROAD ROUTE FROM MONTREAL TO TORONTO, ETC., VIA GRAND TRUNK RAILWAY.

As the Grand Trunk Railway of Canada has recently been opened from Montreal to Toronto, and from the latter place is in rapid progress of completion to Port Sarnia, situated at the foot of Lake Huron, we give the following description of the route from Montreal westward, ascending the noble St. Lawrence.

The depôt is situated at the termination of the *Victoria Bridge*, about one and a half miles from the center of Montreal, subjecting the traveler to a long ride from the hotels or steamboat landing. On leaving the depôt the La Chine Canal is soon passed, and then the Montreal and La Chine Railroad, the track of the Grand Trunk Railway extending westerly across the fertile island of Montreal, passing in sight of *Lake St. Louis*, formed by the junction of the Ottawa and St. Lawrence rivers.

St. Anne's, 21 miles from Montreal, is a French-Canadian village, of some four or five hundred inhabitants. Here is a Roman Catholic church, and a number of picturesque edifices situated near the water's edge. The rapids, government lock for steamers, and the railroad bridge, together with the beautiful Ottawa and islands, altogether afford a magnificent view, almost unrivaled for river scenery. A few miles westward may be seen the hills giving the name to the *Lake of the Two Mountains*.

Isle Perot, about two miles in width, is next passed over by the upward train, and another branch of the Ottawa crossed when the cars stop at the

Vaudreuil Station, situated about half a mile below the village of the same name. Here a lovely view is obtained of the

Ottawa, its islands, and the hills of the Lake of the Two Mountains in the distance. The railroad track, on leaving the Ottawa, runs through a fertile tract of country for several miles, the village of the CEDARS being passed on the left, some two miles distant.

COTEAU STATION is 37 miles from Montreal and one and a half miles from the landing; here is a scattered settlement of French Canadians, numbering about 500 inhabitants.

LANCASTER, 54 miles from Montreal, is situated on the north shore of Lake St. Francis, an expansion of the St. Lawrence River. Here is a population of about 700 inhabitants, mostly of Scotch descent.

CORNWALL, 68 miles from Montreal, is a thriving town, situated at the foot of the Long Saut Rapids. It contains about 2,500 inhabitants. Here the trains usually meet, and the passengers are furnished refreshments. This is also a convenient steamboat landing, where the Royal Mail Line of steamers stop daily on their trips up and down the St. Lawrence.

Dickinson's Landing, 77 miles; *Aultsburg*, 84 miles; *Williamsburg*, 92 miles; *Matilda*, 99 miles, and *Prescott Junction*, 112 miles, are soon reached and passed by the ascending train.

The line of the Grand Trunk Railway from Vaudreuil to Brockville, a distance of 100 miles, runs through a level section of country, from a half to two miles distant from the St. Lawrence River, which is only seen occasionally from the passing train of cars.

The town of PRESCOTT, 113 miles from Montreal, and 60 miles from Kingston, is advantageously situated on the north bank of the St. Lawrence, opposite the village of Ogdensburgh. It contains a population of about 3,000 inhabitants. (*See page* 259.)

The *Ottawa and Prescott Railroad*, 54 miles in length, extends from Prescott to Ottawa City, intersecting the Grand Trunk Railway one and a half miles from the St. Lawrence River. On leaving Prescott the railroad runs through a level country to *Kemptville*, 23 miles, and thence to Ottawa City, a further distance of 30 miles. This is now the most speedy and favorite route from Montreal to the Upper Ottawa, passengers' baggage being checked through, *via* Prescott.

Brockville, 125 miles above Montreal, and 208 miles below Toronto, is one of the most important stations on the line of the *Grand Trunk Railway*, it being a flourishing town of about 8,000 inhabitants. The *Brockville and Ottawa Railroad* will extend from this place to Pembroke, situated 100 miles above Ottawa City. The railroad route from Brockville to Kingston, 48 miles, continues along the north shore of Lake Ontario to Cobourg, 90 miles farther, and thence to Toronto, 70 miles; being a total distance of 333 miles

For further information in regard to Kingston, Cobourg, Toronto, etc., see *Trip from Hamilton and Toronto to Kingston, etc.*

MONTREAL.

The City of Montreal, the largest and chief seat of commerce of British America, is favorably situated at the head of ship navigation on the left bank of the St. Lawrence River, here about two miles in width. It lies 170 miles above Quebec and 350 miles below Toronto, by water, in N. lat. 45° 30′, and W. long. 73° 25′ from Greenwich. The site, although not so commanding as Quebec, is in every other respect superior, lying at the foot of a romantic eminence from which it derives its name, called *Mount Royal,* which hill rises in picturesque beauty, about one mile from the city, to the height of 550 feet, forming a prominent object in the picture from every point of view. The streets, although somewhat irregular, present a fine and clean appearance. Notre Dame Street, the Broadway of Montreal, is the principal promenade and seat of the fashionable retail trade; it is about one mile in length and has many elegant stores, built of stone in the most durable manner. St. Paul Street, lying nearer the water, is mostly filled with wholesale stores. Great St. James Street is a wide and beautiful avenue, where are located most of the banks and insurance offices; together with hotels and other substantial buildings. McGill Street is filled with stores and offices of different kinds, running across the streets enumerated above. Water Street, Commissioners' Street, and Common Street extend the entire length of the city, facing on the St. Lawrence River and La Chine Canal; at times presenting a pleasing and lively appearance when the harbor and canal are filled with steamers and sail vessels of different kinds. From whatever side the city is approached, either by water or land, the scene is one of much interest; if from the St. Lawrence, Victoria Bridge and islands first attract attention; then the splendid towers of the Cathedral, the tall spires of other churches, the elegant front of Bonsecours

Market, the magnificent stone quay, and the long range of cut-stone buildings which front the river, form at once a *tout ensemble* which is unequaled.

The public buildings in Montreal are numerous; many of them massive and costly edifices. The most noted is the Roman Catholic or *French Cathedral*, situated on Notre Dame Street, fronting the Place d'Armes; it is built in the Gothic style of architecture, 255 feet in length by 134 in breadth; it has six towers, of which the three belonging to the main front are 220 feet in height. The principal window is 64 feet in height and 32 in breadth. The interior has several desks or altars, and is capable of accommodating from 6 to 7,000 persons, who can disperse by several outlets. "This church boasts the possession of a magnificent set of bells, one of which, weighing thirteen tons, is hung in the western tower, and is the largest bell in America. Under the church, the entire space is occupied by a cemetery—in which the more wealthy of the Roman Catholics are interred." The Seminary of St. Sulpice, adjoining the Cathedral, is a substantial stone building, at present only finished to the extent of half the proposed plan. In this building is transacted all the parochial business, and also the secular affairs connected with the very valuable property belonging to the priests of the seminary. There are several other Roman Catholic churches, mostly belonging to the order of St. Sulpice, to the members of which Montreal chiefly owed its foundation, and who still hold the seigniory of the island on which it stands.

The Protestant churches, consisting of the Church of England or Episcopal, the Church of Scotland (Presbyterian), the Congregational, the Baptist, the Methodist, and other persuasions, are numerous; Montreal being justly celebrated for its church edifices and church-going people. There are also a great number of nunneries and charitable institutions in the city, both under Roman Catholic and Protestant management. The court-house and prison are new and substantial stone buildings, occupying the site of the former college of the Jesuits. The government house, barracks, ordnance office, six banks, and five market-houses, the principal of which is the Bonsecours Market, are among the remaining public buildings. Nelson's Monument, a colossal statue of the hero of the Nile, is placed on a Doric column, the pedestal of which has bas-reliefs representing naval actions. McGill College is beautifully situated at the base of the mountain, and is richly endowed. Here are also a Baptist college and two Roman Catholic colleges, besides numerous other educational institutions. Montreal has a theater-royal, an exchange building, a penitentiary, a house of industry, a hospital, water works, gas works, a custom-house, a board of trade, scientific institutions, religious and benevolent institutions, and numerous well-kept hotels.

The favorable position of Montreal for trade and commerce, both foreign and domestic, makes it a great thoroughfare for men of business, as well as of the pleasure-seeking community. The facilities afforded by means of the St. Lawrence and Ottawa rivers, in connection with the Grand Trunk Railway and other railroads, open a ready communication, not only with all parts of Canada, but with Portland, Me., Boston, and the city of New York; the latter city being only 400 miles distant, and connected during the season of navigation by two popular lines of travel. The harbor, though not large, is safe and convenient; vessels drawing 15 feet may lie close to the quay, which is a most substantial stone structure of upward one mile in length. The *La Chine Canal*, nine miles long, admits steamers of a large size on their upward trips, they usually running the Rapids on their downward trips from the Lakes above and the Ottawa River. Besides steamers of a large class running to Quebec, steamships run regularly, during the season of navigation, between Montreal and Liverpool, making quick and profitable voyages. The trade through Lake Champlain, mostly by means of the *Champlain and St. Lawrence Railroad*, 44 miles in length, is immense—so much so as to require a ship canal from Caughanawa, or opposite Montreal, to the navigable waters of the Richelieu River, the outlet of Lake Champlain.

The *Montreal and Plattsburgh Railroad*, 52 miles in length. uniting with the La Chine Railroad, forms a direct line of travel to Plattsburgh, situated on the west shore of Lake Champlain. The *Montreal and Ottawa Railroad*, under construction, will add greatly to the advantage of Montreal.

The *Victoria Bridge*, now erecting across the St. Lawrence River, immediately above the city, when completed, will form one of the wonders of the age; it is to cross the river from Point St. Charles to the south shore, a total length of 10,284 feet, or about 50 yards less than two miles. It is to be built on the tubular principle, and will have a track for railroad cars in the center, while on the outside of the tube there will be a balcony on each side, with a footpath for passengers. The bridge will rest on 24 piers and two abutments of limestone masonry; the center span being 330 feet long, and 60 feet high from summer water-level, descending at either end at the rate of one in 130. It is in every respect to be built in the most substantial manner, and, when completed, will cost the enormous sum of £1,250,000 sterling, or $6,250,000. The contents of the masonry will be 3,000,000 of cubic feet. The weight of iron in the tubes 8,000 tons. The following are the dimensions of tube through which the trains pass in the middle span, viz.: 22 feet high, 16 feet wide; at the extreme ends, 19 feet high, 16 feet wide. This gigantic structure is in rapid progress of construction, and, it is understood, will be completed in 1859, or early in 1860.

The drives and inviting excursions about Montreal are numerous, and highly appreciated by visitors from more southern climes. The foremost stands the excursion around the mountain, which stands as a beacon to point out the true position of the city on nearing or departing from this romantic city. Other drives up or down the St. Lawrence, or on almost any part of the fertile island of Montreal, are attended with pleasure and delightful emotions. "Besides these excursions, the tourist will find his time well repaid by a visit to the Saut-au-Recollect, which is a series of Rapids at the northern side of the island, on a branch of the Ottawa called La Riviere des Prairies. Here, besides the beauty of the scenery, he may see the rafts from the Ottawa making the descent—an exciting exploit both to the spectators and hardy crews, though from the rarity of accidents we must conclude that the skill of the *voyageurs* has taught them to avoid any real danger."

POPULATION OF MONTREAL—1852.

Males	27,586	Other countries	1,457
Females	30,129		
		Roman Catholics	41,466
Total population	57,715	Protestants	16,196
French Canadians	26,020	Number of houses	7,420
British Canadians	12,494	" families	9,990
English, Irish, & Scotch	17,77.4		

GRAND TRUNK RAILWAY OF CANADA.

THE GRAND TRUNK RAILWAY, the greatest scheme of its kind in America, embraces in its ramifications the construction of a continuous line of railway from Trois Pistoles, C. E., about 150 miles below Quebec, on the southern side of the river St. Lawrence, the point at which a junction with the proposed *Halifax Railway* is looked forward to—and Port Sarnia, C. W., on Lake Huron, a distance of upward of 800 miles—also a branch line of 50 miles in length, from Belleville to Peterborough, C. W. —and the leasing of the railroad then already built between Montreal and Portland, Me., so that the products of the western points of the Province might be conveyed through Canada to the Atlantic seaboard, without break of guage or bulk. The total length of unbroken railway communication which will thus be obtained, when the St. Lawrence River is spanned by the Victoria Bridge, a structure unequaled in the history of engineering, either in size or in massive proportions—is upward of 1,100 miles. The original capital of the company was £9,500,000, but this being found insufficient, it has been determined to increase this amount to £12,000,000 sterling. or $60,000,000. Of this sum the Province has an interest in the undertaking, in the shape of a guaranty, to an amount of upward of £3,000,000 sterling, or $15,000,000. Of the works proposed, however, it was found necessary, from several causes, to place in abeyance the prosecution of three different sections of the work, viz., the distance between St. Thomas to Trois Pistoles, 100 miles; from Belleville to Peterborough, 50 miles; and from St. Mary's to Sarnia, 68 miles. But these sections will doubtless ere long be proceeded with; in the first case, because the Lower Provinces in all probability, assisted by the Imperial Government, will complete their railway communication to Trois Pistoles, in order to connect it with the Canadian railway system; and in the latter two cases, simply because the traffic of the country will very speedily demand the construction of these lines.

With these curtailments, and they are but temporary, the Grand Trunk Railway is now composed of the following sections, viz.:

Montreal to Portland	292	miles.
Richmond to Port Levi, opposite Quebec, St. Thomas.	137	"
Montreal to Toronto	333	"
Toronto to Stratford	88	"
Making a total mileage of	850	miles.

The works throughout the whole of this great length of line have been pronounced by competent authorities, both English and American, to be altogether unequaled by any railway on this continent, and reflect much credit, not only on the engineer of the company, but also on the several agents of the contractors. On an average, there is a station to every six miles, two men to every three miles, and a locomotive to every four miles.

Apart from the through travel between the East and the West, which must be very large, the junctions between other railways and the Grand Trunk Railway throughout the Province are very numerous, and will provide a heavy traffic, both of passengers and freight.

TRIP FROM MONTREAL TO OTTAWA CITY AND THE UPPER OTTAWA RIVER.

TOURISTS who design to visit the Ottawa River, and view its varied and beautiful scenery, should leave Montreal by steamer, or by the *Grand Trunk Railway*, in the morning for St. Anne's, 21 miles; there taking a steamer for Ottawa City, 90 miles farther; or if desired, continue the railroad route to Prescott, 113 miles from Montreal, and proceed by *Ottawa and Prescott Railroad*. The *La Chine Railroad* also conveys passengers to La Chine, nine miles, from whence steamers depart daily for Ottawa City.

At ST. ANNE'S, 14 miles above La Chine, the steamer passes through a lock 45 feet wide and 180 feet long. Here is a succession of rapids in the river, and several small islands. The village is handsomely situated on the southwest end of the island of Montreal, and is the place where the poet Moore located the scene of his admired *Canadian Boat Song*.*

CANADIAN BOAT SONG.

BY THOMAS MOORE.

Faintly as tolls the evening chime,
Our voices keep tune and our oars keep time;
Soon as the woods on shore look dim,
We'll sing at St. Anne's our parting hymn.
Row, brothers, row, the stream runs fast,
The Rapids are near and the daylight's past.

Why should we yet our sail unfurl?
There is not a breath the blue wave to curl;
But when the wind blows off the shore,
Oh! sweetly we'll rest our weary oar.
Blow, breezes, blow, the stream runs fast,
The Rapids are near and the daylight's past.

---

* The *voyageurs*, in passing the Rapids of St. Anne, were formerly obliged to take out a part, if not the whole, of their lading, owing to the small depth of water here afforded. It is from this village that the Canadians consider they take their departure on ascending the Ottawa, as it possesses the last church on the island of Montreal, which is dedicated to the tutelar saint of *voyageurs*.

Ottawa's tide! this trembling moon
Shall see us float over thy surges soon.
Saint of this green isle! hear our prayers,
Oh! grant us cool heavens and favoring airs.
  Blow, breezes, blow, the stream runs fast,
  The Rapids are near and the daylight's past.

Two miles west of St. Anne's commences the *Lake of the Two Mountains*, being an expansion of the Ottawa, about ten miles long and eight miles wide. Here a branch of the river diverges toward the northeast, forming the west boundary of the island of Montreal. Two hills to the north, elevated 400 or 500 feet above the river at the distance of a few miles, give the name to this body of water.

The INDIAN VILLAGE of the Two Mountains is situated on the north side of the Ottawa, about 25 miles west of La Chine. Here reside the remnants of two tribes, the Mohawks and Algonquins. The settlements are divided by a Roman Catholic church, standing near the river side. On the hill toward the north are situated three or four chapels. The highest summit of the hill or mountain, one or two miles distant, is called Calvary, and is visited by the Indians and whites on certain religious festivals of the Roman Catholic Church. Here the river contracts in width to about half a mile, for a distance of one mile, when it again expands, forming the *Upper Lake of the Two Mountains.* About nine miles farther west the river again contracts to half a mile in width.

On the south is passed the settlement of REGAUD, and a mountain of the same name.

CARILLON, eight miles farther, is on the north side of the Ottawa. Here are rapids in the river, and the navigation by steamboat is continued by means of a lock and canal, 12 miles in length.

At POINT FORTUNE, opposite Carillon, passengers going to the Caledonia Springs usually take a stage for L'ORIGINAL, a distance of 18 miles, along the south bank of the Ottawa, which affords some picturesque views.

At GRENVILLE, 12 miles from Carillon, navigation is resumed on the Ottawa River, for a further distance of 58 miles.

The RIDEAU FALLS (the *Curtain*), so called from their resemblance to drapery, is formed by the waters of the Rideau River precipitating itself into the Ottawa, a short distance below the city of Ottawa. This is a beautiful fall of 30 feet, and attracts much notice, being seen to advantage from the steamer ascending the Ottawa.

CHAUDIERE FALLS (the *Boiling Pot*), which are second only to those of Niagara in grandeur and magnificence, are on the Ottawa, immediately above the city. These falls, in connection with the surrounding scenery, render this section of Canada very attractive to tourists seeking health or pleasure.

The City of OTTAWA, C. W., formerly called *Bytown*, occupies a most romantic position on the southwest side of Ottawa River, being 120 miles distant from Montreal, and 54 from Prescott by railway. It is in a naturally strong situation, and could be easily rendered almost impregnable. The city is divided into two parts, like Quebec, known as the Upper and Lower Towns, which are about half a mile apart. The *Rideau Canal* commences here, and is spanned by a handsome stone bridge, forming part of the street which connects the two portions of the town, and it is also connected with HULL, on the Lower Canada side of the river, by a fine suspension bridge.

The city is justly celebrated as being a great mart for lumber, in which the Ottawa country abounds. In the neighborhood is found beautiful pale-gray limestone, of which material many of the edifices are constructed, giving a handsome and solid appearance to the place; the streets have been laid out with great regularity, and are very wide. Barrack Hill, a commanding site, is retained by the government, which, if judiciously improved, the inhabitants might have beautiful grounds for purposes of health and recreation. Here are situated the county buildings, ten churches of different denominations, four or five banking-houses, several well-kept hotels, together with numerous stores and extensive grist-mills, saw-mills, and other manufacturing establishments.

The *Ottawa and Prescott Railway*, 54 miles in length, ter-minutes at Prescott, situated on the St. Lawrence River, directly opposite Ogdensburgh. No other road of its length in America possesses greater advantages than this railway, if right'y turned to account, pointing as it does to the State and city of New York.

Stages and *Steamboats* run daily from Ottawa City to different places on the river above the city, affording romantic excursions during the summer and autumn months.

The Union Line of steamers runs from AYLMER, nine miles above Ottawa, to JOACHIN, 150 miles above the city. The proprietors have three iron steamers, with fifty-horse-power engines: one running from Aylmer to Chatts; one from Amprior to Portage Du Fort, and one from Portage Du Fort to Joachin. These boats are not sufficient to do the business that is now offered; and it is a remarkable fact, that while goods are carried in winter on sleighs over this route for 50 cents per 100 pounds, the steamboat charge is $1 25.

VILLAGES ON THE UPPER OTTAWA RIVER.

AYLMER, nine miles above the city on the Lower Canada side, is situated at the outlet of Chaudiere Lake, through which the river flows, has about 1,000 inhabitants, and is the shire town of Ottawa County. Is at the foot of steamboat navigation above the city. There is a good McAdam road from the city to Aylmer.

FITZROY and CHATTS—these villages are connected, and situated 32 miles above the city, with about 500 inhabitants; the river at this place has a fall of 52½ feet.

AMPRIOR, 40 miles above the city. This place has sprung into existence within the last two years; has now 60 dwellings, and 40 more under contract. A railroad is now under contract from Ottawa City to Amprior, to be completed in 1858, and I understand that this is also the point where the Brockville and Pembroke Railroad comes to the river. The river has a fall here of twelve feet. To hear the descriptions which are given of this section of the country, one would think that it was the Garden of Eden, and that it was soon to be reclaimed. Those engaged in building up Amprior, predict that it is soon to become the Chicago of Canada.

PORTAGE DU FORT is 60 miles above Ottawa City. The river here has a fall of twelve feet, affording good water-power.

PEMBROKE, 100 miles above the city, is the next place on the river, and is a point of great importance.

The *Brockville and Ottawa Railroad*, when completed, will terminate at this place, and afford great facilities to the settlements on the Upper Ottawa River and its tributaries.

OTTAWA RIVER.

Copied from the Canadian Tourist.

"This river, and the vast fertile territory which it drains, has hitherto been, in a great measure, abandoned to the operations of the lumberman, and the comparatively few farmers who have followed his steps; but, latterly, its capabilities as an agricultural country have gradually attracted a greater degree of attention, which the proposal of connecting its waters with Lake Huron and the Far West will greatly increase. Of the magnitude of the river, the riches of its banks, and the beauty of the scenery, we can not better speak than by making use of the excellent Report lately made by a Committee of the Canadian House of Assembly on Railways:

"'The length of the course of the Ottawa River is about 780 miles. From its source it bends in a southwest course, and after receiving several tributaries from the height of land separating its waters from the Hudson Bay, it enters Lake Temiscaming. From its entrance into this lake downward the course of the Ottawa has been surveyed, and is well known.

"'At the head of the lake the Blanche River falls in, coming about ninety miles from the north. Thirty-four miles farther down the lake it receives the Montreal River, coming one hundred and twenty miles from the northwest. Six miles lower down on the east, or Lower Canada bank, it receives the Keepawa-sippi, a large river which has its origin in a lake of great size, hitherto but partially explored, and known as Lake Keepawa. This lake is connected with another chain of irregularly shaped lakes, from one of which proceeds the River du Moine, which enters the Ottawa about a hundred miles below the mouth of the Keepawa-sippi.

"'From the Long Saut at the foot of Lake Temiscaming, two hundred and thirty-three miles above the city of Ottawa, and three hundred and sixty miles from the mouth of the Ottawa, down to Deux Joachim Rapids, at the head of the Deep River, that is, for eighty-nine miles, the Ottawa, with the exception of seventeen miles below the Long Saut, and some other intervals, is not at present navigable, except for canoes. Besides other tributaries in the interval, at a hundred and ninety-seven miles from Bytown, now called Ottawa, it receives on the west side the Mattawan, which is the highway for canoes going to Lake Huron by Lake Nippissing. From the Mattawan the

Ottawa flows east by south to the head of Deep River Reach, nine miles above which it receives the River du Moine from the north.

"'From the head of Deep River, as this part of the Ottawa is called, to the foot of Upper Allumettes Lake, two miles below the village of Pembroke, is an uninterrupted reach of navigable water, forty-three miles in length. The general direction of the river in this part is southeast. The mountains along the north side of Deep River are upward of a thousand feet in height, and the many wooded islands of Allumettes Lake render the scenery of this part of the Ottawa magnificent and exceedingly picturesque—far surpassing the celebrated Lake of the Thousand Islands on the St. Lawrence.

"'Passing the short rapid of Allumettes, and turning northward round the lower end of Allumettes Island, which is fourteen miles long and eight at its greatest width, and turning down southeast through Coulonge Lake, and passing behind the nearly similar islands of Calumet to the head of Calumet Falls, the Ottawa presents, with the exception of one slight rapid, a reach of fifty miles of navigable water. The mountains on the north side of Coulonge Lake, which rise apparently to the height of fifteen hundred feet, add a degree of grandeur to the scenery, which is in other respects beautiful and varied. In the Upper Allumettes Lake, a hundred and fifteen miles from Ottawa, the river receives from the west the Petawawee, one of its largest tributaries. This river is a hundred and forty miles in length, and drains an area of two thousand two hundred square miles. At Pembroke, nine miles lower down on the same side, an inferior stream, the Indian River, also empties itself into the Ottawa.

"'At the head of Lake Coulonge the Ottawa receives from the north the Black River, a hundred and thirty miles in length, draining an area of eleven hundred and twenty miles, and nine miles lower on the same side the river Coulonge, which is probably a hundred and sixty miles in length, with a valley of eighteen hundred square miles.

"'From the head of the Calumet Falls to Portage du Fort, the head of the steamboat navigation, a distance of eight miles, are impassable rapids. Fifty miles above the city, the Ottawa receives on the west the Bonnechère, a hundred and ten miles in length, draining an area of nine hundred and eighty miles. Eleven miles lower it receives the Madawaska, one of its great feeders, a river two hundred and ten miles in length, and draining four thousand one hundred square miles.

"'Thirty-seven miles above Ottawa there is an interruption in the navigation, caused by three miles of rapids and falls, to pass which a railroad has been made. At the foot of the rapids the Ottawa divides among islands into numerous channels, presenting a most imposing array of separate falls.

"'Six miles above Ottawa begin the rapids terminating in the Ottawa *Chaudière Falls*, which, inferior in impressive grandeur to the Falls of Niagara, are, perhaps, more permanently interesting, as presenting greater variety. The greatest height of Chaudière Falls is about forty feet. Arrayed in every imaginable variety of form—in vast, dark masses, in graceful cascades, or in tumbling spray—they have been well described as a hundred rivers struggling for a passage. Not the least interesting feature which they present is the Lost Chaudière, where a body of water, greater in volume than the Thames at London, is quietly sucked down, and disappears under ground.

"'At the city of Ottawa the river receives the Rideau from the west, running a course of a hundred and sixteen miles, and draining an area of thirteen hundred and fifty square miles.'

"The city of Ottawa is, perhaps, situated more picturesquely than any other in North America, with the exception of Quebec. The view from the Barrack Hill—embracing, as it does, in one *coup d'œil*, the magnificent Falls of the Chaudière, with its clouds of snowy spray, generally spanned by a brilliant rainbow; the Suspension Bridge uniting Upper and Lower Canada; the river above the great Falls, studded with pretty wooded islands, and the distant purple mountains, which divide the waters of the Gatineau from those of the Ottawa—is one of the most beautiful in the world.

"The city, now containing about fourteen thousand inhabitants, sprung up, about thirty years ago, from a collection of shanties inhabited by the laborers and artificers employed by the Royal Engineers to construct the *Rideau Canal*. This canal (terminating at Kingston) was intended by the government of England to be a means of communication between the Lower St. Lawrence and the Lakes, in case the communication on the front should be interrupted. The canal was designed by Colonel By, of the Royal Engineers, and the present city of Ottawa was named Bytown in memory of its founder, until, about two years ago, the inhabitants petitioned the Provincial Parliament to change the name.

"The canal is a splendid specimen of engineering skill, and the masonry of the numerous locks is generally admired for its finish and solidity. Eight of these locks rise one above another directly in the center of the city, the canal being crossed by a handsome stone bridge just above them. The canal, in fact, divides the city into two parts, the Upper and Lower. A large part of the Upper Town is comprised in what is called the Barrack Hill, on which is a small barracks for troops, and some storehouses, the property of the Imperial Government; there is here a parade-ground of several acres, and the summit of the hill, from which is to be seen the beautiful view which we spoke of before, is one of the finest promenades in the world. A few very simple fortifications on this hill would make the city of Ottawa almost as impregnable as Quebec.

"Within the last few years a small hamlet has sprung up near the Suspension Bridge, in consequence of the abundant water-power existing there, of which several enterprising persons have availed themselves to erect saw-mills. There is also here a very large iron foundry and machine manufactory.

"Here also are the slides, erected by government, for the passage of timber, in order to avoid the great fall, over which the pieces of timber used to be precipitated singly, to be again collected below at a great trouble and loss. Throughout the whole summer, from morning to night, the 'cribs' of timber, each manned by three or four hardy raftsmen, may be seen darting down these slides; while from the lofty summit of the Barrack Hill the huge rafts, gay with bright streamers floating from their many masts, may be seen on the smooth, dark bosom of the river, the golden-colored timber flashing in the sunbeams.

"In the Lower Town are the principal mercantile establishments, the court-house and jail, the Roman Catholic Cathedral, the Bishop's Palace; a nunnery, to which the General Hospital is attached, and a Roman Catholic college; the Protestant hospital, the Terminus of the Prescott and Ottawa Railway, and the steamboat wharf. Among the objects well worth seeing in this part of the town is a steam saw-mill, of great size, recently erected by an enterprising citizen. In Central Ottawa are the town-hall, the post-office, telegraph office and news-room, to which are attached a library and museum, the latter containing some very interesting geological specimens. In Upper Ottawa are the Episcopal church and the office at which all the business connected with timber cut on the lands of the Crown is transacted. The banks of Upper Canada, British North America, Montreal, and Quebec have agencies in the city.

"During the summer months steamers run daily on the river between Ottawa and Montreal, and between Ottawa and Kingston, by the way of Rideau Canal. A railway train leaves the city every day for Prescott, where those passengers who intend to go to Montreal change into the cars of the Grand Trunk line, and so reach Montreal by railway.

"Travelers who wish to proceed farther up the river can take a carriage or omnibus for Aylmer, a pretty village about nine miles from Ottawa, between which place and Aylmer there is an excellent turnpike road, where they will find a steamer which takes them to the Chatts; from this there is a railway about two miles; they then proceed by another steamer to Portage du Fort; here wagons are used for a short distance. and another steamer takes them to Pembroke, and again another from that point to Deux Joachim, where for the present navigation ceases for any thing larger than a canoe A railroad is under construction, extending from Pembroke to Brockville, situated on the St. Lawrence River.

"Immediately below the city of Ottawa the river Rideau discharges into the Ottawa, falling gently over the edge of a limestone precipice like a beautifully transparent '*curtain*' of water, from which resemblance its name has been derived; the fall is divided into two portions by a small rocky island, which adds greatly to the picturesqueness of the scene. The Rideau Falls are best seen from a boat.

"A mile lower it receives from the north its greatest tributary, the *Gatineau*, which, with a course probably of four hundred and twenty miles, drains an area of twelve thousand square miles. For about two hundred miles the upper course of this river is in the unknown northern country. At the farthest point surveyed, two hundred and seventeen miles from its mouth, the Gatineau is still a noble stream, a thousand feet wide, diminished in depth, but not in width.

"Eighteen miles lower down the Rivière au Lièvre enters from the north, after running a course of two hundred and sixty miles in length, and draining an area of four thousand one hundred miles. Fifteen miles below it the Ottawa receives the North and South Nation rivers on either side, the former ninety-five and the latter a hundred miles in length. Twenty-two miles farther the river Rouge, ninety miles long, enters from the north. Twenty-one miles lower the Rivière du Nord, a hundred and sixty miles in length, comes in on the same side, and lastly, just above its mouth, it receives the river Assumption, which has a course of a hundred and thirty miles.

"From Ottawa the river is navigable to Grenville, a distance of fifty-eight miles, where the rapids that occur for twelve miles are avoided by a succession of canals. Twenty-three miles lower, at one of the mouths of the Ottawa, a single lock, to avoid a slight rapid (St. Anne's Rapid), gives a passage into Lake St. Louis, an expansion of the St. Lawrence above Montreal.

"The remaining half of the Ottawa's waters find their way to the St. Lawrence, by passing in two channels behind the Island of Montreal and the Isle Jesus, in a course of thirty-one miles. They are interrupted with rapids, still it is by one of them that all the Ottawa lumber passes to market. At Bout de l'Isle, therefore, the Ottawa is finally merged in the St. Lawrence, a hundred and thirty miles below from the city of Ottawa.

"The most prominent characteristic of the Ottawa is its great volume. Even above the town, where it has to receive tributaries equal to the Hudson, the Shannon, the Thames, the Tweed, the Spey, and the Clyde, it displays, when unconfined, a width of half a mile of strong, boiling rapid; and when at the highest, while the north waters are passing, the volume, by calculated approximation, is fully equal to that passing Niagara—that is, double the common volume of the Ganges.

"Taking a bird's-eye view of the valley of the Ottawa, we see spread out before us a country equal to eight times the State of Vermont, or ten times that of Massachusetts, with its great artery, the Ottawa, curving through it, resembling the Rhine in length of course, and the Danube in magnitude.

"This immense region overlies a variety of geological formations, and presents all their characteristic features, from the level uniform surface of the Silurian system, which prevails along a great extent of the Ottawa, to the rugged and romantic ridges in the metamorphic and primitive formations, which stretch far away to the north and the northwest.

"As far as our knowledge of the country extends, we find the greater part of it covered with a luxuriant growth of red and white pine timber, making the most valuable forests in the world, abundantly intersected with large rivers, fitted to convey the timber to market when manufactured.

"The remaining portion of it, if not so valuably wooded, presents a very extensive and advantageous field for settlement. Apart from the numerous townships already surveyed and partly settled, and the large tracts of good land interspersed throughout the timber country, the great region on the upper course of the western tributaries of the Ottawa, behind the red pine country, exceeds the State of New Hampshire in extent, with an equal climate and superior soil. It is generally a beautiful undulating country, wooded with a rich growth of maple, beech, birch, elm, etc., and watered with lakes and streams affording numerous mill-sites and abounding in fish. Flanking on the one side the lumbering country, which presents an excellent market for produce, and adjoining Lake Huron on the other, the situation, though comparatively inland, is highly advantageous. In the diversity of resources, the Ottawa country above described presents unusual attractions alike to agricultural and commercial enterprise."

LAKE GEORGE, OR HORICON

THIS romantic sheet of water, whose beauties are almost indescribable, lies mostly in the county of Warren, N. Y., 27 miles north of Saratoga Springs. It is justly celebrated for its varied and beautiful scenery, and for the transparency and purity of its waters. It is 36 miles long, north and south, and from two to three miles wide; and is elevated 243 feet above the tide-water of the Hudson, although its waters flow north into Lake Champlain. It is surrounded by high and picturesque hills, sometimes rising to mountain height, and dotted with numerous islands, said to count as many as there are days in the year; some are of considerable size, and cultivated; while others are only a barren rock, rising majestically out of the surrounding waters. The wild and romantic scenery of this lake is nowhere surpassed. The bed of the lake is a handsome yellowish sand, and the water is so pure and transparent as to render the bottom visible from 30 to 40 feet. Here the delicious salmon-trout, that weigh from five to twenty pounds, are found in great numbers, and of the finest quality. Silver trout, brook trout, pike, pickerel, perch, and several other kinds of fresh water fish, are also abundant. Travelers on the tour from the Springs to Canada should not fail to visit Lake George; by the French called *Lac Sacrament*, on account of the purity of its waters. The steamboat "Minnehaha" runs through the lake, from Caldwell to the landing near the village of Ticonderoga, whence stages run to *Fort Ticonderoga*, at the steamboat landing on Lake Champlain; where steam passage boats, on their route from Whitehall to Burlington and Rouse's Point, touch daily during the season of navigation. This route is varied in scenery, and deeply interesting in historical incidents.

The romantic village of CALDWELL, lying at the south end of the lake, contains a court-house and jail, two churches, and a number of handsome private residences, besides *Fort William Henry Hotel* and the *Lake House*, two popular public houses, which are usually thronged with fashionable visitors during the summer months.

"Lake George abounds with small and beautiful islands, among the most important of which are Diamond Island, Tea Island, and Long Island. Roger's Rock or Slide, and Anthony's Nose, the former on the west and the latter on the east side, are two precipices worthy of note. Howe's Landing, just behind an island at the outlet of the lake, denotes the spot where the unfortunate expedition of Abercrombie landed, and derives its name from Lord Howe, who accompanied and fell in that expedition, in 1758.

"This lake and its vicinity has been the scene of several important battles. One which has been generally known as the *Battle of Lake George*, was fought at the head of the lake in 1755, between the French under the Baron Dieskau, and the English under Sir Wm. Johnson. Dieskau attacked the English in their encampment, but was defeated and slain. The loss of the English was 130 slain, and that of the French about 700.*

"The most shocking transaction in the vicinity of this lake was the *Massacre* at Fort William Henry in 1757. A British and Provincial army having been collected at Fort Edward and Fort William Henry under Gen. Webb, for the reduction of the French works on Lake Champlain, the French sent a large army up the lake under Gen. Montcalm, for their defense. Gen. Webb, then at Fort William Henry, learning from Maj. Putnam that this force had entered Lake George, returned immediately to Fort Edward, and the day following sent Col. Monroe, with his regiment, to reinforce the garrison at the lake. The day after Monroe's arrival the French appeared at the fort, laid siege to it, and demanded its surrender. The garrison, consisting of 2,500 men, defended themselves with much bravery for several days, with the expectation of succor from Fort Edward. But as none came, Monroe was obliged on the 9th of August to capitulate. By the articles of capitulation, all the public property was to be delivered to Montcalm, and the garrison were to march out with their arms and baggage, and to be escorted to Fort Edward, on condition of not serving against the French within the period of eighteen months.

"The garrison had no sooner marched out of the fort than scene of perfidy and barbarity commenced, which it is impossible for language to describe. Regardless of the articles of capitulation, the Indians attached to the French army fell upon

* See Thompson's Vermont, Part II., page 8.

the defenseless soldiers, plundering and murdering all that fell in their way. The French officers were idle spectators of this bloody scene; nor could all the entreaties of Monroe persuade them to furnish the promised escort. On that fatal day about 1,500 of the English were either murdered by the savages or carried by them into captivity never to return.

"The day following these horrid transactions, Major Putnam was dispatched from Fort Edward with his rangers to watch the motions of the enemy. He reached Lake George just after the rear of the enemy had left the shore, and the scene which was presented he describes as awful indeed. 'The fort was entirely destroyed; the barracks, out-houses, and buildings were a heap of ruins—the cannon, stores, boats, and vessels were all carried away. The fires were still burning—the smoke and stench offensive and suffocating. Innumerable fragments of human skulls, and bones and carcasses half consumed, were still frying and broiling in the decaying fires. Dead bodies mangled with scalping-knives and tomahawks, in all the wantonness of Indian barbarity, were everywhere to be seen. More than 100 women, butchered and shockingly mangled, lay upon the ground still weltering in their gore. Devastation, barbarity, and horror everywhere appeared; and the spectacle presented was too diabolical and awful either to be endured or described.'"

STEAMER ON LAKE GEORGE.

A NEW steamboat is being built on Lake George in the place of the JOHN JAY, burned in July last. She is 145 feet long and 26 feet wide. The boiler and furnace are placed in compartments, incased in iron, entirely fire-proof, no expense being spared in order to make her a beautiful and safe passenger boat.

Her name, "MINNE-HA-HA," a romantic one, is selected with great appropriateness from Longfellow's HIAWATHA:

"With him dwelt his dark-eyed daughter,
Wayward as the Minnehaha;
With her moods of shade and sunshine,
Eyes that frowned and smiled alternate,
Feet as rapid as the river,
Tresses flowing like the water,
And as musical a laughter;
And he named her from the river,
From the waterfall he named her
Minne-ha-ha—*laughing water.*"

The FALLS OF TICONDEROGA, situated on the outlet of Lake George, are well worthy the attention of tourists. Here are two important cascades within the distance of two or three miles, surrounded by mountain scenery of great historic interest. The *Upper Falls*, near the village of Alexandria, are formed by a succession of descents of upward of 200 feet within the distance of a mile, affording water-power unsurpassed by any other locality in the State for safety and a steady flow of water, the stream not being subject to freshets. The *Lower Fall*, in the village of Ticonderoga, has a perpendicular fall of 30 feet, being much used for hydraulic purposes. The ruins of old *Fort Ticonderoga*, two miles below this place, are situated on a point of land at the entrance of the outlet of Lake George into Lake Champlain, standing on an eminence of about 60 feet, overlooking the lake; the ruins are plainly visible from the water, presenting a conspicuous and interesting object. About 1,800 yards southwest stands *Mount Defiance*, rising 750 feet above the lake, overlooking and commanding the site of Fort Ticonderoga. A public house, for the accommodation of visitors, stands near the steamboat landing.

DISTANCES FROM CALDWELL TO ALBANY, *via* SARATOGA SPRINGS.

CALDWELL	0	0	ALBANY	0	0
Glenn's Falls, *Stage*	9	9	TROY	6	6
Moreau Station "	5	14	Cohoes	3	9
SARATOGA SPRINGS	15	29	Waterford	1	10
Ballston Spa	7	36	Junction Albany R.R.	2	12
Mechanicsville	13	49	Mechanicsville	6	18
Junction Albany R.R.	6	55	Ballston Spa	13	31
Waterford	2	57	SARATOGA SPRINGS	7	32
Cohoes	1	58	Moreau Station	15	53
TROY	3	61	Glenn's Falls, *Stage*	5	58
ALBANY	6	67	CALDWELL "	9	67

LAKE CHAMPLAIN.

One of the most interesting and lovely bodies of water in North America lies between the States of New York and Vermont, through which runs the boundary line from near Whitehall to lat. 45°, being a distance of 116 miles; it may be said to extend four miles farther, into Canada, making the whole length of the lake 120 miles; varying from half a mile or less to twelve miles in width. Its direction is nearly north and south, and it is a long, narrow, and deep body of water, dotted with a number of islands, the largest of which belong to Vermont. From Whitehall to Crown Point the lake is quite narrow, but here it begins to expand, and soon becomes three miles wide, still increasing northward until near Burlington, where it spreads to its greatest width. *Missisquoi Bay*, an extension of Lake Champlain on the northeast, lies mostly in Canada, above the 45th degree of north latitude. Steamboats of the first class, and sloops of from 50 to 100 tons burden, navigate Lake Champlain its whole length, thence down the Sorelle, or Richelieu River, its outlet, to St. John's, Canada, where steamboat navigation ceases; a total distance of about 140 miles. This lake is also connected with the navigable waters of the Hudson, by means of the Champlain Canal, which extends south, a distance of 63 miles. As you approach near the center of Lake Champlain, a large body of water presents itself to view, bordered by scenery of the most picturesque description; the headlands which are seen to great advantage, and the vast ranges of mountains on either side, are truly grand and romantic. The highest peak of the Green Mountains, called the "*Camel's Hump*," is seen on the east, while the high ranges of the mountains of Essex County are seen on the west. This latter range of mountain peaks, the *Adirondack group*, contains the highest land in the State of New York, rising in some places to the height of 5,000 feet and upward, abounding with iron ore and timber of large growth. In the streams which flow into this lake are frequent waterfalls of great beauty; and the fine headlands, with numerous indentations and bays of singular beauty, only need to be seen to be admired. Its waters are well stored with salmon, salmon trout, sturgeon, pickerel, and other fish.

"Lake Champlain was discovered by Samuel Champlain in July, 1609, having founded the colony of Quebec in 1608; in June, 1809, he, with a number of French and Indians, proceeded in a shallop up the St. Lawrence and river Iroquois, now Richelieu, till stopped by the Chambly Rapids. From this place he determined to proceed in Indian canoes, but the Frenchmen manifested great reluctance, and only two would be persuaded to accompany him. With these and about sixty of the natives, having transported their canoes by the rapids on the 2d of July, and, proceeding southward, on the 4th of July e entered the lake.

"CHAMPLAIN and his party proceeded along the west shore, advancing by water during the night and retiring into the forests by day, to avoid being discovered by the Iroquois, between whom and the Canada Indians a war was then carried on. As they drew near the enemy's country they proceeded with great caution, but on the 29th of July, in the evening, they fell in with a large war party of the Iroquois. Both parties drew up to the shore, and the night was spent in preparation for battle, and in singing and taunting each other. In the morning an engagement took place, but the Frenchmen being armed with muskets, it was decided in favor of Champlain and his party, a large number of the Iroquois being slain and several taken prisoners. With these they returned immediately to their shallop. Champlain says that this battle was fought in lat. 43° and some minutes, and the place is supposed to have been on the west shore of Lake George. The present name of Lake Champlain was given by its discoverer during his first visit, as he informs us in his journal. He was not drowned in its waters, as has been sometimes said, but died at Quebec in 1635. One of the Indian names of this lake was *Petawa-Bouque*, signifying alternate land and water, in allusion to the numerous islands and projecting points of land. Another is said to have been *Caniaderi-Guarunte*, signifying the mouth or door of the country. If so, it was very appropriate, as it forms the gate-way between the country on the St. Lawrence and that on the Hudson. In more recent times the Indians called it *Corlear*, in honor of a Dutchman who saved a war party of Canada Indians from being destroyed by the Mohawks in 1665.

"The first steamboat built on this lake commenced running in 1809. The *line* boats have always been favorably known to travelers either for business or pleasure, for the manner in which they have been managed—their neat and orderly appearance—obliging and attentive officers and efficient crews. At present there are daily lines to and from Whitehall and Rouse's Point, stopping at Ticonderoga, Burlington, Plattsburgh, and intermediate places, connecting with the various railroads —also numerous ferry boats, propellers, and tow boats, besides more than 300 sloops, canal boats, barges, etc."

Champlain Canal connects the waters of the Hudson with Lake Champlain. It is 64 miles long, 40 feet wide at the top and 28 at the bottom, with a navigable *feeder* at Sandy Hill 11 miles long. It has 21 locks, 14 by 90 feet. Rise from the Hudson, 134 feet, fall to the lake, 54; was begun in 1816, finished in 1819, and cost $1,079,872. The route of this canal is interesting on account of its passing through a section of country rendered memorable by important military operations. It passes in part along the line of Burgoyne's advance from Lake Champlain—near the scene of his principal battles—and of his final surrender. It passes near Fort Miller—Fort Edward—the spot where Miss M'Crea was murdered—Fort Anne—the tree to which Gen. Putnam was bound in 1757, etc.

HEIGHT OF THE PRINCIPAL MOUNTAIN PEAKS IN VERMONT—GREEN MOUNTAIN RANGE.

NAME.	Altitude above Sea.
Chin, or North Peak, Mansfield Mountain	4,279 ft.
Camel's Hump, Huntington	4,183 "
Shrewsbury Mountain	4,086 "
Nose, or South Peak, Mansfield Mountain	3,983 "
Killington Peak, Sherburne	3,924 "
Equinox Mountain, Manchester	3,706 "
Ascutney Mt., Windsor	3,320 "

ALTITUDE OF THE PRINCIPAL MOUNTAINS NORTHERN NEW YORK—ADIRONDACK GROUP.

NAME.		Altitude above Sea.
Mount Marcy,	Essex County.	5,467 ft.
Mount McIntire	Essex County.	5,183 "
Mount McMartin	Essex County.	5,000 "
Dial Mountain		4,900 "
Whiteface Mt.		4,855 "
Mount Seward, Franklin Co.		4,600 "
Mount Lyon, Clinton Co.		4,000 "

Surface of LAKE CHAMPLAIN, above tide	90 feet.
" LAKE GEORGE " "	243 "
" LAKE ONTARIO " "	234 "

LIST OF STEAMERS BUILT AND RUNNING ON LAKE CHAMPLAIN SINCE 1809.

Built.	Name	Tons.	Where built.	Remarks.
1809	Vermont*	167	Burlington, Vt.	sunk Oct., 1815.
1815	Phœnix (1st)	336	Vergennes, Vt.	burnt Sept., 1819.
1817	Champlain	128	Vergennes, Vt.	burnt 1817.
1819	Congress	209	Vergennes, Vt.	broken up.
1820	Phœnix (2d)	346	Vergennes, Vt.	broken up.
1825	Gen. Greene	135	Burlington, Vt.	broken up.
1827	Franklin	312	St. Albans, Vt.	broken up.
"	Washington	134	Essex, N. Y.	broken up.
1828	M'Donough	138	St. Albans, Vt.	lost 1841.
1832	Winooski	159	Burlington, Vt.	broken up.
"	Water-Witch	107	Fort Cassin, Vt.	changed to schooner.
1837	Burlington	482	Shelburne, Vt.	broken up.
1838	Whitehall	461	Whitehall, N. Y.	broken up.
1842	Saranac	331	Shelburne, Vt.	broken up.
"	Bouquet	81	Essex, N. Y.	
1845	Francis Saltus	373	Whitehall, N. Y.	
1847	United States	566	Shelburne, Vt.	
"	Ethan Allen	500	Shelburne, Vt.	
1851	Boston	219	Shelburne, Vt.	
1852	America	681	Whitehall, N. Y.	
1853	Canada	718	Whitehall, N. Y.	
1856	Montreal	416	Shelburne, Vt.	
"	Oliver Bascom	360	Whitehall, N. Y.	

STEAMERS BUILT ON LAKE GEORGE.

Built.	Name.	Where built.	Remarks.
1817	Caldwell, (1st)	Ticonderoga	burnt 1821.
1824	Mountaineer.	Caldwell	condemned 1837.
1838	Caldwell, (2d)	Ticonderoga	broken up.
1852	John Jay		burnt, July, 1856.
1857	Min-ne-ha-ha	Caldwell.	

AMERICAN STEAMERS RUNNING ON LAKE CHAMPLAIN, 1857.

(DAY AND NIGHT LINE.)

Name.	Tons.	From and To.
AMERICA, Capt. Flagg	681	Whitehall to Burlington and Rouse's Point.
CANADA, Capt. Davis	718	" " "
UNITED STATES, Capt. Wm. Anderson.	566	" " "
FRANCIS SALTUS, Capt. L. Chamberlin.	373	Whitehall to Plattsburgh.
MONTREAL, Capt. Mayo	416	Burlington to Plattsburgh.
BOUQUET, Capt. Barker	81	Plattsburgh to St. Albans, Vt.
BOSTON, Capt. Hinkley	219	Burlington to Rouse's Point.

* Built and run by Capt. John Winants. Fare $7 from Whitehall to St. John's, Can.

FREIGHT BOATS.

Ethan Allen,	Capt. Wright, 500	Whitehall to St. John's, Can.
Oliver Bascom,	" Eldridge, 300	" "
James H. Hooker. Propeller		" "

STEAMBOAT AND RAILROAD ROUTE FROM WHITEHALL TO BURLINGTON, ROUSE'S POINT, AND MONTREAL.

Landings, etc.	Miles.	Stations, etc.	Miles.
WHITEHALL, N. Y. ..	0	MONTREAL, Can.	0
Benson, Vt..........	13	St. John's, "	21
Orwell, "	7–20	*Rouse's Point*, N. Y...	23–44
Ticonderoga, N. Y....	4–24	Plattsburgh, " ..	25–69
Larabee's Point, Vt...	1–25	Port Kent, " ..	15–84
Crown Point, N. Y....	8–33	BURLINGTON, Vt. ...	10–94
Port Henry, " ...	8–41	Essex, N. Y..........	14–108
Westport, " ...	9–50	Westport, "	12–120
Essex, " ..	12–62	Port Henry, N. Y.....	9–129
BURLINGTON, Vt.....	14–76	Crown Point, "	8–137
Port Kent, N. Y......	10–86	Larabee's Point, Vt...	8–145
Plattsburgh, "	15-101	Ticonderoga, N. Y. ...	1–146
Rouse's Point, N. Y. .	25-126	Orwell, Vt...........	4–150
St. John's, Can.......	23–149	Benson, "	7–157
MONTREAL, "	21–170	WHITEHALL, N. Y. ..	13–170

USUAL TIME from Whitehall to Rouse's Point, 9 hours.
" " " *Fare*...................... $3 00
Rouse's Point to Montreal, 2 hours.
" " " *Through Fare* 4 50

RAILROAD ROUTE FROM WHITEHALL TO ALBANY.

Stations.	Miles.	Total Miles.
WHITEHALL	0	0
Fort Anne	11	11
Fort Edward	12	23
Moreau Station	1	24
SARATOGA SPRINGS	15	39
Ballston Spa	7	46
Mechanicsville	13	59
Waterford	8	67
TROY	4	71
ALBANY	6	77

Usual Time, 3½ hours. Fare, $2 38.

The village of WHITEHALL, 77 miles north of Albany by railroad route, is situated in a narrow valley at the head of Lake Champlain, and at the junction of the Champlain Canal with the lake, being a secure and important naval station in time of war. The village was incorporated in 1820, and now contains four churches, three hotels, a bank, 30 stores of different kinds, several storehouses, and extensive forwarding houses; two ship-yards and two dry docks, where are built and repaired steamboats, lake craft, and canal boats; machine-shops, brick-yards, tanneries, and other manufacturing establishments. Population about 4,000.

Besides the daily line of steamers running from Whitehall to Burlington, Plattsburgh, and Rouse's Point on the north, the *Saratoga and Whitehall Railroad* extends 40 miles south, to Saratoga Springs, and a branch railroad extends east to Rutland, Vt., connecting with the Rutland and Burlington Railroad, thus forming speedy facilities for reaching New York and Boston by railroad routes.

In the immediate vicinity of Whitehall are high and rugged hills, while to the south lies the valley formed by *Wood Creek*, heading near the banks of the Hudson. Through this valley, during the old French War of 1759, and the Revolutionary War of 1776, the French, the British, and the American armies each marshaled their forces preparatory to attack, or on their retreat. This place was formerly called *Skeenesborough*. The Indian name was said to be *Kah-sha-quah-na*, or *place where dip fish*. Here, during the Revolutionary War, for a time, was the rendezvous of the American forces; this point and Lake George being the only two accessible approaches from Canada, by the invading foe, under Gen. Burgoyne. Here, too, during the old French War, Gen. Putnam distinguished himself, both in battle and in an adroit escape from Indian foes, having, it is said, plunged into the lake about one mile north of Skeenesborough, and swam his horse to the opposite shore, thus eluding their pursuit. Peaceful pursuits and pleasure now render this place a great thoroughfare.

TRIP FROM WHITEHALL TO BURLINGTON AND ROUSE'S POINT.

THIS excursion, during the summer months, is the most grand and interesting of any of similar extent in North America—passing through a romantic lake, with high mountains in the distance, and past scenes rendered classic by their associations with events that occurred during the old French and Revolutionary wars.

On leaving the new steamboat wharf, about one mile north of Whitehall, an interest is at once excited in the breast of all intelligent travelers. The hills rise abruptly to the height of several hundred feet, while the lake or outlet of Wood Creek is hemmed in for several miles by rocky cliffs. The *Elbow*, the *Narrows*, the *Pulpit*, and other names, are given to the most interesting points.

BENSON, 13 miles below Whitehall, is the first steamboat landing. Here the waters begin to widen to about half a mile in width.

ORWELL, seven miles farther, is another steamboat landing. Here the lake widens from one to two miles.

TICONDEROGA, 24 miles north of Whitehall, and four miles east of the foot of Lake George, is a sacred and romantic spot, where is a convenient steamboat landing and a good hotel, besides the celebrated ruins of the old Fort.

FORT TICONDEROGA.—The ruins of this old fortification are situated in the town of Ticonderoga, Essex Co., on the west side of Lake Champlain, at the entrance of the outlet of Lake George, 24 miles north of Whitehall. This place was originally called *Che-on-der-o-ga* by the Indians, signifying, in their language, *noise*, and applied to the falls in the outlet of Lake George; its name was afterward slightly changed by the French into its present appellation, which it has borne ever since it was first occupied and fortified by them in 1756. The fort was at first named *Fort Carillon*, but afterward called Fort Ticonderoga by the English and Americans. This fortification cost the French government a large sum of money, and was considered very strong, both by nature and art. It stands on a point of land elevated 70 feet above Lake Champlain, being surrounded on three sides by water, and on the northwest it was defended by strong breastworks. *Mount Independence*, on the opposite or east side of the lake, was also fortified, and some of the intrenchments are still visible, elevated 110 feet above the lake, and overlooking the peninsula of Ticonderoga. After several sanguinary conflicts in this vicinity, and under the very walls of the fort, in which several thousand lives were sacrificed, this important military position was tamely evacuated by the French in 1759, and given up to the British army under Lord Amherst; who retained possession until it was taken by surprise by Col. Ethan Allen, of the American army, in 1775. He is said to have entered the fort through a subterraneous passage from the south, extending to the lake; surprising the commandant in his bed before he was aware of his danger, and in his characteristic way required the officer to surrender. He asked to whom? "*Why, to Jehovah and the Continental Congress, to be sure*," was his laconic reply. In 1777, the British army, under Gen. Burgoyne, on their route to Saratoga, appeared in array before Ticonderoga, when Gen. St. Clair, the American commander, was forced to evacuate; the enemy having erected a battery on *Mount Defiance*, in the rear, elevated 720 feet above the lake, which overlooked and completely commanded this fortification, which was before considered almost impregnable; it then remained in the hands of the British until the close of the war. Since that time it has been suffered to go to decay, and now presents one of the most interesting ruins of the kind in this country, and is annually visited by a great number of travelers. Near by, delightfully situated on the lake shore, is a well-kept hotel for the accommodation of visitors. Here steamboats, during the season of navigation, daily land and receive passengers on their route from Whitehall to Rouse's Point.

The following account of the DEFEAT OF THE BRITISH AT TICONDEROGA, IN 1759, is taken from the "*Memoirs of an American Lady*," written by Mrs. Grant:

"The army, under the command of Gen. Abercrombie, crossed Lake George on the 5th of July, and landed without opposition. They proceeded in four columns to Ticonderoga, and displayed a spectacle unprecedented in the New World. An army of sixteen thousand men, regulars and provincials, with a train of artillery, and all the necessary provisions for an active campaign or regular siege, followed by a fleet of batteaux, pontons, etc. They set out wrong, however, by not having Indian guides, who are alone to be depended on in such a place. In a short time the columns fell in upon each other, and occasioned much confusion. The advance guard of the French, which had retired before them, were equally bewildered, and falling in with each other in this confusion, a skirmish ensued, in which the French lost above three hundred men, and the English, though successful in this first rencontre, lost as much as it was possible to lose, in one man—for here it was that the valiant Lord Howe, the second in command, fell mortally wounded. He was shot from behind a tree, probably by some Indian; and the whole army were inconsolable for a loss they too well knew to be irreparable.

"The fort is in a situation of peculiar natural strength; it lies on a little peninsula, with Lake Champlain on one side, and a narrow opening communicating with Lake George on the other. This garrison, which was well prepared for attack, and almost impregnable from situation, was defended by between four and five thousand men. An engineer sent to reconnoiter was of opinion that it might be attacked without waiting for the artillery. The fatal resolution was taken without consulting those who were best qualified to judge.

"I can not enter into the dreadful detail of what followed. Certainly never was infatuation equal to this. The forty-second regiment was then in the height of deserved reputation, and commanded by a veteran of great experience and military skill, Col. Gordon Graham, who had the first point of attack assigned to him. He was wounded at the first onset, and of the survivors, every officer retired wounded off the field. Of the fifty-fifth regiment, ten officers were killed, including all the field officers. No human beings could show more determined courage than this brave army did—standing four hours under a constant discharge of cannon and musketry from barricades, on which it was impossible for them to make the least impression. Gen. Abercrombie saw the fruitless waste of blood that was every hour increasing, and ordered a retreat, which was very precipitate; so much so, that they crossed the lake, and regained their camp on the other side, the same night. Two thousand men were killed, wounded, or taken in this disastrous engagement; which was, however, quickly succeeded by the dear-bought conquest of Quebec, where fell both the rival commanders, WOLFE and MONTCALM."

Mount Defiance, about one mile southwest of Fort Ticonderoga, on the south side of the outlet to Lake George, is a bold promontory, elevated about 800 feet above the level of the lake. While the ascent from the water or eastern face is quite steep and difficult, the approach from the west is easy. It was from this quarter that Gen. Burgoyne, in 1777, ascended this mountain and planted several pieces of artillery—obliging the Americans to evacuate the fort, which was before considered almost impregnable. The top of this eminence gives a grand view of Lake Champlain and the surrounding country, and is well worthy of a visit, which can easily be accomplished on foot.

The village of TICONDEROGA, two miles west of Lake Champlain, is situated on the outlet of Lake George, where is a thriving settlement, surrounded by picturesque mountain scenery. One or two miles farther west, on the road to Lake George, is situated another village, called *Upper Ticonderoga*, or *Alexandria*. Here is a most beautiful fall of water, affording immense hydraulic power, a small part of which is only used for propelling machinery. The steamboat landing, at the foot of Lake George, is about one mile west of the latter place, the whole distance to Lake Champlain being four miles. The distance to Caldwell, at the head of Lake George is 36 miles.

LARABEE'S POINT, Vt., one mile from the landing at Fort Ticonderoga, on the opposite side of the lake, is a regular steamboat landing. Here the lake expands from one to two miles in width.

CHIMNEY POINT, nine miles north of Ticonderoga, is also another landing on the east side of the lake, although not now frequented by the steamers.

"Here the French commenced their first settlement upon the lake in 1731. When Crown Point fell into the hands of the English, in 1759, this settlement was abandoned, and the remains of the chimneys, which they had erected in their huts, probably suggested to the first English settlers the name of *Chimney Point.* The *stone windmill*, mentioned by Kalm as being one or two musket-shots to the east of Fort Frederick, and as having five or six small cannon mounted in it in 1749, and which has been supposed to have given name to this point, was most probably at the place opposite, marked by the ruins of what is called *Grenadier's Battery.*"

Crown Point, ten miles north of Ticonderoga, on the west side of Lake Champlain, presents an interesting appearance from the water. The ruins of the old fortifications are situated on a neck of land running into the lake; the embankments are visible, and indicate an immense amount of labor expended to render this point invulnerable to an approaching foe, whether by land or water; yet it was taken by surprise at the commencement of the Revolutionary struggle.

"The French first established themselves here in 1731, and erected a fort which they called *Fort St. Frederick*, from Frederick Maurepas, the French Secretary of State. At this place the French kept a garrison, and from it, during the colonial wars, sent out their parties of French and Indians to destroy the frontier English settlements and massacre the inhabitants. When Kalm visited this place in 1749, there was considerable settlement around the fort, with well-cultivated gardens. Within the fort was a neat little church. The fort was built upon the brow of a steep bank of the lake, but a short distance from the water, and the remains of its bomb-proof covered way, ovens, etc., are still to be seen, though in a very dilapidated state. The small circle to the southeast of this denotes the site of Grenadier's Battery, and the two small parallelograms to the southwest of the latter place, the situation of two strong redoubts.

"On the approach of the British army under Gen. Amherst, in 1759, the French abandoned this fort and retired to the north end of the lake. Amherst took immediate possession, but instead of repairing the old works, began a new fort, which was called *Crown Point*, about 200 yards to the southwest, on higher and more commanding ground. This fort was never completed, as is evident from an examination of the ditch, glacis, etc., at the present day, although it has been said that the British government expended here no less than £2,000,000 sterling.

"This fort was taken by surprise by a party of Green Mountain Boys, under Seth Warner, on the same day that Ticonderoga surrendered to Ethan Allen.

"The width of the peninsula upon which these works stood is one mile, and is in no part much elevated above the site of the principal fort, but there is a considerable mountain on the west side of Bulwagga Bay, the nearest summit of which is only 1¾ miles from the fort, and elevated 400 feet above it. The highest is distant 2¾ miles, and elevated 900 feet. The whole peninsula is made up of dark limestone, covered in most parts with only a slight depth of earth, so that works upon it can not be assailed by regular advances. The width between Crown Point and Chimney Point is only about half a mile. From Crown Point to Split Rock the average width of the lake is about three and a half miles."

PORT HENRY, on the west side of the lake, is situated on *Cedar Point*, at the mouth of *Bulwagga Bay*, which separates Crown Point from the mainland. Here are the works of the *Port Henry Iron Company*, with iron ore of good quality in the vicinity

WESTPORT, 50 miles north of Whitehall, is situated on Northwest Bay, on the west side of Lake Champlain. It contains 700 or 800 inhabitants, and is a thriving place. A horse ferry-boat here plies across the lake, running to Basin Harbor, Vermont.

BASIN HARBOR, one of the best on the lake, is in the town of Ferrisburgh, Vt., and is five miles west from the city of *Vergennes*, and is the landing for it

FORT CASSIN, three miles north of Basin Harbor, and on the north side of the mouth of Otter Creek, was formerly a landing place of passengers for Vergennes. It is eight miles from the city of Vergennes, where Macdonough's fleet was fitted out, with which he gained his victory. Fort Cassin takes its name from Lieut. Cassin, of the navy, who, with a small breastwork at this place, and less than 200 men, commanded by himself and Capt. Thornton, of the artillery, on the 14th of May, 1814, repulsed a large British force in an attempt to enter the creek for the purpose of destroying the American flotilla before it should be ready for service.

SPLIT ROCK has been regarded as one of the greatest natural curiosities on the lake, and is one which did not escape the notice of the earliest French explorers. *RocherFendu* occupies a conspicuous place on Charlevoix's map of 1744. The part detached contains about half an acre, rises about 30 feet above the water, is covered with bushes, and is separated about twelve feet from the main rock. Some have supposed the chasm to have been produced by the breaking off of the promontory in consequence of being undermined by the lake, or by some great convulsion of nature. But the slightest examination shows that the rocky point was here originally crossed by what geologists call a dike, the materials of which have been washed out, forming a chasm in the more solid rock, through which the lake flows when high. The chasm, instead of being unfathomable, as some have represented, is so shallow that no water flows through when the lake is low. A few rods south of Split Rock stands a light-house. The width of the lake between Split Rock and Thompson's Point is only about a mile From this place the width of the lake increases toward the north, and at *McNeil's Ferry*, between Charlotte landing and the village of Essex, it wants 20 rods of three miles.

The village of ESSEX, 61 miles from Whitehall, is handsomely situated on the west side of Lake Champlain, opposite *Charlotte Landing*, with which it is connected by a horse ferry-boat. Population about 700. The lake here expands to three or four miles in width, and presents a large expanse of water toward the north. The *Green Mountains* of Vermont, and the *Adirondack Group* of Essex County, are here seen stretching north and south in vast mountain peaks and ridges. The *Camel's Hump*, being one of the highest peaks of the former, is overlooked by Mount Marcy, on the New York side of the lake, the latter being elevated 5,467 feet, or upward of one mile above the tide waters of the Hudson; and near it this noble river has its most northern source.

FOUR BROTHERS are four small islands lying about seven miles southwest from Burlington, and being out :f the usual line of navigation, they are resorted to by gulls and other water-fowl for the purpose of raising their young. On Charlevoix's map of 1744 they are called *Isle de Quatre Vents.*

Juniper Island lies about three miles southwest from Burlington—is composed of slate rock, with precipitous banks about thirty feet high, and covered with about a dozen acres of good soil. A light-house was erected here in 1826.

Rock Dunder is a solitary rock rising out of the water, between Juniper Island and Pottier's Point, to the height of about thirty feet.

Burlington, Vt., 76 miles from Whitehall, 25 miles from Plattsburgh, and 50 miles from Rouse's Point by steamboat route, is delightfully situated on Burlington Bay, on the east shore of Lake Champlain, and is the most important place in the State. It possesses a convenient and safe harbor for steamboats and lake craft. The United States government have here erected a breakwater, which protects the shipping from westerly winds, and is a great addition to the security of the harbor. In 1850 it contained a population of 6,110 inhabitants; the University of Vermont, founded in 1791, occupying four spacious edifices, and having a medical school attached to it; the Episcopal institute, a court-house and jail, eight churches of different denominations, an academy, and two female seminaries; three banking-houses, several well-kept hotels, and a number of stores of different kinds, besides several factories and mills, and almost every kind of mechanic establishments About 1½ miles distant, on the falls of the Onion River, is a thriving manufacturing place called *Winooski*, where are located several large factories and mills.

Burlington is, no doubt, destined rapidly to increase in wealth and population, from the fact of here centering several important lines of railroad travel, extending from Boston by two routes, through Montpelier and through Rutland. This railroad and steamboat communication extends across Lake Champlain to Plattsburgh and Rouse's Point, running north to Montreal, Canada, and west to Ogdensburgh, N. Y.

Termination of the Rutland and Burlington, and Vermont Central Railroads at the Steamboat Landing, Burlington, Vt.

Its advantages are now great, and its situation most beautiful, overlooking the lake, with its bays, islands, and adjacent scenery—the passing steamboats and other vessels—and possesses a beauty of location probably unsurpassed by any other place in the Union. In trade and commerce it is closely allied with the interests of the State of New York. Steamboats stop here daily on their route from Whitehall to Rouse's Point; a steamboat also plies from this place to Port Kent, on the opposite side of the lake, a distance of ten miles, and thence to Plattsburgh, 25 miles.

The principal hotels in Burlington are the American Hotel, the Exchange Hotel, and the Howard House.

Travelers wishing to visit *Mansfield Mountain*, 20 miles northeast of Burlington, or the *Camel's Hump*, in the town of Huntington, about the same distance in a southeast direction, can easily obtain conveyances to either of the above romantic resorts. From the summit of both are obtained beautiful and sublime views of the surrounding country and Lake Champlain, said to fully equal the prospect from the White Mountains of New Hampshire. The Vermont Central Railroad route, between Burlington, Montpelier, and Windsor, runs near the base of the latter mountain.

The *White Mountains* of New Hampshire, about 120 miles east of Burlington, are reached from this place by railroad and stage, passing over the *Vermont Central Railroad* to White River Junction, and from thence up the valley of the Connecticut River to Wells' River, where commences the *White Mountain Railroad*, extending to Littleton, N. H. From Littleton stages run to the Notch of the White Mountains, a farther distance of 20 miles. This line of travel can be extended through to Portland, Me., passing over a romantic section of country.

PORT KENT is advantageously situated on the west side of Lake Champlain, 12 miles south of the village of Plattsburgh. It contains about 400 inhabitants, 50 dwelling-houses, one church, two taverns, three stores, and two warehouses. The site of this place is beautiful, commanding one of the finest views on Champlain, extending to the opposite shore of Vermont. It is contemplated to construct a railroad from Port Kent to the Au Sable Forks, a distance of 16 miles, passing through the villages of Keeseville and Clintonville.

Immediately south of the landing at Port Kent lies *Trembleu Point*, the commencement of the Clinton range of mountains.

KEESEVILLE, situated on both sides of the Au Sable River, is four miles west of Port Kent. It contains about 3,000 inhabitants, 400 dwelling-houses, one Congregational, one Baptist, one Methodist, and one Roman Catholic church; an incorporated academy, one banking-house, two taverns, and 20 stores and groceries. The water-power at this place is very great, and advantageously used by several extensive manufacturing establishments. There are two flouring-mills, four extensive saw-mills, which make annually about half a million of market boards, an iron foundry, one furnace, and a machine-shop, together with most other kinds of mechanic workshops.

At BIRMINGHAM, two miles below Keeseville, is a succession of picturesque falls, in all about 150 feet descent. Immediately below the lower falls the river enters a deep ravine of singular and romantic beauty. Through the chasm thus formed by the wearing of the waters, or some convulsion of nature, the rocks rise from 75 to 150 feet, almost perpendicular, for a distance of about two miles, averaging about 50 feet in width, altogether forming a great natural curiosity. In addition to the above, there are other ravines in this vicinity of singular formation

From Port Kent to Plattsburgh the course is along the western shore of the lake, passing several islands.

PORT JACKSON, the only intermediate landing place, is nearly west of the south end of *Valcour Island*, noted for a severe naval conflict, on the 11th of October, 1776, between the American flotilla under General Arnold, and the British under Capt. Prindle. The battle was fought a little north of Port Jackson.

"Five or six miles nearly east from Port Jackson was the scene of the conflagration of the steamer Phœnix on the 5th of

September, 1819. On the morning of the accident, the Phœnix left Burlington about one o'clock, against a strong north wind. About 3 o'clock, while off nearly west of the south end of Grand Isle, the boat was discovered to be on fire, and all efforts to extinguish it were unavailing. There were at this time 44 persons on board, 31 of whom entered the small boats, and succeeded, with considerable difficulty, in reaching a small island about a mile to the windward, called Providence Island. The remaining 13 were soon obliged to commit themselves to the water upon bits of plank and such other things as were within their reach. The small boats returned just after daylight, and succeeded in saving six of those who had managed to keep themselves afloat. The remaining seven were drowned. The wreck drifted southward and lodged on a reef extending from Colchester Point. This is the only accident worthy of notice which has occurred during 46 years of steam navigation on this lake."

PLATTSBURGH, Clinton Co., N. Y., is situated on both sides of the Saranac River, 100 miles north of Whitehall and 25 miles south of Rouse's Point by steamboat route It was incorporated as a village in 1815, and now contains about 4,000 inhabitants, 500 dwelling-houses, a court-house, jail, and county clerk's office; a town-hall, one Presbyterian, one Episcopal, one Methodist, and two Roman Catholic churches; an incorporated academy, 50 stores of different kinds, and six public houses, the principal of which are the Cumberland House and Fouquet's Hotel; two banks and one insurance office. Here are situated, on the Saranac, using water-power, two flouring-mills, one woolen factory, one fulling-mill, two saw-mills, two machine-shops, and one foundry; there are also two tanneries, one soap manufactory, three printing-offices, together with almost every other kind of mechanic workshops. The water-power at this place is very great, the Saranac River here having a succession of falls, making a total descent of about 40 feet. The surrounding country is rich in agricultural and mineral productions; iron ore of fine quality is procured in different parts of the county. This is also a United States military post, where the government has erected extensive stone barracks, near the lake shore, and a permanent breakwater for the protection of the harbor in Cumberland Bay

Steamers run daily, during the season of navigation, from Plattsburgh to Burlington and Whitehall on the south, and to St. Albans and Rouse's Point on the north, connecting with different railroads. The *Plattsburgh and Montreal Railroad* extends in a northerly direction to Mooer's Junction, and thence across the Canada line to Caughnawaga and Montreal, a total distance of 62 miles.

RAILROAD ROUTE FROM PLATTSBURGH TO MONTREAL.

Stations.	Miles.	Total Miles.
PLATTSBURGH	0	0
West Chazy	10	10
Mooer's Junction	10	20
Hemingford, Canada	6	26
St. Remi	15	41
Caughnawaga	11	52
La Chine	2	54
MONTREAL	8	62

Usual Time, three hours. Fare, $2 10.

Plattsburgh was the scene of an important engagement between the British and American armies, in September, 1814, which resulted in the defeat of the British, under the command of Sir George Prevost, and the capture of the British fleet under Com. Downie, who was killed in the action. The American army was commanded by Maj. Gen. Macomb, and the fleet by Com. McDonough.

NAVAL ENGAGEMENT AND BATTLE OF PLATTSBURGH, SEPT. 11, 1814.

Copied from Palmer's "HISTORY OF LAKE CHAMPLAIN."

"WHEN the British army reached Plattsburgh, their gunboats had advanced as far as the Isle La Motte, where they remained, under command of Capt. Pring. On the 8th Sept., Captain Downie reached that place with the rest of the fleet, and on the morning of the 11th the whole weighed anchor and stood south to attack the Americans, who lay in Cumberland Bay, off Plattsburgh.

"As the British vessels rounded Cumberland Head, about

eight o'clock in the morning, they found McDonough at anchor a little south of the mouth of the Saranac River, and abreast, but out of gun-shot, of the forts. His vessels lay in a line running north from Crab Island, and nearly parallel with the west shore. The brig *Eagle*, Captain Henley, lay at the head of the line, inside the point of the Head. This vessel mounted twenty guns and had on board one hundred and fifty men. Next to her, and on the south, lay McDonough's flag-ship, the *Saratoga*, mounting twenty-six guns, with two hundred and twelve men. Next south was the schooner *Ticonderoga*, of seventeen guns, Lieutenant Cassin, with one hundred and ten men, and next to her, and at the southern extremity of the line, lay the sloop *Preble*, Lieutenant Charles Budd. This vessel carried seven guns, and was manned by thirty men. She lay so near the shoal extending northeast from Crab Island, as to prevent the enemy from turning that end of the line. To the rear of the line were ten gun-boats, six of which mounted one long twenty-four pounder, and one eighteen pound Columbiad each; the other four carried one twelve pounder. The gun-boats had, on an average, thirty-five men each. Two of the gun-boats lay a little north and in rear of the Eagle, to sustain the head of the line; the others were placed opposite the intervals between the different vessels, and about forty rods to their rear. The larger vessels were at anchor, while the gun-boats were kept in position by their sweeps.

"The British fleet was composed of the frigate *Confiance*, carrying thirty-seven guns,* with over three hundred men, commanded by Captain Downie; the brig *Linnet*, Captain Pring, of sixteen guns and 120 men; the sloop *Chub*, Lieutenant McGhee, and the sloop *Finch*, Lieutenant Hicks, carrying eleven guns and about forty-five men each. To these vessels were added twelve gun-boats of about forty-five men each. Eight of them carried two guns, and four one gun each. Thus the force of the Americans consisted of one ship, one brig, one schooner, one sloop, and ten gun-boats, manned by eight hundred and eighty-two men, and carrying in all eighty-six guns. The British had one frigate, one brig, two sloops, and twelve gun-boats, manned by over one thousand men, and carrying in all ninety-five guns. The metal of the vessels on both sides was unusually heavy. The Saratoga mounted eight long twenty-fours, six forty-twos, and twelve thirty-twos, while the Confiance had the gun-deck of a heavy frigate, with thirty long twenty-fours upon it. She also had a spacious topgallant forecastle, and a poop that came no farther forward than the mizen

* There were thirty-nine guns on board the Confiance, but two of them were not mounted.—*Cooper*.

mast. On the first were a long twenty-four on a circle, and four heavy carronades; two heavy carronades were mounted on the poop.

"When the British fleet appeared in sight, the Finch led and kept in a course toward Crab Island, while the other vessels hove to opposite the point of Cumberland Head, to allow the gun-boats to come up, and to receive final instructions as to the plan of attack. The vessels then filled and headed in toward the American fleet, passing inside of the point of Cumberland Head; the Chub laying her course a little to windward of the Eagle, in order to support the Linnet, which stood directly toward that vessel. Captain Downie had determined to lay the Confiance athwart the Saratoga, but the wind baffling, he was obliged to anchor at about two cables' length from that ship. The Finch, which had run about half way to Crab Island, tacked and took her station, with the gun-boats, opposite the Ticonderoga and Preble.

"As the British vessels approached they received the fire of the American fleet; the brig Eagle firing first, and being soon followed by the Saratoga, and the sloop and schooner.* The Linnet poured her broadside into the Saratoga as she passed that ship to take her position opposite the Eagle. Captain Downie brought his vessel into action in the most gallant manner, and did not fire a gun until he was perfectly secured, although his vessel suffered severely from the fire of the Americans As soon, however, as the Confiance had been brought into position, she discharged all her larboard guns, at nearly the same instant. The effect of this broadside, thrown from long twenty-four pounders, double shotted, in smooth water, was terrible. The Saratoga trembled to her very keel; about forty of her crew were disabled, including her first Lieutenant, Mr. Gamble, who was killed while sighting the bow-gun.

"Soon after the commencement of the engagement, the Chub, while maneuvering near the head of the American line, received a broadside from the Eagle, which so crippled her that she drifted down between the opposing vessels and struck. She was taken possession of by Mr. Charles Platt, one of the Saratoga's midshipmen, and was towed in shore and anchored. The Chub

* The first gun fired on board the Saratoga was a long twenty-four, which McDonough himself sighted. The shot is said to have struck the Confiance near the outer hawse-hole, and to have passed the length of her deck, killing and wounding several men, and carrying away the wheel. In clearing the decks of the Saratoga, some hen coops were thrown overboard, and the poultry permitted to run at large. Startled by the report of the opening gun of the Eagle, a young cock flew upon a gun slide, clapped his wings and crowed. The men gave three cheers, and considered the little incidence as a happy omen.—*Cooper's Naval History and Niles' Register.*

had suffered severely; nearly half of her men having been killed or wounded. About an hour later the Finch was driven from her position by the Ticonderoga, and, being badly injured, drifted upon the shoal near Crab Island, where she grounded. After being fired into from the small battery on the island, she struck, and was taken possession of by the invalids who manned the battery.*

"After the loss of the Finch, the British gun-boats made several efforts to close, and succeeded in compelling the sloop Preble to cut her cables and to anchor in shore of the line, where she was of no more service during the engagement. The gun-boats, emboldened by this success, now directed their efforts toward the Ticonderoga, against which they made several very gallant assaults, bringing the boats, upon two or three occasions, within a few feet of the schooner's side. They were, however, as often beaten back, and the schooner, during the remainder of the day, completely covered that extremity of the line.

"While these changes were taking place at the lower end of the line, a change was also made at the other extremity. The Eagle, having lost her springs, and finding herself exposed to the fire of both the Linnet and Confiance, dropped down and anchored between the Saratoga and Ticonderoga, and a little in shore of both. From this position she opened afresh on the Confiance and the British gun-boats, with her larboard guns. This change relieved the brig, but left the Saratoga exposed to the whole fire of the Linnet, which sprung her broadsides in such a manner as to rake the ship on her bows.

"The fire from the Saratoga and Confiance now began materially to lessen, as gun after gun on both vessels became disabled, until at last the Saratoga had not a single available gun, and the Confiance was but little better off. It therefore became necessary that both vessels should wind, to continue the action with any success. This the Saratoga did after considerable delay, but the Confiance was less fortunate, as the only effect of her efforts was to force the vessel ahead. As soon as the Sara-

* Mr. Alison (History of England, vol. 4), referring to this event, says: "The Finch, a British *brig*, grounded out of shot and *did not engage*;" and again, "The Finch struck on a reef of rocks and could not get into action." Had Mr. Alison taken the trouble to read Capt. Pring's official account of the engagement, he would have found in it the following statement: "Lieutenant Hicks, of the Finch, had the mortification to strike on a reef of rocks, to the eastward of Crab Island, about the middle of the engagement, which prevented his rendering that assistance to the squadron that might, from an officer of such ability, have been expected." It is very convenient for the English historian to convert a small sloop of eleven guns and forty men into a *brig*, and to keep that large vessel out of the action altogether, but, as I have before said, such statements are unnecessary to preserve the well-earned reputation of the British navy for bravery or gallantry in action.

toga came around she poured a fresh broadside from her larboard guns into the Confiance, which stood the fire for a few minutes and then struck. The ship then brought her guns to bear on the Linnet, which surrendered in about fifteen minutes afterward. At this time the British gun-boats lay half a mile in the rear, where they had been driven by the sharp fire of the Ticonderoga and Eagle. These boats lowered their colors as soon as they found the larger vessels had submitted; but not being pursued, for the American gun-boats were sent to aid the Confiance and Linnet, which were reported to be in a sinking condition, they escaped, together with a store sloop, which lay near the point of Cumberland Head during the battle.

"The engagement continued for two hours and a half, and was the most severely fought naval battle of the war. The Saratoga had twenty-eight men killed and twenty-nine wounded; the Eagle thirteen killed and twenty wounded; the Ticonderoga six killed and six wounded, and the Preble two killed. The loss on the gun-boats was three killed and three wounded. Total killed and wounded, one hundred and ten, being equal to every eighth man in the fleet. Besides, the Saratoga had been hulled fifty-five times, and was twice on fire; the Eagle was hulled thirty-nine times. The carnage and destruction had been as great on the other side. The Confiance had forty-one men killed and eighty-three wounded; the Linnet reported her casualties at ten killed and fourteen wounded, but the killed and wounded probably exceeded fifty; the Chub was reported at six killed and ten wounded, and the Finch at two wounded. No account is given of the loss on the gun-boats, but from their close and severe contest with the Ticonderoga, it must have been large. The total of killed and wounded on the British side was equal to at least one fifth of the whole number of men in their fleet. The Confiance had been hulled one hundred and five times. So severe had been the contest, that at the close of the action there was not a mast in either fleet fit for use.*

"Among those killed on the side of the British were Captain Downie, who fell soon after the action commenced, Captain Alexander Anderson of the Marines, Midshipman William Gunn of the Confiance, and Lieutenant William Paul and Boatswain Charles Jackson of the Linnet. Among the wounded were Midshipman Lee of the Confiance, Midshipman John Sinclair of the

---

* I could only look at the enemy's galleys going off, in a shattered condition; for there was not a mast in either squadron that could stand to make sail on; the lower rigging being nearly all shot away, hung down as though it had been just placed over the mast head.—*McDonough's Report of the Battle.* Our masts, yards, and sails were so shattered, that one looked like so many bunches of matches, and the other like a bundle of rags.—*Letter of Midshipman Lee o the Confiance.*

Linnet, and Lieutenant James McGhee of the Chub. The American officers killed were Peter Gamble, 1st Lieutenant of the Saratoga, John Stansbury, 1st Lieutenant of the Ticonderoga, Midshipman James M. Baldwin, and Sailing Master Rogers Carter. Referring to the death of three of these officers, Mr. Cooper, in his History of the Navy, says: 'Lieutenant Gamble was on his knees, sighting the bow-gun, when a shot entered the port, split the quoin, drove a portion of it against his breast, and laid him dead on the quarter-deck without breaking his skin. Fifteen minutes later one of the American shot struck the muzzle of a twenty-four on the Confiance, dismounted it, sending it bodily inboard against the groin of Captain Downie, killing him also without breaking the skin. Lieutenant Stansbury suddenly disappeared from the bulwarks forward, while superintending some duty with the springs of the Ticonderoga. Two days after the action, his body rose to the surface of the water, and it was found that it had been cut in two by a round shot.'

"It is said that scarcely an individual escaped on board of either the Confiance or Saratoga without some injury. Macdonough was twice knocked down; once by the spanker-boom, which was cut in two by a shot, and fell upon his back as he was bending his body to sight a gun; and again by the head of a gunner, which was driven against him, and knocked him into the scuppers. Mr. Brum, the sailing-master of the Saratoga, had his clothes torn off by a splinter while winding the ship. Mr. Vallette, acting Lieutenant, had a shot-box, on which he was standing, knocked from under his feet, and he too was once knocked down by the head of a seaman. Very few escaped without some accident, and it appears to have been agreed on both sides, to call no man wounded who could keep out of the hospital.* Midshipman Lee of the Confiance, who was wounded in the action, thus describes the condition of that vessel: 'The havoc on both sides is dreadful. I don't think there are more than five of our men, out of three hundred, but what are killed or wounded. Never was a shower of hail so thick as the shot whistling about our ears. Were you to see my jacket, waistcoat, and trowsers, you would be astonished how I escaped as I did, for they are literally torn all to rags with shot and splinters; the upper part of my hat was also shot away. There is one of our marines who was in the Trafalgar action with Lord Nelson, who says it was a mere *fleabite* in comparison with this."†

---

* Cooper's Naval History.

† Letter to his brother, published in *Niles' Register*, vol. 8. The result of the engagement depended, from the first, upon the Saratoga and Con-

The officers, on both sides, who fell in the several encounters by land and water, on the memorable occasion above mentioned, were buried in the public cemetery adjacent to the village of Plattsburgh; but their graves were left, under the pressing exigencies of that time, without any permanent monument, or stone of memorial. That community, long discontented with an omission which seemed to betoken an apathy not at all in unison with real feelings, at last determined to make amends for their neglect, and fulfill all the rites of sepulture. Accordingly, a little previous to the return of the anniversary of the battle, in 1843, meetings were held at which it was resolved to celebrate the day, by placing marble monuments, with appropriate inscriptions, at the several graves, and thus render to the brave and devoted dead the remaining public honors so eminently their due, and so long left unpaid. This design was carried into effect under the superintendence of the Clinton County Military Association, and the anniversary rendered deeply interesting by the placing of these monuments, with appropriate ceremonies and religious services, accompanied by commemoration addresses.

The graves are arranged in the form of a parallelogram, with that of Capt Downie, the commander of the British flotilla, in the center, as the officer of highest rank. The names of the others, so far as known, are as follow: Of our own countrymen, Lt. George W. Runk, of the U. S. A.; Lt. Peter Gamble, U. S. N.; Lt. John Stansbury, U. S. N.; Sailing Master Rogers Carter, U. S. N.; Midshipman James M. Baldwin, U. S. N.; Pilot Joseph Barron, U. S. N., and another pilot, name not known. Of the British army, Col. Wellington, 3d Regt. Buffs, Capt. Purchess, 76th Regt., Lieutenant R. Kingsbury, 3d Regt. Buffs; and of the British navy, Capt. Alex. Anderson and three Lieutenants, names not known.

---

fiance. When McDonough anchored his vessel, he not only attached springs to the cables, but also laid a kedge broad off on each bow of the Saratoga, and brought the hawsers in upon the two quarters. To this timely precaution he was indebted for the victory, for without the larboard hawser he could not have brought his fresh broadside into action.

The beautiful lines of an Irish poet of the last century (Collins), can never be more appropriate than to this occasion:

"How sleep the brave who sink to rest,
By all their country's wishes blest!
When spring with dewy fingers cold
Returns to deck their hallowed mold
She there shall dress a sweeter sod
Than fancy's feet have ever trod.
There honor comes, a pilgrim gray,
To bless the turf that wraps their clay,
And memory shall awhile repair
To dwell a weeping hermit there.

CUMBERLAND HEAD is a peninsula extending two or three miles into the lake, opposite the village of Plattsburgh, forming *Cumberland Bay*, into which empties the Saranac River.

CRAB, or HOSPITAL ISLAND lies two miles south, and near the track of the steamers on their way to and from the landing at Plattsburgh. It was on a line nearly north and south between Cumberland Head and Crab Island that the British and American fleets encountered each other, on the 11th of September, 1814, a day which brought so much honor to the American flag.

SOUTH HERO and NORTH HERO are the names of two Islands belonging to the jurisdiction of Vermont. The former is connected by a ferry, and on the east side with the main shore of Vermont by a bridge.

CHAZY LANDING, 16 miles north of Plattsburgh, is a convenient steamboat landing, on the west side of Lake Champlain.

ISLE AU MOTTE, opposite the above landing, is a fine island, also attached to Vermont. It is 6 miles long and 2 miles wide, containing much good land, and a valuable quarry of marble.

The village of ROUSE'S POINT, in the town of Champlain, 25 miles north of Plattsburgh, and 125 miles from Whitehall, is situated on the west side of Lake Champlain, about one mile south of the Canada line, and has a convenient steamboat landing, a very large depôt building, and a well kept hotel. It is surrounded in part by a level and fertile region, which extends west to the St. Lawrence River. One mile north of the village is a fort and military position commanding the navigable channel of the lake. In 1815 the government of the United States commenced the construction of a strong fortress at Rouse's Point; but on running out the boundary line between the United States and Canada, under the treaty of Ghent, this point was found to be north of the 45th degree of north latitude, and the works were suspended.

United States Boundary Line.—"This line was fixed in 1842, by treaty negotiated by Lord Ashburton and Mr. Webster, on the old line formerly supposed to be the 45th parallel of latitude. Immediately after the close of the last war the United States government commenced building a fort on a low point to the northward of Rouse's Point landing, which should completely command the passage up the lake. By the survey of this line in 1818, it was found that this point was north of the 45th parallel, and the work was consequently abandoned; but by the late treaty the fort was secured to the United States, and the work has recently been resumed. An opening through the woods like a road, on the east side of the lake, and about 200 rods north of the fort, marks the place of the *Line* as now established."

At Rouse's Point is erected a long and substantial drawbridge, crossing the foot of Lake Champlain, for the accommodation of the railroad traffic passing from Montreal and Ogdensburgh to New York and Boston. During the winter months this bridge affords the exclusive thoroughfare at this point between Canada and the Eastern States.

The railroads which here terminate are the *Vermont and Canada Railroad*, connecting with the Vermont Central Railroad; the *Northern Railroad* of New York, 118 miles in length, terminating at Ogdensburgh; and the *Champlain* and *St. Lawrence Railroad*, 44 miles in length, terminating opposite Montreal.

On arriving and departing from Rouse's Point, travelers are subjected to the inconvenience of having their baggage examined by custom-house officers; this is a great port of entry as well as thoroughfare.

The town of ALBURGH, Vt., is a triangular body of land projecting from Canada into Lake Champlain, by which it is surrounded, excepting on the Canada side. On the eastern shore lies the village of *Alburgh*, a port of entry, and a few miles north is *Alburgh Springs*, where is a small settlement and several hotels. This justly celebrated watering-place lies near the Missisquoi Bay, and is easily reached by railroad, being situated seven miles east of Rouse's Point and 16 miles west of St. Albans, Vt.

HIGHGATE SPRINGS, three miles from Swanton Station and 17 miles from Rouse's Point, near the village of Highgate, Vt., is another and favorite watering-place, attracting much attention. It is situated near Missisquoi Bay, affording fine fishing-grounds, and an opportunity to enjoy aquatic sports and hunting.

MISSISQUOI BAY, connecting with Lake Champlain on the north, is a large and romantic sheet of water lying mostly in Canada, or north of the 45th degree of north latitude. This bay and its surrounding shores afford most romantic and delightful scenery, varied by high land and picturesque points Hunting, fishing, or pleasure sailing can here be enjoyed by those fond of such sports, while the invigorating climate gives strength and elasticity to the weak and debilitated. During the summer and autumn months a steamer runs around the bay, landing at *Phillipsburgh*, Can., *Highgate*, Vt., and other landings.

ASH ISLAND, four miles north of Rouse's Point, is considered the foot of Lake Champlain. Here the Richelieu, or St. John's River, as the outlet of Lake Champlain is called, is about half a mile wide. The land on both sides of the stream seems almost level with the water, and presents this low and flat surface for many miles.

ISLE AUX NOIX, situated in the Richelieu River, 12 miles north of Rouse's Point, is the first steamboat landing after entering Canada. Here is a strong fortification commanding the channel of the river and occupied by British troops.

RAILROAD ROUTE FROM ROUSE'S POINT TO OGDENSBURGH, *via* NORTHERN RAILROAD.

Stations.	Miles.	Total Miles.
ROUSE'S POINT	0	0
Mooer's Junction	12	12
Chazy	11	23
Summit	14	37
Chateaugay	9	46
MALONE	11	57
Brush's Mills	11	68
Stockholm	14	82
Potsdam Junction	11	93
Lisbon	16	109
OGDENSBURGH	9	118

USUAL TIME, 5 hours. FARE, $3 50.

On leaving Rouse's Point for St. John's and Montreal, the line of the *Champlain and St. Lawrence Railroad* extends along the west side of the Sorel or Richelieu River, over a level and productive section of country, passing La Colle, six miles from Rouse's Point.

ST. JOHN'S or DORCHESTER, 150 miles from Whitehall, is advantageously situated on the west side of the Richelieu River, at the foot of navigation; a bridge connecting it with the village of *St. Anthanase*, on the opposite shore. It is 23 miles north of the American line, 22 miles southeast of Montreal, and contains about 2,200 inhabitants, 275 dwelling-houses, a custom-house, and extensive barracks for soldiers, one Episcopal, one Roman Catholic, and one Methodist church; ten hotels and taverns, ten stores, and two forwarding houses, one extensive glass factory, one stone factory, two tanneries, and mechanics shops of different kinds.

The *Chambly Canal* extends from St. John's to Chambly, on the northwest side of the Richelieu River, a distance of 12 miles. It was completed in 1843, at a cost of about $400,000. There are nine locks on this canal 120 feet long, 24 feet wide, and six feet deep; lift ten feet each, making a total descent of 90 feet in 12 miles. This canal was constructed by the Provincial government. It affords navigation for vessels of 100 tons burden between Lake Champlain and the St. Lawrence River, thus furnishing an uninterrupted water communication from New York to Quebec.

The railroad from St. John's to Montreal, 21 miles in length, extends over a level section of country, the St. Lawrence River soon coming in sight.

The aspect of the St. Lawrence is truly grand and interesting, as you approach it on the south from Rouse's Point. Toward the west is seen the La Chine Rapid, one of the most dangerous on the river. Opposite Montreal it is two miles wide, embosoming the beautiful island of St. Helen, which is fortified and garrisoned by British troops.

As you approach Montreal by water, the new Victoria Bridge, the city, shipping, and wharves are seen to great advantage. The latter—the wharves—probably exceed any thing of the kind in America, consisting of a range of massive and solid masonry extending along the river for upward of a mile.

THE following beautiful lines, descriptive of one of the sources of *human happiness*, is from the gifted pen of N. P. WILLIS, and may be appropriately inserted at this place:

" 'Tis to have
Attentive and believing faculties;
To go abroad rejoicing in the joy
Of beautiful and well-created things
To love the voice of waters, and the sheen
Of silver fountains leaping to the sea;
To thrill with the rich melody of birds,
Living their life of music; to be glad
In the gay sunshine, reverent in the storm;
To see a beauty in the stirring leaf,
And find calm thoughts beneath the whispering tree;
To see, and hear, and breathe the evidence
Of God's deep wisdom in the natural world."

TABLE OF DISTANCES BETWEEN ALBANY AND MONTREAL.

Places.	Miles.	From Albany.	From Montreal.
ALBANY	0	0	248
TROY	6	6	242
Saratoga Springs	32	38	210
Whitehall	40	78	170
Ticonderoga	24	102	146
BURLINGTON, Vt.	51	153	95
Plattsburgh, N. Y.	25	178	70
Rouse's Point, "	25	203	45
St. John's, Canada	23	226	22
MONTREAL	22	248	0

TABLE OF DISTANCES FROM MONTREAL TO QUEBEC, BY WATER.

MONTREAL	0	0	
To Varennes	0	15	Miles.
WILLIAM HENRY	30	45	"
Lake St. Peter	8	53	"
St. Francis	30	83	"
THREE RIVERS	7	90	"
St. Anne	20	110	"
Richelieu Rapids	15	125	"
Cape Sante	15	140	"
Cape Rouge	22	162	"
QUEBEC	8	170	"

RAILROAD ROUTE FROM MONTREAL TO QUEBEC, WHITE MOUNTAINS, AND PORTLAND, MAINE, *via* GRAND TRUNK RAILWAY.

Stations.	Miles.	Total Miles.
MONTREAL	0	0
Longueuil	2	2
St. Hyacinthe	30	32
Richmond	42	74
QUEBEC	97	171
Sherbrooke	24	98
Boundary Line	30	128
ISLAND POND, Vt.	17	145
Northumberland	27	172
GORHAM (White Mt. Station)	31	203
South Paris	43	246
Danville Junction	20	266
PORTLAND	28	294

RAILROAD ROUTE FROM MONTREAL TO TORONTO, *via* GRAND TRUNK RAILWAY.

Stations.	Miles.	Stations.	Miles.
MONTREAL	0	TORONTO	0
Blue Bonnets	5	York	6
Pointe Claire	15	Scarboro'	13
St. Anne's *(Ottawa River)*	21	Port Union	17
Vaudreuil	24	Port Whitby	29
Cedars (road to)	29	OSHAWA	33
Coteau Landing	37	Bowmanville	43
River Beaudette	44	Newcastle	47
Lancaster	54	Port Britain	59
CORNWALL	68	PORT HOPE	62
Dickinson's Landing	77	COBOURG	70
Aultsville	84	Grafton	77
Williamsburg	92	Colborne	84
Matilda	99	Trenton	101
Edwardsburg	104	BELLEVILLE	113
Prescott Junction	112	Shannonville	120
PRESCOTT	113	Napanee	134
Maitland	120	Ernestown	145
BROCKVILLE	125	Collins Bay	153
Mallorytown	137	KINGSTON	160
Lansdowne	146	Kingston Mills	164
Gananoque	155	Gananoque	178
Kingston Mills	169	Lansdowne	187
KINGSTON	173	Mallorytown	196
Collins Bay	180	BROCKVILLE	208
Ernestown	188	Maitland	213
Napanee	199	PRESCOTT	220
Shannonville	213	Prescott Junction	221
BELLEVILLE	220	Edwardsburg	229
Trenton	232	Matilda	234
Colborne	249	Williamsburg	241
Grafton	256	Aultsville	249
COBOURG	263	Dickinson's Landing	256
PORT HOPE	271	CORNWALL	265
Port Britain	274	Lancaster	279
Newcastle	286	River Beaudette	289
Bowmanville	290	Coteau Landing	296
OSHAWA	300	Cedars (road to)	304
Port Whitby	304	Vaudreuil *(Ottawa Riv'r)*	309
Port Union	316	St. Anne's	312
Scarboro'	320	Pointe Claire	318
York	327	Blue Bonnets	328
TORONTO	333	MONTREAL	333

USUAL TIME, 15 hours. FARE, $10.

TRIP FROM MONTREAL TO QUEBEC.

THIS interesting trip is, during the warm season, one of a most delightful character. To be fully enjoyed, however, it should be performed during daylight; but, unfortunately, the evening line of steamers usually alone performs the trips, leaving Montreal at seven o'clock P. M., and Quebec two hours earlier. "Both banks are low and uninteresting in a scenic point of view, but lined with the neat, whitewashed cottages of the French-Canadian peasantry, built so closely to each other as to suggest the idea of a continuous village on either bank; with here and there a thicker grouping of houses round the parish church. Darkness, however, soon closes the view, and the traveler only knows that he is rapidly borne along on the now united and smooth waters of two mighty rivers, better known by the inhabitants on its banks as the *La Grande Rivière*."

On leaving Montreal for Quebec and the intermediate landings, in one of the many splendid steamers which navigate the St. Lawrence, you have a fine view of the beautiful fortified island of ST. HELEN, situated mid-stream opposite the city; and as you are borne along on the majestic current of the mighty river, its thickly settled and cultivated shores compel the admiring attention of the traveler, by the aspect presented by their lines of settlements on each side, for the whole distance of 170 miles from city to city.

LONGUEUIL, on the opposite side of the river from Montreal, is connected with the city by a commodious ferry—this being the present terminus of the *Grand Trunk Railway*, leading to Quebec and Portland, Me., the two routes diverging at Richmond, C. E.—thus forming a speedy line of travel both to *Quebec* on the northeast, and the *White Mountains* of New Hampshire on the southeast.

The RAPIDS OF ST. MARY are entered immediately below St. Helen's Island; and, although not formidable to steam vessels, they often retard the ordinary river craft for many days in ascending.

LONGUE POINT and POINT AUX TREMBLES, on the island of Montreal, are successively passed on the left, and BOUCHERVILLE on the opposite shore.

The ISLAND OF ST. THERESA lies in the St. Lawrence, a short distance from the northern termination of the *island* of Montreal, and 15 miles below the *city*, near the lower mouth of the Ottawa River.

VARENNES, on the southeast side of the river, 15 miles from Montreal, is a beautiful place, and was formerly much resorted to for the mineral springs in its vicinity. The massive church, with its two spires, surrounded by a cluster of neat dwellings, presents a fine appearance from the river. Other objects of interest are seen in the distance; the hills back of Montreal are still visible; and the *Mountain of Rouville*, rising grandly in the southeast, its summit crowned with an immense cross, seen for many miles, greatly exalts the character and expression of the whole prospect.

WILLIAM HENRY, or SOREL, 45 miles below Montreal, stands on the site of an old fort, built in 1665, at the mouth of the Richelieu River. It is regularly laid out with streets crossing each other at right angles. This town was first settled in 1685, and now contains about 3,000 inhabitants. It is no doubt destined to increase, as a canal, with locks, is now constructed from Chambly to St. John's, affording an uninterrupted water communication with Lake Champlain. The fort at this place was taken and occupied, in May, 1776, by a party of the American army, in their retreat from Quebec on the death of Gen. Montgomery.

Leaving the mouth of the Richelieu and proceeding down the St. Lawrence, several islands are passed in succession, and then you enter

LAKE ST. PETER, 50 miles below Montreal. This sheet of

water, which is but an expansion of the river, is about 25 miles long and 12 to 15 miles wide, while the average breadth of the river proper, from Montreal to Quebec, is about two miles, and the scene which its waters present has some features peculiar enough to be noticed. In addition to the more customary forms of steamboats, of ships, and other sea-going vessels, and of the craft usually employed in the navigation of large rivers, the waters of the St. Lawrence, more than any other even on this forest-covered continent, are frequented by enormous timber-rafts, commonly borne along on their way to market by the force of the current alone, though occasionally aided by spreading a sail, or by huge oars called sweeps. These floating islands of timber, with huts here and there rising from their low surface, for the accommodation of the raft-men, and another singular sort of craft with long, low hulls, nowhere else known, and designed chiefly for the transport of timber of great length, contribute the more remarkable and picturesque features to the animating spectacle presented by the navigation of this noble river; while, from its high latitude, and from the characteristic phenomena of northern skies, the ordinary, as well as the more grotesque, features referred to are accompanied by contrasts in the golden grandeur of the sunsets, and in the varied splendor of the northern lights, both of which are so frequent and so remarkable, that they may be very fairly regarded as habitual, and from which the scenery of the St. Lawrence derives a magnificence and beauty probably unequaled.

Port St. Francis, 83 miles below Montreal, is the next steamboat landing. Here the river again contracts to its usual width.

Three Rivers, about half way between Montreal and Quebec, is situated on the north side of the St. Lawrence, at the mouth of the river St. Maurice; nearly opposite to which, and of smaller volume, enters the river Becancour. Three Rivers is an old town, having been settled by the French in 1618. Here is a court-house and jail, a convent, a Roman Catholic church, and three Protestant churches; a mechanics' institute, an academy, several public houses, 40 stores, lumber-yards, a ship-yard and foundry; also, other manufacturing establishments. The town contains about 5,000 inhabitants, and is a place of considerable trade and importance.

This place has become a great lumber mart, caused by the opening up of the great timber country in its rear, on the banks of the St. Maurice. A visit to the wild and romantic *Falls of Shawanagenne*, about 25 miles up this river, will be found interesting; it may be easily accomplished in one day, the road leading through a forest for most of the way, with here and there a hamlet to vary the scene. A part of the journey is usually performed in a bark canoe propelled by Indians. On arriving at the falls, nothing but grandeur and solitude strikes the imagination.

St. Anne, 25 miles below Three Rivers, stands on the north bank of the St. Lawrence, at the mouth of a river of the same name.

The Richelieu Rapids, 45 miles above Quebec, extend some eight or ten miles. The channel of the river is here very narrow and intricate, huge rocks being visible in many places during low water. In order to guide the mariner safely through these rapids, beacon lights are stationed at the more critical points of the passage.

Cape Sante, 30 miles from Quebec, is on the north side of the St. Lawrence, and on the opposite side is a settlement called St. Trois. The banks of the river are here elevated some 60 or 80 feet above the water, and are almost perpendicular, from which the land extends away for many miles, with an almost level surface.

Cape Rouge, eight miles above Quebec, is next passed on the left, when the citadel of Quebec comes into view, presenting a sight at once grand and deeply interesting, from the historical events with which it is associated.

The Chaudiere River, on the right, is much visited for the sake of its beautiful falls, situated a short distance from its entrance into the St. Lawrence

Wolfe's Cove, two miles above Quebec, on the same side, is an interesting spot to strangers, for here the lamented *Wolfe* landed with his gallant army, in 1759, and ascended to the Plains of Abraham, where he fell a victim to his heroic enterprise. But he fell not alone. France mourned an equal loss in the fall of the brave and generous *Montcalm*.

As the steamer approaches the wharf, the line of shipping, extending usually for two or three miles, gives life and interest to the scene below—while the towering citadel above produces emotions of wonder and delight. The city, or Lower Town, only as yet partly seen, soon opens to view, hugging the base of the rocky promontory.

QUEBEC.

The City of Quebec, a seaport, and most important naval and military depôt, is situated on the left bank of the river St. Lawrence, at the point where it is joined by the St. Charles, 170 miles below Montreal, and about 400 miles from the Gulf, in N. lat. 46° 49′ 12″, W. long. 71° 15′ 45″. Population in 1831, 25,916; in 1844, 32,876; in 1852, 42,000, and in 1856, estimated at 46,000, of which about two thousand are soldiers.

As a fortress, Quebec may be justly ranked in the first class. Words can hardly express the strength of its position without the aid of technical terms. The citadel, the Gibraltar of America, is approached by a zigzag pathway, with thirty-two pounders staring you in the face at every turn. When inside the fortress, it looks like a world of itself. The officers' barrack is a fine building, overlooking the St. Lawrence. The soldiers quarters are under the ramparts. The armories, magazines, and warlike implements are immense. The military authorities are energetically at work putting the fortifications of Quebec into repair. The Quebec *Mercury*, of a late date, says: "There is hardly a point at which the fortifications are not being repaired or improved. A new and very strong blockhouse is making below the flag-staff, and very extensive works, of by no means ancient construction, above that point, have been condemned, and are now rebuilding in a more formidable manner, near where a new battery and draw-bridge outlet from the citadel have lately been constructed, communicating with the city over the northeastern glacis."

"The city is built on the extremity of a ridge terminating in the angle formed by the junction of the two rivers on the point called Cape Diamond, which here rises to the height of about 340 feet above the St. Lawrence. The cape is surmounted by the citadel, and the city extends from it principally in a N.E. direction, down to the water's edge. The old town, which lies wholly without the walls, partly at the foot of Cape Diamond, and around to the St. Charles, has narrow and, in parts, steep streets. The ascent from the upper to the lower portion of the city which crosses the line of the fortifications is by a winding street and by a flight of steps; the streets in this section, though narrow, are generally clean, and well paved or macadamized. The public buildings and most of the houses are built of stone. The line of the fortifications stretches nearly across the peninsula in the west, and runs along a ridge between the upper and lower parts of the city. It is intersected by five gates, and has an inner circuit of about 2½ miles. Beyond the ramparts on the west are the extensive suburbs of St. Roch, St. John, and St. Louis. Durham Terrace commands a picturesque view, having the lower part of the city in the foreground; and the shores and waters of the St. Lawrence extending far in the distance. The Public Garden, on Des Carrieres Street, contains an elegant monument erected to the memory of Wolfe and Montcalm. It is 65 feet high, and its design is very chaste and beautiful. This spot attracts great attention, and should be visited by every stranger. The Esplanade, railed off from, and situated between D'Auteuil Street and the ramparts, affords delightful views of the surrounding country and river scenery.

"There are 174 streets in the city and suburbs, the principal of which are the following: St. John Street, the principal seat of the retail trade; St. Louis Street, occupied by lawyers' offices and private dwellings, is handsome and well-built; D'Auteuil Street, facing the Esplanade in the upper town, and in the lower town, St. Peter Street, in which most of the banks, insurance companies, and merchants' offices are situated. There are also many other fine streets, and the appearance of the city has been much improved since the great fire of 1845 when nearly 2,000 buildings were destroyed, which have been replaced by others of a superior description. The streets are lighted with gas, and the city is well supplied with water from the St. Charles River. The Parliament House (destroyed by fire 1853) was an elegant pile of buildings, forming three sides of a square, now about being rebuilt in a much improved style. The Court House and City Hall are substantial stone edifices, St. Louis Street, upper town. The Marine Hospital, a fine stone building, will accommodate 400 patients. The Lunatic Asylum at Beauport, 2½ miles from the city, is an extensive building, inclosed in a park of 200 acres. The Quebec Musical Hall, recently erected, is a substantial and well-built edifice, fitted for musical entertainments, etc. The Quebec Exchange, the Canadian Institute, the Literary and Historical Society, the Quebec Library Association, the Advocates' Library, etc., are among the most noted and interesting institutions of Quebec.

"The Roman Catholic Cathedral is a large and commodious building, but with no great pretensions to beauty of architecture; the interior is handsomely fitted up, and has several fine paintings; the church will seat 4,000 persons. It has a fine choir and a good organ. The Episcopal Cathedral is a handsome edifice, 135 feet by 75 feet. It was erected in 1804, and will seat between 3,000 and 4,000 persons. Trinity Church is a neat stone building, erected in 1824; it is handsomely fitted up. St. Andrew, Presbyterian Church, is 95 by 48 feet, and will accommodate about 1,200 persons. There were, in 1852, one Baptist, one Congregational, four Episcopal, one Free Presbyterian, two Methodist, one Presbyterian, and five Roman Catholic churches. Quebec has three banks, and several bank agencies, two savings' banks, and a number of insurance agencies. The hotels are numerous, and several of them well-kept, being usually thronged with visitors from the United States and foreign parts during warm weather.

"There are three nunneries, one of which, the Hotel Dieu, is a very valuable hospital; the nuns acting as nurses to the sick in these establishments, and as instructresses of young females. There are numerous religious and benevolent institutions, an exchange, a board of trade, a mechanics' institute, etc. Among the establishments for educational purposes, the first place is due to the University of Quebec; it has a principal, and professors of theology, rhetoric, and mathematics, with five regents for the Latin and Greek classes.

"Though not a manufacturing town, Quebec has various distilleries, breweries, with tobacco, soap and candle works, and numbers of fine vessels have been launched from its ship-yards. The climate, though on the whole good and healthy, is extremely hot in summer and cold in winter. The majority of the population is of French extraction, and the French language is mostly spoken in the best circles, and the Roman Catholic religion predominates."

Steamships and other sea-going vessels of the largest burden come up to the wharves of Quebec. Its harbor or basin between the city and the island of Orleans is of great extent, having in general about 28 fathoms water, the tide rising from 16 to 18 feet at neaps, and from 24 to 30 feet at spring tides. The commerce of the city is very extensive, the lumber trade alone giving employment to a great number of ships during the season of navigation, from May to November. Quebec has a regular intercourse, by means of steamers, with Montreal and ports higher up the St. Lawrence and the Ottawa River; also with Halifax, Liverpool, and other ports on both sides the Atlantic.

The *Grand Trunk Railway* is now so far finished as to afford speedy communication with St. Thomas, 49 miles below Quebec, with Portland, Me., Montreal, Kingston, Toronto, etc. Its passenger and freight depôts are situated at Point Levi, opposite Quebec, the two places being connected by steam ferries. Steamers also run to different ports below Quebec, and during warm weather make trips to the lower St. Lawrence and Saguenay rivers.

The following description of the city of Quebec is taken from Mr. Buckingham's late interesting work on CANADA, etc.:

"The situation of Quebec is highly advantageous, in a commercial as well as a military point of view, and its appearance is very imposing, from whatever quarter it is first approached. Though at a distance of four hundred miles up from the sea, the magnificent river on which it is seated is three miles in breadth a little below the town, and narrows in to about a mile in breadth immediately abreast of the citadel; having, in both these parts, sufficient depth of water for the largest ships in the world—a rise and fall of twenty feet in its tides—and space enough in its capacious basin, between Cape Diamond on the one hand, and the Isle of Orleans on the other, to afford room and anchorage for a thousand sail of vessels at a time, sheltered from all winds, and perfectly secure! A small river, the St. Charles, has its junction with the St. Lawrence a little to the north of the promontory of Cape Diamond, and affords a favorable spot for ship-building and repairs, as well as an excellent winter-harbor for ships lying up dismantled.

"The citadel of Quebec occupies the highest point of Cape Diamond, being elevated 350 feet above the river, and presenting almost perpendicular cliffs toward the water. The city is built from the water's edge along the foot of these cliffs, round the point of the promontory, and ascending upward from thence to the very borders of the citadel itself. It is divided into the Lower and Upper Town, the former including all that is below the ramparts or fortified lines, the latter comprehending all that is above and within that barrier. Besides these, there is a large suburb, separated from Quebec proper by the ramparts, and some open lawn beyond these on the west, called the suburb of St. Roch, on the right bank of the river St. Charles, the only portion of the whole that is built on level ground.

"On landing at Quebec, therefore, the traveler has to wind his way up through steep, narrow, and tortuous streets, with still narrower alleys on his right and left, till he reaches the fortified line or barrier. Here he enters by Prescott Gate, on the right of which, after passing through it, he sees the imposing structure of the New Parliament House (since destroyed by fire), with its lofty cupola and fine architectural front; and on the left, a double flight of mean and straggling wooden steps, leading to one of the oldest streets, as an avenue to the Place d'Armes. Going across this last, he passes the English and French cathedrals, the government offices, and palace of justice on his right; and has the site of the old castle of St. Lewis, and the platform overlooking the harbor, on his left. Passing by these, and continually ascending for about half a mile beyond, he reaches the ramparts and gates on the upper side of the city; and going through these, he comes to the open lawn in front of the glacis, beyond which is the suburb of St. Roch, on the level ground along the southern bank of the St. Charles River.

"The plan of the city is as irregular as the greatest enemy of symmetry could desire. The steepness of the ascent from the river to the plain above is no doubt one cause of this, because it was only by making the ascending streets winding and tortuous that they could be got over at all; but besides this, the inequalities in the surface even of the Upper Town led to other irregularities in the form and direction of the streets; while the large space occupied by the old religious establishments, still further curtailing the lines in different directions, so cut up the area, that there is not a single street in all Quebec which can compare in length, breadth, or general good appearance to the King Street of Toronto or the Notre Dame of Montreal. The streets of Quebec are, therefore, in general short, narrow, crooked, steep, wretchedly paved in the center, still worse provided with sidewalks, and not lighted with lamps at night. The private dwellings are in general destitute of architectural beauty, and small and incommodious; some few are of wood, none of brick, but the greatest number are of rough-hewn stone, with high, steep roofs, containing a double row of projecting garret windows, very lofty chimneys, and the roofs principally covered with sheets of tin. The shops are also small and mean, and greatly inferior in the extent and variety of their contents to those of Montreal and Toronto; though the prices charged are, as we thought, higher here than in either of these.

"The public buildings are scattered over the city with so much irregularity, that their position seems to be as much the effect of accident as design. Several of them, however, are so prominently placed and advantageously seen, that they relieve, in some degree, the general monotony of the mass of ordinary houses, and are thus far ornamental to the town; while the spires of the churches, the dome of the Parliament House, and other elevated points rising from the general surface, with their tinned roofs glittering in the sun, give a liveliness and variety to the picture presented by the city, from every point of view, which no other place in Canada, and indeed few places on the globe, present.

"The earliest of the public buildings erected in Quebec was undoubtedly the castle of St. Lewis, of which Champlain laid the foundation on the 6th of May, 1624. The position chosen for it was a most commanding one, on the very edge of an almost perpendicular precipice of rock 200 feet above the river, yet close to its edge; as, between the cliff and the stream, there is only just room enough for one narrow avenue, called Champlain Street. The castle erected here was regarded as the palace of the French governors, who received in it the fealty and homage of the several seigneurs holding their lands according to the feudal tenure of the times. Nor is this practice discontinued; for, according to Mr. Hawkins, in his *Picture of Quebec*, the sovereignty of England having succeeded to that of France, with all its ancient rights and privileges, the king's representative, in the person of the English governor, receives the same homage at the present day as was paid by the seigneurs of former times; this being one of the conditions on which the feudal tenure is sustained. His words are these:

"'Fealty and homage are rendered at this day (1834) by the seigneurs to the governor, as the representative of the sovereign, in the following form: His Excellency being in full dress, and seated in a state-chair, surrounded by his staff, and attended by the Attorney-General, the Seigneur in an evening dress, and wearing a sword, is introduced into his presence by the Inspector-General of the Royal Domain and Clerk of the Land Roll. Having delivered up his sword, he kneels on one knee before the Governor, and placing his right hand between those of the Governor, he repeats aloud the ancient oath of fidelity; after which a solemn act is drawn up in a register kept for that purpose, which is signed by the Governor and Seigneur, and countersigned by the proper officers.'

"In this castle the French and English governors resided till 1809, when it was found necessary to erect a temporary new building for their use while the old one underwent repair; and £10,000 were expended for this purpose under the administration of Sir James Craig. After this it continued to be the seat of government as before; and all the proclamations and ordinances issued, and all the messages sent to the legislative assemblies by the governor in the king's name, were dated from the castle of Quebec. It was also the scene of all the public levees and private entertainments of the governors and their families; and was therefore the constant resort of all the gay and fashionable society of the province. In 1834, however, this ancient edifice was entirely destroyed by a fire, which broke out on the 23d of January, in the depth of winter, when Lord Aylmer occupied it as his official residence; and notwithstanding every exertion made to save it, the thermometer being at 22° below zero, and the fire-engines only capable of being worked by a constant supply of warm water, the castle was soon reduced to ashes. It has never since been rebuilt; but Lord Durham, during his short stay here, had the site cleared of the ruined heaps that still covered it, and the whole area of the former edifice leveled, floored with wood, and converted into a beautiful platform, with a fine iron railing at the edge of the precipice, making it one of the most beautiful promenades imaginable—commanding an extensive view of the St. Lawrence down as far as the island of Orleans—the harbor filled with ships immediately before it, and the opposite bank of the river, with Point Levi, the village of D'Aubigny, and the road leading up through one continuous line of cottages to the Falls of Chaudière.

"The site on which the Parliament House stood is of even earlier date than that of the castle of St. Lewis; there being good reason to believe that it occupied the first spot of ground which was cleared by Champlain for his fort, on founding the city in 1608. Here, too, as at the castle, the site stands on a mass of rock made level by art, and extending to the brink of a perpendicular precipice, of about 100 feet above the river, the narrowest part of which is commanded by its guns. Along the edge of this precipice, beyond the area occupied by the late Parliament House, still runs the Grand Battery of Quebec, the promenade on which, and the view from its platform, is scarcely inferior to that already described on the site of the old castle of St. Lewis."

Plains of Abraham.—This celebrated battle-field lies a short distance southwest of the citadel. A monument is here erected on the spot where Gen. Wolfe is said to have died, with this simple inscription: "*Here fell Wolfe victorious.*" A beautiful monument is also erected, of recent date, to the memories of both Wolfe and Montcalm, within the city walls, with this inscription: "*Immortal memory of Wolfe and Montcalm.*"

WOLFE'S MONUMENT—QUEBEC.

"HERE FELL WOLFE VICTORIOUS."

A broken column! few and brief
The words inscribed upon its stone;
Yet speaks it of the dying chief,
Triumphant tales alone!

It tells unfading glory shed
Upon the hero's parting hour;
Dying beside the host he led,
To victory and to power!

The trumpet's tone, the battle shout,
All sounds of triumph come again,
As shines the brief inscription out,
Upon the storied plain.

The clashing sword, the cannon's roar,
The beating of the wild war drum;
And the last shout, "They fly!" once more
On fancy's vision come.

And marching round the hero's bed,
With banners floating free and fair;
Are seen the host he nobly led
For England's glory there.

But years have passed, and silence reigns
Where once was heard the battle cheer;
Of all the trophies naught remains—
This, only this, is here.

A broken column! brief, yet high
The eulogy its words convey;
Thus in the triumph hour to die,
Breathes not of earth's decay.

Wolfe fell in the moment of victory, and Montcalm, who was mortally wounded in the action, expired soon after. The French, panic-struck by the loss of the battle and the death of their commander-in-chief, surrendered the city before even a single battery had been opened against it. This important event, which transferred the possession of Canada from the French to the English nation, occurred on the 13th Sept., 1759.

The following is an English account of the attack on Quebec by Montgomery and Arnold, in 1775 and 1776:

"At the period of the American Revolution, it is well known that Canada did not join the revolted colonies, but continued firm in her allegiance to the Crown; and hence it became the land of refuge to the many loyalists who were driven from the United States by the success of their war of Independence. As it was believed, however, by the Americans of that day, that an attack on Quebec would be successful, and if so, would induce all Canada to join their cause, such an attack was planned, and its execution committed to two American generals, Montgomery and Arnold. The British troops usually retained in Canada for its defense had been sent on to Boston, so that the province was almost destitute of military force, there being scattered throughout all Canada only about 800 men. In this state of things Gen. Montgomery advanced from Lake Champlain on St. John's, and after a short resistance took it; he then marched on against Montreal, which being perfectly defenseless, surrendered to the American arms on the 12th of November, 1775. At the same time Gen. Arnold was known to Montgomery to be advancing toward Quebec, from the New England States, by way of the Kennebec River through Maine, which at this late period of the year was a most daring undertaking. After passing thirty-two days in the wild forests and swamps, and suffering almost incredible hardships and privations in this hitherto untrodden wilderness, Arnold and his followers reached the banks of the St. Lawrence, by the Chaudière River, on the 4th of November, in the same year. From thence they descended to Point Levi, opposite to Quebec, where they arrived on the 9th, crossed over on the night of the 13th, and landed 500 men at Wolfe's Cove without being perceived either by the sentries or from the ships of war.

"On the 1st of December this force was joined by a much larger one under General Montgomery, from Montreal. By these two the city was invested, and several bombardments of it made with shot and shells, but without producing much effect. A night attack was at length determined on by Montgomery on the southern, and Arnold on the northern, side of the Lower Town. Both attacks were made with great courage and impetuosity, but both failed. In the former, Gen. Montgomery and nearly all his personal staff were killed; in the latter, Gen. Arnold was wounded, and with most of his followers taken prisoners. The loss of the Americans in these attacks was upward of 100 killed and wounded, and of the British, only one naval officer killed, and seventeen men killed and wounded. The Americans did not, however, give up the attempt to reduce Quebec; as, during all the winter following they continued to receive reinforcements, and to invest the town; and in the spring of the year ensuing, May, 1776, they renewed their attack on the citadel. Gen. Carleton, the English commander of the garrison, having received an important accession to his force by the arrival of a small squadron under the command of Sir Charles Douglas, bringing to his aid provisions, ammunition, and men, was enabled to baffle every attempt made on the city, and ultimately to make a sally on the enemy, when they retreated, and abandoned their post.

"This was the last attack made on Quebec by any foreign foe, and as since that period the citadel has been gradually strengthened and improved, under every successive governor of the province, it is now in a condition to resist ten times the force ever yet brought against it, and could not, so long as it contained supplies of provisions, and an adequate number of brave and faithful men, be conquered by any force likely to be brought against it from this continent."

General Montgomery.—A tablet has been placed on the rock of Cape Diamond, near the spot where General Montgomery fell, with his two aids-de-camp, Majors McPherson and Cheeseman, at Pres-de-ville, in the attack upon Quebec by the American forces, in the winter of 1775–6.

The tablet is raised about fifty feet from the road, and bears the following inscription:

HERE

MAJOR-GENERAL MONTGOMERY FELL,

DECEMBER 31ST, 1775.

"It has long been a matter of surprise to our neighbors of the United States, who, during the summer months, pour in a continual stream of visitors to our celebrated city, that no clue could be found by them to indicate the spot where Montgomery fell. The event must ever remain memorable in our colonial history as terminating the last hostile struggle before the city of Quebec.

"Quebec is much indebted to the late Mr. Hawkins for the labor he has bestowed in bringing before the public the various historical reminiscences connected with the city, and this tablet, erected by him, is a fresh proof of the interest he takes in perpetuating the recollection of every incident connected with the many warlike and memorable events illuming the annals of our American Gibraltar." *See* Hawkins' Quebec.

VICINITY OF QUEBEC.

Quebec, the *Ultima Thule* of most travelers, stands not alone in regard to attractions of interest. In the Vicinity, within a few hours' ride, are located waterfalls and varied scenery of the most romantic character, while the banks of the Lower St. Lawrence and Saguenay rivers stand unrivaled in scenic grandeur.

EXCURSION TO CAPE ROUGE.

On this excursion you leave the city by the St. Lewis Gate, and cross the Plains of Abraham to the right of the spot where Wolfe fell. A mile from the gate is the *Race Course*, which is thronged during the spring and fall races; and a mile farther, a road branching to the left leads to *Wolfe's Cove*, celebrated as the place where he landed with his army previous to the capture of Quebec, but now occupied by an extensive ship-yard and lumber-yard. The road beyond runs for some distance through a fine grove, with avenues leading to various pleasant country residences overlooking the river, of which you catch as you pass along occasional glimpses, together with the opposite shore in the neighborhood of the Chaudière Falls.

Returning by the St. Foi road, and facing toward the city, the prospect is far wider and more magnificent. Below and to the left stretches the fine cultivated valley of the St. Charles, bounded on the northwest by a picturesque range of mountains, the settlements reaching to their very base, with villages and church spires scattered over the intervening region; in another direction appear the Falls of the Montmorenci and the Isle of Orleans, and in front spreads the harbor of Quebec, with the bold cliffs of Cape Diamond and Point Levi rising perpendicularly on each side, the former crowned with impregnable bulwarks.

The Falls of Lorette, situated eight miles northwest of Quebec, are visited by many strangers with delight, though but a small volume of water. They have a descent of about 50 feet, and are surrounded by very fine scenery, peculiar to this section of Canada.

The *Indian Village*, at the falls, is inhabited by the remains of the once powerful tribe of the Hurons.

The hills or mountains on the northwest of Lorette may be said to be the bounds of white settlements in North America, although, at no distant period, the upper Saguenay River and Lake St. John will, no doubt, be reached in this direction by railroad.

FALLS OF MONTMORENCI.

In going to the Falls of Montmorenci, which should be visited by every lover of picturesque natural scenery, you pass through the suburbs of Quebec, mostly inhabited by French Canadians, and cross the river St. Charles, near its mouth, by a wooden toll bridge. Here are situated on the roadside several pretty country residences, on the route to *Beauport*, which is a long scattered village about half way between Quebec and Montmorenci, although for most of the distance there are dwellings so continuous as to appear like one continued settlement. At Beauport there is a Roman Catholic church with three spires; and a little farther north may be seen a neat monument and cross near the road, where are frequently found persons kneeling at their devotions.

The celebrated Montmorenci Falls, situated eight miles below Quebec, is a grand cataract. The river is but 60 feet wide, but the height of the falls is 240 feet. The effect on the beholder, says Professor Silliman, is delightful. All strangers at Quebec proceed to visit Montmorenci.

"The effect of the view of these falls on the beholder is most delightful. The river, at some distance, seems suspended in the air, in a sheet of billowy foam, and, contrasted as it is, with the black frowning abyss into which it falls, it is an object of the highest interest. The sheet of foam, which first breaks over the ridge, is more and more divided as it plunges and is dashed against the successive layers of rock, which it almost completely vails from view; the spray becomes very delicate and abundant from top to bottom, hanging over and revolving around the torrent till it becomes lighter and more evanescent than the whitest fleecy clouds of summer, than the finest attenuated web, than the lightest gossamer, constituting the most airy and sumptuous drapery that can be imagined. Yet, like the drapery of some of the Grecian statues, which, while it vails, exhibits more forcibly the form beneath, this does not hide, but exalts, the effects produced by this noble cataract.

"Those who visit the falls in the winter, see one fine feature added to the scene, although they may lose some others. The spray freezes, and forms a regular cone of one hundred feet or upward in height, standing immediately at the bottom of the cataract, like some huge giant of fabulous notoriety."

The *Natural Steps*, in the vicinity of the falls above, are an object of much interest, and there are many excellent fishing places on the river, rendering it a favorite resort of the lovers of angling and romantic scenery. There are also historical incidents connected with this neighborhood, which render it almost classic ground.

There are extensive saw-mills on the south bank of the river below the falls, which are propelled by water-power taken from the stream above, and conveyed for about half a mile in a raceway. These mills have upward of a hundred saws in motion at a time, and are said to be capable of completing an entire cargo of planks in a single day! In winter, the spray rising from the falls is congealed, and often presents a conical mass of ice 100 feet and upward in height. It was on the high grounds north of the falls that Gen. Wolfe met his first repulse, when he attacked the French, a short time before his triumph on the Plains of Abraham. He was here driven back, and compelled to re-embark, with the loss of 700 engaged in the assault.

On returning to Quebec there is afforded a splendid view of the city and citadel; the St. Lawrence, and the opposite shore above and below Point Levi; the beautiful island of Orleans, opposite the falls, and the rich valley of the St. Charles.

The Falls of St. Anne are situated on the river of the same name, on the north side of the St. Lawrence, 24 miles below Quebec, and presents a singular variety of wild and beautiful scenery, both in themselves and their immediate neighborhood. By leaving Quebec early in the day, the tourist can visit the Falls of Montmorenci, and the objects contiguous, and reach St. Anne the same evening, leaving the next morning to visit the falls, and the remainder of the day to return to Quebec.

LAKE ST. CHARLES, 13 miles north of Quebec, is a favorite resort of tourists, particularly of those who are fond of angling, as the lake abounds with fine trout. Parties intending to remain any length of time would do well to bring some of the good things to be found in the larders of Quebec with them, as it is not at all times that the supplies in the vicinity are all that can be desired.

The CHAUDIERE FALLS, on the river Chaudière, nine miles above Quebec, situated on the opposite side of the St. Lawrence, are very beautiful, and much visited. They are 130 feet high. The cataract is a fierce and noisy one. The following is Col. Bouchette's description:

"The continued action of the water has worn the rock into deep excavations, that give a globular figure to the revolving bodies of white foam as they descend, and greatly increase the beautiful effect of the fall; the spray thrown up being quickly spread by the wind, produces in the sunshine a most splendid variety of prismatic colors. The dark-hued foliage of the woods, that on each side press close upon the margin of the river, forms a striking contrast with the snow-like effulgence of the falling torrent; the hurried motion of the flood, agitated among the rocks and hollows, as it forces its way toward the St. Lawrence, and the incessant sound occasioned by the cataract itself, form a combination that strikes forcibly upon the senses, and amply gratifies the curiosity of the admiring spectator."

On visiting the above falls, the tourist crosses the river to *Point Levi,* and then obtains a conveyance for the excursion, passing up the St. Lawrence for a few miles.

DISTANCES FROM QUEBEC TO KAKOUNA, CHICOUTIMI, ETC

		Miles.
QUEBEC to	GROSSE-ISLE	30
"	ST. THOMAS	10 40
"	River Ouelle	32–72
"	MURRAY BAY	12–84
"	KAMOURASKA	6–90
"	RIVIERE DU LOUP	20–110
"	KAKOUNA	10–120
"	TADOUSAC	130
"	HA-HA BAY	54–184
"	CHICOUTIMI	16-200

TABLE OF DISTANCES BETWEEN QUEBEC AND KINGSTON, *via* ST. LAWRENCE RIVER.

Places.	Miles.	From Quebec.	Places.	Miles.	From Kingston.
QUEBEC	0	0	KINGSTON	0	0
Richelieu Rapids	45	45	Gananoque	22	22
THREE RIVERS	35	80	(Thousand Islands.)		
Lake St. Peter	30	110	BROCKVILLE	30	52
WILLIAM HENRY	15	125	Maitland	5	57
MONTREAL	45	170	PRESCOTT, or		
LA CHINE, *via* Canal	9	179	OGDENSBURGH	7	64
Beauharnois	18	197	Gallop Rapids	6	70
Cascade Rapids	1	198	Point Iroquois	6	76
Split Rock "	3	201	MATILDA	2	78
Cedar "	2	203	Rapid Plat	5	83
COTEAU DU LAC	5	208	WILLIAMSBURG	2	85
Lancaster	16	224	Farren's Point	11	96
St. Regis	13	237	Dickinson's Landing	4	100
(N. Y. State Line.)			(Long Saut Rapid.)		
CORNWALL	3	240	CORNWALL	10	110
(Long Saut Rapid.)			St. Regis	3	113
Dickinson's Landing	10	250	(N. Y. State Line.)		
Farren's Point	4	254	Lancaster	13	126
WILLIAMSBURG	11	265	COTEAU DU LAC	16	142
Rapid Plat	2	267	Cedar Rapids	5	147
MATILDA	5	272	Split Rock "	2	149
Point Iroquois	2	274	Cascade "	3	152
Gallop Rapids	6	280	Beauharnois	1	153
PRESCOTT, or			LA CHINE	18	171
OGDENSBURGH	6	286	MONTREAL	9	180
Maitland	7	293	WILLIAM HENRY	45	225
BROCKVILLE	5	298	Lake St. Peter	10	235
(Thousand Islands.)			THREE RIVERS	35	270
Gananoque	30	328	Richelieu Rapids	35	305
KINGSTON	22	350	QUEBEC	45	350

DISTANCE from QUEBEC to NIAGARA FALLS, 570 miles. Descent in the St. Lawrence River, from Kingston to Quebec, 234 feet.

Cape Trinity and Point Eternity, Saguenay River.—Canada.

TRIP FROM QUEBEC TO THE SAGUENAY RIVER.

As a trip down the St. Lawrence to Riviere du Loup, Kakouna, and the far-famed river Saguenay has, within the last few years, become a fashionable and exceedingly interesting steamboat excursion, we subjoin an account of such trip made by the author some few years since.

As the steamboat left the wharf, she took a graceful turn up stream, passing a 74 gun-ship of the Royal Navy, and then descended, running close under Point Levi, affording a fine view of the city and citadel of Quebec.

The beautiful line of settlements below the city, on the same side of the river, next attracts attention ; the view in the distance being bounded by hills, apparently elevated 1,500 to 2,000 feet above the waters of the St. Lawrence.

The romantic *Falls of Montmorenci*, seven miles below Quebec, are seen to great advantage from the deck of the steamer, plunging over an almost perpendicular precipice of 240 feet directly into this great river. Immediately below, on the bank of the St. Lawrence, was fought a severe battle between the English and French armies, a short time previous to the capture of Quebec by Gen. Wolfe, in 1759, in which the British were repulsed with considerable loss.

The ISLAND OF ORLEANS is next passea on the left, descending the river through the principal ship channel. This is a fertile tract, 20 miles long by five or six wide, and in part covered with a beautiful growth of forest. It rises from 50 to 100 feet above the water, and the stream of the St. Lawrence being here divided, the aspect of the shores at once reminds you of the scenery of the Hudson River above the Highlands. It has a population of about 7,000 souls, and produces the finest fruit in Lower Canada, excepting that raised in the vicinity of Montreal.

St. Patrick's Hole, eleven miles below Quebec, on the Orleans shore, affords a fine anchorage for vessels of the largest size. It was here, some 30 years ago, that the immense timber ship was built, supposed to be the largest vessel, by far, that ever crossed the Atlantic.

The Parish of St. Laurent, 14 miles below Quebec, is handsomely situated on the southeast side of the island, which is settled exclusively by French Canadians, mostly engaged in cultivating the soil. The dwellings have a remarkably neat look, being one story high, with both roof and sides painted white.

The southeast shore of the St. Lawrence, for many miles below Point Levi, presents a succession of villages and hamlets, consisting each of a cluster of houses with a church standing in the midst, and with its aspect of guardianship and guidance to the families dwelling around, imparting to the landscape a moral expression, which greatly enhances its picturesque beauty.

The vessels usually seen on this part of the St. Lawrence are of the larger class of merchant ships. The arrivals at the port of Quebec average some 1,400 to 1,500 annually, mostly from Great Britain, and besides other colonial produce, they carry back immense quantities of timber and lumber.

Madam Island, 26 miles from Quebec, is one of several small islands lying below Orleans. The river here widens to ten miles, which gradually increases all the way to its mouth; and for most of the distance there are two ship channels, called the *north* and *south channels*, the latter being the best and most navigated.

Cape Tourment, 30 miles below Quebec, is a bold promontory on the northwest side of the river rising to the height of about 2,000 feet, and seen at a great distance. Here the scenery is truly grand.

Grosse Island, opposite Cape Tourment, is the *Quarantine station* for vessels ascending the river, and it has a hospital, a Roman Catholic chapel, and other buildings usually connected with such an establishment.

St. Thomas, 40 miles from Quebec, on the southeast shore, is situated at the mouth of a stream called *South River*. The shore of the St. Lawrence is lined with a succession of dwellings for many miles below, with high grounds rising in the distance, beyond which may occasionally be seen the hills formerly claimed by the Americans, as the boundary between the State of Maine and Canada. Here terminates the *Grand Trunk Railway* for the present, but will be extended soon some 100 miles farther, to Trois Pistoles.

Crane Island, 45 miles below Quebec, is fertile and settled. Its north end is adorned with the delightful residence of the *Seigneur*.

Goose Island, 50 miles from Quebec, is owned by the Nuns, and is cultivated as a farm, by tenants.

The Pillars, 60 miles below Quebec, is the name given to several small rocky islets, on one of which stands a light-house. Here the scenery is peculiarly grand and interesting. The vast estuary of the river below looks indeed like an opening to the ocean. The shores for some ten miles onward are studded with shining residences, while the hills in the distance, on both sides, resemble very much the scenery bordering the widest part of Lake Champlain.

Sixty-five miles below Quebec is the remarkable channel called the *Traverse*. A floating light guides the mariner by night through this narrow and dangerous passage.

Isle aux Coudres (Isle of Filberts) is a large body of land lying toward the north shore, opposite the Bay of St. Paul's, and about 65 miles from Quebec. It is said that when Jacques Cartier anchored here, on his first voyage of discovery up the St. Lawrence, he gave this island the name it yet bears, from the quantity of filberts, or hazel nuts, which he found there.

St. Anne stands on the southeast shore, on a bay of the same name. Here is a Catholic college and a settlement of considerable size, about 70 miles from Quebec.

As you approach Goose Cape, 75 miles below Quebec, the banks of the river seem to decline in the distance; the river now being free of islands, presents a large expanse of water, here being about 18 miles wide.

MURRAY BAY, 80 miles below Quebec, lies on the northwest side of the St. Lawrence, at the mouth of a river of the same name. This is a fine section of country, producing wheat and other kinds of grain in abundance. Beyond this place is seen a beautiful range of hills, terminating at Cape Eagle and Cape Salmon on the east. This delightful place has become, within a few years, a fashionable summer resort for the Canadians.

KAMOURASKA, situated 90 miles below Quebec, on the southeast side of the river, contains about 1,500 inhabitants, and is surrounded by a fruitful district. Vessels can land here only at high water; at low water, passengers are taken ashore in small boats. In the rear of this village are seen abrupt and sterile hills with little or no verdure. In front are two or three small islands, chiefly resorted to for fishing and bathing, this being a favorite resort, during the summer months, for the citizens of Montreal and Quebec, and is no doubt destined to become a fashionable watering-place, where sea-bathing can be enjoyed by invalids and seekers of pleasure.

About 105 miles below Quebec are the *Pilgrim Islands*, a group of rocky islets which are passed to the right. On the left, a few miles below, is *Hare Island*, near the middle of the river.

The settlement at the RIVIERE DU LOUP, 110 miles below Quebec, on the southeast side of the St. Lawrence, contains about 1,500 inhabitants. Here commences the great road from the St. Lawrence River to the St. John's, by the way of the Madawaska River and settlement.

CACONA or KAKOUNA, 120 miles below Quebec is a fashionable sea-bathing resort.

RED ISLAND lies off the mouth of the Saguenay, this being the first island of the small group met on ascending the St. Lawrence. It is destitute of a light, and has caused many shipwrecks during the prevalence of fogs and storms, so frequent on the lower part of the river and Gulf of St. Lawrence. GREEN ISLAND lies nearly opposite Red Island, on the southeast.

RIVER DU LOUP AND KAKOUNA.

From the pen of a talented Correspondent of the Montreal Gazette.

"RIVIERE DU LOUP is a prettily situated village, taking its name from its river, which river has been made available for the purposes of an extensive saw-mill, a water-power being created by its precipitation over a ridge of rocks, which form the very beautiful Riviere du Loup Falls. There are a few "English" settlers (the word being used in its general sense as distinguishing from "French"), and a clergyman of the Church of England is stationed here. Six miles from Riviere du Loup is the village of "KAKOUNA," to adopt the Indian and more euphonious name, which is effectually supplanting the corruptions of "Cacona" and "Cocona" now in vogue. Kakouna is formed into a village, from the invariable custom of placing the houses on the front of the farms. It is prettily situated on a high ridge, along which passes the highway. Behind the ridge on which the village stands, gently slopes a valley, which is well cultivated, ascending gradually till it attains a considerable elevation at the rear concession, where another village and church are placed. In front of the Kakouna ridge a curtain of trees intervenes between the village and the beach. The view from Kakouna is very pleasing. The river stretches out before it in a noble width of twenty-five miles. The farther shore is a continuous succession of mountains. Amid them opens up the scarcely visible embouchure of the Saguenay. Up the river the pilgrim rocks look grim and solitary. Midway, *Hare Island* rises from the surrounding waters. Below, Kakouna Island projects into the river, forming a bay. Sunset at Kakouna sometimes presents an enchanting spectacle. The gently rippling waters gleam and shine with the sparkling luster derived from the rays of the declining sun. The brilliant coloring and changeful hues of the evening sky appear to rest upon the somber mountains, which, begirt midway with a zone of gray mist, contrast strangely with the gleaming dark blue river which laves their base. Far as the eye can reach, the wide expanse glitters, as if set with gems of every hue—its calm repose unbroken, save by the numerous vessels which, with their white sails floating on the breeze, proclaim the industry of man and his power over the elements, or by the shores of the islets which, bathed in light, rise from its surface. When a storm, too, rises, the river wears a peculiar grandeur, and the mind is irresistibly impressed with a sense of its majesty, and led to a contemplation from nature up to nature's God.

"But, to pass on from this digression, a word or two as to the advantages of Riviere du Loup and Kakouna as watering-places. Now easy of access, with a telegraph at Riviere du Loup and a daily mail, these places are every year becoming more resorted to. There is now much increased accommodation at Kakouna, where are two large and commodious hotels, and a good boarding-house. These contain many visitors, but many families are accommodated in the farm-houses—renting these and providing for themselves. This is a comfortable and independent plan. The houses are improving in accommodation; the practice is beginning to be established of the Canadian families having a smaller house, to which they betake themselves so as to give to the visitors control of the whole of the farm-house. A few home comforts will naturally be wanting, but life in Kakouna is not without its attractions, and the deprivation of a few comforts makes one appreciate them more keenly when regained. A baker leaves regularly at the houses good bread. Beef, poultry, mutton, salmon, herrings, pigeon, sardines, eggs, milk, and butter present a bill of fare that shows there is no danger of starving, while strawberries, raspberries, and blueberries are besides to be had in the greatest abundance. The strawberry grows in peculiar profusion, and of a singularly excellent quality, attaining often a large size. The children of the village reap a harvest while they continue. The sportsman will not find much game, through trout are abundant in the streams and lakes. There are, it may be remarked, attractive places for walks and drives, however. But the main recommendation of the two places in question, is the comparative moderation of the temperature, and the fact that open air exercise can, at all periods of the day, be enjoyed. The heat is never excessive, but the air of the evening is often decidedly cool. On the whole, these watering-places of the St. Lawrence will no doubt continue to attract a steady annual stream of visitors, desirous of luxuriating in a cool atmosphere and enjoying sea-bathing, while other places on the Lower St. Lawrence, presenting equal or greater advantages, will no doubt in due course come into notice, and prove desirable places of resort so soon as the necessary facilities for reaching them shall have been supplied."

As you approach the mouth of the SAGUENAY RIVER, the waters take a very black hue, perceivable for many miles below, and extending far into the St. Lawrence. Just within the mouth of the river, near Tadousac, there is a round mountain peak, called *Tête du Boule*, about 800 feet high, while on the opposite bank there is another bold eminence.

TADOUSAC, 140 miles below Quebec, is situated on the northwest shore of the St. Lawrence, at the mouth of the Saguenay River. This is a post belonging to the Hudson Bay Company, and is the residence of one of its partners and an agent. They alone are allowed to trade with the Indians in the interior, who occasionally visit this place, but more frequently Chicoutimi, at the head of navigation on the Saguenay, and the post at the Lake of St. John, where some of the company's agents also reside. At Tadousac is a Roman Catholic chapel, a store, and warehouse, and some eight or ten dwellings. Here is erected a flag-staff, surrounded by several pieces of cannon, on an eminence elevated about 50 feet and overlooking the inner harbor, where is a sufficient depth of water to float the largest vessels. This place was early settled by the French, who are said to have here erected the first dwelling built of stone and mortar in Canada, and the remains of it are still to be seen. The view is exceedingly picturesque from this point. The southern shore of the St. Lawrence, may be traced even with the naked eye for many a league—the undulating lines of snow-white cottages stretching far away, both east and west—while the scene is rendered gay and animated by the frequent passage of the merchant vessel plowing its way toward the port of Quebec, or hurrying upon the descending tide to the Gulf—while from the summit of the hill upon which Tadousac stands, the sublime and impressive scenery of the Saguenay rises into view.

We extract from the Report of the Commissioners for exploring the Saguenay, published in 1829, the following:

"Upon landing at Tadousac, we proceeded immediately to examine a few of the geognostical characters of the country. The only place of residence here is erected on a bank of sandy alluvium, elevated about fifty feet above the river, and forming a flat terrace at the base of the mountain, which suddenly emerges at a short distance behind. The rocks of which these mountains are composed is granite, either of a red or gray color, depending upon that of the feldspar. On the shore were seen small deposits of magnetic iron. Here bases were measured, and the requisite angle taken, for determining the height of the most elevated point, on either side of the Saguenay, at its mouth, and this was found to be 912 feet on the westerly side, and 588 on the opposite."

L'Ance a L'Eau, or Water Harbor, situated on the Saguenay, about a half a mile above Tadousac, is the name of a settlement where is an extensive lumber establishment.

The St. Lawrence River, below the mouth of the Saguenay, assumes an imposing appearance, gradually widening until its breadth exceeds one hundred miles.

THE SAGUENAY.

"This river has its mouth, according to common computation, 130 miles below Quebec, on the north shore of the St. Lawrence, in latitude 48 deg. 6 min. 38 sec. long., 70 deg. 40 min. west from Greenwich. It discharges a much greater body of water than any other river that falls into the St. Lawrence. Indeed, it is the largest river in North America, the St. Lawrence excepted, east of the Alleghanies.

"It takes the name of Saguenay only below *Lake St. John*, which lies about 120 miles N. by W. of Quebec. From Tadousac, a distance of about 140 miles to the lake, the course of the river is nearly east and west, Tadousac being, as before stated, in lat. 48 deg. 6 min. 38 sec., and the south side of Lake St. John in 48 deg. 23 min. 12 sec., giving only 16 miles to the north of Tadousac."

This lake, which is nearly circular, is about 40 miles across, and it is the center of an extensive region, the waters of which flow into it from the north, the west, and the south, in twelve principal rivers, being discharged to the east by the Saguenay.

The streams which flow into this lake from the south, the west, and the northwest have their sources in a mountainous tract which ranges nearly east and west for a long distance, and then, far in the west, bends northwardly, separating these waters from those which seek the St. Lawrence above Quebec and the Ottawa; and regarding them in their still wider relations, they are part of the extensive range of highlands which divide the basin of the St Lawrence from that of Hudson Bay and its tributaries.

"The country, the waters of which are discharged into the St. Lawrence by the Saguenay, is more extensive than all the rest of Lower Canada; but it has till lately contained, probably, not more than a few hundred Indian families, who live by hunting and fishing, and exchange their surplus with lessees of the King's Post, for a few articles of imported produce.

"The passage of the waters of the Saguenay from below the Ha-Ha Bay to the St. Lawrence, a distance of fifty miles, is one of the wonders of nature. They penetrate through a mountainous tract, composed of sienite granite, forming an immense canal in many places, with banks of perpendicular rocks rising from a thousand to fifteen hundred feet above the surface of the river, which is from a hundred to a hundred and fifty fathoms deep nearly the whole way, and from a mile to three miles broad. The power and pride of man is as much humbled in some parts of this tremendous chasm, as in the immediate presence of Niagara Falls. In many places the largest vessel may run close to the perpendicular rocks, with 100 fathoms water. There are, however, several coves with good anchorage. In Ha-Ha Bay the navy of England might ride, in from five to eighty fathoms. At twelve miles below Chicoutimi, which is distant 68 miles from Tadousac, the spring tide rises 18 feet, and there is from 10 to 50 fathoms at low water. The tide rises and the river is navigable seven miles above Chicoutimi, where the rapids of the outlet of Lake St. John commence. At this point a range of highlands crosses the Saguenay, extending along the head waters of the Malbay, the Gouffre, the Jacques Cartier, St. Anne, Batiscan, and St. Maurice, and forming the south and western side of the basin of Lake St. John, with the Hudson Bay highlands on the north and east.

"It is only within a few years that there have been any agricultural settlers in the Saguenay country. At present there are a few hundred families of *squatters* from the north shore below Quebec, chiefly induced to go in by employment in lumbering, etc., for Mr. Price's numerous saw-mills. At Ha-Ha Bay there is a church, and about 150 families, and openings are made at various places on the river. The soil is of disintegrated clay and granite, with limestone in some places. The general level of the land above Ha-Ha Bay, as far as the eye can reach from the river, is not higher than the island of Orleans, although more broken. The timber mixed, hard and soft, and of a middling growth. The climate is milder, if anything, than at Quebec. With the exception of the ridge crossing below Lake St. John, already mentioned, the country to a great extent round the lake, but particularly on the southwest side, is of the same character.

"On entering the Saguenay from Tadousac, which is about one mile wide at its mouth, the hills soon rise abruptly from the water's edge, from 500 to 1,000 feet above the tide-way, presenting an appearance somewhat similar to the entrance from the north into the 'Highlands' of the Hudson River, with which most travelers are familiar, divested, however, of all appearance of habitation for many miles, and the Saguenay averaging twice the width of the Hudson."

TETE DU BOULE, a round mountain peak, rises on the north side of the river, about one mile from its mouth. Here the rocks and hills are mostly bare, but the verdure increases as you ascend.

About three miles from Tadousac, the river inclines to the north for a few miles, then resumes its western course to Chicoutimi, a distance of sixty-eight miles from the St. Lawrence, and being in many places three miles in width, with a great depth of water, until you arrive at the bar, about sixty miles from its mouth.

The TWO PROFILES, seen on the north shore, a few miles up, and elevated several hundred feet above the water, bear a striking resemblance to the human face.

ST. LOUIS ISLAND presents a rocky and rugged appearance. It lies eighteen miles above Tadousac, and may be passed by large vessels on either side. Here, it is said, fine trout may be taken in large quantities.

At the mouth of the river Marguerite, on the north shore, and at St. John's Bay, on the south, are lumber establishments —the latter 28 miles above the mouth of the Saguenay.

At the distance of 34 miles from Tadousac, on the south shore of the river, are two enormous masses of rock called ETERNITY POINT and CAPE TRINITY. They rise from the water's edge to the height of some 1,500 feet, and so abruptly that they can almost be touched with the hand from the deck of the passing steamer. The aspect of these mountain cliffs is beyond expression grand. No man can pass along their base, and lift his eyes up their vast height, without awe—without experiencing the most intense emotions of sublimity. Sheltered between them is a lovely recess of the shore called Trinity Cove, its sequestered and lonely beauty enhanced by its strong contrast with the wild grandeur of the rest of the scene. (*See Engraving.*)

TRINITY CAPE takes its name from the three peaks of its summit, bearing some resemblance to three human heads; and the name of ETERNITY POINT is abundantly indicated by the huge pile of ever-during rock of which it is composed. The whole scene—the majestic river, a hundred fathoms deep, rolling along the base and in the shadows of the vast and beetling cliffs, bearing on their rocky fronts the impress of Almighty power and everlasting duration—the whole scene at this place is unsurpassed for its magnificence and solemn beauty.

Continuing up the Saguenay, STATUE POINT is next passed, where formerly was to be seen a rock in a niche, high above the water, which resembled a huge human figure. The niche is still visible, but the figure has fallen into the deep water.

The TABLEAU is an upright rock, rising almost perpendicularly from the water, to the height of several hundred feet, situated on the south shore.

The scenery in this vicinity, and for several miles below, is exceedingly grand and picturesque—high and precipitous hills, clothed with a stunted growth of forest trees, and all around a wild solitude, unbroken by a sign of habitation or life, except occasionally a huge porpoise showing his back above the wave, and the water-fowl peculiar to these northern latitudes.

Fifty-eight miles from Tadousac opens the HA-HA, or GREAT BAY, as it is sometimes called. It is entered on the left, while the Saguenay proper comes down on the right. At the head of the bay there is a large settlement, with several extensive saw-mills.

The Bay of Ha-Ha—a name by no means euphonious or worthy of the locality—contains a numerous population for so new a country. Two villages appear at the farther extremity, the population whereof must number at least five hundred souls; it is situated about sixty miles above the entrance, and so closely does it resemble the Saguenay, that it is only when the traveler has arrived at its extremity that the mistake is perceived. The streams which flow into this bay furnish the various saw-mills with the power of preparing deals for the

English market—and it is not an uncommon occurrence to behold three or four square-rigged vessels busily engaged loading on English account. All the lumber establishments throughout the country are owned by the firm of Messrs. Price & Co., of Quebec, and although they entered the trade in the first instance with the intent of furthering their own interests, the result has been that the men they employed have become settlers, and brought into cultivation a large tract of arable land.

From the entrance to Ha-Ha Bay to Chicoutimi, a distance of about twelve miles, the banks of the river are less rugged and are clothed with more verdure, and openings may now be seen on both shores, with occasionally a habitation. About eight miles below Chicoutimi there is a bar, which can be passed by vessels of a large size only when the tide is up, this being the first impediment to navigation in ascending this noble river, which for grandeur of scenery and depth of water may vie with any other stream on the American continent.

Chicoutimi, 68 miles from Tadousac, situated at the junction of the Chicoutimi River with the Saguenay, where is a picturesque water-fall, is another post occupied by the Hudson Bay Company, which has a resident agent stationed here. The settlement now contains an extensive saw-mill, a few dwellings, and a venerable-looking Roman Catholic chapel, of small dimensions, erected in 1727. It is one of those stations where, in former days, the indefatigable Jesuits established a home for themselves; a church yet remains to attest their religious zeal. This edifice is believed to have been one of the first erected in Canada. The locality selected is singularly picturesque and romantic. On one side the Saguenay pours down its mighty flood, the shores on either side covered to the water's edge with the most luxuriant foliage, while, on the other side, a safe and commodious bay receives the mountain torrent of the Chicoutimi River.

The church, a peculiarly agreeable object in so remote a spot, stands about 100 yards from the margin of the stream, in the center of a plat of green-sward set out with shrubbery, and forest trees crown the rising ground in the rear. Here assemble at stated periods the children of the soil; some from the region of the far north—the faith which their fathers were taught in earlier ages leading them to reverence a spot hallowed by traditional associations.

The steamboat navigation of the Saguenay ends here, as the river above this is obstructed by rapids and falls. Fifty miles above Chicoutimi, the river issues from LAKE ST. JOHN, which is a fine expanse of water of about 30 miles in length, and, in the widest part, the same in breadth, its superficial area being over 500 square miles. The rivers *Mistasine*, *Assuapmoussoin*, *Peribonea*, and *Ouatchoanish*, all of which are large streams, and many smaller ones, empty into Lake St. John, and as its only outlet is the Saguenay, which also receives many considerable streams in its course, the great depth and volume of water in that river may be thus accounted for. A *portage road*, or foot-path, runs from Chicoutimi to the Hudson Bay Company's station on Lake St. John.

Lake St. John, the *Saguenay*, and the rivers which they receive, abound in excellent fish, consisting of white fish, bass, trout, doré, carp, pike, eels, and others; the favorite salmon, during the spring and summer months, ascends the Saguenay for a considerable distance, and are taken in large quantities and shipped to Quebec; also cured and sent to European markets.

"The region of the Saguenay can not long remain silent and unoccupied. It is destined to become the home of an active and enterprising race. The climate is well adapted to the purposes of agriculture, and the virgin soil can not fail to repay the labors of the farmer. The aspect of the country around Chicoutimi is divested of the rugged and rocky character which distinguishes the banks of the Saguenay for the first 50 miles, and as the traveler advances inland, the appearance of the country indicates a superior soil—while the climate in the vicinity of Lake St. John approaches very closely to that of the Montreal district."

Taken altogether, few excursions can afford more interest to the tourist and seeker of pleasure, than a visit to Chicoutimi and its vicinity. Besides having a view of the magnificent scenery of the St. Lawrence, here may be seen a picturesque water-fall, and if fond of angling or hunting, the visitor may enjoy himself to his heart's content—surrounded by a vast wilderness, as yet almost unbroken by the haunts of man.

MURRAY BAY—TADOUSAC—HA-HA BAY, ETC.

The following letter was written by a gentleman of Phila delphia:

"On Wednesday morning, 25th July, 1855, we left Quebec for the lower St. Lawrence and Saguenay rivers. At eight o'clock, precisely, the steamer Saguenay shot out from the landing, and rounding under the stern of the French frigate *La Capricieuse* made her way down the St. Lawrence. The tin roofs and spires of Quebec gradually grew smaller in the distance, and the blue tops of the Green Mountains, miles away in Vermont, broke on the sight. As we steamed down the river, we had a fine view of Quebec with its precipitous hill, crowned with battlements, whose immense guns were leveled at us in the harbor. The magnificent basin before the city was dotted with craft laden with other tributaries of the St. Lawrence. A few miles below Quebec the river is divided by the island of Orleans, which is at first hilly and covered with trees, but as we pass along, its shores becomes flat and under cultivation. Its lands are held under the old French tenure, and its inhabitants are Canadian French. A singularity of division in lands which the tourist will observe through Eastern Canada, presents itself very prominently in this island. The lands of the French population, at the owner's death, are divided equally among the children; and in order that each child may have a portion of the river front, a farm is cut up into narrow strips running sometimes a mile in length by twenty yards in breadth. Upon the front the house is built, and the island shore is therefore a continuous line of little wooden houses, backed by cultivated fields.

"In about an hour after passing the island of Orleans, we came to Grosse Isle, upon which is located the Quarantine Station of Canada. Several large vessels were anchored in the stream, undergoing the precautionary measures against infectious or contagious diseases. Ample accommodations are erected upon the shore for emigrants suffering from ship-fever or similar disorders, and the Lazaretto arrangements of Quebec seem to be of the most perfect kind. On the mainland, behind Grosse Isle, Cape Tourment lifts its cloud-capped summit 1,800 feet into the air. The boat stopped at *Murray Bay* to land passengers and freight. This place seems to be the Cape May of Canada, where the citizens of Quebec and Montreal resort in great numbers, for salt-water bathing. The long pier that stretches into the river was crowded with ladies expecting friends and relatives by the boat. During the summer, the ladies of Canada, of every class, when at watering-places, wear straw hats, with rims of enormous breadth, which afford a marked contrast to the minute fixtures which American ladies affect. The scene was highly picturesque, and called forth much complimentary notice from traveling Americans who were aboard. We arrived at *Riviere du Loup*, another watering-place, about dusk, and anchored in the stream to await daylight. At three o'clock we again started for the mouth of the Saguenay, which is directly across the St. Lawrence from Riviere du Loup. The St. Lawrence is twenty-one miles wide at this point. About five o'clock we reached *Tadousac*, which is situated on the point of land formed by the confluence of the Saguenay and St. Lawrence. At this place the French first settled in Canada, and a little red-spired church was pointed out to us as being the first church erected north of the St. Lawrence, and the oldest ecclesiastical edifice in America.

"Leaving the St. Lawrence at this point, we plunged between high ridges into the Saguenay, and continued for five hours to float over its mirror-like expanse. It is a singular fact that the depth of the Saguenay is about seven hundred feet greater than that of the St. Lawrence, into which it empties, and in certain parts a fathom line of one thousand feet fails to touch bottom. The perpendicular mountains that hem it in, rise directly out of the water, without an intervening shore, and the steamboat can glide rapidly along within a yard of the solid land. *Cape Eternity*, about thirty-five miles above Tadousac, is one of the most striking objects upon the route. It is a huge mass of granite, without flaw or fissure, rising eighteen hundred feet in the air. Hardy birches and pines cling tenaciously to its barren sides, giving the only indication of life in the vicinity. The boat arrived at this point while we were at breakfast, and the pilot ran into a little cove beside it, so as to give the passengers a view of it from every side, then rounding directly beneath the overhanging mass, we shot out into the stream to gaze at its heavy summit from the distance. There was a feeling of indescribable awe in watching the receding boulder, as we sped up the stream, and many an admiring gaze was flung backward, even after a sudden bend in the river had hid it from our view. Tête du Boule, the Two Profiles, the Tableau,

Cape Trinity, and Statue Point, are each attractive objects that excite the admiration of the tourist.

"Near eleven o'clock in the forenoon we arrived before the little town which lies at the head of *Ha-Ha Bay*, about 60 miles from the St. Lawrence, and having dropped our anchor, the passengers were sent ashore by the ship's boats. The town is merely an establishment for lumbering purposes, and is owned by William Price, Esq., of Quebec, who is the most extensive lumber merchant in Canada. All the saw-mills upon the Saguenay belong to this gentleman. He keeps constantly employed at his various mills about 3,000 persons, and freights over 100 vessels annually with lumber. As only a few minutes were allowed us, before starting on our return to the St. Lawrence, we preferred remaining upon the steamer's deck and inspecting the town and adjacent country with the aid of a lorgnette. About Ha-Ha Bay the cliffs almost disappear and some indications of agricultural attempts are manifest, but a sterile soil and a bleak atmosphere always militate with tillage and farming in this region The Governor-General of Canada, Sir Edmund Head, was expected to visit the Saguenay on this trip, and as we ran up before the town a salute of guns was fired, and the English colors run up the flagstaff on shore. In return for the compliment, Capt. Simard decorated his steamer with flags of almost every nation, and we left Ha-Ha Bay about noon, in a gala attire of floating bunting. At five o'clock in the afternoon we touched at Tadousac, and in two hours after anchored at the pier of Riviere du Loup, to wait for the morning. Early on Friday, July 27, we started for Quebec, and made the 114 miles before four o'clock in the afternoon.

"The greater part of American tourists make a great mistake in omitting the Saguenay River. They miss the finest scenery on this continent, which they can view by an additional expense of $12 only. The fare on board the boat is of excellent quality, and the berths large and comfortable. It is worth a visit to the Saguenay to taste the salmon, that but an hour before was gliding in its native element. As a matter of information to those wishing to make the trip in future seasons, we may say that a thick over-coat is an absolute necessity. From eleven o'clock in the morning until four in the afternoon the temperature is agreeable, but not too warm; during the other hours of the day and night it will compare exactly with our November. Coming from warmer climates, the tourist can not be too careful to prepare for sudden changes of temperature. We can not close our imperfect sketch of the Saguenay without a word of thanks to Capt. Simard, who commands the steamer Saguenay. To our numerous questions he politely returned us full and satisfactory answers, and we are greatly indebted to him for much valuable information We cordially commend him and his boat to the attentions of all American travelers who may hereafter visit Quebec. From all classes of Canadians, both French and English, we met with the politest treatment, and can vouch for their hospitality and good-will. In conversation with numerous intelligent persons from Quebec and Montreal, we discover that the American character is greatly admired in Canada, and an earnest hope is indulged that the amicable commercial relations now in process of formation between the two countries will tend to introduce some of our finer national characteristics into Canadian affairs. While they are eminently loyal to their sovereign, they yet rejoice in the active energy of the Yankee race, and esteem it a privilege to live in such close juxtaposition to a nationality whose rapid rise and hardy vigor reflect honor on the Anglo-Saxon blood. The kindly feeling beyond doubt is reciprocated in the United States, and that, too, from a nobler motive than commercial and mercantile gain—from the fraternal feeling inseparable from nations descended from a common stock. Whether or not the time will ever come when Colonial Canada will be a sovereign State, and part of our rapidly expanding confederacy, remains to be seen. If the course of events should take such a turn, we will acquire a territory rich in mineral and agricultural resources, and one geographically adapted for unexampled greatness; if not, we are sure of a faithful ally and a firm unwavering friend." J. M. G.

ANTICOSTI

ANTICOSTI, about 400 miles below Quebec, is a large and important island in the Gulf of St. Lawrence, lying W.S.W. and E.S.E., in the widest part of its estuary, between the meridians of 61° 45′ and 64° 15′ W., and dividing the entrance of the river into two channels, from twenty to forty miles in width. It is about 125 miles in length; its extreme breadth is 30 miles; its superficial area 1,530,000 acres. Its surface is in general low, and covered with forests of stunted fir, white cedar, and poplar, or alluvial flats clothed with cranberry and blueberry bushes; but the timber is of inferior quality, and the soil is mostly poor. Bears, foxes, hares, martins, sea-otters, partridges, curlews, plover, and snipe are numerous. The geological formation is a shell limestone mixed with clay, and in some places wholly composed of encrinites. The northern coast is bold and high, presenting magnificent limestone cliffs, which sometimes rise to the height of 500 feet. The severity of the climate is so great that any grain is usually nipped in the bud. In the month of June, ice of considerable thickness is frequently formed during the night; and summer is always far advanced before the snow disappears. Winter commences in the early part of November, and continues till the middle of March; the thermometer ranging during this season from 20° above to 20° below zero. The shores are then surrounded with ice, and all communication with them is cut off. Its shores present a few small creeks, but throughout an extent of 300 miles there is neither bay nor harbor sufficient to protect ships; while the powerful stream setting constantly from the St. Lawrence, the shoals which surround this island, and the heavy snow-storms which here occur in the fall of the year, with its position across the mouth of the river, render it the frequent scene of shipwrecks, and the sailing past it "the worst part of the voyage to or from Canada." (Bonnycastle.) "The bearings of its extreme points are as follows: west point, N. lat. 49° 52′ 29″, W. long. 64° 36′ 54″; variation 22° 55′ W. East point, N. lat. 49° 8′ 30″, W. long. 61° 44′ 56″; variation 24° 38′ W. North point, N. lat. 49° 57′ 38″, W. long. 65° 14′ 1″. Southwest point, N. lat. 49° 23′, W. long. 63° 43′. An elevated and magnificent light-house, with a revolving light, now occupies this point of the island; and another has been erected on the E. coast. Spring tides rise ten feet; neaps, seven feet. This island formerly belonged to Labrador, but was annexed to Lower Canada in 1825, and now forms part of the county of Saguenay. Its name is probably a corruption of the Indian name *Naticostee.* It is first noticed in 1535, by Cartier, who gave it the name of Assumption." (Bouchette.)

Gulf of St. Lawrence.—On passing along the south side of the island of Anticosti, entering the Gulf of St. Lawrence, the shores of Gaspe are seen in the distance. This is an important district and headland, jutting out into the Gulf, and running round into the *Bay of Chaleurs*, comprehending 350 miles of coast; the whole extent is said to abound with fish of different kinds, and during the fishing season a large number of vessels and men are engaged in taking and curing fish for exportation.

Below where the Saguenay joins the St. Lawrence, the distance from shore to shore across the latter stream exceeds twenty miles, and the width goes on increasing till it expands to forty miles, from Cape Chatte to Cape des Monts Pelles, some three hundred miles below Quebec. From thence it goes on still further expanding, till it reaches the breadth of about 120 miles from shore to shore, in a line drawn from the extreme point of Gaspe due north across the western edge of the island of Anticosti, and so on to the coast of Labrador.

The grand trip from the Upper Lakes to the Gulf of St. Lawrence is thus spoken of by a late writer, on terminating the voyage: "Through this magnificent mouth of the river we passed into the *Gulf of St. Lawrence*, having thus traced the noble stream, from the island of Mackinac, in the strait of Michilimackinac, at the head of Lake Huron, down to the island of Anticosti, a distance of at least 2,000 miles, through a chain of the most splendid lakes in the world, and with almost every variety of scenery along its majestic course."

For further description of the Gulf of St. Lawrence and voyage to Halifax, see BUCKINGHAM'S CANADA, NOVA SCOTIA, etc

VALUE OF MONEYS.

The following information will be found valuable to strangers visiting Canada, and particularly to emigrants bringing with them sterling money.

Value of Colonial Moneys.

The basis of the currency is the imperial gold standard, differing from sterling money in the different nominal value of the pound and its constituents.

The pound sterling is by law fixed at Twenty-four shillings and fourpence currency. At this rate all large transactions are settled, and remittances, with the correction of the day for exchange, are calculated.

One pound currency,	contains	four dollars.
One dollar "	"	five shillings.
One shilling "	"	two sixpences.
One sixpence "	"	six pennies.
One penny "	"	two coppers.

The value in sterling of the pound currency is rather over	16s. 5¼d.
The dollar currency rather over	4s. 1¼d.
" shilling " "	9¾d.
" sixpence " rather under	5d.

But in retail transactions an approximation is made to the value of the coins current in Britain and the United States, and in small purchases the following are the rates at which such coins are usually paid away:

BRITISH.

The sovereign	£1 4s. 6d.
The crown	6s. 1d.
Half crown	3s. 0½d.
Shilling, called Trente-Sous	1s. 3d.
Sixpence, " Quinze-Sous	7½d.

AMERICAN.

Eagle	£2 10s.
Dollar	5s. 1d.
Half dollar	2s. 6½d.
Dime, or ten cents	6d.
Real, or *York shilling*	7½d.

A shilling sterling and a quarter of a dollar are taken in the stores as equal. The exchangeable value of the dollar, of course, varies with the course of exchange between the Provinces and the United States, which is principally ruled by that between New York and London. In general, its value is about 5s. 1d. currency, or 4s. 2d. sterling.

GRAND PLEASURE EXCURSION

FROM NEW YORK TO NIAGARA FALLS, TORONTO, MONTREAL, ETC.

PLEASURE travelers leaving New York at 7 o'clock A.M., or 6 o'clock P.M., by steamboats running on the Hudson River, can leave Albany almost immediately after their arrival, and proceed direct to *Schenectady*, 17 miles; *Utica*, 95 miles; *Rome*, 109 miles; or *Syracuse*, 148 miles from Albany, *via* New York Central Railroad.

At Schenectady the *Saratoga and Schenectady Railroad* commences and extends north to Saratoga Springs, 22 miles.

At Utica the *Black River and Utica Railroad* commences and extends north, 16 miles, to Trenton Falls, and thence to Boonville, a total distance of 35 miles. The above railroad, when finished, will run to Clayton, situated on the St. Lawrence River, 109 miles from Utica.

At Rome commences the *Watertown and Rome Railroad*, extending northward to Cape Vincent, 97 miles, forming a direct line of travel to Kingston and other places in Canada.

At Syracuse the New York Central Railroad is intersected by the *Syracuse and Binghamton Railroad* and *Oswego and Syracuse Railroad;* the latter railroad running north to the city of Oswego, 35 miles. Fare from Albany to Syracuse, $3. Usual time, 6 hours. Fare from Syracuse to Oswego, $1. Usual time, one hour and thirty minutes.

Travelers can proceed by railroad to *Rochester*, 81 miles from Syracuse, and there take a steamer for Toronto or Lewiston, or proceed direct through Lockport to the *Suspension Bridge* or *Niagara Falls.* From Niagara Falls, passengers desiring to go to Montreal or Quebec are conveyed by steamer from Lewiston or Niagara, Can., through Lake Ontario to *Kingston* or *Cape Vincent*, and thence down the St. Lawrence River.

Another new and favorite mode of traveling for those who wish to avoid the lake travel is to proceed to *Toronto*, and take the cars of the *Grand Trunk Railway* for Kingston. There take an American or British steamer for *Montreal*.

Steamers of a large class run daily from Oswego morning and afternoon. The morning boats leave Oswego for Sacket's Harbor, Kingston, Ogdensburgh, etc.; while the afternoon boats run direct to Charlotte, at the mouth of the Genesee River, and from thence direct for Toronto, Lewiston, etc., affording travelers a choice of routes if going *west* to Detroit, Chicago, etc., or if proceeding *north* to Kingston, Montreal, etc. Pleasure travelers are also conveyed direct to Niagara Falls, Buffalo, etc.

SACKET'S HARBOR, 45 miles from Oswego, is the first place at which the passenger boats stop to land and receive passengers; usual time, 3 hours.

KINGSTON, 40 miles farther, is usually reached in about the same time, where passengers can stop, or proceed direct down the St. Lawrence River, passing the "Thousand Islands" and magnificent rapids by daylight.

The American steamers, on leaving Kingston, run through the *Kingston Channel* to Clayton or French Creek, and thence to Ogdensburgh. The British steamers run on the north or *Canadian Channel*, stopping at Gananoque, Brockville, Prescott, etc., on the downward and upward trips.

Kingston being the best point for pleasure travelers to start from in order to see the "*Thousand Islands*" to advantage, we subjoin the following description of the trip to Prescott and Ogdensburgh, performed in June, 1857. The American steamers leave Kingston at about 3 o'clock P.M., descending the St. Lawrence, stopping at Ogdensburgh, 62 miles; while the British mail line of steamers leave at 6 o'clock A.M., running through to *Montreal*, 180 miles, by daylight.

On leaving Kingston the steamer runs between Howe and Grand Islands, both belonging to Canada, for a distance of about 15 miles. When at the foot of the former island, the steamer veers westward, passing through a beautiful group of small islands, and approaches GANANOQUE, 20 miles from Kingston. Several light-houses or beacons have recently been erected by the Canadian authorities to mark this intricate channel.

Other beautiful groups of islands are passed below Gananoque, when the *Fiddler's Elbow* is approached, 12 miles distant. Here is a light-house and another group of small islands.

ALEXANDRIA BAY, 34 miles below Kingston, is passed in sight on the right, the British steamer passing through the middle channel of the river. This favorite summer resort is reached by the American line of steamers.

The *Sisters* and *Scotch Bonnet* are a pretty group of islands situated in the middle channel, some 8 or 10 miles above Brockville. Here the stream of the river begins to narrow, and soon the labyrinth of islands are passed by the descending steamer.

The pleasure is greatly enhanced by an observing traveler to vary his routes, when an opportunity offers, in voyaging through the Lakes and down the St. Lawrence River, thus not only affording an opportunity to see the different points of interest on the route, but also see a different class of passengers—the Southern planter, the Northern financier, and the English or French Canadian resident, each possessing distinctive characters; while the intelligent ladies are always alike attractive.

BROCKVILLE, 52 miles below Kingston, is a fine Canadian town, situated immediately below the commencement of the Thousand Islands. The *Brockville and Ottawa Railroad*, now in progress of construction, will afford a direct and speedy route to the Upper Ottawa country.

PRESCOTT and OGDENSBURGH, 12 miles below Brockville, are important towns situated opposite each other, being closely connected by two steam ferries. Here navigation for sail vessels may be said to terminate, while steamers descend the rapids with the utmost safety.

For a further description of the Rapids of the St. Lawrence, see pages 69 and 74.

TRIP FROM "MONTREAL TO QUEBEC AND RETURN," JUNE, 1857.

THE above was the wording of the *pass* received from the Managers of the Grand Trunk Railway in the early part of June, 1857, but preferring to descend the "*La Grande Rivière*" in one of the swift steamers which run between Montreal and Quebec daily, leaving in the evening, I embarked on board the QUEBEC, the crack boat of the Royal Mail Line. Distance, 170 miles; cabin fare, $2 50.

On leaving Montreal, *St. Helen's Island* is soon passed, being in part covered with a rich growth of forest trees, while the fort and breastworks on the north end are seen to advantage. Then comes *Longueuil*, the present terminus of the Eastern Division of the Grand Trunk Railway, it being now reached by steam ferry-boat; but as soon as the *Victoria Bridge* is completed, running across the St. Lawrence River some two miles above, then will passenger and freight trains be transported over the above noble structure, to be finished in 1859.

A number of low islands are next passed on descending the stream, when the beautiful village of Varennes is soon reached and passed, situated on the right bank of the stream. Here is a mineral spring of some celebrity and a good public house.

The north point of the island of Montreal and northern branch of the Ottawa River are passed about 16 miles below Montreal, where are to be seen several picturesque islands, concealing in part the mouth of the Ottawa.

Here the St. Lawrence assumes its most majestic appearance for a stretch of several miles, the stream being from two to four miles in width—flowing onward in majestic grandeur, with here and there a square-rigged sail vessel and immense timber rafts, such as are alone seen on the lower St. Lawrence, being on their way to Quebec from the Ottawa River.

Before reaching Sorel, or William Henry, the stream contracts to about one mile in width, with more elevated banks. The river Richelieu, the outlet of Lake Champlain, enters the St.

Lawrence at *Sorel*, or *William Henry*, 45 miles below Montreal, this being the first regular landing for the Royal Mail Line. Here is situated an old and handsome town, enlivened by English and French residents and the busy Yankee, who is slowly making his way into the lower Province of Canada.

After leaving Sorel a number of islands are again passed, and the steamer soon enters the broad waters of *Lake St. Peter*, an expansion of the St. Lawrence. Here again the square-rigged vessels, the timber rafts, and the more fleet steamer may often be seen threading their way up or down the river.

Three Rivers, 90 miles below Montreal and 80 miles above Quebec, is an old and important town, being advantageously situated at the mouth of the river St. Maurice, on the left bank of the river.

This is considered the head of tide-waters on the St. Lawrence, although the *Richelieu Rapids* are below, where is a strong current when the tide is receding, the river flowing over a rocky and dangerous channel for several miles—the stream alternately running to the right and the left, with banks somewhat elevated. *Point aux Trembles*, on the left bank, is a bold headland, which, when passed, the stream again widens for a number of miles—the shores for the entire distance of 170 miles being dotted with picturesque residences of the French habitans and churches of the Roman Catholic persuasion.

Cape Rouge, 10 miles above Quebec, is another interesting point, situated on the left bank of the river. Next comes in sight Point Levi and the frowning fortress of Quebec—then opens the Lower Town, with its numerous shipping, its steam-tugs, and ferry-boats—altogether affording, during the summer months, one of the most grand and enlivening scenes to be witnessed on the continent of America.

Without entering into a description of Quebec, which is fully described in its proper place, we will allude to the hotels now open for the accommodation of tourists. Russell's Hotel in Palace Street, Upper Town, is an old, popular house; while the Clarendon House, kept by H. O'Neill, on Lewis Street, near the

Durham Terrace, is a new and popular resort for pleasure seekers visiting Quebec.

There are several other good hotels in both the Upper and Lower Town, while Norman's Victoria Hotel at Point Levi, opposite Quebec, is also a favorite resort for both English and American visitors. It is situated near the terminus of the Grand Trunk Railway, from whence steamers are almost constantly crossing to Quebec, affording an opportunity to see the fortress and city, together with the adjacent country, from Cape Rouge to the island of Orleans.

The trip from Quebec to the Lower St. Lawrence and Saguenay Rivers is fully described in another part of this work. See page 153.

RETURN TO MONTREAL.

On leaving Quebec for Montreal, *via* Grand Trunk Railway, passengers can proceed at 6 A.M. or 4 P.M., crossing the St. Lawrence by steamer to Point Levi, one or two miles distant. Near the depôt is situated the Victoria Hotel, a well-kept public house, surrounded by handsome grounds.

This is a most speedy route, the cars going through from city to city in six hours; 170 miles. The first station is the *Chaudiere Junction*, 8 miles from Point Levi; here the Chaudiere River is passed a few rods above the romantic falls on this stream, the spray arising from the waters alone being visible from the cars. For the next 40 or 50 miles the country is level and uninviting, with only a few residences in sight, being for the most part clothed with a stunted forest.

Stanfold, 55 miles from Point Levi, is a small settlement surrounded by good farming land, which continues until *Warwick*, *Danville*, and *Richmond* are reached and passed. At the latter station the passenger trains usually connect with trains from Portland and Montreal, making this an important point on this great railway of Canada. Passengers bound for the White Mountains or Portland, Me., here change cars.

After leaving Richmond for Montreal, the line of the road descends toward the St. Lawrence, passing through several thriving villages.

St. Hyacinthe, 30 miles from Montreal, is handsomely situated on the Yamaska River, about 40 miles above its entrance into the Lake St. Peter.

St. Hilaire, 17 miles from Longueuil, is another delightful village, situated near Beloeil Mountain, a bold eminence rising from the plain to near one thousand feet in height, being plainly seen from Montreal. A most beautiful lake lies near its summit; the outlet flows westward into the Sorel River.

Other hills or mountains are seen in this vicinity besides the one above mentioned. *Mount Rouge* and *Mount Johnson* rise on the south, while *Boucherville Mountain*, also adorned by a most beautiful lake, lies a few miles northwest of St. Hilaire, forming altogether a most interesting and picturesque group of hills or mountains, being visible from the St. Lawrence River for many miles, which, in connection with *Mount Royal*, on the island of Montreal, are most grand and attractive objects to the observant traveler.

The *Sorel* or *Richelieu River*, the outlet of Lake Champlain, is next passed, and the traveler soon arrives at *Longueuil*, where a commodious steam ferry-boat plies regularly to and from Montreal, landing near the center of the city, where cabs and carriages are always to be found in readiness running to the different hotels.

The Grand Trunk Railway also affords the most speedy and direct route to the White Mountains of New Hampshire, as well as to the Ottawa River and Upper St. Lawrence and Lake country.

Montreal to Island Pond, Vt.	143 miles.
Montreal to White Mountains, N. H.	201 "
Montreal to Portland, Me.	292 "

Montreal to Prescott, C. W.	113 miles
Montreal to Ottawa City, *via* Prescott	167 "
Montreal to Toronto, C. W.	333 "

MONTREAL TO BOSTON AND NEW YORK.

PASSENGERS can leave Montreal for Boston or New York, and proceed, *via Champlain and St. Lawrence Railroad*, to Rouse's Point, N. Y., a distance of 45 miles, where they have the choice of proceeding by steamer to Plattsburgh, Burlington, etc., or take the cars of the *Vermont and Canada Railroad*, and proceed direct through by rail to Boston or New York, or any intermediate station.

Trains of cars also run twice daily from Montreal, *via Montreal and Lachine* and *Montreal and New York Railroads*, direct to Plattsburgh, N. Y., a distance of 62 miles, here connecting with steamers running to Burlington, Ticonderoga, and Whitehall.

On arriving at Burlington by any of the above routes, passengers have the choice of proceeding by steamer, or take the cars of the *Vermont Central Railroad*, if bound for the White Mountains or Boston; while the *Rutland and Burlington Railroad* runs both toward Boston and New York, forming a link in the great line of railroads running from the Eastern and Northern States into Canada.

On leaving Burlington by steamer, proceeding toward Whitehall, a most magnificent view is obtained, in a clear day, of the *Green Mountains* of Vermont and the *Adirondack Group* of New York, lying in the counties of Essex and Clinton. The latter are the most elevated peaks, rising to the height of 5,467 feet above the ocean; while the Mansfield Mountain peak of Vermont rises to the height of 4,279 feet, there being lesser peaks on both sides of the lake in full view. The surface of Lake Champlain is elevated 90 feet above tide-waters of the ocean, while Lake George is elevated 243 feet—there being a fall of 153 in the outlet of the latter lake within the distance of 4 miles.

Lake Champlain and the landings on its shore are fully described in a preceding part of this work. See page 101.

The steamboat landing at old Fort Ticonderoga is the point

where passengers disembark when bound for Lake George. A good hotel is located near the landing for the accommodation of travelers, while stages are always in readiness to convey passengers to the foot of Lake George, about 4 miles distant.

Passengers destined for Whitehall, Saratoga Springs, or New York continue on board the steamer until they arrive at the former place, when, if destined south, they take cars for Saratoga Springs, Troy, or Albany.

LAKE GEORGE AND ITS STEAMERS.

Extract from the Glen's Falls Republican.

LAUNCH OF THE "MINNEHAHA" ON LAKE GEORGE, JUNE 12, 1857.

"THIS beautiful steamer was securely launched on Thursday afternoon, the 12th inst., amid the plaudits of the multitude who assembled to witness the spectacle. The day was as fine as could be desired, and every thing conspired to lend interest to the eventful occasion. At a few minutes before one o'clock the invited guests and the ladies assembled upon the forward deck, while a large crowd occupied the bank, which rose like an amphitheater around the bow of the boat. The tops and windows of the surrounding houses were also occupied with spectators. The ceremonies commenced with an announcement from Mr. Thomas Thomas, the respected President of the Fort William Henry Hotel Association, that all was ready, the ringing of the bell which swung from a temporary turret on the shore, and a gun from the new and elegant brass piece placed on the lawn in front of the Fort William Henry Hotel. A series of signals were so planned that the gun never failed to speak when its term came in the programme, and its reverberations lingered around the mountains that surrounded the lake as if loth to depart.

"Edward P. Clark, Esq., of New York city, Secretary of the Fort William Henry Hotel Association, next stepped upon the platform and delivered a short address, of which the following is the substance:

"FELLOW-CITIZENS—We congratulate you upon the completion of a new steamer for this beautiful lake. We would, moreover, take this opportunity to publicly express our thanks to the builders of the boat, and to the persons who have been employed upon her, for their industry in getting it to its present state of completion in so short a period of time. Upon this occasion it may not be uninteresting to you to look back into the history of the steamers which have hitherto traversed this lake. There are many present who are doubtless more familiar with their history than myself, but the few facts we have collected will no doubt be interesting on the present occasion and serve for future reference.

"Previous to 1700 the surface of this beautiful lake had never been broken by any vessel, save the bark canoe of the native Indian.

"From the period of the French and English wars, in 1756, when only yawl gun-boats and batteaux were employed, down to 1815, we can learn of no boats having been built or seen upon the lake. During that year Elijah Dunham, of Dunham's Bay, built a sloop called *Queensbury Packet*. It was built for carrying lumber, and was from sixty to seventy feet long.

"In 1817 the first steamboat was built on Lake George. It was called *James Caldwell*, and was built by a company of individuals at Ticonderoga, above the rapids. The *James Caldwell* made a trip through the lake on one day and returned on the next. She started from the dock called the Harris Dock, just below the Lake House. The travel was so small that the boat did not pay. She was burnt at the dock in front of the Lake House, and no vestige of her remains.

"In 1824 the steamer *Mountaineer* was built, to take the place of the *James Caldwell*, by John Baird and Capt. Jahazel Sherman, of Vergennes, Vermont. Mr. Baird then owned the Lake House. This boat ran until 1836, when she rotted down, and her wreck now lies in Lake George, above the rapids at Ticonderoga. Her machinery was taken out and put into the *William Caldwell*, which boat succeeded the *Mountaineer*. The *Caldwell* was one hundred and two feet long and twenty-five feet wide on deck. She was commenced in March, 1837, and completed in August of the same year. She ran eight miles per hour, and made one trip up and down the lake daily. She was abandoned in 1850, and what remains of her now lies in the cove just below the Lake House.

"In 1849 the *John Jay* was built at Ticonderoga (at the foot of the lake) by Mr. John Jay Harris. She was three years in building, and cost from twenty-five to twenty-eight thousand dollars. The hull was built by Ferris Collyer; Dunham & Company were the engineers. She was one hundred and forty-two feet long and twenty-four feet wide, and purchased from Mr. John J. Harris in 1853 by the Lake George Steamboat Company for eighteen thousand dollars. This company was organized January 14th, 1854. This boat ran from that time to 1856, when she was burned on the 29th day of July, 1856, near Hague, on the lower part of the lake, when rounding the point called Anthony's Nose—the lamentable particulars of which sad catastrophe we are all too familiar with. The wreck of this boat lies on the west bank of Lake George, about one mile below Hague.

"THE MINNEHAHA.—The keel of the new boat which we are about to launch was laid on the 7th of November, 1856, at Caldwell, New York, on the west shore of Lake George. The hull was built by Thomas Collyer; Joseph Belknapp was engineer. The carpenter work was done by F. M. Wright. This vessel is one hundred and forty feet long, twenty-four feet breadth of beam, forty-four feet on deck, and seven and one half feet depth of hold. It cost about twenty-six thousand dollars.

"The public will not miss the popular commander or notables of the *John Jay*. She will be *watched* over by 'OLD DICK,' with his red cap and rattlesnakes.

"We commit her to her native element—long may she float—may she never strike her colors. We have selected a name for the boat which, we hope, will please all its friends. It is the MINNEHAHA, and we thus name her. *Minnehaha*, or *Laughing Waters*, is the name given by the Indians to a beautiful waterfall, about forty feet in height, on a stream that empties into the Mississippi, between Fort Snelling and the Falls of St. Anthony.

"When the name of the boat was announced, the speaker was interrupted by vociferous cheers, the ringing of the bell, and a gun. Mr. Clark next introduced Mrs. Daniel Gale, the wife of the worthy proprietor of the Fort William Henry Hotel, who stepped upon the platform and, according to ancient usage, broke the bottle. A bottle of champagne, elegantly decked with ribbons, having been set upon the bulwarks, and attached by a ribbon to the flag-staff, Mrs. Gale threw it off; it was broken, and its contents sprinkled upon the bow of the vessel, amid the shouts of the multitude, the ringing of the bell, and the sound of the gun from the hotel. The ceremonies being concluded, notice was given to the crowd to prepare for the launch. A block or two was knocked away, and this beautiful steamer gently slid into the crystal waters where she is destined to float. She would have passed quite across the lake if the anchor had not been thrown. She was 'brought to' about the middle of the lake, and safely towed to her dock, in front of the Fort William Henry Hotel, where the boiler lies ready to be introduced. When this useful appendage is added and the wheels are put in, all of which may be done in two weeks, Lake George has as complete, as pretty, and as commodious a steamer as can be built."

For a further description of Lake George, etc., see page 97.

On leaving Lake George for Saratoga Springs, Troy, Albany, or New York, passengers are conveyed fourteen miles by stage, passing through the romantic village of GLEN'S FALLS, where is a beautiful cascade, being one of several falls occurring on the upper waters of the Hudson River, here a rushing torrent, alternately gliding through mountain passes, and then plunging over a rocky surface into the plain below.

MOREAU STATION, opposite *Fort Edward*, situated on the east bank of the Hudson, is the place where passengers take the cars of the *Saratoga and Whitehall Railroad*, and from thence proceed southward to Saratoga Springs, a farther distance of 15 miles.

Starting from *Saratoga Springs* the tourist can proceed to *Albany, via* Schenectady, or Troy, a still farther distance of 32 miles. On arriving at Troy or Albany, the traveler has the choice of proceeding by railroad to *Boston* or *New York*, or proceeding direct to the latter city by steamers navigating the tide-waters of the Hudson River, for a distance of 150 miles above the city of New York.

For a further description of Routes from New York to Saratoga Springs, Lake George, etc., see HUDSON RIVER GUIDE.

APPENDIX

TO

SECOND EDITION,

TRIP THROUGH THE LAKES, ETC.

EXTRACT FROM AN ADDRESS ON THE PRESENT CONDITION, RESOURCES, AND PROSPECTS OF BRITISH NORTH AMERICA, DELIVERED IN GLASGOW BY THE HON. JUSTICE HALIBURTON, 25TH MARCH, 1857.

THE British Territory in North America, Mr. Haliburton says, contains about four millions of square miles, and is larger than all Europe, and exceeds in extent all the United States. This calculation, however, includes Newfoundland and New Britain, or the Hudson Bay Territory, of which Mr. Haliburton says it was unnecessary to speak, as the customs returns of the first would tell all that his hearers required to know, and the Hudson Bay Company would tell them nothing they wished to know. *Prince Edward's Island* contains 1,365,000 acres of excellent land, so free from stone as not to yield sufficient for building purposes. It contains 67 townships, with a population amounting to 70,000.*

Of the island of *Cape Breton* Mr. Haliburton speaks in the most enthusiastic terms. It is separated from Nova Scotia by

---

* "*Prince Edward Island* is so called in honor of the late Duke of Kent, the father of her present Majesty, who was Commander-in-Chief of the Forces in these Provinces in 1779, when its present name was substituted for that of St. John, which it originally bore. Though forming a separate government, as a colony it is comparatively small, being in its greatest length 135 miles, and in its greatest breadth 34 only. In one place it is not more than a mile wide; and its coast on both sides presents so many bays that there are few parts of the island in which it is more than ten miles across from the head of one bay to the head of some other. The whole area of the island exceeds 1,000,000 of acres, and as there are no very lofty mountains, while there is an abundance of wood, and many little lakes and streams, it is fertile and inhabitable throughout. The climate is milder and softer than that of Canada, without the fogs of Newfoundland and Nova Scotia, and the health and longevity of its inhabitants are remarkable."

the narrow Strait of Canso, only a mile wide, is a hundred miles long, eighty-five wide, and two hundred and seventy-five in circumference. The *Bras d'Or*, a navigable lake, nearly divides it in two. It contains extensive coal-fields, brine-springs. large and commodious harbors, a superabundance of fish, and superior land for tillage. Mr. Haliburton, closing his observations on the island, says: "Let the poor, unemployed man seek it, where God has given him good soil to cultivate, coal for his fuel, fish for his food, and salt to cure it."

Of *Nova Scotia* Mr. Haliburton speaks in a very favorable manner. It contains 10,000 square miles. It abounds in mineral riches—coal, iron, gypsum, slate, grindstone, lead, manganese, copper, etc. At a short distance from the coast the land is of a superior quality, and some portions of inexhaustible fertility. On the 31st December, 1850, the number of vessels owned and registered in the Province of Nova Scotia was 2,791, of 163,692 tons. The value of fish taken was largely over $1,000,000. The quantity of coal raised was 115,000 chaldrons, all of which may now be calculated at a much higher ratio. There is, however, a rare advantage which Nova Scotia possesses, namely, that the harbor of Halifax is less frequently b ocked up with ice than any harbor in North America Such an event seldom occurs, and when it does, is never of long duration.

New Brunswick contains an area of about 30,000 square miles, and is as large as Ireland. Its population is 200,000. Its surface is undulating, diversified with lakes, rivers, and noble forests. The river St. John is 450 miles long, and, with its tributaries, drains seventeen millions acres in New Brunswick, the State of Maine, and Canada. Our space will not permit our following Mr. Haliburton through his descriptions of New Brunswick, its vast mineral treasures, harbors, roads, markets, cities, towns, etc. He says great ignorance prevails in Great Britain relative to this splendid Province, only equaled by that young lady's knowledge of botany who declared she knew the names of two flowers only—" Aurora Borealis" and " Delirium Tremens."

Canada proper, according to Mr. Haliburton, is 1,600 miles long, with an average breadth of 230 miles, being one third larger than France or Prussia, and three times as large as Great Britain and Ireland. It contains an area of 350,000 square miles, or 240,000,000 of acres. With regard to the health of Canada, he gives the following comparative statement of the proportion of deaths to population: France, 1 to 43; Spain, 1 to 40; England, 1 to 46; United States, 1 to 74; Upper Canada, 1 to 102. The population of the United States, in fifty years from the year 1800, increased from 5,305,925 to

23,191,876, being an increase of nearly five times; while in Upper Canada, from 1811 to 1851, a term of forty years, the population increased ten times—about double the increase of the whole United States. In the ten years preceding 1855 the wheat crop of the United States increased 48 per cent.—in Canada, in the same period, 480 per cent. The total imports of Canada on the 1st January, 1854, divided among her whole population, amounted to £3 14s. 10d. to each individual—in the United States, £2 7s. 0d. to each individual. Her exports £2 15s. 0d. to each individual—in the United States, £2 7s. 2d. to each individual.

Mr. Haliburton complains in very emphatic language of England's neglect of her possessions in North America. He complains that the five Provinces have no common bond of union, no common interests, no power to prevent the oppressions of strangers, no voice in the regulation of their trade—are involved in war without their consent, peace concluded without their being consulted—that they have no representatives in Parliament, nor delegates in the Colonial Office—that their territory has been ceded away without their consent, etc. He says this state of things can not last—that there are four remedies, viz.: 1st. Annexation to the States. 2d. Federal Union of the Provinces, with a Colonial Board of Control—that is, delegates in Parliament to advocate Colonial rights, and vote on them and them only. 3d. Incorporation with Great Britain and a fair share of representation. 4th. *Independence.*

EXPORTS OF WHEAT AND FLOUR.

The following shows the exports of wheat and flour to foreign ports from Canada, for the year 1856, as published in the Trade and Navigation returns:

Ports.	Wheat, bus.	Flour, bbls.
Bayfield	155,359	—
Brantford	—	12,492
Chippewa	—	7,777
Coaticook	—	108,299
Cobourg	75,271	18,305
Port Credit	99,904	30,118
Dalhousie	78,647	55,684
Dover	118,339	15,164
Dundas	85,461	9,533
Dunnville	66,878	14,839
Fort Erie	—	9,113
Port Hope	127,895	—
Hamilton	559,005	130,306

Ports.	Wheat, bus.	Flour, bbls.
London..................	118,091	—
Montreal.................	448,084	189,438
Oshawa..................	—	10,533
Newcastle................	96,554	—
Oakville..................	282,206	—
Quebec...................	187,193	83,931
Stamford.................	189,332	61,990
Port Stanley..............	172,553	—
Toronto..................	1,661,545	83,351
Whitby...................	379,756	6,140
Woodstock................	111,986	—
Other ports...............	433,437	35,859
Total exports..........	4,997,656	878,775

Value of wheat, £1,744,460—flour, £1,502,451—total value in dollars, $12,997,648—nearly thirteen millions of dollars! Of this quantity $2,103,938 was sent to England, $689,540 to North American Colonies, and the remainder, nearly ten millions, was sent to the United States. Admitting that these government statistics are correct, which it is hardly safe to do, as they are almost invariably below the mark, the Provincial export is very satisfactory. Comparing the past with previous years, the following is the result:

	Wheat.	Flour.	Value.
1854...........	933,756	668,623	£842,620
1855...........	8,193,748	643,936	2,932,691
1856...........	4,997,656	878,775	3,240,912

RAILWAY TRAFFIC IN CANADA.

From a statement in *Herapath's Railway Journal* we learn that though the progress of railways in Canada has not equaled that of the United States, yet Upper and Lower Canada alone now number 1,419 miles. The increase has been as follows:

	Miles opened.		Miles opened.
1847....................	24	1852....................	86
1848....................	30	1853....................	132
1849....................	—	1854....................	431
1850....................	—	1855....................	304
1851....................	42	1856....................	370

The Canada Railways in operation are, miles....... 1,419

RAILWAY TRAFFIC—*Continued.*

	Miles open in Upper and Lower Canada.
Buffalo and Lake Huron	84
Champlain and St. Lawrence	49
Cobourg and Peterboro'	28
Erie and Ontario	17
Grand Trunk (Canada portion)	701
Great Western	284
London and Port Stanley	24
Montreal and New York	37
Ontario, Simcoe and Huron	96
Port Dalhousie and Thorold	4
Port Hope, Lindsay and Beaverton	41
Total	1,419

SURVEY OF THE OTTAWA AND FRENCH RIVER ROUTE,

EXTENDING FROM OTTAWA CITY TO LAKE HURON.

THIS grand project of uniting the waters of Lake Huron and the Ottawa has been recommended by the Provincial Parliament of Canada, and minute survey made of the proposed route. The report of the engineer says:

"The old canoe route of the *voyageurs* of the northwest follows the Ottawa for about 180 miles above Ottawa City to the mouth of Matawan River, ascending which stream, nearly due west, to its head waters on Trout Lake, about 40 miles, it there crosses the height of land separating the waters flowing to the Ottawa from these tributaries to the Lakes and St. Lawrence. The width of the dividing ridge may be taken at three miles, and it is washed on the west side by Lake Nipissing; crossing which we descend its outlet, the French River, to the Georgian Bay. The distance from the mouth of the Matawan, where we leave the Ottawa, to that of French River, is about 125 miles—being a total of 305 miles from Ottawa City."

The above described route is pronounced perfectly practicable for a ship canal route. "Of the 180 miles from Ottawa City to the Matawan, about 85 miles are navigated, in three distinct sections, by steamers of from 5 to 5½ feet draught of water; the highest point to which they now ascend being 'Les Deux Joachims' Rapids, 135 miles above the city of Ottawa." The engineer adds:

"This old canoe route is that which will be adopted for any larger scheme of navigation that the growing wants of the country may require to be perfected by the valley of the Ottawa."

EXTRACTS FROM REPORTS, ESTIMATES, ETC., RELATIVE TO IMPROVEMENTS OF THE NAVIGATION OF THE RIVER ST. LAWRENCE, 1856.

RAPIDS OF THE ST. LAWRENCE RIVER.

ESTIMATES of cost of procuring a navigable channel throughout the whole of the Rapids of the river St. Lawrence, from Prescott to the head of the Lachine Canal, by removing the obstructions; that channel to be 200 feet wide, and between 12 and 13 feet deep at low summer water:

	Feet.	In.	Est. Cost.
1. Galops Rapids (Isle au Galops to Point Iroquois)..	14	9	£11,232
2. Rapid Plat........	11	6	——
3. Long Sault (North Channel)........	48	0	17,198
4. Coteau Rapids (Lake St. Francis to Pte. au Diable)	84	0	40,365
5. Cedar Rapids (Pte. au Diable to Pte. au Moulin)..			12,500
6. Cascade Rapids (Pte. au Moulin to Lake St. Louis)			98,705
7. Lachine Rapids........	44	9	——
Total........	203	0	£180,000

It results from the examination made by the undersigned, and upon which they have the honor of reporting above:

1st. That the river St. Lawrence, in its present condition, may be considered navigable, during low summer water, from Prescott to the foot of Lake St. Francis, for vessels drawing eight feet; also, through Lake St. Louis, for vessels drawing eight feet or even ten feet, and between Lake St. Francis and St. Louis for vessels drawing six feet, and during the higher stages of water by vessels respectively of a somewhat heavier draft, however, not exceeding 8½ and 6½ feet.

2d. That to make it perfectly navigable throughout, from Prescott to the head of the Lachine Canal, for vessels drawing ten feet, will require the removal of obstructions in the Galops Rapids, the north channel of the Long Sault, the Coteau, Cedar, and Cascade Rapids.

3d. That the practicability of removing those obstructions by means of sub-marine blasting, etc., has been ascertained by actual experiment in different portions of the Coteau Rapids; and,

4th. That the cost of the whole improvement will not exceed £180,000, or $720,000.

(Signed) B. MAILLEFERT, W. RAASLOFF, } Engineers.

RAPIDS, ISLANDS, ETC., BETWEEN PRESCOTT AND MONTREAL, GIVING THE DISTANCES FROM PRESCOTT.

SOUTH OR AMERICAN SIDE.		NORTH OR CANADA SIDE.
OGDENSBURGH,		PRESCOTT,
Northern Railroad.		*Ottawa and Prescott R. R.*
Chimney Islands, 5 miles.		Isle aux Moutons.
		Drummond's Island.
Tibbet's Island, 6 miles.		Duck Island.
Isle aux Galops, 7 miles.	Boundary Line, or Channel of the River.	**Galops Rapids.**
		Port Cardinal, 10 miles.
Long Point.		Tousson's Island, 12 miles.
Rapid.		Port Iroquois, 14 miles.
Ogden's Island, 18 miles.		**Rapid Plat.**
WADDINGTON.		WILLIAMSBURG.
Goose Neck Island, 24 miles.		Chrysler's Farm.
Chrysler's Island, 27 miles.		
Cat Island, 31 miles.		Cat Island.
Croyles Island.		Farren's Point, 33 miles.
Long Sault Island, 36 miles.		DICKINSON'S LANDING, 38 m.
Long Sault		**Rapids,** 40 miles.
Barnhart's Island.		Sheek's Island, 41 miles
Rapids.		*Rapids.*
		Cornwall Island.
45 degrees N. lat.		CORNWALL, 50 miles.
ST. REGIS.		St. Regis Island, 53 miles.
Squaw Island, 61 miles.		Butternut Island.
LAKE		ST. FRANCIS,
2 to 6 miles		in width.
		COTEAU DU LAC, 80 miles.

North Side.		South Side.
MacIntyre Island.		Giroux Island.
Maple Island.		French Island.
Coteau		**Rapids,** 82 miles.
Thorn Island.		
Pig Island.		Fish Island.
Broad Island, 84 miles.		Prisoner's Island.
La Pierre Island.		Isle aux Vaches.
Isle a l'Ail.		Cedar Village, 90 miles.
Cedar		**Rapids.**
St. Timothy.	Channel of the River.	Isle aux Quacks.
Isle aux Noix.		Isle de la Grande Chute.
		Pointe aux Moulin.
Split Rock River.		Round Island.
Cascade		**Rapids,** 94 miles.
Beauharnois, 96 miles.		Isle aux Cascades.
Mouth of Ottawa River.		Isle Perrot.
Lake		St. Louis,
4 to 8 miles		in width.
Caughnawaga,		Lachine, 112 miles.
Montreal & New York R.R.		*Lachine Railroad.*
Lachine		**Rapids,** 116 miles.
Isle aux Diable.		Isle aux Heron.
La Prairie.		Nun's Island.
Victoria		*Bridge.*
St. Helen's Island.		MONTREAL, 122 miles.

www.ingramcontent.com/pod-product-compliance
Lightning Source LLC
LaVergne TN
LVHW020117110826
845151LV00001B/190

* 9 7 8 1 4 2 5 5 4 2 5 7 3 *